BOOKS BY JOHN HOHENBERG

The Pulitzer Prize Story

The Professional Journalist

*Foreign Correspondence: The Great Reporters
and Their Times*

The New Front Page

*Between Two Worlds: Policy, Press and Public Opinion
in Asian-American Relations*

The News Media: A Journalist Looks at His Profession

Free Press/Free People: The Best Cause

New Era in the Pacific

AN ADVENTURE IN
PUBLIC DIPLOMACY

by John Hohenberg

SIMON AND SCHUSTER : NEW YORK

327.7305
H68N
84638
Sept 1973

For : HOWARD PALFREY JONES
C . M . LI
RICHARD H . NOLTE

Contents

Foreword

This book is an adventure in public diplomacy.

It undertakes to examine the new United States position in Asia, its risks and advantages, and some of its probable consequences for the American and Asian peoples. It is also an inquiry into the broad new relationships that are taking form between the United States, China and the Soviet Union; Japan, the Indochina states, India and other Asian nations bordering the Pacific and Indian oceans.

What I have attempted to do here is to consider both American and Asian options at first hand with some of the major sources of foreign information that are available to American policy makers and, in elaboration, to present as much relevant material as I could about each country. This book, therefore, places both the principal problems and some of the materials of policy making before the concerned citizen in the period when the United States and China are making a long-deferred adjustment to each other, looking toward the post-Vietnam War period.

THE SOURCE OF THE INQUIRY

My preparations for this work began at the East-West Center in Honolulu during the summer of 1967 and culminated in an eight-month 40,000-mile journey in the Indo-Pacific area in 1970, my sixth sojourn in Asia since 1950. In the course of more than three hundred interviews with influential citizens in Asian lands, ranging in importance from heads of states to revolutionary student leaders, I made it a point to determine not only what they thought of the declining American presence in Asia but also what they wanted to do about it.

During my four months at the Chinese University of Hong Kong in 1970–71, and subsequently, I had ample opportunity to study at close range some of the consequences of the re-emergence of China and its effect on the other three major Pacific powers—the United States, the Soviet Union and Japan.

While the result cannot rival in volume the information that floods the American government's communications system, it is perhaps more selective. As to the validity of the judgments made herein, the reader will have to determine that for himself. In any event, I offer the book as a modest contribution to public knowledge in the field of foreign policy.

At the very least, it illustrates the complexity of the process of putting together new American policies for the Indo-Pacific region after ten years of unsuccessful war in Indochina. At best, it may stimulate a better-informed public discussion of what these policies should be in years to come. And it may possibly dissuade a few of the more downhearted among us from mounting fearfully into our national attic and taking refuge in the dark closet of isolation with the shades of Warren Gamaliel Harding, William E. Borah and Henry Cabot Lodge, Sr.

ACKNOWLEDGMENTS

Let me express my gratitude here to those who helped me with this study. While it is impossible to list them all, I do wish to thank in particular the Asian leaders who took the time and trouble to receive me for interviews, including Indira Gandhi, Y. B. Chavan and Swaran Singh of India; Sirimavo Bandaranaike and A. R. Ratnavale of Ceylon; Eisaku Sato, Yasuhiro Nakasone and Kiichi Miyazawa of Japan; Ferdinand Edralin Marcos, Carlos P. Romulo and S. P. Lopez of the Philippines; Tran Thien Khiem of South Vietnam; Tun Abdul Razak and the Tunku, Abdul Rahman of Malaysia; Lee Kuan Yew and S. Rajaratnam of Singapore; Adam Malik of Indonesia, and Thanat Khoman of Thailand. I owe a great deal, as well, to the American ambassadors and their staffs in each of the countries I visited, to Asian editors, university presidents, business and military people and students who gave so freely of their time, and to my old friends, the foreign correspondents, en masse.

I wish to thank the Ford Foundation for an Asian travel-study grant and both the East-West Center and the Chinese University of Hong Kong for their generosity and support. To Columbia University, I am indebted once again for that durable academic institution, sabbatical leave. But had it not been for the gentle guidance, the steadiness and the wise counsel of my adored traveling companion, my wife, Dorothy Lannuier Hohenberg, this work could not have been completed. Together, we take the traditional steps of absolving all herein of responsibility for the statements and views in these pages.

If this exercise in public diplomacy sheds a small, steady light along the tortuous path of American foreign policy in the Pacific in the years to come, I shall feel gratified.

JOHN HOHENBERG

January 10, 1972
Columbia University,
New York City.

New Era in the Pacific

I. The American Dilemma

1. A STATEMENT OF THE PROBLEM

A distinguished American military commander stood before a large wall map, pointer in hand, and pondered the problem of the United States position in the Pacific in the 1970s. He had just concluded an hour's formal briefing for me on the probable elements of change in our posture and invited my questions.

"How far are we prepared to retreat in the Pacific?" I asked.

He thoughtfully surveyed the once formidable string of American bases from Thailand and Indochina to Japan as well as the great red blob that marked the presence of China, now blockaded by hostile Soviet and Indian power. "I wish I knew," he said.

I put it to him as bluntly as I could. "Do you think we could withdraw as far as Guam, the Pacific Trust Territory and Hawaii?"

He shrugged. "After what has happened in Vietnam and considering the state of public opinion in the United States today, I suppose anything is possible. But I hope we don't have to go back that far. We could have riots over Saipan, too, you know."

It was and is perfectly true. Despite the vast reach of American air and naval power, no made-to-order defense line exists in the Pacific for the United States as defined by traditional military concepts. In the Trust Territory of the Pacific islands, handed over to the United States by the United Nations as a strategic trusteeship and held by the American Navy, protests even now are rising and demands are being made for independence. It is a cause that will appeal to restless university campuses in the United States. Without doubt, it, too, will become a national issue one day—along with others arising from the American withdrawal and belt-tightening process.

The End of an Era

What all this symbolizes to Asians is the end of the era of American expansion in the Pacific. Within a decade, they have seen the might of United States armed forces frustrated in Vietnam by a relatively small Asian army. They have witnessed the decline of American economic power in competition with Japan and the forced devaluation of the dollar. They have observed the debacle of American diplomacy, which could not save Pakistan from dismemberment by a resurgent, Soviet-supported India. And finally, they have noted the swift descent of American prestige at the United Nations with the admission of China over American opposition and the effort of an American President to soften twenty-two years of hostility to Peking with a week's visit.

There is no way of minimizing these defeats by waving the flag and trumpeting the unbroken might of the United States as a world power. Nor is there any concealing the continuing advance of the Soviet Union, the armorer of developing lands from the Red Sea to the farthest reaches of the western Pacific Ocean. To Americans, it is evident enough that the brief moment of empire, nurtured by such diverse figures as Homer Lea and Douglas MacArthur, is over, and new accommodations must be sought in varying ways with China and Japan, and with the Soviet Union and India.

For the world at large the shifting fortunes of the United States mean that a realignment of global power is under way and the ultimate outcome can be only dimly foreseen. Whatever happens, it will be impossible for the centers of influence—American, Soviet and West European plus Britain—to enter into any kind of new arrangement without first insuring a peaceful settlement of differences over Asia. Indeed, if this brave new world is ever to come into being, the principal powers of Asia will have to give it their active support.

What Is the National Interest?

In the formulation of new American policies for the Pacific, the basic question is: What is the national interest? The answers to date have not been very conclusive. Neither Presidential trips to Peking and Moscow nor currency juggling and other high-pressure economic measures are likely in themselves to determine the American course in the Pacific for the long tomorrow.

For beyond Hawaii, Alaska and Guam, at least a part of the American public believes we should have no interest in the western Pacific and some are even doubtful about Guam. Should the United States follow this line, we would be cowering behind a continental atomic defense in the foreseeable future—a "Fortress America" dependent on long-range missiles. It would make a mockery of all the grand American talk about collective security. Worse still, in view of the probable Soviet lead in this department, we would be No. 2 and we wouldn't be trying harder.

As for the other extreme, it is today very close to what it always has been—resistance to Communist aggression and expansion at all costs. This was the cold war line that inspired John Foster Dulles' containment policy against the Soviet Union, now in ruins from Cuba to Cairo and from New Delhi to Hanoi. It also led to the unhappy notion, propagated by President John Fitzgerald Kennedy among others, that the United States could be the world's policeman, the guardian for every beleaguered nation on earth. The assumption here was that the American national interest would not permit Communist nations, in all their diversity, to make gains anywhere without crippling American liberties.

Neither of these extremes seems practical in the vast revolutionary world of today in the Indo-Pacific. The United States cannot long remain a world power of the first rank if, on the one hand, it leaves the Pacific to Japan, China and the Soviet Union or if, on the other, it commits its military strength in opposition to every developing insurgency against every friendly government in Asia. Nor can the

American posture be determined on the basis of the demands of violent elements in American public life, regardless of the self-proclaimed nobility of their motivation. No nation that permits its policies to be dictated by street mobs can long endure.

The basic question that must be answered remains: What is the national interest? If there is any hope whatever of attaining a national consensus on this, then two other questions naturally follow: What options are available to the United States to protect this interest? and, What forces should be committed to safeguard it—and where?

The Role of Morality

In an expanding United States, there was seldom much trouble about the justification for an aggressive foreign policy. The pious old America of Manifest Destiny invariably adhered to its stated moral purpose of civilizing backward mankind and allowing the unfortunate wretches of this earth to labor for the democratic glories of the United States.

It was, in a sense, the American statement of the "white man's burden" as Rudyard Kipling later defined it for the British Empire. Long after Manifest Destiny had served its purpose, the moral pronouncements that justified the aims of American foreign policy continued to roll forth in sonorous language from Washington. The American public had come to expect it. They wanted to know, as Mr. Dooley said of the second Hague Peace Conference, "how future wars shud be conducted in th' best inthrests iv peace."

Thus, from the crusade of World War I to make the world safe for democracy to the enlistment of the United Nations (including Generalissimos Stalin and Chiang Kai-shek) in the cause of the four freedoms during World War II, every American war had to be fought in terms of a holy cause. The presumption was that God, in His infinite wisdom, would not suffer defeat for American arms.

The string went taut in Korea and finally snapped in Indochina. When the state of Bangladesh was born, it was over the opposition of the United States. From now on, in consequence, all the self-serving pronouncements about fighting for the self-determination of small peoples will be bound to have a certain hollow sound for an increasingly disenchanted American public. Morality in itself can no longer justify foreign policy; in recent years, it has been a sorry sham. Something a great deal more realistic will have to be presented to the American people. The time has long since passed when the national interest can be stated in high-sounding moral terms.

The Economic Factor

What, then, of economics? If trade follows the flag, or vice versa sometimes, can a successful appeal be made to the self-interest of a largely middle-class public in the United States? Is it valid to believe that a trillion-dollar economy is worth defending with military power?

Alas for the faith of the righteous in the American free-enterprise system! It has been hedged about with controls to cushion the shock of dollar devaluation and a readjustment of American foreign trade. But in formulating a new economic policy, no one in Washington talks about protecting the right of Americans to trade abroad. As an eminent American ambassador told me in Asia, "We may believe in American business but we won't fight to protect American business overseas."

It is one thing for the American government to give industry tax breaks at home plus a stiff dose of protectionism, and quite another to call out the Marines to frustrate the takeover of American oil companies abroad. The giant American financial interests trade overseas at their own risk.

The Protection of Citizens

From Stephen Decatur's war on the Barbary pirates to the picturesque Rooseveltian demand, "Perdicaris alive or Raisuli dead,"[1] the American citizen abroad has always seemed to be a very special person deserving of his government's full protection.

Except in the most extraordinary cases, it is true no longer.

[1] The message, sent by John Hay for Theodore Roosevelt in 1904, led to the freeing of Ion Perdicaris, an American citizen, by Raisuli, a Berber bandit who had held him for ransom.

American citizens are imprisoned abroad, often without justification. Americans in official positions have been kidnaped, held for ransom, and even killed. Castro's Cuba has captured an American commercial vessel. Peru has harassed American fishing trawlers. North Korea has made off with an American naval vessel and held its crew captive. Many times in any given year, whole planeloads of Americans are hijacked and flown to foreign landing fields. In the Middle East, political brigands even blew up a hijacked aircraft and got away with it.

The protection of American citizens, clearly, is no longer a cause for extreme governmental action except in instances where the United States is performing a humanitarian act and is unlikely to be involved in an open conflict as a result.

What of the Aggressor?

If morality, trade, the protection of American citizens and even the supposedly sacred character of the flag are no longer good measurements of the national interest, what standards remain? There is, of course, the direct act of an aggressor, such as the Japanese attack on Pearl Harbor, that challenges the survival of the United States as a nation. But in an age when the guerrilla is deified by the young and infiltration and subversion are the favorite weapons of the aggressor, the possibility of another Pearl Harbor is remote. Professor Henry A. Kissinger has even argued that the "Pearl Harbor psychosis" is a handicap to American military planning. At the height of the cold war, he wrote that all-out preparation to resist a surprise nuclear attack by the Soviet Union on the continental United States had made us more vulnerable to limited warfare. As matters turned out, he was right.

"By concentrating on measures to defeat a Soviet attempt to neutralize us physically," he pointed out, "we have given the Soviet leadership an opportunity to neutralize us psychologically by so graduating their actions that the provocation would never seem 'worth' an all-out war, the only form of war our doctrine took into account."

Kissinger's strategy at the time was to shift to more flexible forms of national defense and make greater preparations for a limited nuclear war, among other measures, on the theory that American "daring and leadership" would overwhelm a static Soviet force in such a conflict.[2] Fortunately, his novel theory has never been tested. In almost a generation that has passed since he laid down his semi-nuclear posture, there has been no atomic attack, limited or otherwise. In Vietnam, the forces of Hanoi did very well with conventional Soviet arms.

Is Faith in the Atom Misplaced?

The American public never seems to tire of being reminded that two American atomic bombs, one at Hiroshima and the other at Nagasaki, ended the Pacific war in 1945. If Americans could only see the never-ending columns of grim-faced Japanese who visit the scenes of atomic horror in the great museum at Hiroshima, they might have second thoughts about entrusting their future to atomic arms.

Nevertheless, in every military treatise, there is an opening observation that the United States today is the mightiest power on earth (now a moot question), with an atomic arsenal that could destroy its enemies many times over. Necessarily, the Soviet Union could do the same thing. With their smaller atomic armories, the British, the French and the Chinese could cause a horrible amount of damage if they chose and there are at least twenty nations, including tiny Israel, that could produce an atomic weapon within a short time.

The principal use of all this terrible array of weaponry to date has been to induce a feeling of deterrence—a "balance of terror," as it has been called—between the United States and the Soviet Union as well as the other members of the atomic club. That is good as far as it goes, and for as long as there are realistic negotiations to limit the spread of atomic arms and to curb their uses. But once the atomic truce is broken, the chances of world survival are exceedingly dim.

The issue is still what Bernard M. Baruch said it was on June 14, 1946, when he addressed the opening meeting of the Unted Nations Atomic Energy Commission as the American delegate:

[2] Henry A. Kissinger, *Nuclear Weapons and Foreign Policy* (New York: Harper, 1957), pp. 29–30, 399–400.

"We are here to make a choice between the quick and the dead.

"That is our business.

"Behind the black portent of the new atomic age lies a hope which, seized upon with faith, can work our salvation. If we fail, then we have damned every man to be the slave of Fear. Let us not deceive ourselves: We must elect World Peace or World Destruction."

Salvation is still far off, despite the modest advances of the strategic arms limitation talks. And there is no sign that the atomic arms race is slackening perceptibly. For all its atomic strength, the United States is so internally divided on the issue that its public, as a whole, would be hard put to decide where its national interest really lies, and what overt enemy act would be a basis for atomic war. And this is even more true of the Congress of the United States than it is of the electorate at a time when the entire nation is sick of war.

Realistically, on the basis of what happened during the Cuban missile crisis, neither Congress nor the public may ever have a chance to intervene under current circumstances.

The Chimera of Disarmament

It might be expected, therefore, that eager promoters, taking advantage of the passionate American interest in peace, would try to stimulate a mass movement toward unilateral disarmament. Almost every other zany cause has its wild-eyed followers, particularly in California, but the United States has been spared this ultimate folly to date. Of course, it cannot be completely ruled out; a renewed war in Indochina, for example, or a mistaken American involvement in military affairs elsewhere could produce any number of unpleasant reactions. Perhaps the only reason nobody has tried to burn down the Pentagon is that nobody has thought of it. Or if they have, they aren't sufficiently attracted to martyrdom to take the inconvenient consequences that come with arrest, trial and conviction.

Whether the American public follows the Pied Pipers into a crusade for disarmament or not, such a policy offers no hope for the foreseeable future of averting the risk of new wars in Asia or elsewhere. Since the United States obligingly sank the main strength of its Navy after the Washington Arms Limitation Conference of 1921–22, while the Japanese and the British looked on in approval, unilateral disarmament hasn't been a favored topic of American statesmen. All the talk of disarmament in the League of Nations from 1935 on did not deter Hitler, Mussolini or Tojo; nor has the resumption of the annual disarmament debates in the United Nations done anything to avert some threescore wars since 1945.

True, there have been modest advances toward some distant accommodation between men, nations and armaments. The continuing talks on arms limitation also could produce striking results if both the United States and the Soviet Union saw their way clear. But the chimera of total disarmament, at this stage in the world's history, can only delude mankind.

The Dominant Issue

There is no escape for the United States from the responsibilities of world power, no refuge in morality, no release through disarmament. In recasting its policies in the post-Vietnam era, the continuing American concern with the Indo-Pacific is bound to cause a great deal more soul-searching and even misery. For it will not be easy to plan new involvements in Asia against the conviction of millions of Americans who believe the nation's vital interest lies largely elsewhere. Nor will it be simply a matter of time and education before this national myopia can be overcome. The wars in Indochina, and the nature of American policies in the Pacific that flowed from them, have left a bitter heritage that will haunt the United States for years to come.

The effect is particularly noticeable on the young America and the young Asia that are emerging today. Except for the long conflict in Vietnam, neither has very much knowledge of the other. It is not strange, therefore, that with few exceptions neither has very much trust in the other. The chasm between them is very broad and it will not easily be bridged by the current system of exchanges, which so often serves to confirm long-held prejudices instead of removing them.

To approach the situation realistically, it might better be said that there are several young Americas, going by political interests and regional and social groupings, and numerous young Asias, accepting the old standards of nationalities, castes, tribes, religions and political and economic groups, and the newer swing toward dynamic international action.

But whether the forces are two, several or many on the rim of the Pacific and Indian oceans, the home of one-third of mankind, the dominant issue is still the same. How are these giant continents to live together in peace in the remaining years of this century and the long and desperate uncertainties of the next? The animosities born of three Asian wars over the past three decades will not easily be laid to rest among the generations that had to fight.

A Problem of Attitudes

Unlike the many historic ties that bind Western civilization together, there is little in the way of common heritage between Americans and the peoples of the Indo-Pacific. Asian studies only recently have begun to attract major attention in the nation's colleges and universities. Moreover, the flow of Asian immigrants to the United States mainland was a mere trickle until revised immigration laws provided a modest increase.

For the bulk of the American public, Asia has represented the mysterious East, vaguely bounded by Mount Fuji, Manila Bay, the Great Wall of China and the Taj Mahal. Even in the state of Hawaii, where Asians and Americans of Asian descent are in the majority, I have found a relatively small commitment to Asian peoples. To most Hawaiians, events in Asia are important only when related to family ties. To them, as to their fellow Americans in large part, the people of Asia represent the eternal stranger.

In the words of a disillusioned young foreign correspondent, "What readers of my paper want from me is stuff about war in Asia, scares about Red China and stories about funny little people, from geishas to snake charmers."

But for most literate Asians, the United States holds intense interest, although reactions in general are not often favorable. The youth culture in Asian lands is powerfully influenced by the long-haired and casually attired style of American youth. The older Asian generations may deplore it, but the Asian teen-ager seems fascinated by American rock music and American dancing, as well as the latest in American movies and television, where available. To Asian intellectuals, this may be the appeal of what they call the "Coca Cola civilization," but its strength in every cosmopolitan center is undeniable. And scornful as most intellectuals may be of the United States, not many of them will turn down a chance to study at American colleges and universities if it comes to them.

Regardless of the impact of American life on Asian societies, however, the existence of a substantial anti-American attitude throughout the Indo-Pacific must be conceded at the outset of any examination of American policies, old or new. Nor is this merely the by-product of radical turmoil, the urge to attract attention by centering on some prominent target like the American embassy in an Asian capital or the nearest American military base. For to a certain extent, the American also represents the eternal stranger to the mistrustful Asian. He is the symbol of a predominantly white civilization, the inheritor of the power of all the fallen imperialisms that have preyed on Asian lands for centuries past. He was the first to use the atomic bomb, and he used it against Asians—and Asians alone. Scant wonder, in developing Asian lands, that the American is often looked upon as a rich and unwelcome intruder, and in industrialized Japan, Hong Kong and Singapore as a ruthless competitor.

Yet, it would be a mistake to conclude that either American indifference or Asian hostility is so pervasive that no progress can be made in establishing a better balance between the peoples of the two continents. I remember being quite discouraged after a long period of interviewing in Tokyo, and traveling with my wife to Kyoto to look up an old friend, the Reverend Graham McDonnell of the Good Shepherd Movement of Japan. Following a pleasant dinner one evening, I told Father Graham that, despite all the fine and challenging things that were happening in Japan, I was mightily depressed because of the persistently anti-American attitudes that both my wife and I had observed. After more than a decade in Japan, Father Graham might have been expected to agree with us but he did not; instead, he remarked cheerfully that we had been seeing too many people who had reason to be anti-American. He was probably right.

That night, to show us another side of Japan, he took us to a mountaintop Buddhist shrine outside Kyoto where we spent a reflective evening listening to our friend, the Catholic priest, discussing the affairs of the spirit with his friend, the Buddhist priest. The warmth and the kindliness with which we were received reassured us, even if the discussion in Japanese and mingled snatches of English was difficult to follow. It was another side, and a better side, of Japan. When we departed next day, we were better prepared than we had been to try to maintain our perspective.

Truly, attitudes are becoming increasingly important in the era of the postindustrial state, with its emphasis on communications and changing philosophy. But they are not, and cannot be permitted to become, decisive. Every great power arouses a certain amount of antagonism merely by reason of its existence and growth, as the Japanese are discovering anew. Only Americans, however, seem to be surprised by it.

The American Image

There is more to the American image in the Indo-Pacific than meets the eye. To those who look upon Uncle Sam as a weary colossus, packing up in Vietnam and elsewhere and moving out in disillusion and defeat, it is difficult to account for the confident advance of the great American corporations in the principal centers of industrialized Asia. And to others who would arouse hatred against the United States as a symbol of imperialism, the selfless service of missionaries and physicians, teachers and other young people from the United States in impoverished areas invariably comes as a surprise. Any Asian who takes the trouble to do so finds out soon enough that neither the oncoming tourists nor the retreating soldiery are fully typical of America, that land and people are as diverse in origin and outlook as the Asians themselves. Even more so in some places.

All this makes the United States a puzzlement.

It becomes very difficult, for example, to reconcile the notion of an American pullout in Asia with plans for enormous military aid loans and grants in fiscal year 1972 to such client states as South Vietnam, Cambodia, South Korea, Laos and Thailand.[3] The practical-minded Asian can't help but wonder why the United States is putting

[3] State Dept. figures for these countries, issued July 9, 1971, totaled more than $1 billion but were later scaled down.

out its billions without making better arrangements for the defense of its interests. Nor can he understand why the United States wants non-Communist Asians to hasten their industrial development but at the same time forces a revaluation of their currencies in large part to reduce their competition with American goods.

Such apparent inconsistencies account for a lot of the doubt about American motives and skepticism toward the announced policies of the United States. Almost everywhere I went in Asia, I found a disheartening and ever-widening credibility gap between Americans and Asians. The intelligent Asian invariably asked me, sooner or later, "What are you Americans *really* going to do?"

The declining status of foreign economic aid as a focal point of American policy is also disturbing to Asian opinion, as is the rise of the United States' major ally in the Pacific, Japan, as a trading giant. If there is any satisfaction over Japanese-American trading squabbles, which burst into the open from time to time, it is speedily dissipated by the fear that it will give rise to American protectionism and close off the great American market to Asian goods. Nor do the developing lands in Asia accept with any degree of equanimity the promotion of a Pacific Free Trade Area to bring together the United States, Japan, Canada, Australia and New Zealand. Even without the prospect of mutual tariff concessions among the five, their total intraregional trade already is about 40 per cent of their total trade.[4] Such selective trading among the chief industrialized nations of the Pacific would spell death to the infant industries of many a developing nation.

If the American image in Asia is less than noble, these are some of the reasons for it. There are many others, notably the prospect that a nation of the size and power of the United States would try to go into isolation because events in Asia didn't work out quite as Washington had intended. And this is the most puzzling prospect of all to thoughtful Asians.

The Notion of Isolation

I cannot conclude this opening statement of the American problem without recalling an afternoon's conversation with a wise and dis-

[4] *Pacific Community*, July, 1971, p. 727.

cerning Asian statesman in the foothills of the Himalayas. It was quiet in Katmandu that summer's day. We talked of many things—of the problem of China, the enormous potential of Japan, the disorderly array of Southeast Asia, the effect and meaning of the American withdrawal in the Pacific. I tried to make the point that Asians, on the whole, were far more fearful of a policy of American isolation than was the American public itself. At length, my diplomatic host said, "I do not know whether the United States intends to go into isolation or not, and perhaps Americans don't know, either. In any case, we are a non-aligned country and we believe in a continuing policy of non-alignment. But I must ask myself, 'Will the world be a better place if the United States withdraws from the Pacific and goes into isolation?'"

A corollary to that question might also be posed: Will the United States be any better off with a sharply and even a dangerously reduced commitment in the Pacific?

That, too, is a part of the American dilemma. There will be many such questions in these pages and the American people and their government will be able to supply only a part of the answers. For in the long view, the peoples on the rim of the Pacific and Indian oceans are becoming increasingly interdependent and the Asian and American continents must take far better account of each other in these critical years. How to do it is the problem.

2 . THE DECLINE OF AMERICAN POWER

What brought the United States to the brink of national paralysis over the conduct of the long and unpopular war in Vietnam?

Assuredly, it was not the overpowering attack of a superior armed force, for North Vietnam remains nothing more than a fourth-class military power. Nor was it due to the machinations of international Communism, directed by the Soviet Union as the chief supplier of arms for Hanoi and abetted, in this instance, by China despite its troubles with Moscow.

More than anything else, the United States failure in Vietnam was due to the inability of successive American governments to impress their concept of the national interest in Asia on the American public. This was more than a credibility gap. It was a breakdown in the relationship between the governors and the governed without parallel in the United States since the Civil War. This tragedy did not burst upon the nation all at once. It was many years in the making.

"Bring the Boys Back Home!"

Even before the Japanese surrender on the deck of the U.S.S. *Missouri* on September 2, 1945, in Tokyo Bay, there were insurrections at major American troop centers. Regardless of the effect on American military power, then at its apex, a violent and unreasoning mass movement had developed in the United States to "bring the boys back home." As the pressure increased, the Under Secretary of War, Robert P. Patterson, had to go on a personal tour to quiet the enraged soldiers and a point system had to be devised to facilitate discharges from the service.

But nothing could placate American public opinion. It insisted on tearing down American military might in order to bring sons, husbands, fathers and boy friends back to the family hearth at once. Radio disc jockeys were in the forefront of the movement, rallying their listeners to action with shrill invective. In very large sections of the popular press, the biggest headlines were devoted to stimulation of the cause.

Congress buckled under the accumulated pressure of mail, telephone calls and personal visits from frenzied wives, girl friends and parents. Nobody heard very much then about all the implausible theories of amiable but impractical philosophers who hold the power of public opinion in a democratic society to be a pleasant and harmless myth. President Harry S Truman himself, after less than five months in the White House, had to announce at a press conference that he was doing everything within his power to "bring the boys back home." The fighting had stopped only nine days before in the Pacific war.

The few voices of reason that dared to cry out in alarm were all but lost in the rising clamor.

General Matthew B. Ridgway denounced the mob attack as a

"shameful demobilization."[5] *The New York Times* declared ominously that the "present pellmell rush out of Europe and Asia, under Congressional pressure, is nothing less than a new retreat into isolation."[6] When Army discharges alone reached seven million out of a force of twelve million the following spring, President Truman sardonically announced it was "the most remarkable demobilization in the history of the world, or 'disintegration,' if you want to call it that."[7]

The United States was to pay a terrible price for a stampede to an uncertain peace and a return to business as usual, but the public will could not be thwarted under the circumstances. In a matter of months, it reduced to near impotence the mightiest military machine the world had ever seen up to that time—a conquering force that was able to sustain a million casualties, including nearly 300,000 battle deaths in all theaters of war, and the loss of $350 billion in military and civilian property.

Within five years, schoolboys had to be instructed in the meaning of Pearl Harbor, Guadalcanal, the Coral Sea, and Iwo Jima, over which the Marines raised the flag on Mount Suribachi for the most memorable of all war pictures. The banners of the victorious American divisions were furled and forgotten. And even the foot-slogging GI himself was remembered only in the funny pages as a monumental "sad sack."

No wonder that Stalin consolidated the Soviet Union's position in North Korea and Kim Il Sung bided his time for attack! No wonder that Mao Tse-tung had no fear of American retribution as he savagely battered the wavering forces of Nationalist China! No wonder that Ho Chi Minh, the surprise beneficiary of secret American aid in the closing days of the war in Indochina, made his preparations for a major campaign to force the French into the sea!

American military power, once a mighty force to be feared and

[5] Matthew B. Ridgway, *Soldier* (New York: Harper & Bros., 1956), p. 157.

[6] Meyer Berger, *The Story of The New York Times* (New York: Simon and Schuster, 1951), p. 534.

[7] Harry S Truman, *Memoirs* (New York: Doubleday, 1955), Vol. I, pp. 506–510.

respected, had surprisingly vanished from Asia almost overnight with the exception of Japan. The new masters of Asia must have mused on the strange and unpredictable ways of this form of government called American democracy. But, with alacrity, they took advantage of its weakness.

The Acheson Doctrine

Another critical instance of governmental conflict with the public will, not unexpectedly, developed from the first; such phenomena seldom are isolated occurrences. There was one confusing element, however, in the new chapter that was to be enacted in the complicated drama of Pacific power—a speech by the Secretary of State, Dean Acheson, before the National Press Club in Washington on January 12, 1950.

In the light of decisions made by the Joint Chiefs of Staff, Acheson publicly excluded both Korea and Formosa from the American defense perimeter, which, he said, ran "along the Aleutians to Japan and then . . . to the Ryukyus [and] from the Ryukyus to the Philippine Islands . . ." He went on to say, "So far as the military security of other areas in the Pacific is concerned, it must be clear that no person can guarantee these areas against military attack. But it must also be clear that such a guarantee is hardly sensible or necessary within the realm of practical relationship."

Then came a specific declaration of intent, which foreshadowed another doctrine nearly twenty years afterward: "Should such an attack occur—one hesitates to say where such an armed attack should come from—the initial reliance must be on the people attacked to resist it and then upon the commitments of the entire civilized world under the Charter of the United Nations, which so far has not proved a weak reed to lean on by any people who are determined to protect their independence against outside aggression."[8]

It doesn't matter so much today that Acheson was wrongfully blamed by the Republicans, led by Senator Joseph R. McCarthy, for virtually "inviting" the Communists to attack in Korea. After the

---

[8] W. W. Rostow, *The United States in the World Arena* (New York: Harper & Row, 1960), p. 235.

passage of twenty years, most fair-minded Americans accept the thesis that the Secretary of State was trying, within the conventional wisdom of the era, to limit American responsibilities in the Pacific and to that end he publicized the decisions of the Joint Chiefs of Staff.

What *does* matter is that when the attack came on June 25, 1950, President Truman realized almost at once that the doctrine of placing "the initial reliance . . . on the people attacked" simply couldn't work in Korea. He had to decide within hours whether to honor American commitments by intervening with whatever military strength we could muster or to stand aside and let the Communists take all of Korea—a dagger pointed at the heart of Japan.

Why the Public Backed the Korean War

Should the President have turned to the Senate to "advise and consent" before he plunged the United States into war? It is an academic question today. And, while there is little doubt that he was constitutionally obliged to do so, it is also true that the situation scarcely offered time for the luxury of a full-scale Senate debate between "hawks" and "doves."

In any event, Truman took the gamble of ordering General Douglas MacArthur's slender American forces into action against the North Korean invaders without any assurance that either the Senate or public opinion would support him. Nor did he have any notion what the United Nations would do, even though he had authorized a United States appeal to the Security Council. The fact is that the American defenders had been in action for more than twelve hours at the time the Council met that bright and beautiful Sunday at Lake Success.

It was only through a freak of history that the United States won the priceless moral support of the United Nations against the aggressors. Despite the crisis, the Soviet Union chose to continue the boycott it had been conducting against the U.N. for months to protest the exclusion of Communist China. The United States argued successfully the fine legal point that an absence by a great power in the Security Council could not be construed as an automatic veto.

Thereby, at three momentous Council sessions within a month, the Americans won a condemnation of North Korea as the aggressor and were given the authority to command a United Nations army to oppose the North Koreans.

This was the decisive stroke that insured President Truman of the support of the Senate and a majority of the public in the summer and fall of 1950. To the conservatives, ever in favor of fighting Communism, it wouldn't have mattered what the United Nations did. The American right would have been for armed opposition to the North Koreans in any case, particularly with their idol, General MacArthur, leading the U.S.-U.N. crusade. It was to dominant liberal opinion in the eastern United States, the old interventionists of World War II, that the United Nations' blessings made the difference.

Thus, it came about that President Truman, instead of facing a threat of impeachment, became a folk hero for at least a few months of the Korean War. While there were no flag-waving parades in the streets of American cities, with pretty girls chanting martial songs, nobody thought of organizing protests, burning American flags, or marching with North Korean banners and portraits of Kim Il Sung. On American campuses, all was docile, too. When students were called up by the reserves or were caught in the draft, they went quietly if not willingly. There is no known instance of a faculty member rising in righteous wrath to protest that students' constitutional rights were being violated in the absence of a declaration of war.

South Korean incompetence in military affairs and the tightening of dictatorial rule, all perfectly apparent to the outside world, were regretfully accepted in the United States as facts of life. No reporter was denounced for publicizing the woeful weaknesses of our Asian ally. The only point on which there was public vindictiveness was the failure of the United Nations to come to the support of the United States quickly with large contingents of troops.

Here, both the conservative press and conservative politicians made targets of Britain and France in particular; nobody, however, picketed the White House. The Chicago *Tribune,* that pillar of conservatism, groused on its editorial page that the "White House gang" was "enormously popular," a tribute that was richly deserved. But the popularity didn't last.

Stalemate in Korea

The American public, trained by complaisant historians from grammar school up to believe that American arms would triumph despite every setback, found the opening months of the Korean War very much to its liking. There was the fabled retreat at the opening of the conflict, due to the historic inability of the United States to prepare itself against aggression, and the sudden dazzling blow with which General MacArthur hurled his troops at the enemy's rear in Inchon. The North Korean retreat followed under blistering American firepower and purple MacArthurian rhetoric. So far, all was well.

But by September, the Americans were rushing toward the Chinese border and the United Nations allies murmured nervous protests. By October, the Indians were signaling Washington frantically that the Chinese were about to enter the war. By November, disregarding MacArthur's proud prediction that he was about to end the war and "send the boys home for Christmas," the Chinese hurled an initial force of 250,000 crack troops into the war.

Now it was the Americans who had to fall back and a disillusioned public began grumbling. The American right accused the White House of a "no win" policy. MacArthur, the greatest American proconsul in Asia, demanded an immediate attack on China to deny the enemy a "privileged sanctuary." But before anything else could happen in this frightening situation, President Truman moved again. At 1 A.M. on April 11, 1951, he relieved MacArthur of his command, charging insubordination. A few weeks later, the Russians proposed a cease-fire.

The American public, confused and bewildered by a war of limited aims, a war "that couldn't be won or lost," took little part in the proceedings. After the truce talks began on July 10, 1951, the war was usually shoved back inside the newspapers even though hard fighting continued for two years. To all intents and purposes, it became, truly, the "forgotten war."

The Long Truce

The efforts of America's greatest living war hero, General Dwight David Eisenhower, had to be invoked before the fighting ended. A disillusioned public, determined on change and impressed by the old general's promise to end the war if he were elected President, sent him to the White House in 1952. When the truce was signed at Panmunjom the following summer, however, there was no jubilation in the United States. Although the State Department worked very hard to convince the public that the war had been a defeat for Communist aggression, the man in the street didn't see it that way. He knew it was not, by any stretch of the imagination, a glorious American victory of the kind the schoolbook historians had always led him to expect.

The truth was that the Chinese, with minor assistance from the North Koreans, had been able to contain the best efforts of a United Nations force that included 230,000 Americans, 450,000 South Koreans, and contingents from fifteen other countries totaling 50,000 troops. The Chinese casualties were said to exceed 900,000. However, the United Nations losses were heavy, too, totaling 447,000 dead and 550,000 wounded, of which the Americans alone suffered 33,600 battle dead and more than 100,000 wounded.[9]

Despite everything the Democrats could do, the outrageous theory gained ground in the country that American arms had been denied a well-earned victory through treachery in Washington. It was the high tide of the McCarthyite movement that would surely have torn the country apart if its leader, drunk with power, had not challenged the Army and the White House and fallen under the censure of his peers in the Senate.

All the signs of public displeasure with long, unsuccessful wars in remote places were plainly to be seen. But the elite in Washington disregarded the warning. Not too long after the signing of the uneasy Korean truce, the United States was being committed to still another

[9] Matthew B. Ridgway, *The Korean War* (Garden City, N.Y.: Doubleday & Co., 1967), pp. 195, 218; Robert Leckie, *Conflict* (New York: G. P. Putnam's Sons, 1962), pp. 312–313, 429. U.S. casualties are from official Defense Department figures.

Asian war. It was a fatal disregard of the power of American public opinion.

3. THE ROAD TO VIETNAM

At the outset of John Foster Dulles' quixotic effort to build a wall of containment around Communist power, he visited India's great Prime Minister, Jawaharlal Nehru, in New Delhi to explain the proposition to him. Dulles, of course, knew quite well that Nehru's non-aligned sympathies would be for the Soviet Union and against the United States in any crisis. However, President Eisenhower's dour Secretary of State, one of the most distinguished international lawyers of his time, was determined to do his best to make Nehru understand the American position. Unfortunately for Dulles on that less than historic occasion, his oratory failed to win a convert; worse still, when he paused after a particularly brilliant flight of rhetoric, he noted to his utter discomfiture that Nehru had fallen asleep.[10]

Dulles, always a proud man, stomped out of the Prime Minister's mansion and took the next plane out of Palam Airport. Within a short time, he interested Pakistan in the proposition he had tried in vain to sell to Nehru. Thus, on September 8, 1954, the Southeast Asia Treaty Organization was born. Through it, the United States became allied with Pakistan as well as Australia, France, New Zealand, the Philippines, Thailand and the United Kingdom.

Few in the United States were bothered when the pact extended the signatories' military protection to the three successor states in French Indochina, all non-members. It was, the more liberal editorial writers observed wryly, just another instance of what they called Dulles' "pactomania." Yet, this was the instrument through which the United States was led into the longest and most disastrous war in its history.

Why Vietnam?

If many Americans were confused by the war in Korea, they were utterly bewildered by the war in Vietnam. In the first place, most of them did not know where Vietnam was and initially cared even less.

[10] An intimate of Nehru's, a former Cabinet minister, told me the story during a visit in New Delhi in 1970.

In the second, it was a universally held opinion that, after Korea, the United States had no business taking part in any other war in Asia. It was no accident that the 1955 Pulitzer Prize for cartooning went to D. R. Fitzpatrick of the St. Louis *Post-Dispatch* for a drawing in 1954 that showed a hesitant Uncle Sam, gun in hand, standing before a quagmire labeled "French mistakes in Indochina." The caption read: "How would another mistake help?"

Yet by that time, the United States was deeply involved in this "crummy war," to use a phrase of the Chicago *Daily News*'s durable war correspondent Keyes Beech. Alarmed by the Communist victory in China and Ho Chi Minh's successes at the head of his pro-Communist Vietminh in Indochina, the United States decided as early as December 30, 1949, that it must "block further Communist expansion in Asia" and pay "particular attention . . . to the problem of French Indochina." On May 8, 1950, after recognizing the French-supported government of Bao Dai, the United States granted $10 million in military aid to the French. On June 27, President Truman sent a thirty-five-man Military Assistance Advisory Group to Indochina to teach troops in the new French Union State of Vietnam how to use American weapons.

A Mutual Assistance Agreement followed on December 23 and on September 7, 1951, American economic assistance began flowing into Saigon. This was how it happened that by 1954, the last year of France's tottering empire in the Far East, the United States had put up $1.1 billion in military aid for the French side in Vietnam, 78 per cent of French war costs. No wonder the authors of the Pentagon Papers on the Vietnam War wrote, from hindsight, that as early as 1950 the United States was "directly involved in the developing tragedy in Vietnam."[11]

But to most Americans, the war in Vietnam still seemed desperately unreal. Nevertheless, in the last days of the French stand at Dienbienphu, there was such pressure on President Eisenhower to intervene that he authorized a draft resolution asking for Congressional permission to send American troops to Indochina. The main pro-French forces in the Administration, Secretary of State John

[11] Pentagon Papers, *The New York Times*, July 5, 1971, p. 13. Much of this is also in Truman, *op. cit.*, Vol. II, p. 519.

Foster Dulles and Admiral Arthur W. Radford, the chairman of the Joint Chiefs of Staff, evidently had able reinforcement from the then Vice-President of the United States, Richard Milhous Nixon. Appearing before a group of American editors in Washington for a background talk, Nixon warmly advocated American armed intervention to save the French from defeat by the Communists in Indochina.

The Democrats weren't as enthusiastic. The Senate majority leader, Lyndon Baines Johnson, warned against a "blood-letting spree" in which American troops would be fighting "to perpetuate colonialism and white man's exploitation in Asia." And the young senator from Massachusetts, John Fitzgerald Kennedy, bluntly told the French that they were to blame for their own predicament and would get no American military aid.[12]

As early as April 4, 1954, President Eisenhower had decided against American military intervention without Congressional approval and he held resolutely to that course despite all the furor. He made his position publicly known on April 29, in connection with the opening of the Far Eastern Conference at Geneva. And when Dienbienphu fell on May 7, there was no mourning in the United States and no sense of impending catastrophe. Even the persistent Dulles finally gave up trying to get American troops into Indochina on June 15 when he saw that the French cause was hopeless.

The United States did not sign the Geneva agreement of July 21, 1954, under which the French gave up Indochina to the struggling successor states of North and South Vietnam, Laos and Cambodia, but agreed to abide by its terms. The reason for the curious American position was the conclusion by the National Security Council on August 8 and 12 that the settlement was a "disaster" and a "major forward stride of Communism which may lead to the loss of Southeast Asia." The domino theory, under which one Asian country after another would topple into the Communist net, was deeply believed then in Washington. Despite intelligence warnings, the American government approved a Dulles plan for a limited intervention in defense of South Vietnam.[13] And with Dulles' creation of the SEATO

[12] *Congressional Record*, April 6–14, 1954, pp. 4402–4977 *passim*.
[13] Pentagon Papers, *The New York Times*, July 5, 1971, p. 13.

pact at about the same time, the machinery was set up for eventual American intervention.

Soon, the United States was secretly circumventing the Geneva accords. Colonel Edward G. Lansdale of the CIA was sent into South Vietnam with a team of "paramilitary" agents for operations against North Vietnam, which he carried out with skill but little perceptible impact on the war itself. It was the first post-Geneva step in support of the new leader of South Vietnam, Ngo Dinh Diem. While the United States did not direct Premier Diem to refuse to hold the 1956 elections for the unification of Vietnam, provided for in the Geneva pact, the record is replete with American pleas to delay the voting as long as possible. In any event, the election was never held and the insurgency against the South Vietnamese government began the following year.[14]

The United States has always contended that the uprising against Diem was fomented and directed by Hanoi, but the authors of the Pentagon's war history have their doubts. They pointed out that South Vietnamese, in the main, formed the first Vietcong units that fought against Diem in 1957 and Hanoi's decision to intervene came two years later. It was then that the North Vietnamese apparatus in the south, which had been present since 1954, was activated in behalf of the Vietcong, the Pentagon historians concluded.[15] By the time the Kennedy Administration came into power, the insurgency in the south was in full swing. Diem's government already had lost at least half the countryside and was slipping rapidly. The situation in Laos was even worse. But a calculated policy of lying already had been instituted and everything on the surface was made to look good.

The Kennedy Commitment

When John F. Kennedy became President, he had a chance to extricate the United States from Vietnam but couldn't bring himself to do so. The political formula of "fighting Communism" was too appealing; moreover, President Kennedy was by no means as peaceful a man as Senator Kennedy had been.

[14] *Ibid.*, p. 14.
[15] *Ibid.*, p. 12.

Badly mauled politically by the failure of the Bay of Pigs invasion in Cuba, the young President called on April 20, 1961, for action that would prevent Communist domination of South Vietnam. On May 11, against the advice of the intelligence community, he opened a campaign of clandestine warfare against North Vietnam and secretly sent 400 Special Forces troops and 100 additional American military advisers into South Vietnam. That breached the Geneva accords, which limited the United States to 685 military advisers in the south, so nothing was said about it. In the words of the Pentagon's historians, the "limited risk gamble" of the Eisenhower Administration became a "broad commitment" by the Kennedy Administration to save South Vietnam from Communism. But the public didn't know it.

A crisis over Berlin and the Cuban missile confrontation with the Soviet Union probably prevented Kennedy from taking any step for a major build-up in South Vietnam. Nevertheless, the United States had sent in 16,000 reinforcements by October 1963. They didn't help much. For while Diem and his American advisers were proclaiming victory from the housetops of Saigon, they actually were on the verge of losing the country to Ho Chi Minh and only a handful of young foreign correspondents in Saigon had the courage to say so.

Kennedy sent in a new ambassador, Henry Cabot Lodge, Jr., who soon began assisting a group of Vietnamese generals in a plot to overthrow Diem. By October 30, 1963, the White House was cabling Lodge to use his own judgment in the matter but warning that once the coup began, "it is in the interest of the U.S. Government that it should succeed." On November 1, the generals overthrew Diem and his powerful brother, Ngo Dinh Nhu, seized them and killed them. Lodge cabled Washington three days later that it would shorten the war.[16] It didn't. Far from improving the situation, the Diem assassination made things worse and a whole succession of weak military regimes in Saigon tottered from one crisis to another.

The War Goes Up—and Down

With President Kennedy's assassination on November 22, 1963, the initiative for war or peace in Vietnam passed to his successor, the

[16] Pentagon Papers, *The New York Times*, July 1, 1971, pp. 3–14.

Vice-President, Lyndon Baines Johnson. Once again, an American President with an anti-war record on Vietnam could not bring himself to order a retreat in the face of a Communist enemy. To his friends and associates, the new President raised the non-issue that he did not want to become the first President of the United States to preside over a losing war. Without doubt, he also remembered the great scare of the early 1950s when the Democrats had been charged, without justification, with being "soft on Communism." Knowing that his probable challenger for the Presidency in 1964 would be a Republican conservative, Barry Goldwater, Johnson was reluctant to expose a weak chink in his political armor. And so, throughout the campaign, he procrastinated.

The evidence of the Pentagon Papers shows that the President, on February 1, 1964, authorized "an elaborate program of covert military operations" against North Vietnam but hesitated to send in American troops for a year thereafter. The secret war included commando raids into North Vietnamese territory, air raids by CIA-recruited pilots and destroyer patrols in the Golf of Tonkin. While all this clandestine action was going on, Pentagon and State Department planners on May 23, 1964, drafted an elaborate scenario that was intended to lead to full-scale bombing of North Vietnam in a month. On May 25 a draft was even made of a joint Congressional resolution that amounted to a declaration of war.

But President Johnson balked. The intelligence community was unimpressed with the entire business. And action on the whole program was put off, although parts of it were instituted piecemeal.

The public's attention, meanwhile, was being centered on the Presidential campaign, where a curious charade was taking place. Johnson was solemnly depicting himself as a man of peace while his belligerent opponent, Goldwater, was being painted as a desperado anxious for atomic war. And secretly, the North Vietnamese were being pressed into desperate action by every possible means. At length, on July 30, patrols from South Vietnam attacked two North Vietnamese islands in the Gulf of Tonkin and North Vietnamese torpedo boats swarmed to the defense. On August 4, they attacked the American destroyers *Maddox* and *C. Turner Joy*.

It was the break for which the Johnson Administration had been waiting. Within twelve hours, reprisal air strikes were directed against North Vietnam and President Johnson thereafter appeared on television, telling the American people of an unprovoked attack on the two destroyers and his retaliatory action. "We still seek no wider war," he said. On August 7, the long-planned joint Congressional resolution was overwhelmingly approved by both houses, giving the President power "to take all necessary measures to repel any armed attack against the forces of the United States and to prevent further aggression" in Southeast Asia.

It wasn't by any means a declaration of war but the Administration acted as if it had been.[17] Such suspicious critics as Senator Wayne Morse of Oregon, who dared to suggest that the whole thing seemed to have been pretty well planned, were howled down as unpatriotic connivers who sought to undermine the national morale. And so, in bright and shining propaganda armor, the Administration did battle with the dragons of Communism and President Johnson was overwhelmingly elected to a full term in the White House.

After so many ups and downs, the war was about to break wide open.

Escalation

As early as September 7, 1964, a White House strategy conference reached agreement that widespread air attacks would be necessary before North Vietnam could be persuaded to abandon its campaign against the south. On the day of the President's election, November 3, the final stage of planning was begun. And on February 13, 1965, the President finally issued the order for the sustained bombing of North Vietnam.[18] But alas for him and for his optimistic strategists, the bombing only increased North Vietnam's resolution to fight on and stiffened the attitude of Hanoi's allies, especially the Soviet Union. The Pentagon's historians wrote sadly, "After a month of bombing with no response from the North Vietnamese, optimism began to wane."

The next step, so long urged by General William C. Westmoreland, the American commander in South Vietnam, was the massive influx

[17] Pentagon Papers, *The New York Times*, June 13, 1971, pp. 35–40.
[18] Pentagon Papers, *The New York Times*, June 14, 1971, pp. 27–32.

of American ground troops. Both John A. McCone, director of the Central Intelligence Agency, and George W. Ball, the Under Secretary of State, warned that the ground war would be both unwise and fruitless. Ball even proposed that the United States withdraw from Vietnam.

Once again, the best advice was swept aside in the impetuous rush of the Johnson Administration for self-justification in an ill-judged Asian military adventure. The President decided on April 1 to order American ground troops into offensive action in South Vietnam. Five days later, the first increase of 18,000–20,000 troops was authorized. On April 7, as a kind of afterthought, he proposed North Vietnamese participation in the giant Mekong River Valley development project —the Pentagon's historians called it a "billion-dollar carrot" offer— and also offered to negotiate for peace without preconditions. In May, he gave the North Vietnamese an unannounced five-day bombing pause to see if they were weakening.[19] They weren't. By summertime, 125,000 American fighting men were in the beleaguered land and the President was saying, "This is really war."[20]

As the American commitment increased, members of the SEATO pact and others were pressed to contribute troops, with assurances of substantial payment for services rendered. The South Koreans came, 50,000 strong, and the Thais in lesser numbers. The Australians, Filipinos and others sent what amounted to token forces. But the Americans, of course, carried the burden of combat, with more than 500,000 ground troops in action at the peak of the war against North Vietnam and the Vietcong.

Instead of weakening, the enemy waxed stronger and boldly took the offensive at a time when, by all American calculations, Hanoi should have been piteously begging to have the war halted. On January 31, 1968, during Tet, the Lunar New Year, the climactic enemy offensive began with an attack on the United States embassy in Saigon. Nearly every city and most of the principal towns of South Vietnam suffered attack, the worst being against Hué, which was captured and held for almost a month.

President Johnson publicly announced the attack had been antici-

---

[19] Pentagon Papers, *The New York Times*, June 15, 1971, pp. 21–24.
[20] *The New York Times*, July 29, 1965.

pated and that the enemy had suffered a great defeat. But from the evidence of the Pentagon Papers, he was shocked and upset by the North Vietnamese offensive. He received a top-level military report on February 28 conceding that the North Vietnamese and the Vietcong now held the initiative, were operating "with relative freedom in the countryside," and had driven the Saigon government forces back into the towns and the cities. The pacification program, in consequence, was badly damaged, the report said.

The home front, so long deluded, deceived and misinformed, had enough. Seeing nothing ahead but protracted conflict for a cause that aroused little enthusiasm at best, the American public fairly exploded in disapproval. On the nation's campuses, there were riotous demonstrations for peace that spring. And despite the manifold pressures of the Joint Chiefs of Staff for a general call-up of reserves and the virtual placement of the nation on a war footing, it was the public will that prevailed.

On March 31, 1968, President Johnson ended the bombing of all but the southern border of North Vietnam, called for peace talks and announced that he would not be a candidate for re-election. For him, the war in Vietnam had become the end of the road.[21]

4. THE GREAT RETREAT

When Richard Milhous Nixon entered the White House in 1969, he had to deal first of all with a full-blown peace movement encompassing all levels of American society—a huge, unruly, uncontrollable public upheaval. The old anti-Communist fighter and Vietnam war hawk might have been expected to bellow defiance. But he did not. He advised his countrymen first of all to lower their voices and reduce the level of tumult. He promised to do the rest.

It didn't work. Despite the opening of peace talks in Paris, the announcement of a program of "Vietnamization" of the war, and the withdrawal of 60,000 American troops in two operations five months apart, the peace demonstrations in the United States mounted in fervor. For a sensible and realistic politician of Nixon's experience, the message was clear. He realized he had to find a better and a surer

[21] Pentagon Papers, *The New York Times*, July 4, 1971, pp. 15–17.

way to lead the United States out of the Vietnam War and other potentially dangerous commitments in Asia without seeming to knuckle under to the Communists.

The Beginning at Guam

The President made a start on July 25, 1969, in what was, to all outward appearances, a routine press conference on the island of Guam, a stopover during his summer's trip to Asia. The random nature of this first major departure from American policy was emphasized still more when the President invoked the old press conference rule against direct quotation of a part of what he said. He made these two points:

1. The United States intended to keep all its treaty commitments, such as, for example, the agreement with Thailand in the SEATO pact.

2. The United States henceforth would encourage—and had every right to expect—that Asian nations themselves would take over increasing responsibility for their military defense, except when threatened with nuclear war by a major power.

Then he elaborated as follows and permitted later quotation:

"I want to be sure that our policies in the future all over the world, in Asia, Latin America, Africa and the rest, reduce American involvement . . . I believe that we have—if we examine what happened in Vietnam, how we became so deeply involved—that we have a good chance of avoiding that kind of involvement in the future."

There Were No Cheers

The initial pronouncement of what was to become known as the Nixon, or Guam, Doctrine produced scant enthusiasm and a lot of questions. Like Acheson's declaration twenty years earlier regarding the "initial reliance" on the nation that was attacked, it persuaded few people at the outset that the United States really meant what it said. And when Nixon went out of his way a few days later to give a pledge of help for Thailand, which seemed to run counter to his pronouncement at Guam, these doubts redoubled.

The President accordingly rephrased his doctrine on November 3, 1969, in this manner:

"The United States will keep its treaty commitments.

"We shall provide a shield if a nuclear power threatens the freedom of a nation allied with us, or of a nation whose survival we consider vital to our security and the security of the region as a whole.

"In cases involving other types of aggression we shall furnish military and economic assistance when requested and as appropriate. But we shall look to the nation directly threatened to assume the primary responsibility of providing the manpower for its defense."

Here was disengagement, if Nixon meant what he said, and the home front began to respond somewhat grudgingly. But in the Indo-Pacific, all was confusion. For here, nobody could say exactly what the Nixon Doctrine amounted to, and that included most American ambassadors. A shudder of fear went through the anti-Communist regimes of Southeast Asia.

The President elaborated still more. In his "State of the World" message to the Congress on February 18, 1970, he acknowledged that the varying versions of the Nixon Doctrine, put out chiefly by its author, had raised numerous questions. He sought to answer them as follows:

"First, we remain involved in Asia. We are a Pacific power. We have learned that peace for us is much less likely if there is no peace in Asia.

"Second . . . a growing sense of Asian identity and concrete action toward Asian cooperation are creating a new and healthy pattern of international relationships in that region. Our Asian friends, especially Japan, are in a position to shoulder larger responsibilities in the peaceful progress of the area . . .

"Third, while we will maintain our interests in Asia and the commitments that flow from them, the changes taking place in that region enable us to change the character of our involvement. The responsibilities once borne by the United States at such great cost can now be shared. America can be effective in helping the peoples of Asia harness the forces of change to peaceful progress, and in supporting them as they defend themselves from those who would subvert this process and fling Asia again into conflict."

Whatever was happening in Asia, there was no doubt that Nixon now was making progress with the public at home. Through sheer persuasion, he was selling himself to the American public as a prophet of peace and a new order.

The Upset

Then came Cambodia. On March 18, 1970, while Prince Norodom Sihanouk was out of the country, he was overthrown in a bloodless coup organized by General Lon Nol. For once, the "privileged sanctuary" of North Vietnamese and Vietcong forces along the Cambodia border was laid bare for attack. The Vietcong headquarters, the fabled "Central Office," which had been pinpointed for years on Cambodian territory, lost its protector. With a new regime in power, the agile Sihanouk no longer could spin out his furious lies about Cambodian neutrality, which nobody believed but which the United States had chosen to respect.

There was a great temptation in both Saigon and Washington to take advantage of the unexpected opportunity to wreck the enemy's sanctuary, disrupt his supply lines and make him pay heavily in human blood and suffering for his long years of security along the Cambodian frontier. To experienced military leaders, it had always seemed impossible to conduct separate wars in Vietnam, Laos and Cambodia. Once, just after taking over as the American commander in Vietnam in 1964, General William C. Westmoreland had told a luncheon companion, "The only way this war can be won is to fight one campaign in all three countries."

General Westmoreland had since become Army Chief of Staff. With Sihanouk out of the way, intervention at last was possible. President Nixon, after weighing the consequences, took the gamble, authorized the Cambodian invasion on April 30, 1970, and overnight plunged the United States into its worst crisis of the Vietnam War.

Uproar on the Campus

The American public was thunderstruck. As a survey by the Carnegie Commission on Higher Education since has shown, the American academic community erupted overnight. Out of the nation's 2,550 colleges and universities, 21 per cent closed down, 4 per cent had to call in police to put down rioting, and an over-all total of

57 per cent experienced organized dissent in one form or another. At 18 per cent of the institutions, college and university presidents took public positions against the Cambodian intervention.[22]

"No episode or series of episodes had a higher impact in all of our history than the events of April and May, 1970," said Dr. Clark Kerr, director of the Carnegie Fund Study on the Future of Higher Education. When National Guardsmen killed four students at Kent State University in Ohio on May 4, the disturbances intensified. Of all President Nixon's options, this one did the most damage.

Abroad, the best that can be said for the big gamble in Cambodia is that it bought time. When the South Vietnamese Army (ARVN) went into action in Cambodia for the first time and didn't fall apart, as had been its custom at home more often than not, its American military advisers began claiming success for the Nixon program of "Vietnamization"—of gradually turning the fighting over to their ARVN allies. But it was the little untrained army of 30,000 youthful Cambodians, plus thousands of raw volunteers from the cities and countryside, that displayed the greatest courage in the defense of their country against the Vietcong and the North Vietnamese regulars. While the Americans went rummaging through the borderland in search of the enemy's secret bases and forced the North Vietnamese deeper into the Cambodian countryside, the Cambodian Army performed feats of heroism that were recorded on American television and spread throughout the world.

But neither American arms, the newly found fighting qualities of the South Vietnamese nor the heroics of the Cambodians made any impression in the United States. Quite simply, there was no doubt that the bulk of the American public wanted the war to end. The expansion of the conflict into Cambodia and the renewed flare-up of fighting in Laos were widely resented on the home front. President Nixon, in the words of Bob Dylan's famous protest song, didn't need a weatherman to tell him which way the wind was blowing. Before the first shock of the invasion had been absorbed, he went on television to assure the American people that all American troops would be out of Cambodia by the end of June.

[22] From a report of the Carnegie Commission Survey of University Presidents, *The New York Times,* October 3, 1970.

Once more, the roars of protest had had a major effect on American military strategy in the field.

Pullback from Cambodia

President Nixon kept his word. The 30,000 American troops that had surged into Cambodia were pulled out on schedule. Although many a skeptical correspondent had predicted that the roof would fall in with the American withdrawal, it didn't happen in quite that way. The North Vietnamese and the Vietcong, together with their Cambodian allies, the Khmer Rouge, didn't crash Pnom Penh as if they were going to a party. General Lon Nol's young Cambodians stood and fought. Moreover, as the little Cambodian Army grew, the South Vietnamese continued to surprise their detractors for a time. But, as was the case in Laos, Cambodia appeared to be permanently divided and it scarcely seemed possible that it would ever be the same again. Two years later, Communist troops held more than half the country and numerous military observers believed Pnom Penh would fall to them if they made a serious effort to take the capital.

If there was no joy among the anti-Communist regimes of Southeast Asia over the American pullback from Cambodia, a semblance of order was restored temporarily on the American home front. But President Nixon, a gambler to the end, could not resist a major strike against the Ho Chi Minh Trail network in northern Laos to interdict the enemy supply route during the period of major American troop withdrawals. With American air support, 20,000 of the best South Vietnamese troops invaded Laos during the winter of 1971 and did at least a part of the job assigned to them. The quick mobilization of a North Vietnamese defense, buttressed by tanks and anti-aircraft fire, forced the invaders out on March 24 after forty-four days of action.

"We're Leaving!"

The effect of the Laos campaign was to create even more apprehension among the American public over the intentions of its government. The President was fortunate in being able to avoid the kind of public outcry that had toppled the Johnson Administration in 1968 and caused almost as much turmoil in 1970. Very possibly, the limited American participation in the invasion tamped down the public reaction. Then, too, there had been so many anti-war demonstrations for such a long time in the United States that the young participants were close to exhaustion. In any event, the continued American troop reductions served to restore the public's sense of balance until bombing of the North resumed in 1972.

From Tokyo to Saigon and from Manila to Bangkok, the Pentagon's orders to reduce forces took effect with varying consequences. The protests from the anti-Communist governments were loud and continuous, but had little practical effect on the pullout. In fact, when I asked one eminent American general in Saigon what plans he had for the immediate future, he replied sharply, "We're leaving! Those are my plans. And this time, there's no doubt whatever about it!"

President Nixon had begun removing American troops from South Vietnam even before the Cambodian invasion, but it was a slow and intricate process. From a high of 536,000, he had cut American strength there to fewer than 60,000 troops by spring of 1972. Despite Congressional efforts to speed up the withdrawal, he would not be hurried. Nor did he panic over the North Vietnamese offensive of 1972, which pressed into the heart of the South, and new enemy activity at the Paris peace talks plus renewed anti-war activity at home.

It was clear enough, if the President followed his announced objectives, that a residual force of 30,000 to 50,000 Americans would remain in South Vietnam by the end of the American presidential election year of 1972. And he kept open his option to take even these units out if the enemy proved to be more tractable than expected.

The American withdrawals announced for forces based elsewhere in Asia may not have attracted as much attention on the home front, but they were taken very seriously in the countries that were affected. Even the Japanese, so conscious of their vast industrial power and their increasing military strength, welcomed assurances from the Pentagon that their outdated military equipment would be modernized. But despite similar concessions and continued military aid for South Korea and Thailand, there was resentment over the American pullout.

President Nixon found his situation extremely difficult. The rate of withdrawal from Vietnam and the additional troop cuts he had proposed elsewhere in Asia were not enough to placate either Congress or the public. He even had to stave off a serious move to reduce American troop commitments in Europe by unilateral action and fight to extend the military draft.

There was no doubt that American policies in Asia, for all the brave front put up in Washington, were in disarray. The old American program of containment, intervention and war was bankrupt. The Nixon Doctrine, makeshift and jerry-built, was not much of an improvement. As the position was put by Malcolm Fraser, the Australian minister of defense, "We reject the concept of detachment . . . We do not believe there is any security in isolation. You do not make Southeast Asia or the Indian Ocean disappear by turning your back on them."[23]

It was in this extremity that President Nixon sought to ease the pressure on his Administration by resorting to "instant diplomacy" —a series of dramatic and unexpected moves that he concealed from friend and foe alike until he was ready to act. The first was his announcement of July 15, 1971, of his intention to visit China and his disclosure that the way had been prepared for him by a secret visit of Dr. Henry Kissinger, his assistant for national security affairs, to Premier Chou En-lai in Peking. The second was his declaration of the "dollar war" a month later, in which he severed the dollar from its gold base in an unadmitted move to devalue it, clamped a 10 per cent temporary surcharge on imports to force revaluation of foreign currencies, notably the yen, and sought to bolster the sagging economy with a ninety-day price-wage freeze and new tax benefits mainly for an outpriced American industry.

With the coming of Phase II of the new economic policy, featuring more flexible controls for the longer term, the United States reached new monetary agreements with its nine leading industrial trading partners on December 18, 1971, agreed to devalue the dollar and lift the 10 per cent import surcharge.[24] But that was only the beginning

[23] *U.S. News & World Report,* August 31, 1970, p. 21.

[24] By raising the price of gold from $35 to $38 an ounce, a reduction of 8.57 per cent was made in the value of the dollar. Assuming that this and all other agreements of the ten were carried out, this meant an effective reduction of about 12 per cent in the value of the dollar against other leading currencies, excluding the Canadian.

of the long effort to solve the economic crisis. The outlook, for all the cheering in Washington, remained clouded.

5. THE PUBLIC AND FOREIGN POLICY

An impatient and often censorious public seldom sits with folded hands once it becomes aware of an impending upheaval in the United States. From the Boston Tea Party to the riots over Vietnam, that is the American record. In troubled times, it is not often that people are willing to await the descent of some star-spangled Moses from the Hill, Washington's Sinai, with the Word.

Can a Policy Be Imposed?

The apparent belief of three presidents—Kennedy, Johnson and Nixon—that national commitments can be made by executive fiat raises the question of whether a new Asian policy, in part or as a whole, can be successfully imposed. The answer would appear to be no, but there are still pizza-pie Machiavellis in the Pentagon who privately believe that they can lull the public into accepting an American military presence on the Asian mainland in the post-Vietnam era.

This is, of course, a total misreading of the lessons of the American wars in Indochina. Neither the American Congress nor the public, particularly the young, is likely to forget the furtive manner in which the nation became involved in its most disastrous war. Because the venture was undertaken to fight Communism, the military brand of automatic anti-Communism is not going to be very popular for a long time to come. In addition, those Asian leaders who set up a cynical cry of "Communist take-over!" from now on are not going to find the United States ready to rush in at once with men, arms and riches to give them undeserved support.

This scarcely means that more Americans are likely to tolerate Communist philosophy or agree that it is a beneficial form of government. It does mean that relatively few Americans, outside dedicated conservatives of the old school, are going to respond with loud yawps of applause to the ever-familiar political summons, around election time, to a great anti-Communist crusade. A lot of sharp questions are likely to be asked, both today and tomorrow, of the advocates of any policy that is likely to involve the United States in a war, especially a long war in which victory is a remote possibility.

The United States might have arrived at this critical position in its history a lot sooner if Dwight David Eisenhower had not been able to stop the shooting in the Korean War in 1953. For the American public will make a lot of allowances for its government's mistakes in wartime if victory is ultimately achieved. But if war yields only an unpalatable truce, as in Korea, or aimless fighting for indefinite goals, as in Indochina, then the American government forfeits the public trust in part or in whole. And whatever policies it is able to follow, in such an eventuality, must perforce be of a largely negative character—the doleful consequence of any military retreat, no matter what fine words are used to try to disguise it.

The Making of a Policy

What procedures should the United States follow to formulate a set of new and realistic policies to safeguard its national interest in the Pacific for the long tomorrow? There are many possibilities, from the usual ineffable convocation of wise men, real and fancied, in the secret recesses of the White House, State Department and Pentagon to the droning television hearings devised for the benefit of the Senate Foreign Relations Committee. President Nixon, during the spring and summer of 1971, took the additional step of holding regional conferences with editors and others. It was a somewhat tardy recognition of the public factor in the formulation of foreign policy.

Whatever the method, it is not likely to produce an instant Pacific policy, seasoned to the public taste, cooked to Congressional perfection and served up with a flourish by the nation's Chief Executive. Rather, in the bumbling and the muddling through that are characteristic of policy formulation in much of American diplomatic history, both government and people may be expected to proceed haltingly from one trial to another until some uneasy and probably less than triumphant consensus is attained.

"Open Covenants"

President Wilson once championed the cause of "open covenants
. . . openly arrived at," but he did not mean thereby to invite the
public to peer over the policy maker's shoulder. Nor did he approve
of the journalist who filched government secrets, genuine or not, and
broadcast them to the nation. In fact, nobody was more shocked than
the scholar–president by the rough-and-tumble coverage of the press
at Versailles in 1919 and the premature disclosure of Article X of the
Covenant of the League of Nations. It was the weapon Henry Cabot
Lodge, Sr., and his associates used to bludgeon an embittered and
resentful America into isolation.

In all fairness, however, it should be noted as well that other
journalistic disclosures, notably the Dumbarton Oaks Papers, helped
right the balance and stimulated public thinking in favor of American participation in the United Nations at the end of World War II.
Nor was the publication of the Pentagon Papers a blow to the governmental process in the United States. Actually, the disclosures in
the main only served to confirm what many had suspected and
blocked the government from a return to the devious tactics that had
forced an unwilling nation into an unwanted war.

It will not do, therefore, for the American government to try to
separate the public from its press by making out the press to be a
traitorous villain and an enemy of the national interest. These tactics
have been tried often, without distinguished result, in less enlightened
states. True, journalists do not always fight on the side of the angels,
it being notably difficult these days to distinguish heavenly messen-
gers from the myriad who claim to represent the divine will. But in
an open society, the journalist is the guardian of the non-govern-
mental channels through which the public receives much of its trust-
worthy information. And in the United States, for want of a Congressional questioning mechanism, he is also the chief interlocutor of the
government.

No one has ever really tried to bring the government, the public
and the press together through a policy of "open covenants . . .
openly arrived at." There have been many objections whenever
someone suggested giving so idealistic a procedure a trial. The White

House has argued for its right to privacy in its planning, the same right that is routine procedure in business enterprises. The State Department has cried out that it cannot reveal every message between itself and foreign capitals. And the Pentagon has thundered that almost everything it does, from an order for coffee beans to the newest arms sale to some Latin American country, is covered by national security.

It is high time to try to squeeze some of the nonsense out of foreign policy planning and execution. Fortunately, there are a declining number of officials who believe that the making of American foreign policy should be an esoteric exercise of power at the highest levels of government. Policy makers have, for the most part, become aware of the need for public support but too many still argue that certain policies, which are regarded as too sensitive for public discussion, can be "sold" to the American people upon adoption.

It won't do. Sensible people are well aware of the need for privacy in diplomatic negotiations and are as concerned as any general over the safeguarding of the national interest. What is required here is no day-by-day revelation of what the American ambassador in Thailand did or did not say to the foreign minister in Bangkok, but some concrete evidence of the willingness of the American government to consult its people, wherever possible, when dangerous tensions arise in international affairs.

There are many ways in which this kind of thing can be done, and done well. Franklin Delano Roosevelt did it with his frequent news conferences, his fireside chats and his willingness to include Congressional leaders of both major parties in important international negotiations. Had he been as stubborn as Wilson, as devious as Kennedy or Johnson, or as authoritarian as Nixon, he could never have achieved success for his foreign policies. But then, there was a unique bond between FDR and the American people, a feeling of faith and trust that has been lost for more than a generation and will be difficult to restore.

The attempt will have to be made, however, if public confidence in the policy-making process is to be regained and the American dilemma in the Far East resolved. That is the responsibility of government. For a public that is becoming increasingly concerned over the lack of an integrated American approach to the nation's troubles in Asia, the prime necessity is more information and more background on which it may be possible to make sound judgments. This book, in the detailed treatment that follows of the problems of Asian countries and their links with the United States, is an effort to advance that most important cause. It is basic to the building of a stronger and more enduring American relationship with the peoples of the Indo-Pacific.

II. Japan as a World Power

1. ATTITUDES

Toward the close of his illustrious career as Malaysia's first prime minister, Abdul Rahman surveyed the state of Asia and remarked with spirit and conviction, "I'm sure of one thing: the Japanese are not to be trusted. They take twice as much out of a country as they put in."

The old Tunku chuckled and added, "I told them that right to their faces in Tokyo and they didn't like it."

He wasn't alone. Mochtar Lubis, the leading journalist of Indonesia, also had a message for the Japanese on a mission to Tokyo. He told one influential group there: "I don't like Japanese business methods or general aggressiveness. In Indonesia, we wouldn't want you as the defenders of the Strait of Malacca."

What was the Japanese reaction? "They thanked me for my frankness," Lubis said.

Still another point of view came from the Padre Faura, where the Foreign Office is located in Manila. There, Foreign Minister Carlos P. Romulo of the Philippines picked up a souvenir plate tracing the route of four Japanese warships on a recent "show the flag" tour of Asian waters.

"Do you know," he mused, "that this coincides exactly with old Baron Tanaka's East Asian Co-Prosperity Sphere?"

It was a chilling thought for those with long memories who watched a stiff, well-drilled, well-disciplined group of Japanese naval cadets disembark from the warships as symbols of the "new Japan." Nothing could have been less calculated to instill good will and a comfortable, neighborly spirit among the countries that had felt the heel of the Japanese conqueror of another generation.

Of course, there is agreement in the former Co-Prosperity Sphere that the mighty economic Dai Nippon of the 1970s bears no resemblance to the military dictatorship of the 1930s. But there is also a widely held concern for the future among worried Asians who believe that a powerfully rearmed Japan will rise among them once more.[1]

The "Ugly Japanese"

The Japanese are well aware of the fears of their neighbors. Kinji Kawamura, foreign editor of *Asahi Shimbun*, reported after a tour of Southeast Asia that resentment was rising against hard-driving Japanese businessmen, the "Ugly Japanese," as they were called. It was a bitter thrust against both them and the "Ugly Americans," whom they sought to replace.[2]

The *Japan Times*, an authoritative English-language newspaper that sometimes reflects the views of the Gaimusho, the Japanese Foreign Office, wrote: "Our new economic status brings with it many privileges. But it also brings problems and responsibilities . . . We will find ourselves at times in a position comparable to that of the United States often during the past decade, facing many of the same problems and we will find that it is both difficult and trying. We are already finding the charge of the 'Ugly Japanese' rising to haunt us in parts of Asia. We will be subjected to charges of 'himotsuki enjo' [aid with strings], a charge which we ourselves have leveled at the United States in the past . . ."[3]

[1] From my own interviews.
[2] In a talk with Mr. Kawamura.
[3] In an editorial, June 10, 1970.

As the United States has discovered to its cost, such criticism from abroad is amplified and used in a different and even more embarrassing form at home by radical groups, particularly extreme leftist students in their ceaseless gyrations against the Establishment. For example, three radical student groups in Japan—the Chukaku-ha, Kakumaru-ha and Hantei Gakuhyo—attacked the Japanese-American alliance in these terms: "The U.S. imperialists, now being bewildered, consider their rule of Asia in crisis. And the Japanese imperialists, who are in collusion with the American imperialists, are attempting to engage in aggression in Asia."

To this, the Chukaku-ha added the slogan: "Let's turn Japanese imperialist aggression in Asia into a civil disturbance in Japan."[4]

The "New Order"

The trouble with radical rhetoric is that it tends to become obsolete with a fair degree of rapidity in dramatically changing times. For even the most dedicated of the Japanese "New Left," to say nothing of the old, would be hard put these days to produce tangible evidence of the collusion of the United States and Japan to produce aggression in Asia. The truth is that, lamentably, the Japanese-American alliance has fallen into disarray under the multiple pressures of trade rivalry, a currency war and a kind of furtive competition for a better relationship with China.

Eisaku Sato, who served longer as Japan's prime minister than anybody else in the annals of parliamentary government, could not have foreseen so disagreeable a state of affairs when he called for a "New Order" and a "New Pacific Age" in which Japan and the United States would submerge their differences in a calm and beautiful sea of international cooperation.[5]

"Japan," he said, "cannot hope alone to secure the peace of Asia. Along with the efforts of the Asian countries themselves, both the material and moral cooperation of the industrial countries that have a great interest in this area are required . . . Here again we find the shape of the New Pacific Age, where a New Order will be created by

[4] Kiyoaki Murata, *Japan Times*, September 25, 1970, p. 16.
[5] In his National Press Club speech in Washington, November 21, 1969.

Japan and the United States, two countries tied together by common ideals."

These poetic sentiments, which have little to do with reality, came on the same day as the issuance of the Nixon-Sato communiqué on the reversion of Okinawa to Japan in 1972. In the United States, the rising anger over Japan's sharp commercial practices and trade restrictions had not yet surfaced to any degree. As for the Japanese home front, the jubilation over the Okinawa pact was so great that few paid any attention to suggestions that Japanese-American relations were less than perfect and that Japan wasn't doing very much to provide economic assistance to its less fortunate neighbors and smaller trading partners. The only sour notes, therefore, came from Asians who were not particularly attracted to a Japanese "New Order," having terrible memories of a similar age proclaimed under the guns of the World War II Axis powers. The Japanese government was soon to learn, despite its air of assurance, that the cooperation of the United States could not be taken for granted.

A Message from India

There have been other drawbacks to Japan's rise to power. One was the inevitable lecture from India, that most pious moralist among nations. But here the Japanese had a break of sorts. Instead of being verbally battered by the vinegary old anti-American V. K. Krishna Menon, their lecture came from the gentle Durga Das, one of the most respected journalists of India, a friend of Jawaharal Nehru's.

"Indians and Southeast Asians generally feel that the Japanese are selfish," he wrote, "and they make every deal with an eye on maximum benefit to themselves and their country—be it a commercial transaction or a foreign aid deal—and that they lack warmth of human or even neighborly feelings. The smaller nations in Southeast Asia (behind the back of the Japanese of course) do not hesitate to state that they are afraid of the co-prosperity cult reappearing in the guise of economic aid and collaboration."[6]

Durga Das's admonition to Japan represents a broad consensus among Indian editors and business people. As for the government,

---

[6] Durga Das, INFA Syndicate, distributed from New Delhi, June 28, 1970.

there can be no mistake about its mistrust of Japanese intentions even though New Delhi could use more Japanese help. The Pakistanis, relying more on China and the United States, do not bother to disguise their feelings about the Japanese. President Zulfikar Ali Bhutto of Pakistan first called the Japanese "economic animals," a term they resent more than any other.

The Fears of China

Premier Chou En-lai has left no doubt that China fears a rising military spirit and expanding economic power in Japan even more than it fears the million or more Soviet troops on the northern Chinese border. While expressing the kindliest sentiments toward the Japanese people as "diligent and brave," he calls attention on every occasion to China's fifty years of suffering under the heel of the Japanese military. To an American interviewer, he ticked off the reasons for his country's fear of Japanese "reactionaries"—a sharply rising military budget, an expanding nuclear capability, colossal economic power, American aid under the Japanese-American Mutual Security Treaty, and a largely passive acceptance of the situation by the Japanese public.

"When you oppose a danger," Chou said, "you should oppose it when it is only budding. Only then can you arouse public attention. Otherwise, if you are to wait until it has already developed into power, it will be too strenuous. If the Far Eastern situation is really to move toward realization, and if Japan gives up its ambitions of aggression against Korea and China's Taiwan, then it will be possible for China and Japan to conclude a mutual non-aggression treaty on the basis of the five principles of peaceful coexistence."[7]

The Japanese business community and Japanese intellectuals, both of whom desire improved relations with China but for far different reasons, feel the sting of Chinese disapproval the most. Invariably, when the annual Japanese "memorandum trade" agreement is signed in Peking, it is accompanied by denunciations of Japan's military revival. Japan's support of Taiwan, too, is fearfully resented in Peking. As for South Korea, in a typical propaganda statement,

---

[7] James Reston, *The New York Times*, August 10, 1971, p. 14.

Hsin Hua, the New China News Agency, has attacked "the vicious aim of military aggression underlying the infiltration of Japanese monopoly capital" into that country.[8]

The Japanese naturally are both bewildered and resentful. On the one hand, China assails Japanese agreements with the United States on the defense of Taiwan and South Korea as well as the reversion of Okinawa to Japanese rule. And on the other, the United States, as Japan's principal ally, doesn't even bother to inform Tokyo in advance about an announcement of a proposed visit to Peking by an American President or an attack on the yen. The tendency for the Japanese to rely more and more on their own strength is understandable under the circumstances.

As the position was put by one of Japan's leading pro-Chinese intellectuals, who has no love for the United States, "The psychological distance between Japanese and other Asians is greater than between Japanese and Western nations."[9]

The Japanese Are Not Beloved

Japan's rise to world power has won many advantages for its people. But Dai Nippon also has discovered the unpleasant truth that world power has its penalties as well as its rewards, something that has dismayed conquerors from Alexander the Great to Dwight David Eisenhower. However, the Japanese are fundamentally tougher than Americans, who are often resentful that they are not loved in a world that they believe owes them so much. The Japanese are not beloved, either, but they don't worry about it as long as the GNP keeps going up.

While Kiichi Miyazawa was the Japanese minister for international trade and industry, he once remarked that his people were "ambiguous" about attracting the world's love. "The United States," he said, "suffers from a guilt complex whereas in Japan, a totally different kind of society, the dominant reflex action is a sense of shame when there is too much justifiable foreign criticism."

Miyazawa was in a better position than anybody else at the time to know the extent of Asian criticism of Japan for chasing the almighty

[8] *Japan Times*, June 27, 1970, p. 5.
[9] Prof. Kinhide Mushakoji, *Japan Times*, June 24, 1970, p. 6.

yen and sacrificing everything to the constant pursuit of trade. Like nearly all Japanese, he reacted defensively against such terms as "economic animals" and "Ugly Japanese." He said, "It's simply not true. Our future course toward developing nations . . . will be to increase the percentage of our gross national product that goes into foreign economic aid."[10]

That has been done, to some extent, but the developing nations say it's nowhere near enough.

The American Partnership

Until the tumultuous days of the "Nixon shock," as it was called in Japan, the Japanese-American partnership seemed to be impervious to strain. The era of the American occupation and the terms of the peace treaty had been beneficial to Japan on the whole. The Mutual Security Pact had relieved the Japanese of the necessity of defending themselves, enabling them to put all their resources into an unparalleled economic revival. To this, the United States had contributed with an indulgence rare in the annals of a conquering power. Japanophiles in the United States, notably Professor Edwin O. Reischauer of Harvard, had argued, "America has only one vital interest in Asia and that is in a healthy and friendly Japan."[11] The touchy negotiations over the reversion of Okinawa had gone well. Even the once-resented American military presence in Japan had been reduced almost to the vanishing point. And President Nixon had said at the high tide of this era of good feelings: "Our cooperation with Japan will be crucial to our efforts to help other Asian nations develop in peace. Japan's partnership with us will be a key to the success of the Nixon Doctrine in Asia . . . A sound relationship with Japan is crucial in our common effort to secure peace, security and a rising living standard in the Pacific area."[12]

The cost of maintaining the partnership in the expansive style to which the Japanese were accustomed proved, however, to be too much for the United States in the long run. The first symptoms of distress

[10] In my interview with Miyazawa in Tokyo, June 18, 1970.
[11] *Bulletin of the American Society of Newspaper Editors*, June, 1970, p. 14.
[12] Speech, February 18, 1970.

came when a dispute over the volume of Japanese textile imports was blown up into a major crisis and an old anti-dumping regulation of the United States Treasury was invoked to block the sales of cheap Japanese television sets. Nevertheless, the chronic American trouble over balance of payments worsened on a world scale, soaring from a deficit of about $6 billion in 1968 and 1969 to the alarming rate of $24 billion for 1971.[13]

American officials had been muttering for years that the yen was overvalued by perhaps as much as 25 per cent and the Japanese were making far too large profits at American expense. But when the Japanese trade balance hit a rate of $3 billion on the basis of figures for the first six months of 1971, the American government decided it had to act. Viewed against the background of the growing imbalance in American trade with the rest of the world, the Japanese position was intolerable to Washington. It was for this reason, primarily, that the United States cut the dollar loose from its gold base on August 15, the opening of the great "dollar war," and imposed the 10 per cent surcharge on most foreign imports. The Japanese at once recognized the threat to their two-way trade with the United States, which in 1971 was running at the rate of $11 billion. But they didn't cave in right away.

The United States was determined that it must right the economic balance with Japan if the partnership was to survive. While Japanese industrialists expressed their outrage, Eisaku Sato doggedly stuck to his pro-American position, saying: "The basis of our foreign policy is our close relationship with the United States . . . We are in the same ship so we must make every effort not to sink together."

It marked still another crisis for the veteran Prime Minister. Despite President Nixon's grand gesture in greeting Emperor Hirohito in Alaska, the Japanese did not endure the pain of "Nixon shock" in silence. For Japan finally had to revalue the yen by 16.88 per cent (from 360 to 308 to $1) as part of the 10-nation agreement of December 18, 1971, in which the dollar was devalued. It was the price for the removal of the import surcharge.

Despite the gloom in Tokyo over the "new yen," the Ministry of International Trade and Industry wasn't too downcast. For fiscal

[13] *The Wall Street Journal*, August 24, 1971, p. 16.

year 1972, it predicted Japanese exports would rise 17 per cent, instead of the expected 25, and for fiscal year 1973 the outlook was for an increase of "only" 10 per cent over the 1972 level.[14] It was, in any event, quite a change from the black day of surrender in 1945, of which Toshikazu Kase wrote: "Indeed, a distance inexpressible by numbers separates us—America from Japan."[15] The gap of distance has long since been closed. The gap of understanding remains.

2. THE JAPANESE PARADOX

Japan is a nation of monumental contradictions.

It is the only great world economic power that is not also prepared to defend its trading position with great military power.

Although its 105,000,000 people are crowded into an area less than that of California, it is nevertheless using its farmlands to create a new suburbia, massive modern highways and meandering golf fairways.

As the world's third-largest economic power, it pins most of its city dwellers into expensive substandard housing and obliges them to put up with unhealthy conditions in many areas, plus a fearful stench caused by poor sewage. In Tokyo, less than 37 per cent of family dwellers have sewer outlets and fewer than 50 per cent have bathtubs.[16]

Japan hopes to pass the Soviet Union in gross national product by 1980 and to outproduce the United States twenty years later; however, Japanese air pollution is worse than that of other advanced nations, leading the Governor of Tokyo to predict that the citizenry eventually may have to wear gas masks.[17]

Yet, the long-suffering Japanese workman is told that he will surpass both the British and the Germans in average individual

14 *The New York Times*, December 20, 1971, p. 56.

15 Douglas MacArthur, *Reminiscences* (New York: McGraw-Hill, 1964), p. 277.

16 *Economic Survey of Japan*, 1968–69, by Economic Planning Agency, Japanese government: housing, p. 211; sewage, p. 212. See also *Newsweek*, November 9, 1970, p. 53.

17 *Ibid.*, pp. 199–201.

income by 1975, but meanwhile he has a good deal less protection than they have from an admittedly inferior social security system.[18]

The Japanese government and leading industrialists fear a labor shortage, but both support a build-up of the armed forces and a munitions industry.

Production and Pollution

Japan boasts of having the largest steel company in the world and is justly proud of being first in shipbuilding and second in auto production; however, so much factory waste pours into its rivers that water pollution has become a source of national concern.[19]

The Japanese National Railways has the reputation of being the most efficient large line in the world, and its 125-mile-an-hour *Bullet Express* is hailed as a marvel; still, the JNR was on the verge of bankruptcy through overexpansion at the beginning of the 1970s.[20]

The *boomu* in consumer goods has quadrupled auto ownership to 30 per cent in five years, placed color TV in one of every four households, washing machines in 99 per cent of homes, and refrigerators in 95 per cent. However, the average Japanese family also has plunged $1,500 in debt, which considerably detracts from the announced high rate of annual savings.[21]

And, despite a national reputation for revering art and antiquity, the Japanese nevertheless permitted the destruction of Frank Lloyd Wright's architectural gem, the Imperial Hotel in Tokyo, and the construction in its place of a massive ark with a tasteless lobby the size of a football field and bone-chilling air conditioning.[22]

No wonder the respected weekly *The Economist* wrote: "By 1975, Japan will have been setting a spectacular example of economic growth to the rest of the world for three decades. By then it will be needing to set another example, of how to deal with the intensifying

[18] *Ibid.*, pp. 203–206.
[19] *Ibid.*, pp. 200–201.
[20] *Japan Times*, September 18, 1970, p. 16.
[21] "Behind the Consumer Boom," *Japan Times* editorial, June 21, 1970, p. 16.
[22] The new monstrosity of an Imperial has to be seen to be believed.

problems of the physical and social stresses of urbanization, conges-
tion and pollution."[23]

If Japan really intends to tackle its massive problems at home and
also increase its commitments in foreign aid to counteract growing
criticism abroad, then something more is going to be needed than
reassuring public-relations statements. The commitment of substantial sums to accomplish necessary social reforms will mean that some
of the appetite for yen-chasing at the expense of all other considerations will have to be curbed.

The Economic Engine

Japan's economic engine has been running with a wide-open
throttle for well over a decade, but it took some time to rebuild after
the disaster of World War II. Starting with a bombed-out plant and
a defeated people in 1945, Japan went to work with such vigor that it
outpaced every nation in the world. From 1952 until 1960, the
growth rate averaged 10 per cent a year in real terms and the average
national income tripled.[24] But that was just the beginning. From
1960 to 1970, the Japanese economy grew at an annual rate of 11 per
cent in real terms and the gross national product reached more than
$200 billion, exceeded only by those of the United States and the
Soviet Union.[25] In fact, Japanese expectations rose to such a point
that when the growth rate relapsed to somewhere between 6 and 8 per
cent for 1971 under the shock of the "dollar war," it was accounted
by many in Tokyo to amount to an economic recession.

The euphoria over Japan's well-being reached such exaggerated
heights that an American writer with a gift for press agentry,
Herman Kahn, predicted the Japanese would outproduce the United
States. Some Japanese fell for the same notion. Takashi Ihara, president of the Bank of Yokohama, wrote: "If this ratio [of growth] is
projected into the future in a simple formula of figures, it is possible
that Japan will surpass the United States in the 21st century."[26] But

[23] *The Economist*, September 12, 1970, p. 59.

[24] *Far Eastern Economic Review*, July 9, 1964, p. 63.

[25] Takashi Ihara, "Japan's Economic Position in the World," *Pacific Community*, July, 1970, p. 621; *Time*, April 12, 1971, p. 32.

[26] *Ibid.*

the powerhouse of the Japanese Cabinet, Takeo Fukuda, saw storm clouds ahead in the form of Japanese problems with the United States.[27] And it turned out that he was right.

Goals for Japan

Just before the United States flagged down the speeding Japanese economic engine, Japan was headed toward a goal of a $440 billion GNP by 1975, a per capita national income of about $3,300, and a boost in Japan's share of world production from 5.6 per cent to 12.3 per cent. This was the projection of the Japan Economic Research Center, which is sponsored by the prestigious economic newspaper *Nihon Keizai Shimbun, The Wall Street Journal* of Japan. The JERC also looked for a Japanese surplus of at least $5 billion by 1975, with exports rising in value to $42 billion annually on the basis of an anticipated take-over of nearly 20 per cent of the American market. All this was based on the expectation of an annual growth rate of 12.4 per cent.[28]

There appeared to be good reason for Japanese optimism, for its exports were increasing at a rate of around 20 per cent annually and for 1970 had zoomed to almost $20 billion. Of this total, Japan's exports to the United States in 1970 amounted to $5.9 billion, a 21.2 per cent increase over the previous year. And, since the United States exports to Japan amounted to considerably less, $4.6 billion, the Japanese held a $1.3 billion trade advantage over the Americans for a single year—pretty good business. That had been the story from 1965 on, when the Japanese surpluses began building. After Canada, Japan was the biggest of American trading partners and profits were soaring.

For the first half of 1971, the gap between the two leading trading nations of the free world widened even more. Japan's exports to the United States were nearly $3.5 billion, up 32 per cent, while American exports to Japan dropped 6 per cent to under $2 billion.[29] It was

---

[27] Fukuda's views were in a Tokyo dispatch in the Hong Kong *Standard*, December 1, 1970, p. 4, Sec. 2.

[28] Yoshizane Iwasa, president of Fuji Bank, in *Pacific Community*, April 1970, p. 386.

[29] Figures on U.S.–Japan trade from U.S. Commerce Department.

no wonder, therefore, that Japan went into a state of sudden "Nixon shock" on August 15, 1971, when Premier Sato received only seven minutes' notice that the American dollar was being set afloat on world markets and most imports to the United States would be subject to a 10 per cent surcharge. The Japanese fairly reeled. In four days, the Tokyo Stock Exchange lost an unprecedented 412.5 points as the securities of leading companies plunged downward in heavy selling. The government, meanwhile, bought dollars at a furious rate to try to maintain the yen at its historic rate of 360 to $1. It was an economic crisis of the first order.

For almost two weeks, the Japanese held out against mounting pressure. But at last, on August 28, the Japanese government let the yen float between unspecified levels against the dollar. It had been forced to buy about $4 billion in United States currency to make its failing effort to support the yen, but even the decision to cut the yen loose did not amount to unconditional surrender. Although the United States was looking for something between a 15 and a 20 per cent revaluation of the yen, the Japanese managed to keep practical revaluation to less than 10 per cent for some weeks. On December 18, as a part of the ten-nation monetary agreement in Washington, Japan finally accepted the upward valuation of the yen from 360 to 308 to $1, an increase of 16.88 per cent. In return, the import surcharge ended. In all the bargaining that went on with its trading partners to reconstitute the shattered currency system, the Americans found that the Japanese were the toughest in maintaining their position. They had a lot to do with the final decision to devalue the dollar.

Despite the monetary upheaval, Japan's goals did not change. For the immediate future, the Japanese did not foresee any sharp decline in their trade with the United States. In fact, because of the increased volume of their exports, Japan still counted on reaching the $6 billion export level for 1972 and gaining thereafter. Nor did they worry unduly about the outlook for succeeding years.

Japan, Inc.

Where will the Japanese go from now on? It depends in part on how well the Japanese sales force abroad deals with the problems of the revalued yen and the devalued dollar. But there are major problems at home, too. The usually docile Japanese labor force is not likely to continue to let its leaders enter into cozy arrangements with management, especially in an inflationary time. In the long run, what labor does is likely to be more important than the gyrations of the yen. For the whole basis of the Japanese economy is dependent on increasing productivity as well as continued access to Asia's storehouse of materials.

Barring some cataclysmic event that would disrupt Japan's economic system, the chances are that the 1971 blows from the United States will be absorbed and the setback to the economy will be temporary. For fundamentally, the Japanese industrial system is so sound and the cooperative aspect of relations between the new *zaibatsu* and the government so strong that there is every prospect of a $500 billion Japanese GNP by 1975. For fiscal 1973, despite the yen's revaluation, the conservative Sumitomo Bank forecast the growth rate would bounce back to 12 per cent and the temporary recession would be over. As for the per capita national income in terms of a revalued yen, it is almost sure to go to $4,000 by 1975 and perhaps more if labor gets tough.

Consider the Japanese position even in the face of the American protectionist drive: Japanese external reserves reached a high of $12.5 billion before the end of 1971, exceeding America's, and making Japan second only to West Germany as a holder of foreign currency. The Japanese balance of payments also surged ahead, reaching a surplus of $3.3 billion before the end of 1971. In addition, there were record surpluses of $2.63 billion in short-term capital and almost $1 billion in trade.[30]

Despite all favorable indications, however, some realistic Japanese are beginning to be less confident in Japan's future. This is not particularly because the yen has been revalued; revaluations of the mark, the last in May 1971, have not notably checked the progress of West German industry. It is basically because Japan's industrial leaders as a whole do not relish the prospect of another trade war with the United States, but still are reluctant to give up any of their

[30] Sumitomo Bank estimate, *The New York Times*, December 24, 1971, p. 31; figures on Japan's reserves and payments balance from *Reuters* economic report from Tokyo, September 14, 1971.

current advantages. Until the Japanese decide on a lot more liberal trading practices, therefore, a very large question mark is going to hang over their relations with the United States.

What the United States has insisted on in its dealings with Japan, Inc. (a term that denotes the tight cooperation in most matters between Japanese business and industry and their government) is a lowering of the protectionist barriers that surround the giant of Asia. This would include, in addition to liberalized trading laws, an increase in the flow of foreign capital investment in Japan and a loosening of both its exchange rates and capital transactions to conform to modern realities.

Will the Japanese Do It?

They have responded very slowly to the pressures that have been put upon them. One conditionally favorable response is the Japanese government's decision to permit United States and European automobile manufacturers to put up Japanese assembly plants if they hold a 50-50 interest with a Japanese concern.[31] It is on this basis that General Motors, Ford and Chrysler are arranging with Japanese partners to try to open up the long-closed Japanese automobile market. It remains to be seen how successful the auto invasion will be.

The Japanese also have taken initial steps to try to please their less fortunate trading partners. They have stepped up foreign aid, but not to the projected goal of 1 per cent of their GNP, and they have relieved their aid recipients of the necessity of using Japanese products exclusively. As for the long-held Japanese import controls, these have been relaxed to some extent.

Such mild advances do not mean that the high protective wall around Japanese business and industry, erected over a quarter-century with the help of the United States, is going to be dismantled overnight. No Joshua from Washington, with a single blast of his horn, is going to cause the walls of this modern Jericho to come tumbling down. The Japanese don't give up that easily. Nor is it possible that Japanese economic liberalization, a piecemeal business,

---

[31] Toshio Yoshimura, *Far Eastern Economic Review*, December 12, 1970, p. 40, and Koji Nakamura, *Far Eastern Economic Review*, March 6, 1971, p. 21.

will halt the swing toward American protectionism as a defense against the inroads of Japanese competition. The United States Treasury's finding that Japanese TV sets have been dumped on the American market (that is, sold at less than the price on the home market) is a harbinger of things yet to come.[32]

The Trade War

The fear of a trade war between Japan and the United States has not been exaggerated. Nor will the 10-nation monetary agreement in Washington at the end of 1971 remove the danger. From the heat generated by the opening skirmishes, it may be seen that a full-scale economic war in the Pacific could lead to disaster and change the lines of power that now extend over the area. It is a comfortable, but not entirely valid, assumption that the revaluation of the yen will, in Paul Porter's words, "correct the underpricing of Japanese exports and the overpricing of other nations' exports in the Japanese markets."[33]

The Japanese themselves aren't so sure of that. Even before the revaluation of the yen, it was clearly evident that many of Japan's business leaders, in consultation with their government, had reached a working consensus on the range of monetary change that they were prepared to accept and believed they could live with. Yet, the president of the important Fuji Bank, Yoshizane Iwasa, warned of continued trouble in a typically Japanese statement that faced both ways: "Japan-United States economic relations promise to become even closer in the 1970s, and frictions and conflicts are bound to grow more abrasive."[34]

One leading Tokyo industrialist, who talked to me at length privately about the problem, said bluntly that he was losing faith in the United States and thought Japan would have to follow an independent line in the Pacific. I raised the question of whether Japan could win an all-out trade war. To which he responded grimly: "You

---

[32] Toshio Yoshimura, *Far Eastern Economic Review*, September 26, 1970, p. 40.

[33] In testimony before a House subcommittee in Washington, reported in the *Japan Times*, December 6, 1970, p. 1.

[34] Yoshizane Iwasa, in *Pacific Community*, April, 1970, p. 386.

will see that Japan's homogeneous society is much stronger than the heterogeneous society of the United States."[35]

There were such undertones in almost every interview I was able to arrange with people who were involved in the trading rivalry with the United States. I remember one business leader who remarked, half in jest, that the American public did not seem to be greatly aware of their country's responsibilities in the Pacific and he wasn't interested in calling their attention to the importance of the American stake in the area. "If the American people want to ignore the Pacific," he said with a broad smile, "that's good for Japan."

Not much of this crops up in public exchanges, however. The formal line is handed ou⁺ by Nobuhiko Ushiba, Japanese ambassador to the United States: "The United States and Japan share the common cause of establishing in Asia and other parts of the world peace and prosperity founded on the respect for freedom and justice."[36] And the Japanese go right on building factories in Asian lands where there is an even cheaper pool of skilled labor, thus giving them a price advantage, and continue to expand their whopping trade surpluses at the expense of weaker countries. Then they wonder why they are resented!

What Will Japanese Labor Do?

There is an even greater paradox in the Japanese economy than the spectacle of Japanese business and industry fighting the United States, which made their miraculous prosperity possible.

It is the comparatively meek posture—until recently—of Japanese labor. Since the Communist-led strikes in the immediate post-World War II period, labor trouble has been comparatively rare in Japan and the work force has been willing, more often than not, to wait for its share of the benefits that have come to the land. In the process, Suzuki San, the admirable Japanese worker, has accepted wages that are, on the whole, less than those of labor in comparable industries in the West.

Admittedly, the yen has been undervalued and dollar comparisons before the time of revaluation are misleading but they do indicate in a very broad way the dilemma of Japanese labor. For example, despite increases in Japanese wages each year, per capita earnings for 1970 still lagged around the $2,000 mark. They did not by any means keep pace with the inflationary pressures that caused Japanese consumer prices to shoot up 31.9 per cent from 1965 to 1969 and another 7.7 per cent in 1970.

That started the Japanese consumer revolution, spearheaded by Japanese labor.[37] While there were no Japanese Ralph Naders around to blow the whistle on excessive profiteering by Japanese business, the consumer movement was instrumental nevertheless in forcing a change in television set pricing and in making the new *zaibatsu* aware that they weren't going to have everything quite their own way. The pressures increased for a more realistic wage for Japanese labor, particularly after serious shortages developed in several key areas. Some manufacturers, directly after the beginning of the American "dollar war," took advantage of the confused situation by announcing restrictions on hiring. But for the long run, the rising militancy of labor against an inflationary economy was not to be contained by such tactics. The consumer movement was the best indication of that.

Japanese industry was well able to pay its labor a reasonable wage. With the GNP soaring past the $200 billion mark and exports exceeding $20 billion in the early 1970s, the forty leading Japanese corporations were among the strongest and most productive in the world. Japan could boast, as well, of some of the richest and most powerful industries on earth, including steelmaking, electronics, optics, chemicals, shipbuilding and automobiles.[38]

Why did Japanese labor remain so stable until inflation became a real burden? There are many reasons, one of the most important being the peculiar structure of Japanese society. Traditionally, except in times of stress such as the immediate post-World War II period or the inflation of the early 1970s, the work force in Japan is comparatively docile. Suzuki San generally elects to stay with one employer

[37] UPI file from Tokyo in Hong Kong *Standard*, November 11, 1970, p. 4, Sec. 2.

[38] Philip H. Trezise in *Pacific Community*, April, 1970, p. 355.

for life and share in the benefits of his prosperity, often on his terms.

In Japan, this is the way things have been done since the nation's industrialization first began. Under this system, nobody is fired except in extraordinary circumstances. Promotions are guaranteed for all except the most obvious drones. If the salaries are modest, the bonuses can be very large in a good year; and with them, usually, go such perquisites as company-supported housing, restaurants, recreation centers, life insurance, and pensions and other outward evidences of a feudalistic, paternalistic society. It is a part of the ethos of Japan, Inc., and most workers are reluctant to change the system.

Of course it is inefficient. Nearly all factories and businesses are overstaffed, but the practice is still accepted as a part of the Japanese way of life. Takashi Ihara has estimated that it takes from one and a half to two Japanese to do the work of one Briton, German or Frenchman, two Japanese for one Swiss, and three Japanese for one American. Yet, even he is beginning to have his doubts about the system, for he writes: "Loyalty to enterprise . . . is a tradition of labor in Japan . . . It will continue for some time. But we are not sure if it is an inherent virtue of the Japanese people.[39]

Problems of Labor

Through the 1960s, there weren't many such doubts about the system. Pay increases for the work force in general amounted to 11 per cent annually and were generally absorbed by industry due to a continued increase in labor productivity. But with young people staying in school longer and most retirements starting at fifty-five years of age, the size of the work force began declining in the 1970s.[40] A few of the more advanced companies began raiding one another for executive personnel, something that would have been unheard of in an older Japan. In addition, young workers imbued with new ideas were discussing the advantages of job-hopping and a few actually tried it but met with discouraging experiences.[41]

[39] Ihara, *op. cit.*, p. 632.
[40] Takashi Oka, "How the Japanese Succeed," distributed by New York Times News Service, November 15, 1970.
[41] Findings from my interviews with leaders of labor and management.

With the quickening of the inflationary spiral in the early 1970s, less than 65 per cent of the total population fifteen years old or older remained in the Japanese work force. It was a strong incentive for Japan's big business to seek social change, at least in shaping the work habits of labor and stimulating its productivity. For it was clear that a time of rapidly rising wages was approaching and a certain amount of labor unrest was inevitable if labor's demands could not be met within reasonable bounds.

In this extremity, Suzuki San's work practices and general outlook on life came under the microscope of efficiency experts at home and abroad. On the whole, it seemed that numerous Japanese workers were still attracted by the labor practices of big companies and the special benefits they offered for a lifetime of labor. A report on the Toyota Motor Company's 38,500 employees, for example, pointed out that the low average starting wage of $100 a month for a six-day forty-two-hour week was compensated for by annual wage increases as high as 20 per cent, month-long vacations, job security, medical care and company-sponsored recreation. Other companies had even more generous programs.

Until inflation became a major factor in the lives of the Japanese workers, this kind of paternalism tended to keep Japan's 61,000 unions weak and their growth low. Of 50 million workers, 33.7 million were fully employed at the beginning of the 1970s but only 11.6 million were labor union members. It was taken as an ominous sign that the rate of growth among labor union members had been reduced then to two-tenths of 1 per cent a year. The largest, Sohyo, the General Council of Trade Unions of Japan, with 4.2 million members, was growing slowest of all. The Japanese Confederation of Labor (Domei), with 2 million, the Churitsu Roren, or Federation of Independent Unions, with 1.4 million, and even the tiny Shinsam-betsu, or National Federation of Industrial Labor, with 74,000, did better.[42]

It would have been a mistake to assume, however, that unions did not expand because workers in general were satisfied. The govern-ment's own Economic Planning Agency found: "Many people are

[42] Labor statistics from *Japan Times*, November 28, 1970, p. 10; report on Toyota from *Time*, October 5, 1970, pp. 51–52.

dissatisfied over housing shortages and lack of public facilities, in addition to high prices and low incomes . . . Dissatisfaction over rising consumer prices is noted most markedly among housewives and old-age families. The low level of personal income, another cause of discontent, has something to do with the lag of social security in Japan. Although the saving rate is much higher here than in other countries, most of the savings are designed . . . not for investment or other profit-making purposes but for extraordinary payment in case of illness and other emergencies and, to a lesser degree, for the winter of life. Our survey shows that savings for extraordinary expenditure are made by 80 per cent of the households owning savings, while the rest save against their old age.

"These trends indicate that an overwhelming portion of the savings is designed more or less to make up for the inadequacies in the nation's social security system."[43]

Suzuki San, it seems, is not as well off as Japan's cheerleaders would have the outside world believe. In fact, by American standards, he doesn't really do at all well in spite of the percentages of his current and projected wage increases. With continuing inflation and tightening competition for Japanese business in the vital export trade, difficult times lie ahead for Japanese labor. For Japanese employers even now are beginning to stiffen their resistance in the periodic wage negotiations, arguing that greater wage rises will only lead to higher prices and, anyway, Japanese labor isn't maintaining its record for productivity.

In its calculations for the future, Japanese labor will have to count on the eventual imposition of some kind of an incomes policy under government regulation. As for Japanese industry, the time of docility for the work force is rapidly running out. Suzuki San may dislike picket lines, but he may have to get used to them once more.

3. THE SWINGING PENDULUM

The ever-hopeful Eisaku Sato likes to compare Japanese-American relations to a pendulum in constant motion. When the old Prime

---

[43] *Economic Survey of Japan,* 1968–69, by Economic Planning Agency, pp. 210–211.

Minister is in the proper mood, he will recall that it was the U.S. that induced Japan to participate in world trade—a polite way of describing Commodore Matthew Calbraith Perry's successful demands for American trade concessions, negotiated under the guns of his warships at Shimoda in 1853–54. Because Japan did not have either the strength or the inclination to oppose the United States, American-Japanese relations remained cordial on the whole for more than fifty years after that unpromising beginning.

Then, in Sato's view, the pendulum began to swing back. The change in Japanese opinion began with the Russo-Japanese War in 1904 and President Theodore Roosevelt's mediation between the belligerents at Portsmouth, New Hampshire, to restore peace. Japanese dissatisfaction with the peace of Portsmouth, coupled with difficulties over Japanese immigration and American boycotts of Japanese goods, finally culminated in a Japanese decision to cut loose from the United States and go it alone. The eventual result was World War II and Japan's defeat.

Once more, the pendulum changed its course toward improved relations. But it didn't happen at once. A new relationship had to be worked out between the United States and its conquered foe—a relationship that was to change the course of history in the Pacific. What the United States wanted to do, in short, was to insure that Japan never again would be so isolated that its government and people would be tempted to go it alone.

"Democratizing" Japan

During the first phase of American policy development in Japan, between 1945 and 1951, General Douglas MacArthur saw to it that his Occupation regime did everything possible to "democratize" Japan. It was a very large order in a land still dominated by feudal traditions, where equality was not really recognized as a practical goal for the citizenry. Nevertheless, the great American proconsul persisted and he produced remarkable—even astonishing—results.

Between 1945 and 1947, in what was called the "punishment and reform" phase of the American Occupation, Japan was governed under MacArthur's Initial Post-Surrender Policy. As he spelled out the position in two papers sent to Washington on August 29 and November 8, 1945, his purpose was "to insure that Japan will not again become a menace to the United States or to the peace and security of the world."

First of all, he disposed of Japan's remaining Pacific empire and shrank the defeated nation's boundaries to the four home islands. Next came disarmament, the punishment of war criminals and the reduction of the Emperor to a powerless "symbol of state." Land and educational reforms and an effort to break the power of the *zaibatsu,* the Japanese industrialists, were next on the order of American priorities. MacArthur grandly ordered the creation of a free press, something easier said than done, and imposed on the Japanese a set of labor practices patterned after the American model.

All this was undertaken, initially, on the supposition that the five great powers of the United Nations would maintain friendly relations in the postwar period and associate themselves with a genuine effort to preserve peace. But almost as soon as the shooting stopped in 1945, the Cold War began. The United States and the Soviet Union drifted apart and soon were glowering at each other across the boundaries of occupied Germany and occupied Berlin.

And in the Pacific, the United States suddenly realized that it could not depend on a friendly and powerful China as a counterweight to even a "democratized" Japan, for Mao Tse-tung's Communist armies from Yenan were sweeping the country. Clearly, it was only a question of time before Chiang Kai-shek and his weak and wavering Nationalists would be overthrown.

The "punishment" phase of American Occupation policy in Japan came to an abrupt end. The initial alliance with Japanese liberals and radicals, at the expense of the conservatives and the *zaibatsu,* began to weaken perceptibly. Instead of a vassal state, to be kept in perpetual bondage, Japan emerged from its "punishment and reform" phase as a most desirable Pacific ally of the United States.

The Constitution of 1947

The "democratization" of Japan now was placed, to a much larger extent, in the hands of the Japanese people. In the words of the

Japanese Constitution of 1947, which became the basis for the new democracy under Japanese auspices: "Government is a sacred trust of the people, the authority for which is derived from the people, the powers of which are exercised by the representatives of the people, and the benefits of which are enjoyed by the people."

To a nation that had known democratic practices only briefly in the late nineteenth and early twentieth centuries, this was almost unbelievable. Never before in history had a foreign occupying power commanded a defeated people to rise up and govern themselves under the benign eyes of their conquerors. Never before in Asia had a Western power made so impetuous an attempt to impose Western democratic ideals on an Asian people that had had contact with more of the excesses of self-government than its benefits. For even in the most liberal periods of the Meiji reform era, the people never had had very much to say about the practices of government and, more often than not, submitted to the distinctive Japanese process of indirect rule.

The traditional Japanese view of government was best expressed during the Meiji period by Yukichi Fukuzawa, the "Great Enlightener," founder of Keio University and the newspaper *Jiji Shimpo,* when he wrote: "Compared with consideration of [Japan's] strength, the matter of internal government and into whose hands it falls is of no importance at all. Even if the government be autocratic in name and form, I shall be satisfied with it if it is strong enough to strengthen the country."

The new Japanese Constitution swept tradition aside. In place of royal power, all the trappings of parliamentary democracy came into being with suitable American modifications. There was a Bill of Rights, modified, to be sure, by the phrase "within the limits of the law." The last vestiges of Prussianism in the old Meiji Constitution were wiped out with the adoption of Article 9, the so-called "no war" clause, which guaranteed in effect that Japan never again would take up arms against its neighbors. What armed strength there was in the new Japan would be limited to the Self-Defense Forces, which were yet to be created. Protected by the full military strength of the United States, and sheltered by the American atomic umbrella, Japan had no need to be concerned for its safety.

The Japanese Recover

It did not take the Japanese very long to appreciate the scope of their opportunity to revive their old trading empire and broaden it in area and intensity of penetration. Alone among the great trading nations of the earth, Japan did not have to worry about the cost as well as the obligation of self-defense. Even Germany, Japan's former Axis ally, was finding that there would be no "free ride" in the matter of national defense. But Japan did have a "free ride" and took advantage of it.

The Americans, as always in the opening phase of the postwar era, were helpful. Under the Nine-Point Stabilization Program of 1948, the United States sought to restore the basic underpinnings of the Japanese economy through expanded trade and production, better tax collections, credit restrictions, wage and price controls and a balanced budget. While the program did stabilize prices, it also increased unemployment. But all Japanese doubts for the immediate future were removed when the Korean War began in the summer of 1950.

That was the crucial event in the restoration of the Japanese economy. As the center of American troop staging areas, naval and air activity and military procurement, Japan's trade underwent a phenomenal expansion. By the time the Japanese peace treaty was signed by the United States on September 8, 1951, Dai Nippon's recovery was under way.

The Tight Embrace

Eisaku Sato's pendulum now was swinging toward improved Japanese-American relationships with increasing speed. By the time the Occupation ended on April 28, 1952, Japan and the United States were locked in a tight diplomatic embrace that was to continue for the next eight years without a major disturbance. The only threats to this new era of good feeling in the northern Pacific were murmurings among the Japanese against the Japanese-American Mutual Security Treaty, which had been signed on the same day as the peace treaty; the American retention of Okinawa and the Bonin Islands, and American pressures for a certain amount of Japanese rearmament.

But the conservative Liberal-Democratic Party, which assumed control of the new Japanese government and was to maintain its rule through the beginning of the 1970s almost without a break, did not permit these things to disturb a progressively benign relationship with the United States. The "free ride" was proving to be most attractive. And the expanding Japanese industrial network was becoming more and more powerful. It appeared, to the prudent new rulers of Japan, that a modest "low posture" in world affairs would be best calculated to maintain the nation's industrial progress. That meant a minimum of action and discussion; and, if a crisis threatened, an ambiguous attitude would soften its impact on the public.

In consequence, nothing was done about the Mutual Security Treaty for some years despite rising protests by the Japanese left that it "compromised" Japanese sovereignty and involved the country in the Cold War against its will. On Okinawa, there was more movement. The United States recognized what it called Japan's "residual sovereignty" over the big island and the rest of the Ryukyus and, in 1957, authorized the creation of an Okinawan legislature that would remain subject to the veto of the American High Commissioner. As for the American insistence on partial Japanese rearmament, the best that could be obtained was the establishment in 1954 of the Japanese Defense Agency and a Self-Defense Force of more than 100,000 men. To all intents and purposes, Japan still was getting a "free ride" in the American defense system.

The Treaty Riots

The Japanese left, with the enthusiastic support of Peking, began campaigning furiously in the mid-1950s for an end to the security treaty. Almost the entire opposition to the Liberal-Democratic Party concentrated on this issue, from the relatively mild-mannered left-of-center intellectuals to the stalwarts of Japan's Socialist Party and the always clamorous Communists, split now between Peking and Moscow.

The campaign obliged the Japanese Prime Minister, Nobusuke Kishi, a brother of Eisaku Sato, to seek concessions on a relaxation of the terms of the treaty and in 1957 the United States agreed at least to listen. A Kishi-Eisenhower communiqué, made public after a meeting of the two leaders in Washington, called for American consultation with Japan on the disposition of American forces there. At the same time, a joint committee was created to study other problems arising from the treaty. But as for Okinawa, the United States refused to make any concessions. "So long as the conditions of threat or tension exist in the Far East," the communiqué said, "the United States will find it necessary to continue the present status."

Instead of placating the Japanese left, the Kishi mission served only to increase the intensity of the anti-treaty campaign. As the agitation mounted, the radical Zengakuren student movement was brought into the streets to add its youthful "shock troops" to the less demonstrative mass of protestors. Kishi, on his part, intensified his negotiations with the United States for treaty revision and succeeded. Nevertheless, on November 27, 1959, 12,000 students and others forced their way into the Japanese Diet compound in a riotous protest rally. At the beginning of 1960, when Kishi flew to Washington for the successful conclusion of the revised treaty, 700 students violently demonstrated against him at Haneda Airport. The proposed revisions didn't go far enough to please them.

The signing of the revised Treaty of Mutual Cooperation and Security at a White House ceremony on January 19, 1960, went through without a hitch, despite every attempt by the Japanese left to block it. There should have been a certain amount of satisfaction in Japan over the liberalized relationship with the United States, but there wasn't. The treaty opponents complained that it still committed Japan to a policy of military cooperation with the United States and therefore made Japan a party to the Cold War.

The Battle of the Treaty

In reality, the revised treaty was much better than it was made to appear. First of all, it committed the United States to respond to a common danger "in case of armed attack on either party in the territories under the administration of Japan." Second, its duration was limited to ten years, after which it could be abrogated by either party with one year's notice. And, in an accompanying exchange of notes, Japan was assured of prior consultation by the United States in the use of American bases for combat purposes outside Japanese territory and in the commitment and deployment of American forces in Japan. These were considerable concessions by the victor in the Pacific war to the conquered foe, coming only fifteen years after the end of the conflict.

The Japanese Diet, however, was in no hurry to ratify the revised treaty. Throughout the winter, its members droned on in seemingly endless debate while the lines of protest hardened outside. Not only the Japanese left but also some of the most respected elements in Japanese life began to coalesce against ratification of the treaty. *Asahi Shimbun*, the greatest newspaper in Japan, put itself at the head of the opposition, a tremendous gain for the anti-treaty forces.

Kishi saw that he was being boxed in and, in a most un-Japanese maneuver, determined that he would force the issue. It was a major error in strategy. For on May 19, 1960, when he suddenly called up the treaty revision bill for a vote, the Socialists staged a sit-in strike in the Diet to make a plenary session impossible. The frantic Kishi called the police and had them drag out the opposition. Then, he jammed ratification through with the help of the remaining Diet membership, which was almost solidly LDP.

The demonstration that night was appalling in size and force. But much worse was to follow. The Japanese Labor Federation called a general strike June 4. When that produced no result, thousands of demonstrators swarmed to Haneda Airport six days later to imprison James C. Hagerty, press secretary for President Eisenhower, in his automobile after he had arrived to arrange for a state visit by the President. On June 15, an even larger mob burst into the Diet grounds, overturned and burned police vehicles, and had to be driven off by tear gas. A woman student was killed, 400 persons were injured, and Japan was on the point of insurrection.

The excesses of the anti-treaty forces finally alienated their more conservative supporters. *Asahi* abandoned the fight in disgust and most of the conservative Japanese press followed. But the damage had been done. On June 17, Kishi notified President Eisenhower that he would be in danger if he visited Japan; accordingly, the trip was canceled. Four days later, the Emperor signed the revised treaty and the United States Senate ratified it on the following day. Kishi bowed out with his Cabinet, hoping to quiet the disorders, and the Hayato Ikeda government came in to continue the almost unbroken rule of the LDP in postwar Japan.

Gradually, Japan returned to normal. While there was a certain amount of disillusionment with the Japanese left and its methods, it retained its hold on most of the intellectuals and a very large proportion of the university students. It would live to fight another day.

Agreement on Okinawa

The burst of unparalleled prosperity that came to Japan in the decade of the 1960s effectively smothered most attempts to whip up public sentiment against the Mutual Security Treaty in its revised form. Moreover, since the treaty had ten years to run, even the impractical and visionary academics saw there was little use in trying to stage demonstrations for that length of time. The Japanese left concentrated on a kind of virulent anti-Americanism, seeking to capitalize on everything from opposition to the Vietnam War to a growing sentiment in favor of the reversion of Okinawa to Japanese rule.

It was Okinawa, at length, that became the central issue in Japan.

President John Fitzgerald Kennedy sent Professor Reischauer to Japan, hoping thereby to provide the United States with an ambassador who could talk with the Japanese in their own language and bring about a better and smoother relationship with the United States. Reischauer's Japanese was almost flawless, but he couldn't very well talk down the Japanese case for Okinawa. President Kennedy himself took a hand in the issue in the spring of 1962 by calling Okinawa a part of the Japanese "homeland" and maintaining the pledge of eventual reversion to Japanese rule. As if to show that the United States meant what it said, the American and Japanese governments proceeded to coordinate their economic assistance programs for Okinawa.

Had it not been for the Vietnam War, perhaps these gradual moves might have mollified the Japanese. But President Johnson's escalation of the conflict in 1965, and the American bombing of North Vietnam, produced a violent reaction in Japan. Charges were made that Okinawa, being a staging area for American troops in the Far East, might well draw Japan into the war. Ninety-two intellectuals signed a statement on April 20, 1965, that blamed the United States for broadening the struggle in Vietnam and appealed for an end to hostilities.

The American State Department fought back, accusing many Japanese—including the press—of seriously misunderstanding the American position in Vietnam. Ambassador Reischauer even charged the Japanese press with an "unbalanced" presentation of the Vietnam War. If the press was somewhat more subdued for a time, the Japanese left was not. The anti-Americanism that had been the left's trademark from the outset was more in evidence than ever. Consequently, there was danger that the issue of Okinawa's reversion might be tangled up in the anti-war campaign with all manner of unpleasant results for the Japanese government, which had until then loyally maintained its support of the American position.

Sato Takes Charge

It was at this point in Japanese-American postwar relationships that Eisaku Sato emerged from the shadowed obscurity of Japanese politics to assume leadership of the hard-pressed Japanese government in 1964. A protégé of the great Japanese elder statesman and former prime minister Shigeru Yoshida, he was, like Yoshida, bold, forceful and generally optimistic. Like Yoshida, too, he preferred for the most part to keep his own counsel.

The new prime minister was too shrewd to permit his opponents to select the proper battleground and choose the issue on which to contest the long primacy of the Liberal-Democratic Party. He simply took the Okinawa issue away from the left and made it his exclusive property. Within months, in January 1965, he met President Johnson and obtained an agreement to broaden the work of the Joint Committee on Okinawa to include a general effort to promote the welfare of the people of the island. Two years later, after another meeting with President Johnson, the Prime Minister triumphantly brought back the Bonin Islands to Japanese rule. Even more important, he flourished an American pledge to survey the Okinawa problem once again "with a view to the return of administrative rights to Japan."

This was a promise from which the United States could not very well retreat. It meant more to the Japanese than the fulminations of the left against the Vietnam War, particularly after the end of the bombing of North Vietnam in 1968, the retirement of President Johnson, and President Nixon's announcement of a policy of disengagement. For Okinawa had become the symbol of a resurgent Japan—the very marrow of the new giant who was flexing his muscles in northeast Asia.

Truly, as Sato said after obtaining Nixon's agreement to return Okinawa to Japan in 1972, it was the end of the postwar era "in name and in fact."

The American Position

During a Tokyo briefing on the progress of arrangements for the reversion of Okinawa, an American spokesman was asked what the position of the United States would be with respect to Okinawa "after you leave."

The spokesman was puzzled. "But," he said, "we aren't leaving."

That went right to the heart of the matter. For with the return of administrative rights over Okinawa to Japan, the American military position there came under the general terms of the Mutual Security Treaty but was not, for the time being, otherwise affected. In the stuffy language of the Sato-Nixon communiqué, "It was agreed that the mutual security interests of the United States and Japan could be accommodated" within the Okinawan reversion arrangements.

There was even a section that provided for consultations to insure unimpeded American military use of Okinawa in connection with the Vietnam War in the event that hostilities continued after reversion. And while the United States announced that it "understood" Japan's opposition to the positioning of atomic weapons on Okinawa, the American military retained its right to consult Japan on taking so drastic a step in an emergency.

But most important of all, from the standpoint of the United States, was an unprecedented postwar Japanese declaration that the security of the Republic of Korea and Taiwan was directly linked to the security of Japan. This was taken to mean, at the very least, that the United States would be able to use Japanese bases to combat an attack on South Korea or Taiwan.

Following the signing of the Okinawa reversion treaty on June 17, 1971, Japan paid $320 million for forty-six military facilities on the big island but the United States retained eighty-eight of its military installations, including the key Kadena Air base. Soon afterward, some of the American "nuclear facilities" were removed from Okinawa to other unspecified locations.

The atomic argument was not defused by this acknowledgment of the changed status of Okinawa. For as far as the Japanese were concerned, they wanted no nuclear weapons on Japanese soil because of the traumatic attitude of the Japanese public toward atomic warfare. In view of the enormous American missile capability and the operation of numerous American nuclear-equipped submarines, it really wasn't necessary for the United States to keep alive the possibility of using any part of Japan as an atomic base. Just why the Pentagon chose to continue the argument remains a secret that may be locked forever in the dim recesses of the military mind.

The Japanese Position

Inevitably, with the conclusion of the Okinawa pact, a chorus of belittling comment arose from the Japanese left. It was said that the agreement was insufficient, that it would not reduce anti-American feeling in Japan, that it committed Japan even more than before to a policy of support for American militarism in Asia, and that the United States should close all its Japanese bases forthwith and leave the home islands and Okinawa for good. It was said that the Japanese public would become increasingly resentful of the United States if it went on using Japan as a base for American military movements in the Pacific and drew the Japanese ever closer into a military partnership with atomic capabilities.

Without question, these doubts were sincere and represented the feelings of a considerable area of Japanese opinion. The Japan Socialist Party tried to capitalize on them by calling the reversion plan for Okinawa a fraud, the exclusion of nuclear weapons "a lie," and the proposed Japanese protection of the Republic of Korea and

Taiwan a dangerous provocation to China. "Japan," the Socialists warned, "will begin to embark on a dangerous road of increasing its voice in Asian affairs and securing a leading role in Asia."

The Japanese electorate carefully followed the progress of the negotiations on Okinawa and, despite everything the opposition could do, registered its approval. It gave Prime Minister Sato and his Liberal-Democratic Party an overwhelming vote of confidence in the 1969 elections. With 302 seats, the LDP dominated the lower house of the Japanese Diet as never before; as for the confused and divided Socialists, they plunged to an unprecedented low of 90 seats.

It was clear enough to the Japanese public that the possession of Okinawa was what counted, not the continued American military presence. For any thinking Japanese, following the course of American movements in the Pacific and the state of American public opinion, could see that it was only a question of time before the American military presence dwindled or, perhaps, vanished altogether. And even if the American military remained in possession of a part of Okinawa, the Japanese civil administration of Okinawa in time would gain such primacy over its movements that it would be rendered powerless. As for the "scare" propaganda that Japan could be drawn into a war over South Korea or Taiwan, it simply missed its mark. The results of the election showed that the public was willing to trust the government to cross that bridge when and if it became necessary.

The Position of the LDP

As the dominant political organization of Japan, the Liberal-Democratic Party went into the 1970s with many questions dividing its diverse and contentious factions. The leadership of Eisaku Sato, who had been in office longer than any Japanese prime minister, was weakening as he approached the end of his service in 1972. His rivals were taking heart, knowing that he would not be able to stand again for the party presidency after serving four terms of two years each. And under the Japanese system, the party presidency of the LDP determines the identity of the prime minister.

Sato, shrewd politician above all, recognized the signs of the times and reshuffled his Cabinet on July 5, 1971, thereby hoping to quiet the political war over the succession. He put his favorite, the sixty-six-year-old Takeo Fukuda, who had been finance minister, in the key post of foreign minister to handle the matter of Okinawa's reversion. The younger and more energetic Kakuei Tanaka, the secretary of the party, came in as minister of international trade and industry with the responsibility of placating the rising American anger against Japanese competition.

It didn't settle much of anything within the LDP. The party had just suffered crushing defeats in the Tokyo and Osaka gubernatorial elections and the public was becoming increasingly restless because of rising living costs. Such party stalwarts as Masayoshi Ohira, a former foreign minister, and the kingpin of the Japanese Self-Defense Forces, Yasuhiro Nakasone, fresh from the major policy post of director general of the Japanese Defense Agency, were both in the fight to succeed Sato. It was an unsettled time for Japan, an era of change, for relations with the United States had worsened and the old Prime Minister was under increasing criticism within his own party.

Of the sixty-three Cabinets and thirty-nine prime ministers that Japan has had since 1885, Sato's government had been in power the longest—and that was its principal trouble. By winning his fourth term as LDP president on October 29, 1970, Sato had become assured of breaking the Yoshida Cabinet's record of six years and two months of service. But younger men assailed him for holding to his course of cooperation with the United States after the rise of American protectionism and the beginning of the "dollar war." He couldn't ignore them, but he strove mightily to stay on course for the remainder of his final term.

More than any other factor in his policy, Sato depended on cooperation with the United States for the well-being of Japan. As he said after his final Cabinet reshuffle, he wanted "to improve friendly relations" with the United States. It was quite an order at the time. Thus, the pendulum of Japanese-American relations swung restlessly to and fro but every change appeared to worsen the position of the two nations.[44]

[44] Sato Cabinet change, *The New York Times*, July 6, 1971, p. 1; re-election, *Japan Times*, October 30, 1970, p. 1. Also important are Sato's announcement of his intentions, *Japan Times*, September 23, 1970, p. 1; "The Master Mind" by Minoru Shimizu, *Japan Times*, October, 1970, p. 12; and an editorial in the

4 . THE WISDOM OF EISAKU SATO

The Prime Minister's residence in Tokyo is a splendid old brick building that sits in solitary splendor behind its protective fences and hedges in a secluded area near the harsh gray eminence of the Diet building. It is a pleasant place, reminiscent in a way of Frank Lloyd Wright's lamented Imperial Hotel, with a graceful red-carpeted staircase, quiet and well-furnished rooms and a relaxed atmosphere. Here, Eisaku Sato has ruled Japan from the time he took over from Hayato Ikeda on November 9, 1964, without much change in his essential philosophy of government.

There wasn't much ado about security or credentials when I arrived to see the Prime Minister on a rainy Friday in the late spring of 1970. Two gentlemen from the Gaimusho, the Japanese Foreign Office, met me at the door and informed me that a Cabinet meeting was just breaking up. It was then only 11 A.M., and since the subject had been a matter of agreeing on instructions for a new mission to Washington to avert a trade war, it was plain enough that the Japanese Cabinet did not mind early hours.

As we walked up the red-carpeted staircase, Cabinet ministers in dark suits were emerging from the Prime Minister's office suite, looking very grave, and the corridor was lined with their waiting associates. I saw three whom I knew slightly but had no chance to do more than exchange brief greetings or nod; all, it seemed, were in a hurry to get on with their business. My escorts and I waited upstairs in a room jammed with overstuffed chairs, grouped about a long table, in which the Cabinet session had been held. I had just shaken hands with Yasuhiro Nakasone, then the director general of the

---

Japan Times, The LDP Presidency, October 2, 1970, p. 14. I have found Robert A. Scalapino's discussion of "The United States and Japan" (in *The U.S. and the Far East*, 2nd ed., Prentice-Hall, Englewood Cliffs, N.J., for the American Assembly) to be useful and also the companion work, *Japanese-American Relations in the 1970s*, edited by Gerald L. Curtis (Columbia Books, Inc., Washington, D.C., for the American Assembly). As for the judgments that I have made and some of the insights I have attributed to various Japanese leaders, these were derived entirely from my own interviewing in Tokyo, Osaka and Kyoto.

Defense Agency, when one of the gentlemen from the Gaimusho plucked at my sleeve and murmured, "The Prime Minister."

Eisaku Sato had entered the room from his inner office without ceremony, shook hands with me briskly and welcomed me in English, smiling pleasantly all the while. After a brief session of picture-taking, he led me into his office—a large and beautifully furnished oak-paneled room with a large Japanese flag beside his big desk. Facing the desk, about twenty feet from it, was a large globe, turned so that the Prime Minister would be looking at North and South America. A big red button located Washington, D.C. There were quiet Japanese paintings and a big clock on the walls and a small color TV set perched inconspicuously on a table at one side.

We sat in a comfortable group of big chairs about a low table and were served *ko-cha,* the tea most Americans prefer, as we talked. My two escorts from the Gaimusho and a third man, whom I assumed to be the Prime Minister's secretary, all took notes during the conversation, which was brisk and lively and shifted from one subject to another with delightful informality. Now, the only English that was spoken came from me and the Gaimusho's interpreter; the Prime Minister spoke Japanese but seemed to follow my questions almost as rapidly as did the interpreter.

Portrait of a Prime Minister

Eisaku Sato was then sixty-nine years old but would have passed for a vigorous fifty-five or so. He was rather short, but stout and powerfully built, and seemed in the best of health. It was obvious that he paid a good deal of attention to his clothes, for his dark-gray suit was expensive and well-tailored; like his white shirt and blue tie, it was immaculate. The only decoration he wore was a small insignia of honor in his buttonhole.

The Prime Minister's large, unlined face mirrored his moods, as he spoke with the consummate art of a veteran actor. With his iron-gray hair, his large liquid-brown eyes and his generous and expressive mouth, he could be grim, grave, inquisitive, lighthearted and even merry by turn. Often, as the translator was repeating his words in English, he would look at me with raised eyebrows in a kind of comical way to underline a pleasantry. But if his mood was serious, he would survey me gravely and nod his head to emphasize the forcefulness of his words. Now and then, he would gesture lightly with one hand; but actually, he needed no other form of communication but his expression to show his moods.

I have seldom seen a man who could act any part with such ease and could control his voice and face with so little effort. Those who have said that he has a genius for timing and most sensitive antennae for political movements are exactly right.

A Matter of Security

In his genial and unobtrusive way, the Prime Minister tried to put me at ease by telling of an ambassador who had come to Japan for his second term of service and remarked: "Tokyo looks more and more like New York." I said I thought this was true enough, except that in Tokyo my wife could walk the streets without fear while in New York she could not. To which Sato rejoined with a smiling caution about wandering around alone in the Ginza area after midnight.

But at least, I observed, the Prime Minister did not have to warn members of his Diet to be careful about going to their garages for their cars after dark, a subject that President Nixon and the Congress of the United States had worried about. True, Sato said, but because of the tenseness in Japan over the Mutual Security Treaty at the time, he had had to go everywhere with heavy guards to prevent being "hijacked." Upon which we agreed that conditions in the large cities in our respective countries were not markedly different in matters of personal security.

Some Observations on Trade

It was a period when the negotiations over textiles had broken down and there was danger of a full-scale trade war between Japan and the United States, which was very much on the Prime Minister's mind. The forces of protectionism in both countries were trying to impose their will on their respective governments, resulting in a certain amount of ill feeling in Tokyo as well as Washington. Sato took the longer view. The whole objective of Japanese-American trade, he said, was to conduct commercial transactions in such a manner as not to impede relations between the two countries. And that, he remarked, was where the principal difficulty lay.

While he did not minimize the disagreement over textiles, he also refused to let himself be stampeded by it. There would, he said, be other such difficulties, in diverse fields, one being electrical goods. The point was that Japan, in his view, sought in all these areas an economic competition that could be carried on within the framework of the free enterprise system. He emphasized, too, that the rivalry should be friendly—an evident warning against too steep a rise in American protectionist sentiment.

His solution? He had said it before and he has said it many times since: More personal contacts between Japanese and American business and industry to enable them to work out their own problems, better communications between both countries, and a solution of outstanding trade problems on a multinational as well as a binational basis. That, of course, meant recourse to GATT (the General Agreement on Tariffs and Trade) in the ever-difficult matter of reducing import restrictions. But Sato also had other methods in mind, which he intended to try from time to time when the going became difficult.

The important point was that he did not intend to permit a Japanese-American trade war to develop in the Pacific if he could help it. He knew only too well what the consequences would be.

Security in the Pacific

Turning to the broader problems of security in the Pacific, he reminded me that Japan was the only great economic power that was also not a great military power and he proposed to continue to maintain a modest Japanese posture toward armaments as long as he remained in office. The Self-Defense Forces, in consequence, were to be contained in size within the framework of that policy, he said. That, he went on with a cautioning gesture, meant continued reliance on the United States for the defense of Japan.

Unlike his vociferous opponents, he was perfectly content to maintain the strength of the Japanese-American alliance and it did not concern him that he was charged with being a supporter of American military policies in Vietnam and elsewhere. He intended to see that

Japan stood by its commitments, he said. Nor did he believe by any means that Japan was getting a "free ride" any longer under the protection of the American atomic umbrella. Continued Japanese reliance on the armed strength of the United States, he pointed out, would mean that Japan could give increased economic aid to the developing countries of Asia—something that would be to the advantage of both Japan and the United States.

Nevertheless, he observed that the whole question of security in the Pacific was greatly complicated. As a legacy of World War II, he remarked on the continued division of many countries—China, Korea, Vietnam and Germany—as a major cause of the unsettled world situation. Over the long term, despite his usual optimism for the future of the Pacific, he felt that the German problem might be solved sooner than affairs in the Pacific, which were even more complicated. As always since 1945, he said, everything still depended on the ability of the United States and the Soviet Union to work together for peace.

As for mainland China's part in the Pacific equation, he expressed the belief that it remained for the United States and the Soviet Union to convince Peking that it should divert its energies from atomic military development to a broadening of both agriculture and industry. He did not want to say more on China at that particular juncture in history, remarking that China was exceedingly difficult to fathom.

The American Commitment

I asked what Japan would do about defending itself if, as was possible, the United States was obliged by circumstances to withdraw to the mid-Pacific. Did it mean first of all that Japan would be obliged to rearm at a faster pace? Was it possible, as some of Japan's neighbors feared, that Japanese armed forces would move in to fill the vacuum created by the American disengagement?

The Prime Minister shook his head and replied: "The Guam Doctrine is often interpreted to mean that the United States is going to withdraw from Asia. However, it has been made known to all that the United States is ready to stand by the commitments it has already made.

"Even if the United States were to withdraw from Asia, Japan has neither the intention nor the capability to fill the military vacuum which would be created by such a withdrawal. The important thing is for the United States to act in such a manner that all the efforts and sacrifices it has made in this part of the world are not rendered null and void."

The Preservation of Peace

Then, turning to me, he said he wanted to say something to me personally in concluding the interview. With a philosophical air, he remarked that the world was a much smaller place today than it had been only a few years ago and it would take great effort, great will and enormous patience to maintain peace in this smaller and far more dangerous globe.

In the Pacific, he repeated for emphasis, Japan recognized that the actions of the United States, the Soviet Union and China would be crucial toward questions of war or peace. He was well aware that China had been weakened somewhat by internal troubles but he still considered it a major force in Asia and one of the great powers of the world.

Therefore, he concluded, the United States can scarcely afford to say that all its major interests lie in Europe or the Middle East. The American people, he said, also have major responsibilities in the Pacific. To this, I agreed. Having spoken with me for an hour, the Prime Minister arose with a broad smile and wished me well.

His had been a thoroughly professional performance. I had come in with the realization that Sato had a reputation for waspishness and bad temper that made him feared, never loved, by his colleagues. And I had been told that he was no crowd-pleaser; in fact, a subsequent poll showed that only 27.4 per cent of those consulted wanted him to continue in office. Nevertheless, I left the Prime Minister's residence with a lively appreciation of his shrewdness and his keen political sense. I did not then and have not since questioned the basic sincerity of his policy toward the United States.[45]

[45] The interview was on June 19, 1970. The poll by the Kyodo News Service was reported in the *Japan Times*, October 11, 1970, p. 1.

5. THE POLITICS OF CONSENSUS

In a fit of temper over a reporter's question about the zigs and zags of the Soviet policy line, Foreign Minister Andrei A. Gromyko once said, "A great nation does not change its foreign policy every ten minutes."

The observation is doubly true when applied to the foreign policy of Japan in a revolutionary world. While Eisaku Sato has maintained his pro-American posture and his successor may continue it unless the trade war gets too hot, a change is likely by the middle of the decade. Even today, widespread evidence is available in Japan of restlessness over the American alliance. In the manner peculiar to Japan, the leaders of the various important segments of Japanese life already are exploring their options.

It will take time before these obscure and measured consultations produce the kind of consensus on which a future Japanese government will be willing to risk a bolder, stronger and more venturesome posture in the Pacific. It will take even longer to determine whether, in the slow evolution of Japanese political life, the New Right will come to power or whether a weakened Liberal-Democratic Party will have to give way to a resurgent and revitalized New Left. Yet, there can be no doubt either in Tokyo or Washington that change is in the air and the relations between Japan and the U.S. will be quite different a decade hence than they are today. Just how different the situation of the two nations will be, and whether they will come to a parting of the ways, depends very largely on how well they are able to resolve their current difficulties over mutual security, trade, and approaches to other Asian nations.

The Many Wait on the Few

In a homogeneous, tightly knit society such as Japan's, which has always closed itself off from the prying of the *gaijin*, the foreigner, it is difficult to know exactly what forces shape the policy of consensus in determining the Japanese position on a particular issue or set of issues. Nor can it be said with certainty at what point the eminent Japanese who are consulted on such matters are able to come to a meeting of minds. In fact, there is a constant shifting in the identities of the people and groups who make up the consensus, depending on the issues and interests that are involved.[46]

But one thing is certain: On matters of high policy affecting the national interest in Japan, the many still wait on the few. True, in every outward respect, the MacArthurian heritage of "democratization" is accepted and the sometimes painful rituals of democratic society are observed in the Japanese manner. No one can say that the Japanese do not have the right of free speech and free press, freedom of assembly and freedom of religion. Despite the dominance of the LDP, there is a multiparty system. There are free elections. And issues are discussed and duly voted upon in the Diet with binding national consequences.

Yet, behind the scenes, the decision making proceeds in its slow ceremonial way in very much the same manner as the board of directors of a very large and conservative corporation goes about deciding the future of its firm and of the people who depend on its discernment and wisdom. There is respect for public opinion in Japan, as witness the many polls on every conceivable subject that are taken by both the government and private organizations. But except in matters where there is a clear and unmistakable public position, such as the current opposition to atomic development for military purposes, the public's view does not play a key role in the high-level decision making.

It is the government, once its course has been set, that usually shapes public opinion in Japan, with a powerful assist from the news media. The pressure of the public on the government, so familiar in the divided United States of today, is rarely felt in the domain of the island colossus of the Pacific.

It follows that one of the more difficult exercises in diplomacy is to discern the direction that the politics of consensus is likely to take in Japan. The process is made doubly hard to deal with because of the habitual unwillingness of most Japanese to make a frontal approach to an issue and their pleasant if misleading practice of telling a

[46] For an excellent study of the Japanese consensus, see Richard Halloran, *Japan: Images and Realities* (New York: Alfred A. Knopf, 1969).

visitor what they think he wants to hear. In consequence, the best hope there is for arriving at realistic judgments is the private discussion of relevant issues with those Japanese who are experienced in consensus politics.

Thus, while no Japanese Cabinet minister publicly questioned the wisdom of the Sato government's policy of close cooperation with the United States in the Pacific, some were deeply disturbed by it. They did not hesitate to say privately that they did not like the way the United States is using its power in Asia. They also argued that even if the Sato policies are retained through the mid-1970s, a sharp departure from the current alliance system is a virtual certainty.

A Pessimist's View

One of the many pessimists among Japan's present and former Cabinet ministers told me in Tokyo that he believed the American-Japanese relationship was headed downward. He doubted, in fact, that the trend could be reversed. While he agreed that the problems of trade and the Mutual Security Treaty were important, he was even more bothered by the American tactics of withdrawal in the Pacific.

During the Johnson and Nixon Administrations, he said, the shift toward American protectionism had become very strong, particularly when directed against Japan. He recognized that it did not sit well with American business that the United States, which accounted for one-third of Japan's foreign trade, was carrying a 1971 trade imbalance in Japan's favor at the rate of almost $3 billion. He agreed, too, that the Japanese campaign against the United States over the Vietnam War might have made a better impression if 15 percent of Japan's trade with the United States had not come as a result of the war.

Nevertheless, he viewed such matters as a part of the force that was driving the United States away from the western Pacific and toward a greater degree of protectionism. He called it isolation and expressed doubt that even a strong leader would be able to combat the trend successfully.

Had such statements come only from this one Japanese dignitary, I might not have paid so much attention to them. But I heard them repeatedly from Japanese in all walks of life during my stay in their country. They were deeply imbedded in Japanese thought.

I asked my Japanese source whether he was worried by a potential withdrawal of American forces possibly as far as the mid-Pacific and an eventual removal of the American atomic umbrella from Japan and South Korea. As far as he was concerned, he did not see that it would make an immediate difference to Japan. For the next few years, at least, he expressed the opinion that trade would continue to have a higher priority than national defense in the Japanese scheme of things. In fact, he was one of those who did not believe in an immediate and decisive expansion of the Japanese defense forces because he could not see where—and against whom—they would be used.

Even if the United States did embark on a major withdrawal to the mid-Pacific, he maintained that Japan could still depend on the Polaris submarine and land-based Minuteman missiles as credible deterrents to any country that would consider launching an attack against Japan, something he believed to be unlikely in any case. Of course, he well understood that there would come a time when a different leadership and the pressure of events would make a decided change in Japan's policy.

Under the influence of a younger, more aggressive and more nationalistic generation, he said, it was entirely possible that Japan would do away with the sacred "no war" Article 9 of the Constitution and even go for a Japanese atomic weapon. But that would be a far different Japan than the economic powerhouse of today, which bent every major resource toward widening its trade and boosting its GNP. Therefore, he could not conceive of any dramatic change in Japan's military posture in, say, the next five years.

For the long run, he saw Japan locked in increasing rivalry with the United States and the Soviet Union in the Pacific and considered China an uncertain force that might affect, but could not control, the policies of the other three powers. True, he did not like the prospect. No Japanese would. But as a realist, he had to concede the obvious. And he thought that Japan, in one way or another, would be able to adjust its policies to live with its Pacific rivals.

What Conservatives Believe

Many of the themes touched upon by the pessimistic Japanese, an ex-Cabinet minister, appeared in one form or another in the views of a number of distinguished conservatives to whom I talked. There were differences in emphasis, in timing and in the degree of anticipated changes, but two points stood out in the limited soundings I was able to make of Japanese opinion: (1) Japan would have to seek new policies in the Pacific in the years to come, and (2) Japan should maintain its current posture for the short run. Within that rather blurry framework, privately expressed opinions were colorful and almost infinitely varied.

One of Japan's elder statesmen, a familiar figure at most Japanese-American conferences, warned that the Vietnam War and its consequences were the most damaging factors in relations between Japan and the United States. With the increasing American pullback in the Pacific, he thought it inevitable that Japan's Self-Defense Forces (he smiled at the term "Self-Defense") would be measurably increased, particularly at sea and in the air, to safeguard Japanese trade routes. For the present, and he emphasized "present," the protection of the American nuclear umbrella would be needed but he indicated it probably wouldn't be for too long.

As for American bases in Japan, it was his opinion that two naval and two land bases for the American armed forces would be sufficient and that the presence of the American military, in any case, should be limited to a "token force." He wasn't too disturbed by the prospect that American and Japanese trade rivalry in the Pacific would increase; he took it pretty much for granted and didn't see that anything in particular could be done about it. In his view, nature would have to take its course, nature in Japan being a most powerful and growing economy.

The leader of a Japanese trade organization with broad contacts in government and industry agreed, in another conversation, that Japan would considerably expand its sea and air forces in the next decade and continue to maintain a modest but respectable ground force. However, he did not believe that the Japanese public could be persuaded, in current circumstances, to accept an atomic Japan although he could discern a certain amount of propaganda that was intended to slowly change the public's mind. In consequence, he, too, argued that the American atomic umbrella would remain necessary for Japan's defense for some time to come, even if the United States did retreat to the mid-Pacific.

On the economic front, he anticipated that Japan and the United States would become even keener rivals over the next decade but he foresaw a good many difficulties for his country in the fight over trade. Even now, he pointed out, Japan is being made the target of innumerable reproaches by fellow Asians for "trying to hog all the business," a burden the United States has had to bear in the past. In the military field, too, he said that Japan was inheriting a large share of the ill will stirred up by the United States through its intervention in Vietnam. But he thought his country, as a world power, would have to expect such adverse judgments—and a good many more.

The president of one of Japan's major newspapers, in a round-table conference that included leading members of his editorial staff, reluctantly came to the conclusion that an American pullback of major proportions in the Pacific would change Japan's outlook and military policies rather drastically. But he said, without seeming unduly disturbed, that Japan could live with such a situation if it had to do so. He was much more serene, on the whole, about Japanese-American relations than one of his associates, an American-educated editor, who observed, in a sharp tone, that American popularity had sagged in Japan because of American trade policies and the Vietnam War. He left no doubt that he thought Japan should cut loose from the close American embrace—a view that his president did not publicly encourage.

The president of one of the important rival newspapers, a man of an even more conservative nature, simply said he wasn't for change of any kind in Japanese-American relations. He wouldn't hear of a substantially increased Japanese military establishment, believed it utter folly even to think of an atomic bomb for Japan and was one of the few who argued for retention of the Mutual Security Treaty in its present form for a number of years. As for trade relations, he conceded there were difficulties between the United States and Japan but—true rugged individualist that he is—suggested that private enterprise could work out a better solution than the governments concerned.

A conservative military specialist, by far the most outspoken of the diverse group whose opinions I solicited, said there was no doubt whatever that if the current situation continued in the Pacific, Japan would begin rearming in earnest by 1975. He saw no reason why the Japanese defense forces should not be familiar with the most sophisticated weapons and methods in use in the world today. Without saying so directly, he left the impression that he believed such information was being gathered constantly with or without the assistance of the United States. For, in building up a modern military force, he argued, Japan might be able to leapfrog over some of the outworn or outdated techniques in use today and develop a whole family of newer and even more potent sophisticated weapons. It was a chilling view, but it was honest.

Finally, one of the very few academics who favored the conservative cause, a retired professor with close links to both government and business, said rather sadly that Japan's relationship with the United States had been the salvation of his country and he was reluctant to see any change whatever. But, with a sigh, he recognized the nature of the division that was coming about in the Pacific and he indicated, with a shrug of his tired shoulders, that there was nothing he could do about it at his advanced age. "The younger generation," he remarked with a melancholy smile, "is in favor of a lot of changes and so I suppose we will have them, whether we like them or not."

It was not to be expected that any Japanese of importance would go so far at this stage in the proceedings to reckon on the consequences for the United States of things yet to come. Among these possibilities were the change or complete abandonment of the Mutual Security Treaty, the deployment of a strengthened Japanese defense force outside the country, at least by air and sea, a Japanese posture toward China of a radically changed nature, and the thrust of an even greater Japanese trade offensive in time.

A number of years would pass before Japanese attitudes solidified on such crucial questions. For the present, in the laborious politics of consensus, the consultations went on at the highest levels in the land.

What was wrong fundamentally in the long and successful postwar Japanese-American relationship that drove both sides relentlessly toward changes that might not, in the long run, be beneficial for either of them? Many things, most of them not very well understood either by Americans or Japanese. As a Japanese commentator, Kazushige Hirasawa, wrote: ". . . Neither the Japanese nor the American people correctly understand the rapid changes brought about by the U.S. losing its 'almighty' position, on the one hand, and the fast growth of the Japanese economy, on the other . . . The truth is that things have changed in both Japan and the United States, so that they are now disappointed with each other."[47]

6. THE OPPOSITION

The trouble with the Japan Socialist Party, the principal opposition to the ruling Liberal Democrats, is that it has been rent by internal struggles almost since its formation in 1945. In the foreseeable future, still more trouble is in store for the ill-assorted group of Marxist-Leninists of the JSP's left wing and the European-type Socialists on the right. The furiously anti-American Marxists, including a large proportion of intellectuals, teachers and radical students, invariably hammer away at their revolutionary anvils in a land where revolutionary movements are unpopular. The more practical and less radical group on the right seeks to associate itself with the aims of the Japanese middle class. And between them there is constant friction.

The result has been a series of splits and mergers, followed by still more divisions, that have made the JSP a mere patchwork of an organization, ill suited to contest the nearly twenty-five-year reign of the Liberal Democrats. The Socialists' high-water mark came in 1958 when they won 166 seats in the House of Representatives. Then they dropped, successively, to 144 in 1963, 140 in the following year and 90 in 1969, when the Sato-led LDP captured 302 out of the 486 House seats.

[47] *Japan Times*, October 2, 1970, p. 1.

The moderate Democratic Socialist Party, created in 1959 by some of the dissatisfied right-wing Socialists, and the fast-rising Komeito, or Clean Government Party, political arm of the Soka Gakkai Buddhist movement, gained both strength and prestige from the JSP debacle. So did the hard-working Japan Communist Party, which took fourteen seats in the election.

However, the left wing of the JSP learned nothing. The call for a class struggle and all-out opposition to "American imperialism" remained its theme for the twenty-fifth anniversary of the party in 1970 with the party's chairman, Tomomi Narita, accusing Washington of "letting Asians fight Asians under the Nixon Doctrine." Saburo Eda, secretary general of the party, sounded the right-wing's battle cry against the party's ideology, but Narita defeated him at the party's 34th National Convention at the end of 1970.[48]

Because of this basic division, little chance exists in the foreseeable future for a left-wing Socialist government that will try to take Japan into the neutralist third-world camp and strengthen its alignment with the Communist countries. The class struggle, as a political end, simply isn't very attractive to a people who are interested in struggling primarily for the good life.

The Communist Line in Japan

It is the Japan Communist Party, rather than the warring Socialists, that is concentrating on popular issues such as anti-pollution campaigns and demands for better housing. Curiously enough, under the direction of its presidium chairman, Kenji Miyamoto, the old *apparatchiks* who worked for violent overthrow of the government are now out of favor. Some have even been expelled from the JCP in its effort to broaden its popular appeal. The JCP, in short, is a nationalist party that advocates a strictly Japanese approach to Communism.

Miyamoto's slogan is for a "People's parliamentarianism" at home, which means that Japanese Communists for the present are content to allow the public to believe that they will choose to try to

[48] *Japan Times*, October 12, 1970, p. 1; October 13, 1970, p. 3; December 3, 1970, p. 1.

come to power by parliamentary means. On foreign policy issues, the JCP stresses its independence of domination from both Moscow and Peking and its virulent opposition to the United States.

One of the members of the seven-man party presidium, Tetsuzo Fuwa, put the JCP's American position this way: "Our ultimate objective is to create a Communist society in Japan. But this will take time and meanwhile reality stares us in the face—that Japan is an industrially advanced nation, tied to the United States in a position of military and political subservience."

While the Communists are even less of a threat to the Liberal-Democratic Party than the Socialists, the Miyamoto line has made the JCP the strongest and biggest Marxist-Leninist party in any of the non-Communist Asian lands. In addition to its fourteen seats in the House, quite an advance from its single seat in 1953, the Communists have 300,000 members and 400,000 subscribers to their party newspaper, *Akahata*.[49] In the local elections of April 11, 1971, the JCP polled nearly three million votes, a gain of 7.5 per cent over the previous comparable election, and became the third-largest party in local assemblies. By joining forces with the Socialists, they helped defeat the LDP's candidates for governor in Tokyo and Osaka. What is even more important, the Communists gained in strength while the Socialists declined.

The elections to the House of Councilors, or upper house of the Japanese Diet, confirmed the Communists' gains ten weeks later. As a result of the voting on June 27, 1971, the Communists' share of the total was 8 per cent. With their ten seats, however, they were far behind the dominant LDP and the Socialists.

The Outlook

Among thoughtful Japanese, there are some who believe that the Socialists eventually will go out of business because of the split in their ranks. Under this theory, the right-wing Socialists would join their erstwhile colleagues in the Democratic Socialist Party and the Socialist left wing would make common cause with the Communists in a united front-type organization.

There is little reason to believe, however, that either a strengthened

[49] *South China Morning Post*, September 19, 1970, p. 8.

Democratic Socialist Party or a united front of the far left would become an effective opposition to the LDP. Neither has sufficient popular following as yet and neither has the power that the LDP commands through business, industry and the Establishment press. Consequently, left-wing Socialists have been putting out feelers for a merger of all opposition parties against the LDP. But just how the conservative Komeito and the right-wing Socialists would fit with the Marxist-Leninist revolutionaries defies all understanding. Barring a reversal of public attitudes, the Japanese left, both old and new, is destined to remain a secondary political force.

The only issue the left has had over the years is the Mutual Security Treaty, which it violently opposed and sought to overturn. But when the tenth year of the American-Japanese pact passed on June 22, 1970, with a series of peaceful but futile demonstrations and the treaty went into its automatic year-by-year renewal stage, the left was obliged to cast about for some other way to appeal to the public, for the LDP took over the issue of bringing about sufficient changes in the treaty to accommodate Japan's new position of world power. And the same thing happened in the reversion of Okinawa.

As for the China issue, the LDP obviously is improving Japan's relationships with Peking even if it doesn't appear ready yet to go as far as the left desires. But the Japanese public doesn't seem to be upset about this or anything else as long as the yens keep rolling in.

"Japanese Democracy Is Weak"

Among the younger Socialists, the dominance of the Liberal Democrats and the public rejection of the Socialist program of neutralism and non-armament have created a feeling amounting sometimes to despair. One of the most respected of the younger Socialist M.P.'s, Masashi Ishibashi, told me that he believed the whole system of postwar democracy in Japan was now threatened. "Japanese democracy," he said, "is very weak and elected officials are not greatly respected."

I asked Ishibashi why the JSP had not been able to challenge the LDP successfully in recent years. He shrugged. People in Japan, he explained, respected authority and they were generally inclined to vote for the party in power. Consequently, he argued, the government invariably had a built-in advantage because its propaganda was more acceptable to the public. As for the JSP, he felt that it had depended too long for its main support on the Sohyo, the radical labor federation, and would do better by following a more independent course. He pointed out also that in the 1969 elections Sato produced the Okinawa revision agreement with the United States at a psychological moment in the campaign while the opposition was divided between the Socialists and three smaller parties.[50]

In a party brochure, he wrote this darkening view of Japan's future under the conservatives:

"It is certain that Japan's setup for independent defense will be strengthened . . . and it is also clear that, with the backing of increased military forces and economic aid, Japan will begin to embark on a dangerous road of increasing its voice in Asian affairs and securing its leading role in Asia.

"This will not be just for the purpose of lightening the burden of the United States . . . but will be of more positive significance in that this course points to the same road traversed in the past by the old militarists with miserable defeat . . . The only force that can smash such a dangerous ambition is our party's banner of non-armament and neutrality, the forces for the protection of the Constitution and for democracy, rallied around our party."[51]

The argument is sincere, but it has convinced only the Socialist faithful to date.

The Peace Movement

Out of the trackless jungle of opposition politics in Japan, the younger generation sees very little chance that any new force will emerge in the foreseeable future with relevance to its own aims and ambitions. Many young people in Japan have told me this. The majority have found little to attract them in the radical student movement and its doctrine of perpetual violence and anarchy. Nor

---

[50] Interview with Masashi Ishibashi, June 19, 1970.

[51] Masashi Ishibashi, article in *Japan Socialist Review*, Nos. 194–195, January 1, 15, 1970, p. 27. He became Secretary General of the JSP, the party's No. 2 post, on December 2, 1970.

are they particularly impressed with the program offered by the majority LDP.

The one new organization that has an idealistic attraction for many young people in Japan is the Beheiren, the Peace for Vietnam Committee. It began in 1965 as a spontaneous movement of teachers, other intellectuals, students and housewives following the beginning of the American bombing of North Vietnam. It has specialized in monthly rallies against the Vietnam War and attracted the most attention with its one-day combined protest against the war and the renewal of the Mutual Security Treaty on June 15, 1969, when it claimed a 75,000 attendance.

Beheiren is a kind of youth pool of the New Left. It says it has no membership, no paid officials, no organizational trappings of consequence. Oda Makoto, its chairman, takes care of its expenses through voluntary contributions. In one instance, Beheiren raised nearly $7,000 to pay for an anti-war advertisement in *The New York Times* on November 16, 1965. In others, it brought various American radicals to Japan to make common cause with the Japanese peace movement. It boasts that it has helped sixteen deserters from the American armed forces to escape from Japan.

About 250 Beheiren groups now exist in various parts of Japan and there is a monthly publication, *Beheiren News*. It still does not believe in a cohesive action program but tries to stimulate individuals to take whatever action that pops into their minds. It is very much a "do it yourself" peace movement and is, therefore, difficult to estimate as to both size and strength. Some claim it has attracted 1,000,000 young people into its ranks; others argue the permanent roll of peace activists in Japan is much less. But certainly it is a force that is likely to go on in one form or another long after Vietnam.

Its theme is a folk guerrilla song entitled "Friends," which begins:

> *Friend! Burn the fire of struggle,*
> *Since the dawn is coming.*[52]

Like their associates in the United States, the peace activists of Japan are likely to continue to play a largely negative role. They have

[52] Yoshiyuki Tsurumi, "Beheiren," *Japan Quarterly*, Vol. XVI, No. 4, October–December, 1969, pp. 444–448.

no positive program to present to their skeptical elders. And being unable, or unwilling, to bridge the generation gap themselves, the radical-minded young leftists of Japan remain outside the wobbly sphere of consensus politics.

The Japanese Right

The right, as always, is potentially powerful in Japan. The glory of Dai Nippon still has a profound appeal to a proud, cohesive and nationalistic people. In and around Tokyo alone, there are about 300 rightist organizations with a total membership of 105,000; outside the capital, there are perhaps again as many in the guise of sports clubs, military associations and conservative student organizations.

While the radical students who tear their universities apart may monopolize the headlines and TV screens in their own country, they seldom attract much attention abroad. It is only when the extreme right breaks loose in some mad and inexplicable fashion that a tremor of alarm flashes through East Asia and the Western world. For an older generation cannot forget that this is the way militaristic Japan once began an insane sweep toward Pacific conquest. On May 15, 1932, young rightist officers assassinated Prime Minister Tsuyoshi Inukai to remove a human obstacle from their path. And on February 26, 1936, an abortive military coup set the stage for the take-over that eventually brought the feared Hideki Tojo, "The Razor," to power.

There are few who want to connect that kind of a Japan with the Japan of today. And yet, when Yukio Mishima tried to rouse the Army into an attack on the "No War" Constitution and committed suicide in the ceremonial Japanese manner when he failed, a thrill of horror radiated from Tokyo into every major capital in the world. Prime Minister Sato called the man mad in an effort to diminish the importance of the incident. But as *The Times* of London put it, regardless of whether Mishima was mad or actually was attempting a *coup d'état,* "there will be those in many countries who harbor smoldering suspicion [of Japan] from the war years; or who, like the Chinese, have been shouting about a revival of Japanese militarism, and who will take the Mishima incident as the most combustible kind of fuel."[53]

Actually, Mishima caused no damage within Japan itself. The forty-five-year-old novelist and his eighty-member private army, which he called the Tate-no-kai (Society of the Shield), picked the worst possible time and place for their deed. For when he stood on the balcony at Ground Self-Defense Headquarters in Ichigaya around noon on November 25, 1970, and called on 1,200 members of the regiment guarding Tokyo to rise with him to restore Japan's military glory, the troops hooted at him and laughed. It seemed ridiculous to them that they should be asked to follow this dreamer in his self-designed trick uniform. And so, as he had planned, Mishima committed hara-kiri and was beheaded by one of his youthful followers, who was himself beheaded in turn. With the release of the base commander, General Kanetoshi Masuda, who had been held captive by Mishima and his four followers, the three surviving members of the leadership were taken prisoner and the incident was over, or so the police said.

But from the manner in which Cabinet ministers were guarded thereafter and the precautions that were taken to watch every major rightist group, it was clear that fears of a military take-over, once aroused, could not easily be brushed aside. The New Left may have been floundering at the outset of the new decade. But the New Right was marshaling its forces. And though Mishima had failed, he had become a symbol that would not die.

7. JAPAN'S MILITARY REVIVAL

Behind the high thick walls of the Japanese Defense Establishment at Rappongi, thirty minutes from downtown Tokyo, the structure and development of Japan's new armed forces are being planned with infinite care. Dai Nippon's Pentagon is well aware of the anxious

---

[53] *The Times* of London, November 27, 1970. Estimates of Tokyo rightist groups are from the Metropolitan Police Department, *Japan Times*, November 27, 1970, p. 3. Material on the Mishima incident is from the *Japan Times*, November 26–29, 1970.

scrutiny of the Asian lands that were held captive under the banner of the Rising Sun only a little more than a quarter century ago.

Consequently, whatever is said and done about Japan's military revival must of necessity be carefully weighed. The military policies that will guide Japan for the 1970s and thereafter, as a result, may be veiled in ambiguities to avoid needless provocation. In any discussion of what Japan's real intentions are, it is likely that there will be more denials than affirmations and that the Japanese style of discourse, so heavy with innuendo, will confuse matters still more. For the Japanese themselves are still far from a consensus and the Rappongi brass hats do not know how far they can go.

Japan's Military Posture

Nevertheless, this much is known of Japan's military posture for the fourth five-year period of defense build-up, 1972–76:[54]

The expenditures that are formally proposed total $16 billion, more than twice as much as in the previous five years.

While the Self-Defense Forces will be held to a modest 270,000, an increase of 11,000, there will be a determined expansion of ground, naval and air weaponry.

The Ground Self-Defense Force, comprising 13 divisions of 180,000 men, will be armed with 1,000 of the most modern tanks, 230 more helicopters, 270 more armored cars, new amphibious vehicles and Hawk surface-to-air missiles.

The Maritime Self-Defense Force will be composed of 200 warships totaling 245,000 tons, including cruisers, destroyers and submarines. But the new vessels will nearly all be new high-speed rocket ships, small and packed with firepower and highly maneuverable.

The Air Self-Defense Force will have 1,750 modern aircraft with the acquisition from the United States of 100 F-4 Phantom fighters. The ASDF also will receive three more Nike-Ajax surface-to-air missile units and the Badge automatic radar warning and control system, as well as other modern American equipment.

In addition, the Japanese intend to boost their research and

[54] Most of this is from Yasuhiro Nakasone's plan, submitted to the Liberal-Democratic Party October 21, 1970, and the final draft announced April 27, 1971; *Japan Times*, April 28, 1971, p. 1.

development fund by 3.5 times, to nearly $500 million, give the SDF personnel a much-needed pay increase and establish what is termed an "information division"—the beginnings of a new Japanese military intelligence agency—under the Joint Chiefs of Staff.

As for bases, Japan sees no need for continued American occupation of about 120 bases on the home islands and neither does the United States. Accordingly, by mid-1971, only 28,000 American military personnel remained on Japanese home-island bases and 40,000 others on Okinawa. The residual forces will go eventually as the remaining bases are vacated by the United States. Perhaps five bases, and maybe fewer, will remain under some kind of joint authority if Japan's desires are met.

Japan also is moving in on Okinawa with the vanguard of a force of 6,400 SDF troops. The Okinawans may not be enthusiastic about this quick reintroduction of the Japanese military, but there is little they can do about it. The SDF presence is a symbol of Japan's determination to take over all of Okinawa sooner or later.

The Japanese position on the acquisition of nuclear weapons is more difficult to define. Despite all the pledges against nuclear arming, the Japanese government's White Paper on defense, in its original version, contended that Japan had the right to acquire tactical nuclear defense weapons. Under the Nuclear Nonproliferation Treaty, it is also possible for Japan to operate nuclear marine engines, as demonstrated by the nuclear-powered freighter *Mutsu.*

Since the making of atomic fuel for peace or war uses is identical for 75 per cent of the manufacturing process, if follows that the Japanese already are well along the road to atomic development. The joint use of enriched uranium techniques, requested from the United States, is another major step even if it is done cooperatively in a Pacific nuclear power project. And the acquisition of the "New N" rocket series, if licensed by the United States, means that Japan will be able to launch space satellites after 1975—at a cost estimated in the preliminary stages at $600 million.

Thus, the basis for a powerful modern armed force has already been laid. While the Japanese point out that their defense outlays are only 1 per cent of their GNP, that GNP is the third largest and the fastest-growing in the world and makes their military fund the seventh biggest in the world. Under these circumstances, Japan's neighbors cannot be blamed too much if they remain skeptical of the honeyed assurance in the Defense White Paper.

The "Nakasone Whirlwind"

The guiding genius of Japan's military revival, Yasuhiro Nakasone, is a former commander and fighter pilot in the Japanese Imperial Navy during World War II who served as the director general of the Defense Agency in 1970–71. He is a *samurai* of the new school and, at fifty-two, makes no secret of his ambition to be prime minister before the 1970s are over. The press has called him the "Nakasone whirlwind"! He made Rappongi come to life.

. Nakasone, author of Japan's 1972–76 development plan, is a graduate of Tokyo University. After receiving his degree in 1941, he served in the Home Affairs Ministry—seat of the old "thought control" apparatus—but soon went into the Navy. For a young and inexperienced officer, he won promotion very quickly—a testimony to his own military talents.

Once the war ended, Nakasone worked as a superintendent in the Tokyo Metropolitan Police Department. He also ran an anti-Communist group that fought Communist agitators in the postwar period. It is not strange, therefore, that he came to the attention of another vigorous anti-Communist and ex-cop, Matsutaro Shoriki, the publisher of *Yomiuri Shimbun*, who was having his own stiff battle with the Communists at the time in order to save his newspaper from being torn apart. With Shoriki, Nakasone became a founder of Japan's earliest atomic energy research and development program. Soon he was marked by his conservative friends as a man to watch and began his slow rise to eminence in the Liberal-Democratic Party. His first Cabinet post was as state minister in charge of science and technology. Later, he became minister of transport.

Nakasone has had his erratic moments and his defeats. For years, he campaigned for the popular election of Japanese prime ministers and sought to make them far more powerful and less accountable to the Diet than they are today. His friends finally persuaded him to give up what amounted to a hopeless reform campaign. But they couldn't curb his tendencies toward being a political maverick and making damaging off-the-cuff statements. For example, he once called the Pearl Harbor attack a "conspiracy" that he blamed on Franklin Delano Roosevelt. He also denounced the Japanese Constitution at one time as an "effort to prevent the Japanese from ever rising again." It made him some powerful friends on the far right, even if he learned to be more expedient and later moderated his views.

But it soon became clear that Nakasone was no ordinary chauvinist and that he could not be dismissed as a mere rabble-rouser. Step by step, he assumed more responsibility and gained more adherents among the New Right of the LDP. He won the confidence of Eisaku Sato, which was most important of all to his advancement. And in 1967 he assumed the presidency of the rightist Takushoku University for three years—a step toward the establishment of a more imposing image. By the time he was made the boss at Rappongi, he was ready to cut a larger figure in Japan.

Nakasone's Program

Nakasone began modestly enough with a statement of five principles that Prime Minister Sato enthusiastically accepted. They were, briefly stated, a determination to make Japan responsible for its own security, maintain the American alliance in some form, develop a nonnuclear defense program, link it to a broadening diplomatic effort, and remain within the territorial confines of the nation.

But no sooner had he outlined this program before the Diet, to well-merited applause, than he told the top leaders of the Defense Agency that Japan should "wipe out ambiguous expectation and unquestioned dependence on the United States." He left no doubt that he would seek revision of the Mutual Security Treaty and the "Japanization" of the American-held bases in the home islands as well as Okinawa.

Before the Foreign Correspondents' Club of Japan, shortly after taking office, he spoke to the world press about his ambitions for Japan's military development. While he made the usual reservations about building a force solely for defense and abjuring nuclear force, he came right to the point about Japanese-American relationships.

"The day will come," he said, "when Japan can—and should— bear a greater burden of leadership and responsibility in a larger partnership with the United States than now exists—a partnership in which mutual security problems could be dealt with as one part of a broad system of economic, cultural and defense cooperation between the two nations.

"At any rate, it will be necessary for both the United States and Japan to pursue a flexible policy capable of meeting new situations at any time by means of adapting and refining the operations of the U.S.-Japan Security Treaty."

As for bases, he spoke with un-Japanese directness, for his mind had long been made up on this issue and he had both his party and public sentiment with him. "In the seventies," he said, "the management and operation of military bases in Japan, including those on Okinawa after reversion, will be subject to continuous examination with a view toward reduction and conversion to Japanese control."

Nakasone also called for greater respect for the Japanese armed forces, strengthening of Japanese intelligence efforts, promotion of autonomous research and development in the fields of strategy, tactics and weaponry, and the build-up of a munitions and arms industry. No wonder, after such a speech, that the Asians became anxious about their own security!

A Visit with Nakasone

Yasuhiro Nakasone received me at the headquarters of the Defense Agency in Rappongi on a summer's afternoon in 1970 with a mutual friend as interpreter. He was suave, sedate and intensely serious—a tall, lean, young-looking Japanese in the naval tradition. His face was striking, even handsome in a way, with a long straight nose, narrow brown eyes and a thin, controlled mouth. He was dressed neatly but without showiness in a dark-gray suit, well-shined black shoes, a white shirt and striped gray tie. I was impressed by his hands, which were lean and hard, the hands of a working artist or sculptor, I thought. As it turned out, he is an amateur painter in the tradition of another Former Naval Person.

Nakasone's office was plain and unobtrusive in much the same style as the man himself. Near his large clean-looking desk, a big globe was turned in such a way that he faced the Asian continent and the Japanese home islands. On the walls were a calendar, a few paintings and oddments. Plain white curtains framed the windows behind him. The only sign of military activity throughout the visit was at the checkpoint at the head of the red-carpeted stairs leading to the director's office, where two soldiers in uniform greeted me and passed me through.

Nakasone spoke in a low, even voice in Japanese and followed the translation with evident interest, for his English is perfectly good and he could have used it if he had chosen to do so. But it was typical of his pragmatic nature that he had, after a bold beginning, become supercareful about what he chose to say and how he phrased his ideas. He was, and remains, a politician with a keen sense of what he cannot do and what he cannot say publicly. Far from the hawkish, devil-may-care military type that his opposition made him out to be, I found him a good deal more reserved than several recent occupants of high office in the E-ring of the Pentagon. He didn't bother to conceal his mistrust of the United States, which probably accounts for his departure from Rappongi after preparing the fourth five-year military expansion plan.

It was by chance that my appointment fell on the day that marked the end of the ten-year initial period of the Mutual Security Treaty, June 22, 1970. Although the treaty was being automatically renewed, Nakasone pointed out to me that either side may henceforth denounce the pact with one year's notice. That, he reflected, would equalize the position of Japan and the United States.

Since he had discussed changing the treaty so often, I asked him how he proposed to do it. It was quite possible, he explained, to use a joint consultative committee to arrange for changes in base agreements and other measures appropriate to the standing of powers of equal rank. He rejected the notion of a NATO-type base agreement, saying he wanted something more suitable to Japan's needs.

In response to my question over what would happen in Japan if the United States eventually pulled its military strength back to the mid-Pacific, he replied that it would be a grave matter for South Korea and Taiwan, not for Japan. With a show of confidence, he argued that Japan was developing a suitable defense capability and still needed only the American nuclear umbrella. That position, he maintained, would not change through the period of the fourth five-year military plan, ending in 1976. Thereafter, he added, the position would have to be reassessed—and it required no feat of mind reading to understand that he believed Japan then would be ready to move decisively into the Pacific power structure.

As for the development of the Self-Defense Forces, he saw no particular reason at that time to think in terms of total manpower exceeding the 1972–76 ceiling of 270,000—a small, compact, hard-hitting professional force operating with the most sophisticated modern weapons systems. He emphasized naval development above all else. At one point in the discussion, he expressed the hope that he could one day consider the Sea of Japan to be the Lake of Japan. I thought it a rather tall order in view of the known operations of the Soviet nuclear submarine fleet in that general area, but ambitious concepts seemed to be a part of the director general's approach to his job.

Nakasone would not be jarred out of his public adherence to Article 9 of the Japanese Constitution, whatever he may have said—or thought—before assuming office at Rappongi. He was cautious when I asked him what would oblige him to change his five principles of defense. Not, he said, the United States pullback. But, he went on, a nuclear threat or an attack on Taiwan or Korea might be different, depending on circumstances. Asked what would happen if there were a Japanese mass protest against defending Taiwan or Korea, he said doggedly that the Japanese response would be appropriate and within the limits of the Constitution.

The director general gave the impression that he believed the struggle for Okinawa had been resolved with the Sato-Nixon reversion agreement. In any event, he wasn't troubled. Nor did he believe there would be further difficulties from the American side. The United States, he remarked with a rather grim, tight smile, had been having more troubles with Japan over trade than over Okinawa. He concluded with some of the observations he intended to make to the American government on a forthcoming visit to Washington, none of which were particularly surprising.

After my departure, I reflected that I had seen a singularly tame hawk at Rappongi, but scarcely the real Nakasone. He had fashioned himself, for the time being, into a dutiful shadow of Eisaku Sato. But he was far too strong a character to be anybody's shadow for very long.

The American Spectators

For many years, the United States has urged Japan to adopt a more vigorous defense posture and the Japanese government is now obliging Washington. The American position is based on a good deal more than the notion of reducing or terminating the "free ride" the Japanese have been getting through the willingness of the United States to assume the burden of Japanese defense.

Long before there was a Nixon Doctrine or a thought of precipitate American withdrawal from a forward military posture in Asia, the United States was urging Japan to take on a larger role in Asian affairs. The "low posture," a whole corps of visiting American diplomats said, was not fitting for a Japan that had become so great an economic power.

Among the Asians who watched this developing relationship between the conqueror and the loser in the Pacific war of 1941–45, there were cynics who concluded that the United States was preparing the way for eventual departure from the Indo-Pacific area. Such observers, and they included Asian statesmen at the highest level, argued that the United States had no intention of remaining in the western Pacific, wouldn't carry out its commitments, and in any case had no business on the Asian mainland or the big Asian islands twenty-five years after the end of the Pacific war.

During my travels in the Indo-Pacific area over a period of fifteen years, and in my discussions at the United Nations over a quarter century, I met no Asian statesman of consequence who was willing to predict that the United States would stay the course in Asia for a prolonged period. The best they could do was express such a hope.

Whatever motives the various American governments may have had in the long postwar period, the consequences are now emerging with greater clarity. There will be an increasingly powerful Japan in the foreseeable future, both militarily and economically. Only time and circumstance will reveal the nature of long-term Japanese military planning and the extent of Japan's peaceful reconquest of Asia through its newfound economic strength. While the Japanese have continued to protest that they are both unable and unwilling to fill the vacuum that may be left by the United States in the Pacific, their neighbors are becoming increasingly skeptical. The unpredictable Filipino President, Ferdinand Edralin Marcos, once blurted out that he expected Japan to replace the United States militarily in the Pacific.

The distressed Eisaku Sato responded that the Japanese people would "never allow us to take over the role of the United States" and he pointed once again to the "no war" article in the Japanese Constitution. In the first White Paper on Japanese defense, moreover, there were voluble pledges against a revival of Japanese militarism and assurances that Japan would never again commit aggression against its neighbors. But there were some notable deletions in the eighty-nine-page document, made by the government before it was issued, that showed Japan was keeping its options open. These omissions included statements that it was within the "no war" Constitution for Japan to develop tactical defensive nuclear weapons, but this right was not being exercised "at present"; that Japan would never introduce conscription again; and that the Mutual Security Treaty would be in existence "semi-permanently."[55]

Japan meanwhile is reviving its arms industry. Japanese contractors in 1970 alone received more than $1 billion in defense orders, and that was bound to increase. Only ten firms accounted for half the orders, with Mitsubishi Heavy Industries as the top supplier. It should not be imagined, however, that the Japanese at this stage intend to build up a great military-industrial complex at the expense of their trade. The chances are that a combination of Japanese and American military suppliers, with others in South Korea and elsewhere, will share in enlarged Japanese defense orders.

Thus, for a time, the United States is likely to maintain an association with Japanese defense. But whether Japan eventually will allow the Americans to continue as participants, or reduce their role to that of mere spectators, is something that cannot now be foretold. It

[55] The Defense White Paper was issued in Tokyo, October 20, 1970. The reports of the deletions were carried by Reuters in its file for that day. See also Kyoaki Murata, "The Spectre of Conscription," *Japan Times*, November 6, 1970, p. 14, and Hanson Baldwin, "Japan's Arms Industry," in the New York Times News Service for December 14, 1970.

depends entirely on whether the Japanese disregard Eisaku Sato's advice and try once more to go it alone in the Pacific, with all the risks that such a course entails.

The Dialogue of Defense

As long as Sato remained in control of Japan's foreign policy, there was no question about Japan's willingness to continue to depend militarily on the United States. Even when Nakasone paid his first visit to Washington as defense director, he was careful to take a moderate position. On the application of the Nixon Doctrine, he cautioned mildly, "We in Asia hope that you [the Americans] will proceed gradually to avoid the severe shocks of your withdrawal." And on the possibility of Japan's acquisition of atomic weapons, he repeated solemnly that there was no chance of it "as long as the U.S. deterrent functions."

But Japanese commentators complained that Nakasone's reception in Washington was cool even though he brought back an *omiyage* (gift) in the form of the return of one American base and the promise that others would follow. The American reaction was not difficult to explain. After years of concern over the attack on the Mutual Security Treaty from the New Left, the Pentagon was scarcely likely to strew flowers in the path of a far more dangerous and determined opponent of the pact, the leader of the Japanese New Right. No one in authority could forget that Nakasone had given the Diet full warning of his intentions at the outset of his rule at Rappongi: "We need security permanently. But we need not cling to the present Japan-U.S. Mutual Security Treaty forever."

No wonder that Sato was full of assurances to try to ease American concern at the time of the second Nixon-Sato meeting in 1970. "We have no intention of reviving militarism," he said. "I don't think there is any possibility of our conversion of our Self-Defense Forces into full-fledged armed forces." Yet, he added somewhat gloomily, "We will never compete with the U.S. on the military level, but economically there will be a conflict."

Whatever doubts the American military may have entertained privately over Nakasone's future intentions, conservative sentiment in the United States was far more alarmed over the inroads of Japanese trade than over any future defense build-up. Senator Strom Thurmond, the South Carolina Republican who had a certain amount of influence in the Nixon Administration, urged Japan to show more "leadership necessary to the defense" of non-Communist Asia. And, instead of being worried over enlarged Japanese defense expenditures, Thurmond argued that Japan wasn't spending enough to do the job. As for the American liberals, they were so frantic about getting the United States out of its involvement in the Vietnam War that nothing else mattered.

Consequently, the process of dismantling American strength in the northwest Pacific went on. The B-52 bombers that had been used against Vietnamese targets were removed from Okinawa. Rappongi went about its operations for the reduction of American bases in Japan without any undue disturbance. Within the ruling LDP, the New Right quietly looked forward to a campaign for major revisions in the Mutual Security Treaty sometime after 1975. And in South Korea and Taiwan, there was a new awareness of the meaning of Japan's commitment to aid in their defense.

A Matter of Faith

Even though Japanese-American problems are serious and will take time to resolve, it is somewhat ridiculous to hark back to the days of Homer Lea and sound the alarm against a new "yellow peril," as some in the American and European business communities are doing. The Japanese are painfully aware of such extreme sentiments and resent them as much as they always have. As one Cabinet minister put it to me in Tokyo, "We can understand why Americans and Europeans find it more congenial to deal with each other than with us. But we are no 'yellow peril' in any sense." With a rather bitter reference to the unhappy days of the "gentlemen's agreement" with the United States, he went on, "After all, there is no problem of Japanese immigration these days. Japanese people prefer to stay in Japan."

What it all comes down to, as the minister and I agreed, is a matter of faith—the restoration of trust in the relationships between the United States and Japan. And this is the most difficult of all the elements that must be dealt with in the field of international relations, for it cannot be grasped or even clearly defined. It either exists or it does not. It either draws the contending parties insensibly together or it does not. No law can decree the creation of faith and no article in even the most high-flown language of treaties can specify its meaning.

On and off during my visit to Japan, I thought about the problem in an aimless sort of way without coming to any conclusion. And then, one sunny afternoon, in the garish and crowded entrance plaza of Expo '70 at Osaka, a familiar old song came blaring over the public-address system. It was something Cole Porter wrote long ago, based on a theme taken from an Ernest Dowson poem:

> *But, I'm always true to you darlin' in my fashion,*
> *Yes, I'm always true to you darlin' in my way.*[56]

In matters of faith affecting the United States and Japan, perhaps that is the best that can be expected.[57]

8. JAPAN AND THE CHINESE PUZZLE

During the visit of a recent Japanese mission to Peking, a Chinese official asked Tomoo Hirooka, president of *Asahi Shimbun,* how long he thought it would take before China became a great industrial power.

[56] From *Kiss Me Kate,* by Cole Porter, published by Buxton Hill Music Corp., 609 Fifth Ave., New York City. Published with the permission of the copyright owners.

[57] Much of the basic reporting about Japanese defense was developed in my interviewing. For the text of Nakasone's speech March 5, 1970, see the paper of the Foreign Correspondents' Club of Japan, *No. 1 Shimbun,* for April, 1970. I am specially indebted to the anonymous author of three authoritative articles in *Yomiuri,* April 23, 24, 25, 1970, on defense planning. For news reports on Nakasone speeches and his visit to Washington, I consulted the files of the Associated Press. Sato's response to Marcos is in an AP interview July 14, 1970. Sato's assurances to the United States at the time of his second talk with Nixon are in the files of the AP and United Press International. Strom Thurmond's advice is in *The New York Times,* September 21, 1970, datelined Tokyo. The Japanese Defense White Paper was summarized in the *Japan Times,* October 21, 1970, and the announcement of the fourth defense build-up was published next day.

"About twenty-five years," Hirooka said in an offhand manner.

The Chinese official was astonished. "Do you *really* think it will take as long as twenty-five years?" he demanded.[58]

The Uses of the China Trade

Regardless of how long it takes China to industrialize, Japan's interest in the Chinese trade is enormous. That covers China and Taiwan.

Japan is mainland China's largest trading partner; it ran up a $625 million business in 1969 and $820 million in 1970, a gain of more than 30 per cent. It didn't make any difference whether the Japanese worked under the so-called "Memorandum Trade" principle, which was official and amounted to only $70 million, or under an informal "Friendly Firm" formula that China also recognized. The Japanese did well either way.

As for the Taiwan trade, Japan's performance was even better. Following a trading record of $787 million in 1969, the Japanese boosted their business by more than 20 per cent and achieved a new high of $950 million in 1970. Best of all, from Tokyo's point of view, both gave Japan hefty trade balances.

If it weren't for the nasty problem of dealing with two Chinas, the Japanese would be very happy with their current position. Certainly, Japanese business people, with their customary acumen, have found little to worry them in the "four principles" laid down for the "memo trade" by the Chinese Premier, Chou En-lai. These are, briefly, that firms doing business with Peking may not invest in or aid either Taiwan or South Korea, export war materials to South Vietnam, Laos or Cambodia, or enter into joint ventures with American firms. Nor have the Japanese been upset by Peking's wrathful attacks.

To keep on trading with both Chinas at the rate of nearly $2 billion a year, and more than that soon, is balm enough for Peking's insults.

True, about thirty Japanese companies that have been trading with Taiwan no longer can do business with Peking. And about twenty companies engaged in the China trade have been proscribed by

[58] From an interview with Hirooka, June 12, 1970, at *Asahi Shimbun*.

Taiwan.[59] But neither Peking nor Taiwan, despite a number of things that have given them pain in Tokyo's policies, is barring Japanese trade. If anything, Japan continues to send out salesmen in greater numbers than ever to both Chinas.

However, that isn't going to solve Japan's problem. Nor is United Nations action going to make things any easier. The two Germanys, the two Vietnams and the two Koreas have managed to survive outside the United Nations and so has Taiwan. Japan's problem will be to devise means to continue doing business with Taiwan while recognizing China, something that also interests Washington intensely.

"Immobile as a Mountain"

The time has passed when a Gaimusho spokesman in Tokyo could say, as one did to me, "Our China policy should be as immobile as a mountain." For President Nixon's new approach to China in 1972 marked a watershed in both American and Japanese policies toward Peking. The United States finally recognized there could be only one China.

The Japanese could say, as did Zentaro Kosaka, the chairman of the LDP Foreign Research Council, that they should return to the 1951 position outlined by Prime Minister Yoshida, who signed a bilateral treaty with Nationalist China but wrote a letter in which he said it didn't apply to the Chinese continent. The *Japan Times* could argue, as it did in an authoritative editorial, that there was no need for Japan to "rush headlong" into Chinese recognition. The Gaimusho could stress, with typical Foreign Office obtuseness, that sixty-eight countries, including sixty-five U.N. members, still recognized Taiwan, while fifty-three, including forty-eight U.N. members, recognized Peking. But it wasn't convincing, in view of the changed U.N. line-up that admitted Peking.

The public opinion polls in Japan also told a different tale—one that both the Japanese government and the opposition parties were bound to take into account. A *Mainichi Shimbun* poll showed that 47 per cent of the respondents wanted Japan to "normalize" relations with China as soon as possible, 16 per cent asked for immediate

[59] *Far Eastern Economic Review*, September 26, 1970, p. 24; "Made in Japan," *Asia Magazine*, October 4, 1970, p. 13.

normalization, 23 per cent favored gradual improvement in relations and only 4 per cent were against normal relations. Ten per cent had no opinion. In another public opinion survey, by *Yomiuri Shimbun*, 43 per cent favored gradual improvement in Japan-China relations, 19.8 per cent were for immediate recognition, 8.9 per cent were for broader economic contacts, 8.5 per cent wanted the present relationship to continue unchanged, and only .7 per cent were for no contact. No response came from the rest.[60]

The recognition of China was the only issue of consequence that the divided Japan Socialist Party could grasp in its long and unsuccessful pursuit of the Liberal Democrats. Consequently, after four indecisive missions to Peking, the Socialists sent a fifth pilgrimage of sixty members to Peking late in 1970. Premier Chou En-lai obliged the Japanese Socialists with a pledge to enter into a non-aggression pact with Japan as soon as diplomatic relations are restored. Of course, Chou also took his usual dig at the "revival and danger of Japanese militarism," for no love was lost between Peking and the Sato regime.[61]

But the exchange didn't hurt trade, which was a relief to Tokyo.

The Ambassador's Dream

One effect of the Japanese government's awkward position on Chinese recognition at the outset of the 1970s was to revive an old political joke.

The Japanese ambassador to Washington, so the story went, dreamed that he had just received a telephone call from the State Department that the United States had recognized China—and woke up screaming. As an example of black humor, it tickled the Japanese, but their government continued to stick with the United States to bar Peking from the United Nations in 1970. That, however, marked the beginning of the end of the policy of freezing out China. When President Nixon signaled the change in the United States' China policy without even consulting Japan, the joke about the Japanese

---

[60] *Japan Times*, October 16, 1970, p. 14. About 2,000 respondents participated in each poll.

[61] *Japan Times*, November 4, 1970, p. 5.

ambassador's nightmare was no longer anything to laugh about in Tokyo.

In whatever way Japan moved to catch up with the times and normalize Chinese relations, there were difficulties. Peking was outraged by Japan's agreement with the United States to help defend both Taiwan and South Korea. Premier Chou En-lai never let an occasion pass without expressing his deep concern and resentment over such a pledge. In addition, rather pointed remarks were made about the question of Japanese reparations—something Tokyo had tried to ignore in the past. China, however, did not forget. While Marshal Chen Yi was China's foreign minister, he once said of Japan, "The Chinese people have a right to ask for reparations."[62] Even though Japan's China trade soars, the reparations problem will have to be settled one day if the two countries are to resume normal intercourse.

Despite the aura of optimism among the opposition Socialists and others, the notion that the Chinese and Japanese governments will be comfortable with each other under current conditions is not generally accepted in official Tokyo. And probably not in Peking, either. The establishment of a large and potentially active Chinese embassy in Tokyo and Chinese consular offices elsewhere is not something to which the conservatives in Japan look forward. Being familiar with Japanese subversion in China during the first four decades of the century, some of those presently in charge of Japanese policy are uneasy about the consequences of giving a free hand to a far more powerful China in the home islands.

Nor is Japan happy about a veto-wielding China in the United Nations. Before China's admission, Japan even asked the General Assembly "to review the composition of the permanent membership of the Security Council."[63] The move didn't get anywhere. With even the Russians speaking out in favor of Peking's admission to the United Nations, Japan saw that it simply wouldn't do any longer to help the United States shore up the leaking dike against Peking.

There was, nevertheless, a genuine feeling of compassion for

[62] "Asian Commentary," *Far Eastern Economic Review,* July 9, 1964, p. 47.
[63] *Japan Times,* September 19, 1970, p. 14.

Chiang Kai-shek among influential Japanese conservatives that accounted for Japan's lingering effort to support a "two Chinas" policy. Aside from the mounting Japanese trade balances with Taiwan, these Japanese recalled that Chiang did not seek war reparations from Tokyo and helped support the Japanese recovery program. In addition, it has never been forgotten in Tokyo that Taiwan, then called Formosa, was an integral part of the old Japanese empire for fifty years and that a degree of loyalty to Japan still exists among the older Taiwanese. It follows that Japan, no less than the United States, intends to maintain its commitments to Taiwan without regard for the status of its United Nations membership.

Yet, many influential Japanese are now asking themselves, in view of both the changed American and Chinese situations, whether it is realistic for Japan to follow the United States lead on China policy. For if the Soviet Union could strike a bargain of sorts with an ex-enemy, West Germany, could not China eventually become more amenable to turning to Japan for help in economic development? Perhaps, in the long run, it could be the American ambassador to Tokyo, and not the Japanese ambassador to Washington, who will have the nightmare about Chinese recognition. Once the Japanese reach a consensus, they move swiftly.

Does China Threaten Japan?

The Chinese line on Japan was laid down by Mao Tse-tung on February 9, 1961, when he said, "China regards the liberation of Japan as a matter of grave importance. The first revolution in the world was the Russian Revolution. The second was the Chinese Revolution. The third is the Japanese Revolution. If Japan is liberated, the Orient will be liberated and the world will also be liberated."

Mao's remarks are painfully familiar to the Japanese military, who have long memories. A former chief of staff of the Air Self-Defense Force, Minoru Genda, predicted that the Maoist program would be applied by pushing revolutionary operations within Japan, creating domestic confusion and, in the final stages, invoking the threat of "nuclear blackmail to achieve its [China's] ends."

"Communist China's strategy toward Japan," he wrote, "does not lie in destroying Japan's industrial facilities or its cities, but in placing Japan's industrial potential under its complete domination. If Communist China succeeds in revolutionizing Japan, and both countries are organized on a modern basis under a dictatorial regime in the style of Mao Tse-tung, the resulting combination could easily become a frightful force capable of challenging the United States or Soviet Russia on an equal basis and would succeed not only in revolutionizing the whole of Asia but would take a big stride toward turning the entire world Communist."

This is hair-raising stuff, but it bears no resemblance to current realities. For the Chinese theoreticians want no part of the only considerable Communist force in Japan, the Japan Communist Party, which they denounce as "revisionist" (that is, pro-Soviet) and therefore unworthy of recognition. Moreover, Genda concedes that the numerically superior Chinese air force of 2,800 aircraft includes only 150 obsolete Soviet-made IL-28 bombers, scarcely a threat to Japan's modern defense system. As for a Chinese invasion, it is out of the question. And the destruction of Japan's industry by nuclear warfare, if China attempted it, would wreck the very basis for Chinese efforts to win over the Japanese people.

Japan is far more vulnerable to a Soviet attack on its trade routes, which would choke off its raw materials, energy sources and eventually a substantial part of its food supply. For no Japanese military establishment within the decade of the 1970s can hope to stand up against the 120 submarines in the Soviet Far East fleet plus the 150 Arctic submarines that could be called in, the 1,500 Soviet medium and heavy bombers in the Far East, and the estimated force of 350 to 400 missiles that are deployed in Siberia alone. The 13,000 Japanese and 16,000 foreign ships that supply the Japanese home islands would be at the mercy of Soviet air and naval power even if the United States sent its Seventh Fleet into action (always a big question mark in Japanese minds).[64]

The Soviet Union is thus regarded by the Japanese military as a graver threat than China, although the Maoist long-range program of subversion is scarcely underestimated. To an important segment of

[64] Minoru Genda, "Japan's National Defense," *Pacific Community*, October, 1970, pp. 30–48 *passim*.

Japanese opinion, the United States is a bigger question mark in some respects than China, for the degree of American response in the event of Japanese need cannot be calculated. It did not help the United States very much in 1972 to reassure Japan after President Nixon's week-long sojourn in Peking that nothing had changed between Washington and Tokyo. Tokyo didn't believe it.

"Japan Can Deal with China"

There is one other major element in Japan's relations with China that is likely to influence Japanese decision making. This is the feeling, which crops up repeatedly in conversations with representative spokesmen from the far left to the far right, that Japan "can deal with China." In effect, this sentiment is based on the supposition that both nations, being Asian powers, can reach a better understanding among themselves than with outsiders such as the United States, the United Kingdom or the Soviet Union. Of course, it flies in the face of history, for the Japanese have never been notably successful in dealing with China from the war of 1894–95 on. Nor were the Twenty-one Demands any model for peaceful coexistence, foreshadowing as they did nearly a quarter century of war between Japan and China.

The argument today is that Japan has learned its lesson, that Japan has a moral obligation to atone for its misdeeds in China and that Japan has an inherent cultural affinity for China. Naturally, the university professors and other assorted intellectuals of the New Left have a far different set of reasons for promoting Japanese relations with China than do the industrialists, businessmen and military people of the New Right. But they come out pretty much toward the same general objective.

Just a few of the many conversations about China that I had with Japanese in all walks of life serve to illustrate this general proposition.

Kiichi Miyazawa, while serving as the minister for international trade and industry, regarded China as more of an opportunity for Japan than a threat to Japan's survival. He argued that China could not really become competitive with Japan as an industrial power for twenty-five years or more. Today, he pointed out, China's per capita income is still only about $100 and the greatest problem that the Chinese government faces is the feeding of 800 million people. In Miyazawa's view, the per capita earnings in China are not likely to increase substantially until Peking becomes less doctrinaire and more responsible and adopts major birth control practices. At best, his estimates are that China could begin to show a significant per capita increase by 1973.

In the struggle to feed the huge Chinese population, the Japanese authority predicted that Peking would gradually have to place more emphasis on a market economy and individual incentive and less on Mao's doctrine of permanent revolution. In consequence, he saw much that Japan could do for China and very little that Japan had to fear.

Masashi Ishibashi, the Socialist M.P. and "shadow" foreign minister of the Japan Socialist Party, argued the case for China differently but just as effectively. With the growth of protectionist sentiment in the United States, he said, Japan in time would come to depend less on trade with Americans and more on its dealings with Communist nations, mainly China. He also thought China was important to Japan from a moral point of view because he deeply believed that Japan would have to compensate China in some manner for the damage the Japanese had done during World War II. Another of his major points on China was that he thought Japan and China together could help insure peace in Asia, something that would benefit the United States, as well.

A respected industrialist, Ryoichi Kawai, senior managing director of the Komatsu Manufacturing Company, Ltd., was enthusiastic about his travels in China both as a member of Japanese commercial missions and on his own. There were, he said, many compensations for the foreigner who traveled in China because of the low earning standards of the Chinese on the mainland. He talked of excellent dinners for a dollar, haircuts for twenty cents, and a nice room in the Peking Hotel at one-third the cost of a major Japanese or American hotel.

Kawai's main argument for the normalization of Japan's relations with China was that it would help Japan to increase its trade as one means of bringing Peking back into the community of nations. He hoped that the United States would not object too strenuously if the Japanese offered a major development loan to China in the foreseeable future. Asked what Japan could do if China refused the loan, he answered by recalling how long-term credits were extended to the Soviet Union in its earliest and more recalcitrant days. The same strategy, he maintained, should now be applied to China to induce Peking to abandon its truculent approach to the world.

One of the foremost China experts in Japan, Kanae Tanaka, the editor and board chairman of *Mainichi Shimbun,* predicted that it would be fifty years before China could be organized in such a way as to conduct itself as a responsible world power. Nevertheless, he did not regard this as a sufficient reason for Japan and the United States to abandon efforts to improve their relations with China. Once, he said, he had had the notion that Japan could act as a bridge between China and the United States; now, however, he doubted if such a position would be practical for Japan because of Chinese irresponsibility. Moreover, he could envision no circumstance under which Japan could set aside its commitments to help defend Taiwan and South Korea, in both of which there are now massive Japanese commercial interests. He also thought it unlikely that Japan would break away from its close relationships with the United States in the foreseeable future and did not see that these would be harmed in any way by continued Japanese trade with China.

Much the same rationale was adopted by his fellow journalist, Tomoo Hirooka, the president of *Asahi Shimbun,* who put the case this way: "Japan takes an interest in conducting trade with China, but that does not mean Japan is to part from the Free World and associate herself with the Communist bloc. We do take an interest in trade with the Chinese, simply in the hope that a China that has been isolated from international society will open its doors. Consequently, there does not seem to be a possibility that would produce an adverse impact on the relations between the United States and Japan. A rise in Sino-Japanese trade would not necessarily bring about a drop in trade between the United States and Japan."

Such broadly representative views make it evident that Japan already has reached a consensus on continuing to build up the China trade, if it can be done without sacrificing large trading interests elsewhere. But the normalization of Japanese relations with China is something else again, even though public sentiment is pointing steadily in that direction. Inside the government, there appears to be far more willingness to consider diplomatic recognition of China than in the United States. But Peking, after being ostracized by both Tokyo and Washington for more than a generation, is bound to drive a hard bargain.

9. THE GOOD LIFE

For Suzuki San, the Japanese who is making his way into the newly affluent middle class, life these days is a series of bewildering changes. If he wants to keep up with the Yamamotos, he finds he must plan and scrimp to acquire a home and a car. Where he once was able to amuse himself by going out with the boys, he has to contend today with the wife and kids who expect to be taken out for dinner now and then at a city hotel or country drive-in restaurant. Furthermore, if he wants to get ahead at the office, he notes that common sports like baseball or bowling simply aren't in the same class with golf in establishing the proper social status.

Life is no longer either simple or easy for Suzuki San. In the roaring inferno of construction, smog and traffic that Tokyo has become, he buffets his way into crowded trains or buses or fumes on a street corner while waiting for an empty taxi and a discourteous driver. If he has to take a customer out at night, he must plunge into the mad carnival of expensive cabarets, low-down strip joints and 50,000 bars with B-girls or slightly better-style hostesses attached.

There is today a kind of desperation in such an existence for Suzuki San, even if it is scarcely the life of "quiet desperation" of which Henry David Thoreau wrote more than a century ago. Japan's stratified society is breaking down under the pressures of industrialized life. And Suzuki San isn't quite sure whether he likes what is happening or not. Yet, it is the price that he, like most of Japanese urban society, must pay for their country's rise to world power. Neither they nor their neighbors nor their children will ever be able to go back to their old leisurely ways, although the Japanese ceremonial life-style and dress will still be practiced for perhaps another generation in the home. For Japan, in its anxiety to overtake and surpass the West, has fallen victim to some of the worst aspects of Western civilization and lost some of the fascination of its own culture in the process.

The Quality of Japanese Life

When Japan was just beginning to recover from the destruction of World War II in 1950, 46 per cent of the nation consisted of farming households that led a quiet and fruitful rural life and 54 per cent worked in the cities. Twenty years later, the rural population had dropped to 25.6 per cent—26,280,000 people in 5,324,000 households living in 142,689 villages.[65] The majority of 74.4 per cent of Japan's people, or 76,370,000, lived in the cities, with the heaviest concentrations in Tokyo, Osaka and Nagoya, although places like Sapporo, Sendai, Hiroshima and Fukuoka were growing rapidly. Even the ancient shrine city of Kyoto, most charming of all, was beginning—most regrettably—to resemble Paterson, N.J., in some respects.

The process of urbanization was thus accomplished in a single generation with all the attendant consequences—poor housing, polluted air and water, overcrowded transport, inadequate highways and ever-rising costs. A lot of farmers became clerks and delivery people, for in five years clerical workers increased by 35 per cent and those working in distribution and kindred services went up 21 per cent. Some of the city workers did better, for people in managerial positions increased nearly 34 per cent in the same period and specialized workers gained almost 15 per cent.[66]

With a rapidly rising per capita income, the Japanese began buying at a fast rate. They owned close to 25,000,000 motor vehicles, choosing from among 1,044 combinations of color, specifications and parts for passenger cars; 25,000,000 TV sets, 20 per cent color models; and enough washing machines and refrigerators to put one in almost every home. By the beginning of the 1970s, more than

[65] Agricultural-Forestry Ministry survey, in *Japan Times*, October 3, 1970, p. 9.

[66] Government White Paper on People's Lives, 1970, summarized in *Japan Times*, June 27, 1970, p. 5.

500,000 Japanese were going overseas each year, 54 per cent on pleasure and the remainder on business, many to the United States. It was a full-fledged consumer *boomu*.[67]

The Japanese began building roads and expanding into the suburbs at a furious rate, selling 5,000,000 automobiles a year in the process. The Japan Railway Construction Corporation undertook the Seikan Tunnel, linking the main home island of Honshu with northernmost Hokkaido. Three bridges were planned between Honshu and the relatively rural island of Shikoku. Encouraged by the success of the New Tokaido Line's "Bullet Express" between Tokyo and Osaka, the Japan National Railways began dreaming of more such trains and an even faster one to be powered by a linear induction engine.[68]

Life was speeding up for Suzuki San, but that didn't make it much better for him. In some ways, he was worse off than he had been.

The Rocketing Cost of Living

It was bad enough that consumer prices bounced ahead at the rate of 5 to 7 per cent annually, but that could be borne with the continued increase in wages. What hurt was the rocketing cost of land for those who so badly wanted to own their homes rather than rent them, a tremendous ambition for many Japanese families. In the six largest cities, land prices zoomed by 26.4 per cent a year for 1955–60, 24.7 per cent for 1960–65, 12.4 per cent for 1965–69, and 20.1 per cent for 1969. In the early 1970s, prices were still tilting upward with no relief in sight.

What this meant, in effect, was that in the greater Tokyo area, purchase prices for homes averaged 2.1 to 2.6 times the average income of purchasers in public corporation housing developments and 2.2 to 3.2 times as much in private developments.[69] As an illustration of how rapidly land values increased, a tract of land purchased by International Christian University for $300,000 in the

---

[67] *Ibid.* See also *Japan Times*, June 21, 1970, p. 16, and *South China Morning Post*, November 2, 1970, p. 11.

[68] *The Economist*, September 26, 1970, p. 95.

[69] Government White Paper on People's Lives, 1970, summarized in *Japan Times*, June 27, 1970, p. 5.

early 1950s at Mitaka, outside Tokyo, was valued less than twenty years later at $80 million by the university authorities.[70]

The Japanese government's White Paper on People's Lives soberly concluded: "The upsurge of land prices, coupled with the rise in construction costs, brings heavier financial pressure on the housing costs of the people. In addition, the fact that the average commuter takes a longer time getting to work adds to the worsening of living conditions."[71]

But even those who were lucky enough to find a plot of land on which to build in the area around Tokyo, Osaka and Nagoya found that their troubles were only beginning. For they had factories, highways and airports in close proximity to their homes and had to put up with all kinds of annoyances in one of the most densely populated sections of the world. In a single five-year period ending in 1965, for example, the population density in the three key metropolitan areas of Japan increased from 8,698 per square kilometer to 9,908. And Japan defines a densely populated area as one in which there are 4,000 persons per square kilometer![72]

Then, too, the influx of tourists, which approached 1,000,000 annually in the early 1970s, very soon became a complicating factor because the Japanese enjoy traveling in their own country, as well as abroad, and were therefore the first to feel the pinch in hotel accommodations. Under the impetus of the Olympic Games and the Osaka's Expo 70, the Tourism Division of the Transport Ministry began stimulating hotel building, estimating that 65,000 hotel rooms would be needed by 1975. That was an increase of 230 per cent over the 28,000 rooms in 176 hotels that were officially registered with the government in 1970.

The forty-seven-story Keio Plaza Hotel, the nation's tallest and largest, with 1,000 rooms, went up in Tokyo's Shinjuku area. A thirty-story hotel, the Pacific Tokyo, was constructed in front of the

[70] Told to me by Holloway Brown, ICU's public relations director.

[71] Government White Paper on People's Lives, 1970, summarized in *Japan Times*, June 27, 1970, p. 5.

[72] This amounts to 10,240 people per square mile, and puts the current density rate at more than 25,000 people per square mile, double that of the District of Columbia.

Shinagawa Station. And others of twenty-three, sixteen and ten stories respectively were erected in the Oimachi, Kudan and Narita areas, the latter being the site of a second Tokyo International Airport that was to relieve pressure on suffocating Haneda.[73]

Against such competition for city space, Suzuki San is helpless. He has had to push out to the suburbs. There he has surrounded himself with the familiar trappings of suburbia—supermarkets, golf courses, gas stations, swimming pools, bowling alleys and roadside stands. He has also taken up horse racing in a big way; attendance at the various tracks went up 40 per cent in a single recent year.

In many respects, the Japanese "satellite cities," their term for suburbs, are an imitation of the American model. The ultimate insults to the good life—fried-chicken eateries, hamburger joints and smelly drive-ins purveying tough New Zealand beef—have not yet arrived in Japan in large numbers, but they are on the way.

The Dietary Revolution

Japanese diet is changing as rapidly as every other aspect of Japanese life. During the 1960s, the average volume of rice eaten dropped 13 per cent, fruit consumption rose 3.5 times, milk 2.7 times and meat 2.5 times. But Japanese health experts aren't satisfied. They want people to eat 40 per cent more fruit, drink 55 per cent more milk and eat 5 per cent more meat.

At the same time, the Japanese farmer, making up less than 20 per cent of the 50,000,000-strong labor force, is raising more rice per unit than any other country. Japanese rice production is running about 17,500,000 metric tons on an estimated 8,000,000 acres and the government's rice surplus is now approaching 10,000,000 tons. But the rice isn't cheap. In 1971, when the government boosted the rice price for producers by 3 per cent, the Japanese were eating the world's most expensive rice. Under the government subsidy plan, government rice cost 142 yen a kilo (18 cents a pound) and the "free market" price was 200 yen (25 cents a pound).[74] Meat was

[73] *Asahi Evening News*, June 16, 1970, p. 5.
[74] *Japan Times*, May 2, 1971, p. 1. See also *South China Morning Post*, October 12, 1970, p. 2, Sec. 2.

very dear, too, particularly the kind of prime Kobe beef that the Japanese love, but the artificially high price of rice no doubt did help stimulate the interest of Japanese families in Western-style foods.

The burgeoning restaurant industry therefore no longer concentrates on traditional Japanese-style dinners, but generally offers both Western and Japanese menus. It is a common sight in the newer "drive-ins" in suburbia to see Japanese eating Western style on one side of the house and traditional style on the other. Not that this means Japan is going over to a meat-and-potatoes regimen all at once. There aren't enough meat and potatoes yet to go around. But certainly, a start is being made. Already the changed diet has been enough to produce an appreciable increase in the size of the new generation of Japanese milk-drinking, hamburger-eating youngsters.

Schools and Society

Japan was the third-ranking world power in compulsory education at the beginning of the 1970s, after West Germany and the United Kingdom, with an attendance rate of 99.9 per cent. In terms of the number of students who went on to high school, 82 per cent, and to universities, 21.4 per cent, Japan again was third, behind the United States and the Soviet Union.

A government White Paper on Education, issued in November 1970, took justifiable pride in such statistics. In an additional survey by the Education Ministry, it was shown that more than 1,400,000 students were attending 382 four-year institutions of higher learning as of May 1, 1970, with an additional 263,000 in 479 junior colleges. This amounted to 16.2 persons per 1,000 in institutions of higher education, next to the 34.7 persons in the United States and 18.9 persons in the Soviet Union.[75]

Yet, something was badly wrong with Japanese education, for in 1969 and 1970 a small number of student radicals was able to interrupt the functioning of 124 universities and close down the greatest, Tokyo University. Weak administrators, permissive faculties and scheming student revolutionaries all were blamed, as in the United States. But there was one big difference in Japan and that was the

[75] *Japan Times*, November 17, 1970, p. 3; November 28, 1970, p. 12.

system itself. For while the faults of American education were inherent in the American life-style, the shortcomings of Japanese education were due primarily to the kind of educational system that was fashioned for them after World War II by American Occupation authorities.

In theory, the new era for Japanese education was supposed to eliminate all class distinctions and the painful "control of ethics" for students under the Emperor's various edicts. In practice, the reforms failed, for poor administrators, some of them corrupt, weakened many institutions of higher learning by failing to keep up with the times. In the words of Professor Noboro Ito of Tsuda College, they "neglected to democratize the universities while sitting comfortably on the old authority."[76]

Now, a new wave of reform is under way in Japan in the wake of the disastrous 1969–70 riots. Japan's Central Education Council has projected a new educational order that will take at least a decade to implement—if students and faculties will sit still that long, which is doubtful.

Under the leadership of Dr. Tatsuo Morito, a former minister of education, the Council seeks to diversify higher education by creating five groups of colleges, institutes and universities. For public servants and managers, the general universities would remain. There would be separate colleges for engineers and other professions, for teachers and artists. Then would come the two-year general junior colleges and two-year special institutes for vocational training. As for control, the government would yield authority over state and public universities to administrators and faculties, under the Morito plan, and provide generous subsidies to make them as self-sufficient as private universities.

The Council has also proposed massive changes in secondary school education to make life easier for the Japanese high school student. The reason is that the secondary schools have been infected with the virus of revolt to almost as great an extent as the univer-

[76] "Japan's Classroom Counter-Revolution," *Asia Magazine*, October 4, 1970, p. 24. A 1970 Education Ministry report shows 82 per cent of junior high graduates in Japan continue in senior high schools and nearly 25 per cent of senior high school graduates go to college.

sities. One survey showed that 170 junior high school students at forty-seven schools throughout Japan had affiliations with radical groups.[77] Another study disclosed that three out of five students in Tokyo high schools were dissatisfied with both their curriculum and their teachers and that 30 per cent of them couldn't keep up with their work in the classroom.[78] Whether there is any particular correlation between the two findings remains undetermined. But certainly, both are danger signals.

What the Education Council has done for the high schools is to soften up the whole curriculum, offer more optional and fewer compulsory subjects, recognize that in an age of mass education not every student is fit to attend universities, and request administrators to make life more interesting in the secondary schools. It is only a question of time before marching bands and girl cheerleaders become the order of the day in Japanese high schools, some of which already have gone over to the American pattern of entertainment in education.

A Major Casualty: English

One of the more regrettable signs of the times is that, in the massive sweep of educational reform, English has now been dropped as a compulsory subject in Japanese secondary schools. It never was very well taught there as a general rule and Japanese weren't on the whole particularly capable as students of English. But now, the Japanese schoolboy of the 1970s isn't even going to be able to speak in the quaint (and often imaginary) syllables popularized by Wallace Irwin in another era.

Just about the only places where English has been taught well in Japan since World War II have been the secondary schools or institutions of higher learning that are sponsored by religious organizations. And these, of course, will continue to offer English instruction even if the public secondary schools give up except for a few inadequate optional courses. It is a pity that English instruction has

[77] "The Faces of Dissent," *Asia Magazine*, October 4, 1970, p. 22.
[78] *Japan Times*, June 28, 1970, p. 14.

been sacrificed to satisfy the violent anti-Americanism of the professional Japanese teachers' organizations.

The Good Shepherd Movement

There is a demonstrable interest in Japan in acquiring a better command of English than is offered in the schools that are under the jurisdiction of the government. The Good Shepherd Movement, a Catholic social communications project sponsored by the Maryknoll Fathers, has taught 250,000 people to speak English at its English centers in Kyoto and elsewhere. Through its two daily radio programs, one on 109 stations and the other on 77, the Good Shepherd Movement encourages the belief in simple, basic principles of life, such as love, friendship and devotion. It also offers television programs three times a week in Tokyo, Nagoya, Osaka, Kyoto and other cities. The result is a listening and viewing audience of somewhere between 6,000,000 and 10,000,000 people a week, depending on the type of program, in a nation that has less than 1 per cent of Christians among its population.

The interesting part of the English classes, as I discovered during a visit to the project in Kyoto, is that the students are a mixture of working class and university people who pay for their instruction and faithfully attend class in the evening. While there are some American instructors, the strength of the project lies in its American-university-trained Japanese teachers who speak excellent unaccented English.

Father Graham McDonnell, M.M., the director of the GSM English Center in Kyoto, always has at least three English classes going in the evening in the parish house adjacent to the Catholic church in Kyoto. "In addition to teaching English," he says, "we also like to give instruction to our people in the customs, etiquette and ways of thinking they will encounter if and when they are able to travel to the United States or other English-speaking countries."[79]

With the impending disappearance of compulsory English instruction in Japan's secondary schools, the privately financed English schools such as those of the Good Shepherd Movement will have to

[79] See "Light of the Heart," a brochure published by the Good Shepherd Movement, Kawaramachi-Sanjo, Kyoto, Japan.

assume a larger part of the burden if they are able to do so. The "Koka-Kora" English of the teen-agers and the "striku and boru" English of the sports commentators are scarcely good enough for the educated Japanese who wants to be a part of the world.

The Lessons of the World's Fair

The rise of insularity in Japanese education, ironically, comes at a time when the Japanese people have been exposed to more foreign influence than ever before in their history. The spectacular pageantry of the Olympic Games in Tokyo in 1964, the beautifully staged Expo 70 at Osaka, and the Winter Olympics in Sapporo in 1972, much as they impressed world opinion, have had an even greater impact on the Japanese people themselves.

It has been a part of the conventional wisdom of our time that these three great events restored Japan's self-confidence and helped persuade both government and people that it was now best to abandon the humble "low posture" of the postwar era and assume a more fitting attitude toward the world. No doubt that is true. But even more important, the Japanese people were given an unobstructed view of the *gaijin,* the round-eyed, big-nosed foreigners whom they were taught for a century to despise, and found that they weren't quite as devilish as they appeared.

Traditionally, despite their outward show of friendliness, most Japanese have been xenophobic. Lafcadio Hearn's difficult experiences with them, for all his love of Japan, have been repeated many times over among outsiders who have sought in vain to penetrate the inner recesses of Japanese society. Not even those foreigners who married Japanese have been received into the Japanese family fold, in most cases, and this is still as true as ever.

What has begun to change since the Olympics and the world's fair, however slowly and agonizingly, is the Japanese appraisal of the outside world. In a recent poll of public attitudes by *Mainichi Shimbun,* for example, 29 per cent of those questioned thought that Japan should be modeled on the United States and another 29 per cent expressed the belief that Switzerland was the best model. There were 10 per cent who had more admiration for the British, 7 per cent for the West Germans, 4 per cent for the French and the rest, who had no choice, presumably thought that Japan as it now exists is ahead of all other countries.[80]

That is a considerable advance over the fanatical Imperial Japan of the earlier years of this century. It should not be imagined that the Japanese, the most insular and self-centered of all peoples, will change their national character overnight—or even in the remaining years of this century. But the impact of other cultures on the people of Japan is being felt increasingly. If it were not for the enormously difficult Japanese language, the greatest barrier between Japan and the rest of the world, the process of internationalizing Japanese society would be much farther along than it is.

But middle-class Japan increasingly is sallying into the outside world. True, tourists still travel in the familiar Japanese phalanx, as do Japanese journalists, scientists and other professionals, which makes sight-seeing a group experience. Yet, even that represents progress over the old isolation. It will be a long time before the Japanese give up faith in the group creed: "The nail that sticks up must be hammered down."

Why did the world's fair have such an impact? Primarily, it was because most of the 64,000,000 people who attended, and made possible a profit of perhaps as much as $25 million, were Japanese.[81] They did not pay much attention to the fewer than 2,000,000 foreigners who visited the Senri Hills outside Osaka. What did attract them were the foreign exhibits, headed by those of the United States and the Soviet Union. It was obvious that long lines of Japanese did not wait for hours to get into these two pavilions because of any political sympathies. These were the star acts and they received virtually equal billing by popular demand. Using the same standard, Japan's own pavilion, with its futuristic impressions of what life would be like in the twenty-first century, appealed less to the average Japanese than such commercial exhibits as that of Mitsubishi.

On the testimony of the crowds that came, saw and were conquered at Osaka, foreign influences of all kinds are in Japan to stay. If more proof were needed, the national effort that went into the 1972 Winter

---

[80] *Far Eastern Economic Review*, October 24, 1970, p. 43.

[81] *Japan Times*, September 15, 1970.

Olympics in Sapporo shows that Japan is determined to play a leading role in the world from now on. It will take more than two blows from the United States—the change in China policy and dollar devaluation—to force the Japanese off course. The influx of foreign tourists to Japan and the growth of the travel mania among the Japanese themselves will be a further stimulus to keep the new dispensation going. The real meaning of the Olympics and the world's fair is that Japan's isolation from the world will never again be possible—or even thinkable.

10. THE ISSUES FOR JAPAN

Fuji, the snow-topped mountain so revered in Japan, is often veiled these days by dark clouds of soot that swirl from nearby factory chimneys. It is a symbol of the noxious and sometimes fatal pollution of air, land and water that has become the most dramatic of Japan's problems at home.

There Is No Escape

The filth and the sickening vapor that are by-products of the Japanese economic miracle are so pervasive in urbanized Japan that there is no escape from them for millions upon millions of people. For 48 per cent of the Japanese live in the 1.2 per cent of the home islands that are saturated by pollution. The newspaper *Yomiuri Shimbun* illustrated what this means by reporting that in the single month of September, 1971, more than 5,000 Japanese fell ill of diseases attributed to pollution, more than in the entire previous year.[82] Despite pressures from the *zaibatsu*, the government has embarked on a long-delayed cleanup. The action the government institutes over the next few years will show whether it is strong enough to discipline its wealthy supporters among the factory and mill owners who have been getting away with what amounts to murder. Already the cry is going up in Japan from the industrialists that the cost of a cleanup will be so great that they will have to curtail their operations. It is a

[82] George Chaplin, *Honolulu Advertiser* section, December 5–12, 1971, entitled "Japan, What Now?" p. 6.

form of intimidation that is being attempted, as well, in the United States. But the Japanese and American publics are not impressed.

The Japanese form of air pollution is particularly distressing because its base is a noxious chemical that produces an eye-stinging smog and a wheezing effect in breathing that has become widely known as "Yokohama asthma." These symptoms are not confined to Yokohama, but are to be found in every Japanese city where there is a heavy concentration of factories and automotive engines. In an investigation of the phenomenon, the Japanese government concluded:

"The primary cause of air pollution is the sulfur oxides discharged during the burning of heavy oil at industrial plants. Heavy oil consumption has continued to increase since 1957–58 partly because the primary source of energy was switched from coal to petroleum . . . The sulfur oxide content in the air is generally higher in Japan than in other advanced nations because crude oil from the Middle East, used here in large quantities, contains about 3 per cent sulfur . . .

"The second cause of air pollution is the rapid progress made in motorization. Still another cause is the lag in the maintenance of road traffic facilities."

The Case Against "Hedoro"

Bad as the air is in the cities of Japan, the pollution of the waters around them is worse. Here, the wastes of the factories are making sewers of beautiful rivers and cesspools out of beaches. Even well-used harbor channels are silting up with a sludge known as *hedoro,* a combination of the words for "muck" and "vomit," and swimmers are breaking out with mysterious rashes.

Once again, the government is well aware of the causes of *hedoro.* Its report on pollution says: "As for water pollution, increasing quantities of industrial waste water that are discharged into nearby rivers are believed to constitute a major cause. Rivers in and around urban centers have become polluted primarily because huge volumes of waste water used by industries using great quantities of industrial water (e.g., dyeing, spinning, pulp, paper, oil refining) are not adequately treated before being discharged."

No wonder a fifteen-year-old high school boy at Utsunomiya demanded of Prime Minister Sato: "Isn't the government treating the people more or less as livestock?" It wasn't enough for Sato to respond solemnly, "Industry exists for us, not we for industry." The public waited to see whether the Prime Minister and his huge majority in the House of Representatives would take really effective action against the Japanese malefactors of great wealth.[83] The most that could be said was that he and his successors tried.

A Decline in Social Stock

Almost as important as pollution is the issue that is related to what the Japanese call "social stock"—the overhead capital that goes into improvements in housing, sewage systems, water supply systems, medical facilities, roads and parks. In all except medical facilities, Japan appeared to be lagging behind other advanced nations at the outset of the 1970s on the basis of the relationship of such expenditures to per capita national income.

Because of the rapid growth of the gross national product, the ratio of investment in social stock to GNP has actually declined instead of increased. The government frankly admitted its incapacity in these graphic terms:

"Since the Meiji Restoration (1868), Japan has been trying to catch up with advanced nations of the world; she was also eager to build up her military power. In making these efforts, this country has been unable to devote as much attention to improving its social stock, particularly living-related facilities. In other words, living-related social overhead capital has long lagged since the Meiji era . . .

"The biggest reason for the strong sense of want possessed by the Japanese people with regard to social facilities is their rapidly growing realization of contradictions which arise from the widening imbalance between social and personal consumption. The level of social consumption remains at a low level although the people's desire for it has increased because of rising income levels. And the soaring level of private consumption makes the gap appear all the wider . . .

---

[83] *Economic Survey of Japan, 1968–69,* issued by the Economic Planning Agency of the Japanese Government, pp. 199–201. For a colorful report of pollution at Fuji city, see *Time,* October 12, 1970, p. 30. The report of a fifteen-year-old boy lecturing Sato was in *The New York Times,* September 22, 1970, in a story by Tadashi Oka from Utsunomiya.

"The ratio of public investment in this area must, of course, be increased considerably."[84]

The Japanese are a remarkably patient people, not inclined to panic over delays in large matters or frustrations in small ones. Their capacity for effective and devoted work is demonstrated in their industrial progress and their no less remarkable agricultural development, especially in the cultivation of rice. Their response to appeals for self-restraint is evidenced in their willingness to make a national crusade out of the issue of birth control, resulting in a satisfactory decline in their burgeoning birth rate and the stabilization of their population growth.

It may be said with some degree of certainty that neither the ills of pollution nor the delays in the provision of an improved social infrastructure will lead to a Japanese revolution. But certainly, continued failure to deal effectively with these problems will do more than anything else to weaken the thinning fabric of a democratic form of government in Japan. It is not a risk that Japan can afford to take. Nor can the other nations in the Pacific, great and small, be indifferent to the course that these twin domestic issues take in the years to come.

Trade, Aid and Defense

With a projected gross national product of $440 billion by 1975 if all goes well, Japan's planners can scarcely be faulted for making the expansion of trade their first priority for the first part of the decade —and perhaps for the remainder as well. But with the walls of protection rising in the United States and elsewhere and competition increasing from Singapore, Hong Kong, Taiwan and South Korea, where labor is cheap and plentiful, the Japanese are going to have to temper their hard-sell sales techniques with added inducements in the American pattern. Already, Japanese salesmen are being taught how to be nicer to customers abroad and Japanese tourists are being told that they are their country's "ambassadors."

That, however, will not be enough to sustain Japan's sales drive and the government knows it. The Gaimusho is worried about tough criticism of Japanese stinginess in foreign aid from people like

[84] *Ibid.*, pp. 190–195 *passim*.

Abdul Rahman, former prime minister of Malaysia, and Prime Minister Lee Kuan Yew of Singapore, among others. When the Tunku called upon Japan "to show more honest intention" and more generosity in helping other Asians, *Asahi Shimbun* said he was perfectly right. And when Lee Kuan Yew asked the Japanese to loosen up and show that they are not "difficult people to deal with, unkind and ungiving," he, too, was applauded by Tokyo liberals.

But the Okurasho (Finance Ministry) wasn't convinced. It pointed out that Japan boosted its aid from $625 million in 1966 to $1.8 billion four years later. This, it said, put Japan third among non-Communist aid suppliers, after the United States and West Germany. It called attention to a proposal to keep increasing foreign aid at the rate of 20 per cent a year through 1975, but conceded that foreign aid in 1970 was only .92 per cent of the GNP. That earned the Japanese the Dickensian title of "Scrooge" from at least one commentator.[85] In the light of Japan's expanding economic power and its growing investments in other countries, projected at $2.5 billion in 1975, it simply wasn't enough. Not even the revaluation of the yen and tightened competition with the United States for trade could excuse the slenderness of Japan's foreign aid program.

The Foreign Ministry's repeated proposal for the commitment of 1 per cent of the Japanese GNP to foreign aid by 1975 is at least a minimal recognition of Japan's responsibilities. This would mean close to a $5 billion allotment for foreign aid by the middle of the decade if the Japanese GNP expands as projected—nearly three times as much as was spent in 1970. It is a worthy aim. Naturally, the Japanese Treasury people aren't happy about the prospect. They like to play the high-interest game, in which Japanese loans to developing countries carry 4 per cent interest rates—and up.

Yet, if Japan's exports go to $37 billion by 1975, as projected, more development aid and credits will have to be passed around among Asians. The customers for foreign aid may not always be right, but there are too many of them for the Japanese to ignore if Japan is to continue to set up overseas factories and use cheap foreign labor. This won't be done by taking out twice as much as is put

[85] Dick Wilson, "Putting the Screw on Scrooge," *Far Eastern Economic Review*, December 12, 1970, p. 45.

in—Tunku Abdul Rahman's view of Japanese foreign aid.

Japan does have a growing stake in the developing lands. Direct Japanese investment world-wide stood at $668 million in 1970, of which one-sixth was in East and Southeast Asia. Indonesia was the biggest recipient, with $50 million, followed by Taiwan and Thailand. If direct investment goes up annually as projected by the middle of the decade, and the "dollar war" with the United States does not do too much damage to Japan's foreign trade, the Japanese will be in a position to offer considerably more help to their neighbors than they offer today.

The trouble is that the government also faces rising demands for funds to tackle the principal problems of the home front, with which the public is far more deeply concerned. Social security, for example, already had reached 5 per cent of the GNP and more than 20 per cent of the budget in 1970, when the government conceded that the program had to be strengthened. Therefore, a 1 per cent increase of the GNP allotment to social security by 1975 is probably the least that can be done.

As for education, if any Japanese doubts the urgent need for reforms, the statistics for student arrests during university disorders and the rise of juvenile crime are bound to be sobering. In a Justice Ministry White Paper on Crime, released toward the end of 1970, it was shown that 40 per cent of vicious crimes in Japan during 1969 were committed by minors and that the arrest rate for minors was 8.9 per 1,000 population as compared with 3.4 for adults. In actions taken against students during the 1969 university rioting, 20,091 were arrested, 4,225 were indicted, 1,387 had been tried by mid-1970 and all but 20 had been convicted.[86]

Under such circumstances, it follows that educational reforms are bound to be pressed with vigor—a program that is not going to be cheap. For by 1975, in spite of the outlook for a declining student population, 5,000,000 children are expected in primary and secondary schools and 1,500,000 in junior and four-year universities and colleges.

With defense needs, agricultural subsidies and public improvements all demanding a greater share of the GNP, the pressures on the

[86] From a Reuters report from Tokyo, October 28, 1970.

Japanese government are going to be very great indeed. In the annual struggle over the national budget for some years to come, therefore, the political leadership will have to make some hard choices and be prepared to sell them to an increasingly restive Diet. For if the needs of trade, aid and defense come first, then the much-needed campaign to improve life for the Japanese citizen is going to suffer and no member of the ruling party underestimates the political consequences. But if the home front finally is to be given full recognition, then Japan may very well have to review its priorities with all the consequences such a step entails.

Can Japan Win a Trade War?

When George Ball saw that the United States and Japan were on a collision course, he wrote, "Some of us . . . have watched this development like spectators at a Greek tragedy, observing the actors in the drama caught up in an interplay of forces they seemed unable to control."[87] There hasn't been much of this kind of hand-wringing in the higher reaches of the American government, however, as protectionist barriers against Japanese trade began moving into place and the assault against the yen opened. Nor is it likely, despite any temporary adjustments that may be made from time to time, that the essential economic rivalry between the United States and Japan will be lessened.

Japan recognizes that painful reality. It is one reason why the Japanese government has been so dilatory in moving to ease the ills of the home front. Just after the opening of the "dollar war" in 1971, it was not without considerable calculation that Finance Minister Mikio Mizuta warned his people that they would have to endure a time of "glorious suffering" if Japan was to become a "truly strong nation."[88] Americans, somewhat aghast at the unexpected Japanese resistance to Washington's will in the opening stages of the conflict, wondered if Japan really expected to win a trade war in the event that it was permitted to develop. The answer was yes.

Both the United States and Japan are going to have to revise their current belligerent trading tactics if they are to avoid the ultimate

[87] George B. Ball, *Pacific Community*, October, 1970, p. 1.
[88] Takashi Oka, *The New York Times*, August 31, 1971, p. 1.

tragedy of an all-out economic struggle. For such a calamity could scarcely be confined to the Pacific, should it be allowed to develop without letup. Surely, it would spread to the Commonwealth countries and Western Europe as well, disrupting the carefully designed economic arrangements that solidified the Western world after World War II and made possible a time of unparalleled prosperity. No other event short of a major shooting war would produce such monumental changes in global relationships.

The struggle between the United States and Japan has been slow in developing, but there can be no doubt of the determination of either of the economic belligerents. In the years immediately after World War II, the conquering Americans were pretty condescending about the first feeble efforts of the Japanese to return to world markets. It was a time of low posture for Japan, of meekness and humility, of slow recovery from the abyss of national humiliation and defeat. At a time when Japan could barely feed its own people with the help of massive imports, the United States was encouraging its erstwhile foe to work for a trade revival. Everything from diplomatic pep talks to stimulants for the slowly reviving Japanese economy came from the United States. No other conqueror had ever done so much for a defeated foe.

After the Korean War, when the Japanese recovery became a reality, some of the American pep talks lost their fervor. Then, bit by bit, the very measures that some American economists had been advocating to aid Japan began drawing protests from American business. Japanese products were entering the American market by that time in increasing volume and home industry was beginning to feel the pinch. The artificially low valuation of the yen against the dollar helped a lot. But the willingness of the Japanese work force to stay on the job at comparatively low rates of pay was even more decisive in the early stages of what came to be known as the *boomu*.

The American government tried to resolve the competitive issue at first by persuading the Japanese to adopt a series of "gentlemen's agreements" to set up voluntary restraints on certain exports. Nevertheless, trouble mounted over such assorted articles as shoes and grapefruit, television sets and steel, textiles and automobiles. In the tension that resulted from a prolonged argument between the two nations over textiles, the American economic attack broadened to include the entire restrictive system of Japanese trade, industry and finance. The American Commerce Secretary, Maurice H. Stans, warned, "The American trade advantage is largely done and the politics of another day need to be updated."[89]

The goal of the American government at the outset of the 1970s was nothing more nor less than the thoroughgoing reform of Japan's manner of doing business, which severely penalized foreign competition in the Japanese home market while leaving Japanese foreign traders to do more or less as they wished. It was, ironically, the system that the United States had encouraged the Japanese to develop at the outset of their recovery. Now, it had become too powerful for the Americans to oppose in the normal processes of free trade.

The Japanese naturally were resentful. The United States had become their chief market abroad; in the absence of a substantial China trade, they had come to count on American helpfulness and generosity. And when Washington began to turn against them, they first became confused, then angry.

Worse still, the Japanese saw resistance growing elsewhere in the world to their export drive, which directed about one-third of their products to the United States, one-fifth to Southeast Asia and one-tenth to Britain and Australia.[90] Soon Japanese resentment burst all bounds. The financial newspaper *Nihon Keizai Shimbun* wrote: "Even if the economic factors behind Japan's image gap were excluded, the emotional criticism of things Japanese would still remain. . . . Although Volkswagen has gained a large share of the U.S. market, they receive none of the strong blasts of criticism directed at Nissan and Toyota." And a worried Japanese diplomat said of a European trade conference: "The atmosphere is just like that on the eve of World War II when America, Britain, China and Holland surrounded Japan in the Pacific and tried to squeeze Japan by pressing on its supply of raw materials."

From *Asahi Shimbun*, the leader of the Japanese press, came the bitterest denunciation of all: "At the bottom of the U.S. moves to

[89] *Japan Times*, October 11, 1970, p. 10.
[90] *The Economist*, October 17, 1970, pp. 24–27 of a special section, "Japan Means Business."

exclude Japanese goods is the racial prejudice of the white people who regard the Japanese as 'yellow-faced upstarts.' " To which Kiichi Miyazawa, then the trade minister, added: "As things are going, the yellow peril complex can only become more widespread in the U.S."

The Japanese overdid their complaints about racial antagonism. At about the same period, *The New York Times* published a survey showing that racial prejudice in the United States against 500,000 Japanese-Americans and 400,000 Chinese-Americans had all but disappeared.[91] What the *Times* survey did not show, of course, was the essential mistrust of many Americans of Japan's rising eminence in the Pacific, which had less to do with race than with the residue of ill feeling against the Japanese during and after World War II. Still, the Japanese seizure of the racial issue as a weapon against their American rivals was a part of the frenzied spirit of the times.

In the United States, too, emotionalism played a part in the confrontation with Japan but it was hardly rooted in racism. It was a time when unemployment was around 6 per cent and the American economy was boosting living costs to an uncomfortable level for most people. The inflationary spiral showed no sign of yielding to the passive "game plan" originally adopted by the Nixon Administration, which was no plan at all. Despite soothing words from Washington, all was not well and the American people knew it.

When the protectionist forces in the American Congress joined the Nixon Administration in making an issue of Japanese textile competition, the old liberal free traders in the United States reacted in alarm. With the intensification of anti-Japanese propaganda in the field of trade, they saw their government turning its back on more than forty years of free-trading progress. The Washington *Post*, for example, warned that all the blame could not be assigned to Japan. The protests against a revival of protectionism became so strong that President Nixon eventually had to take notice, denying for the record that he really sought "excessive" protection for American industry.

Yet, once the American government began its campaign to retrieve its economic position at home and abroad in the latter part of 1971,

[91] *Far Eastern Economic Review*, November 28, 1970, pp. 63–65, is the source of Japanese reaction. The *New York Times* survey was on December 13, 1970.

there was no doubt that Japan was the major target. And the threat of protectionism was the bludgeon with which the Japanese, among others, were beaten into submission. It soon became evident that the textile issue, while it posed a test of strength, was of less importance than the whole broad range of Japanese-American relationships.

The settlement, far from eliminating tensions between the two nations, served in some ways to intensify them. A touring Japanese editor, asked at the time whether anti-Americanism was increasing among the Japanese public, nodded somberly. "It's getting a lot worse," he said. References to the protective American "atomic umbrella" were dropped from official Japanese pronouncements as a matter of policy. *Yomiuri Shimbun,* one of the "big three" Tokyo dailies, mirrored public displeasure with its headline: "Severity in Japan's Economy; Era of the New Yen Has Arrived." And a leading government official called the terms of the American settlement the "greatest economic shock" to Japan since World War II. Such victories will do the United States no good for the long run. For if Japan runs up against continual American trade hostility, the days of the Japanese-American alliance are numbered.[92]

Japan will never lack for trading partners, regardless of what the United States does. An anticipated $5 billion in trade scheduled with the Soviet Union for 1971–75 and perhaps even more trade with China should provide some indication that Japan does have alternatives to the Washington love-hate relationship. Right now, these alternatives may not seem as attractive as the American market but Japan always has been drawn to the Asian hinterlands. In any event, the higher the American economic protective walls rise, the greater is the probability that there will be a powerful challenge to American economic dominance from the Pacific in years to come.

11. THE ISSUES FOR THE UNITED STATES

The United States cannot continue for very long to make out Japan to be the chief economic villain among its trading partners and expect to retain Japanese loyalty. That is perfectly obvious. In the new

[92] I talked with the visiting editor, who chose not to be identified. Other comments from *The New York Times,* December 21, 1971, p. 56.

Pacific age that both nations have done so much to make possible, they will have to reach a better understanding on economic and political grounds or go their separate ways, with inevitably tragic consequences.

The most immediate issue for the United States is whether to continue to play the dangerous game of semiprotectionism, using temporary import barriers and restrictive "gentlemen's agreements" as bargaining counters, or revert to the free-trade principles that have been the underpinning of American world leadership. There are many forces, union labor among them, that favor a swing to full protectionism, but labor would be the first to suffer from retaliatory measures that would be taken against the United States. For Japan, in concert with the Common Market, is fully capable of meeting such an American protectionist offensive by discriminating against American goods. That kind of a falling-out between the United States and its principal trading partners would be a boon to the Soviet Union, one from which Moscow would gain both prestige and profit.

It would seem, therefore, that the United States might well declare a moratorium on protectionism while a new effort is under way, based on the ten-nation Washington agreement of 1971, to reconstitute the shattered Bretton Woods relationships and rebuild a more realistic system. The damage that has been done to the dollar so far cannot very easily be repaired; in any event, it is futile to declare Japan to be the culprit when the United States itself was the chief author of the ruinous inflation that weakened the American economy.

Sooner or later, Americans are going to have to get used to the idea that the dollar no longer is the king of world currencies, that its value is bound to fluctuate not only against the yen but also the Commonwealth and leading European currencies, and that its price in terms of gold is not fixed for all eternity. The devaluation of the dollar, which once struck such terror into political hearts in Washington, actually turned out to be a relatively mild economic palliative. The heavens did not fall when the value of the dollar in terms of an ounce of gold was raised from $35 to $38, an effective 8.57 per cent devaluation. Franklin Delano Roosevelt had done worse. As long as Washington kept the gold window for trade closed tight, there could be no run on the remaining American gold hoard.

It follows, therefore, that the United States could now take an important step to reassure Japanese opinion by closing out, as gracefully as possible, the remaining vestiges of the Occupation period. More than a quarter century after the Japanese surrender in Tokyo Bay, it is high time. Beginning with the reversion of Okinawa to Japanese sovereignty, the United States could draw up a timetable for the abandonment of all remaining American bases there and in the home islands. Atomic weapons, in any case, no longer will be permitted on Japanese soil except in a national emergency.

The adverse Japanese reaction to the continued American military presence in Okinawa and the home islands cancels out whatever advantages there may be to the American retention of the remaining bases on Japanese soil. Under changing conditions, they are no longer needed as a threat to China—quite the contrary, in view of the changing American posture toward China. They never were much of a threat to the Soviet Union, being vulnerable to Soviet missile attack. And as for their past uses in defense of both South Korea and South Vietnam and the protection of Taiwan, that phase in American history has ended.

The United States will have to reconcile itself to the slow emergence of Japan's military strength as an independent force in the Pacific, probably with its own nuclear deterrent in years to come. But Japan is by no means going to be the American "gendarme in Asia," the substitute policeman to keep order in the Pacific. That is simply not the Japanese style. For a measurable period to come, Japanese forces are not going to be seen very much outside the home islands and Okinawa except on ceremonial occasions, for the Japanese themselves are aware of how greatly their neighbors fear the revival of Japanese military power. The armed forces, therefore, are likely to continue to be small but formidable; the reserves, much larger than may now be anticipated.

Instead of alternating between a public policy of urging Japan to expand its armed forces and a private fear that Japan will go too far, the United States had best come to terms now with Japan on military matters and work out a more acceptable Mutual Defense Treaty. Otherwise, like all outworn instruments, it is likely to fall into disuse and eventually it will be abandoned. The Japanese alliance, for all the strains that have been imposed on it, remains too valuable to be used as a mere bargaining counter in American relations with either China or the Soviet Union. In many ways, it is more important to American interests than the somewhat questionable good-will gestures that may be expected from time to time from either Peking or Moscow.

Of course the Japanese are difficult. Independent peoples generally are; otherwise, they wouldn't be able to maintain their freedom for very long. But it is in the American interest to work with Japan on a mutually agreeable basis. To do it will take time, patience and a willingness to try to understand Japanese problems instead of merely insisting on an all-or-nothing American solution, as has been the case too often in Japanese-American postwar relationships. For all the criticism that has been directed against various facets of the Japanese-American alliance, nothing has yet come along that can replace it. For a long time to come, it is likely to remain indispensable to the structure of peace in the Pacific.

III. Pressure on the Outposts

1. THE VIEW FROM WASHINGTON

From the Han River estuary near the top of the great arc of the Pacific to the South China Sea, the outposts of non-Communist Asia are entering an era of increasing military hazards and political unrest. The American military withdrawal, coupled with new and aggressive American economic policies, have thrown all of them on their own resources to a greater extent than they had anticipated. And these resources, without the resolute support of the United States, are scarcely adequate in a period of perpetual revolution in Asia.

The Cheering Is Over

The cheering for the United States has long since died away, even among America's closest Asian allies. Militarily and politically, the Pacific pullout has been a blow to American power. The damage has been compounded economically by the cut in the purchasing power of Asian lands due to the American "dollar war," which forced a world-wide shift in the value of currencies. For the Asians, particularly the smaller lands dependent on the United States, this was a blow, for most of them had to revalue.

161

Yet, both before and after the currency upheaval of late 1971, Washington's policy was one of cheerful optimism. One of the authors of the new American economic policy, Dr. Arthur F. Burns, chairman of the board of governors of the Federal Reserve System, has always reminded client states of their progress.

"The countries of Asia that have relied basically on the free market system, and have avoided centralization of economic decisions in the hands of government," he says, "have clearly been winning the economic contest. They are the countries that have been most successful in increasing the wealth of their people and in raising their standard of living. The countries that have done the least well have tended to be the ones that either rejected the free market or severely limited it by government controls."[1]

In the light of the American resort to government controls in 1971, however temporary, Dr. Burns's sweet talk has been tinged since with a certain amount of bitterness in numerous Asian lands that have been depending on the United States. For there is clearly a limit to the small economic booms that have come about in South Korea, Taiwan, Hong Kong, Thailand, Malaysia and Singapore, paralleling Japan's economic miracle. During the 1960s, they set a combined record of 6 per cent a year of average increase in real output. And for South Korea and Hong Kong, as in Japan, growth rates in excess of 10 per cent continued through 1970.

Until the United States put on the brakes and the Japanese economy slowed down, the smaller non-Communist Asian lands were exporting at an ever-increasing rate. In South Korea, for example, exports rose annually at the rate of 40 per cent for more than a decade, from $32 million in 1960 to an anticipated $620 million for 1971—and it would have been $50 million more than that if the United States had not enforced its temporary import surcharge. Taiwan boomed along at an annual rate of export growth of 19 per cent, even greater than Japan's. Tiny Hong Kong, with 4,000,000 population, enjoyed annual growth rates of 13 per cent or more and in 1970 alone exported about as much as India, with 550,000,000 people.

[1] Address by Arthur F. Burns, "The Economic Contest Between Freedom and Authoritarianism," Chungang University, Seoul, June 26, 1970, p. 10.

It did not really help very much for Dr. Burns to lecture the Asian lands at the bottom of the scale in terms of the GNP—Ceylon, Burma, India and Indonesia—because each had "experimented extensively with government ownership or control over economic activities."[2] They, as well as others, had a right to ask why the United States, the champion of free enterprise, was doing a certain amount of experimentation itself.

The Need for Precaution

There is, however, no fear that the economies of non-Communist Asia are on the verge of collapse. What is happening now in numerous places is a quiet re-evaluation of policies toward the United States in the light of the American pullout and economic belt tightening, coupled with Washington's approaches to Peking. There is, indeed, need for precaution.

For South Korea, for example, all this means greater dependence on Japan, an end to a policy of uncompromising hostility to Peking, and at least the beginnings of a new approach to North Korea. For Taiwan, the disposal of the twenty-five-year-old myth of great-power status as the holder of China's seat in the U.N. marks an even greater turn in the road. And as for the Philippines, where democracy has run riot, a respected monetary authority has pronounced a lasting economic revival to be impossible as long as monumental disorder and corruption persist in the island republic.[3]

Four Lands in Crisis

There is bound to be concern, therefore, over the situation of lands in Asia that are caught in the middle of so many changes in the power equation—the economic struggle between the United States and Japan, the American military retreat and the slow but continuous Russian expansion, the emergence of China, and the winding down of the Vietnam War. Of these outposts, none are in a more critical position than the Republic of Korea, Taiwan, the Philippines and the Crown Colony of Hong Kong, Britain's remaining possession in East

[2] *Ibid.*, p. 14.
[3] *Pick's Currency Yearbook*, reported in United Press International file for October 25, 1970.

Asia. Each is left vulnerable in a different way by the withdrawal of the United States and each must now consider new policies, or variations of old ones, to take account of the new lines of power that are thrusting into the Pacific.

2. SOUTH KOREA FACES REALITY

Twenty years after the beginning of the Korean War, I was taken on an American helicopter patrol flight along the Demilitarized Zone (DMZ) between North and South Korea on a cool, gray summer's day. It was quiet. As we flew over the highways that spun along the rolling countryside on our way to the DMZ, we could see a steady procession of trucks and automobiles, many of them on military missions. But at the DMZ itself, there was little movement of any kind. The 4,000-meter-wide DMZ, a no man's land covered with two decades of wild growth, was ominously still.

This was a place where there was neither war nor peace, only a gnawing and dreadful uncertainty that had persisted for a generation. While the Americans then on duty did not know it, they were about to be pulled out of the very middle of the defense line and sent home. For the first time in two decades, the South Koreans would face the enemy alone.

The Fence

Along the rugged territory that sloped away from us toward the distant blue-shadowed mountains, a steel, wire and concrete fence wound through the DMZ on the United Nations side. It had been built to span the 151-mile waist of Korea at the DMZ from the Han River estuary on the west to a point just below the 39th parallel on the east. With its protective bunkers and mine fields, this was a formidable obstacle to infiltrators—the Asian equal of the Berlin Wall.

As the chopper whirled along that day, I noticed GIs popping out of their bunkers and foxholes to salute, although we were several thousand yards distant. It was at once an empty testimonial to American military arrogance and a clear indication of the newfound security of the soldiers on sentry duty in what was, for many years, an exposed and dangerous position. The tiny figures, standing so carefully at attention, with arms raised toward their helmets, were symbols of outworn times, an outdated spit-and-polish command, and a rather foolish custom in a semiwar zone.

When we landed and visited a post near the DMZ later, I was told that the fence had so reduced the number of incidents since 1968 that there was very little for the Americans to do. It was now an event if a Communist soldier tried to get through the mine fields, the barbed wire and the steel and concrete obstacles. One had been killed outside the post two nights before and everybody was still talking about it.

As one GI phrased it, "Sure, the chances of an incident up here now are very small, but that doesn't mean you can go to sleep or even relax on duty. You can always get your throat cut."

The fence, a distinctive American contribution to the defense of South Korea, has served its purpose. With its completion, the incident rate dropped almost 500 per cent, from 629 in 1968 to 138 in 1969 and 108 in 1970. The fire fights were reduced proportionately from 356 to 77. The number of Americans and South Koreans killed in action was cut from 197 to 16, the North Koreans killed in action from 321 to 49.

New Tactics by North Korea

Unable to maintain pressure on South Korea across the DMZ for the time being, the North Korean leadership has turned to new tactics and a new and far more venturesome policy. In January 1968, North Korea captured the U.S.S. *Pueblo* and her crew in a major blow at the United States that attracted world attention. A year later, North Korean gunners shot down an American intelligence plane in neutral air space, killing thirty-one aboard.

The program of infiltration from the north has been conducted mainly by sea since, around both ends of the fence. In a single month during the summer of 1970, for example, South Korean intelligence estimated that thirty armed North Korean agents tried to infiltrate the south on ten different missions, with the result at twelve of them were killed. But some always get through, and that is the frightening part of the North Korean program of infiltration and subversion. The people of Seoul still remember the thirty-one-man suicide platoon of North Koreans that raided their city in 1968 and nearly succeeded in getting to the Blue House, the official residence of President Park Chung Hee.

There is good reason to believe that the North Koreans are training around 10,000 agents for both terrorist and espionage missions to be carried out in the south, with a supporting force of 20,000 to supply them with weapons and food when needed. More than one hundred high-speed wooden boats, capable of cruising at thirty knots and difficult to detect on radar, are maintained to transport this force in small groups. In additon, there are a number of AN-2 light aircraft and MI-4 helicopters for the infiltration of agents by air.

Besides flying over and cruising around the big Korean fence, the North Koreans maintain continual contact with sympathizers among the Chosun Soren, the 500,000 Koreans in Japan. And this is a sore point between the governments of South Korea and Japan, for President Park's military advisers are known to believe that the Japanese are not doing enough to halt the traffic in espionage agents and terrorists between the Japanese and Korean coasts. There is, in fact, a Korean Guidance Department in the Korean organization in Japan to care for North Koreans who are in transit.[4]

The Japanese, of course, argue that they are doing all they can to keep out of trouble with both Koreas, but the long coastlines of Japan and Korea make airtight surveillance impossible. That undoubtedly is true. With their growing financial interest and trade in South Korea, there is no particular reason for the Japanese to favor the North, openly or covertly. The hijacking of a Japan Air Lines jet aircraft to North Korea in 1970 by a small group of student fanatics who called themselves the "Red Army" showed rather conclusively that Japanese sympathies do not lie with the government of Kim Il Sung.

A Korean View of Japan

Yet, it is not easy for the Republic of Korea to show much faith in Japanese intentions despite the surface cordiality of their current economic relationships. The rising Korean generation, just as much

---

[4] Kim Myong-sik, in the *Korea Times*, July 5, 1970, p. 3.

as their elders, cannot easily dismiss the miserable record of Japan in its forty-year occupation of Korea and the ill-concealed race prejudice of many Japanese against Koreans. During every visit I have made to Korea, the bitterest and most persistent question Koreans have asked me is, "Why does the United States insist on pushing us into the arms of Japan?"

While the Koreans have always known that the Americans were not on the Asian mainland for good, the notice of the United States' intention to cut its commitments in the Pacific produced a furious reaction in Seoul. Initially, at least, there was less fear of what China or the Soviet Union or North Korea would do than of the revival of Japanese militarism. In a characteristic comment, Professor Hahm Pyong-choon of Yonsei University wrote: "As the United States increasingly wishes to reduce its presence in the Western Pacific, Japan will be called upon by the U.S. and her Asian neighbors to fill the military and economic gap left behind by the retreating Americans. Thus, the increase in the military power of Japan in the coming days will easily be justified as an unpleasant necessity coerced upon Japan against her pacifist intentions . . ."

Recalling the domination of the Japanese military and the *zaibatsu* in the era of the Co-Prosperity Sphere, he demanded: "Is it realistic to assume that the forthcoming Japanese sphere of influence over Asia will be less suffocating and more benign to her Asian neighbors whose national interests may come into competition or even conflict with those of Japan?" If the question was disdainful, the reply was downright hostile: "It requires no elaborate argument to show the fact that economic domination can be as imperialistic and humiliating to those who suffer it as military and political domination."[5]

South Korea Is No Pushover

No catalogue of complaints, however justified, can conceal the fundamental toughness and resilience of South Korea today. For the Korean character, far from yielding to the miseries of self-abasement, is as strong, salty and durable as the formidable national dish,

[5] Hahm Pyong-choon, "The New Japan: The Chrysanthemum and the Transistor?" *Pacific Community*, April, 1970, pp. 436–437.

kimche. The ideal of all Koreans, despite the restraints that have been laid upon them, is still a rugged and uncompromising independence.

Because South Korea is ringed by the great power influences of the United States, Japan, China and the Soviet Union, it will never be the "Land of the Morning Calm," except in the meaning of its ancient name, Chosun. For most of the 4,000 years of its recorded history, it has known only war and conquest.

Mongols, Manchus and Japanese by turn have stormed through its mountainous corridors, ravaged its countryside and reduced its cities to ruin. Not even its 250 years as a "Hermit Kingdom," sealed off from the world, could bring it peace. For in 1905, after the Russo-Japanese War, it became a mere appendage of Japan, a colony degraded by a new Oriental imperialism.

Only after the American defeat of Japan in 1945 was Korea able to regain its national identity, but the price was a cruel division along the 38th parallel between the Communist-dominated North and the United States-supported rule of President Syngman Rhee, who took over as president in the south in 1948. The peace and freedom that all Koreans sought remained as far off as ever. In the United States, there had been hope that the establishment of the Republic of Korea in the south would be an ameliorating influence. But the Communist invasion in 1950, which touched off the Korean War, destroyed whatever slender chance there had been for reunification.

Today, President Park Chung Hee in Seoul and Premier Kim Il Sung in Pyongyang still talk about reunification, but in unrealistic terms. North and South face each other across the DMZ in what seems like endless hostility. The annual U.N. debates on the "Korean question," under such circumstances, become exercises in international humbug. In 1970, the usual Communist resolution calling for the withdrawal of all foreign troops from South Korea was defeated, 60–32, with 23 abstentions, and an American pullout continues to be Kim Il Sung's precondition for negotiations.

Under present conditions, the two Koreas can't be reunited. And few except congenital idiots, of whom there are still quite a few in international life, regard the possibility of another Korean War with anything but horror. For this time, if it happens, it would almost certainly escalate into a great-power conflict in the tinderbox of Asia.

Assuredly, the South Koreans are not going to give up all they have attained. They may not enjoy parliamentary government to the fullest extent, and their press may be under severe restraints, but there is an opposition party, there are elections, and life is far better than it is in Pyongyang. Any renewed frontal aggression by the Communist powers is sure to be fiercely resisted by South Korea, with the gravest consequences for the United States, China, the Soviet Union and Japan.

A Military Stalemate

In a mountainous land that is barely the size of Indiana, 30,000,000 South Koreans for more than a decade have supported an armed force of 600,000—third largest in Asia. Naturally, this never would have been possible without massive financial assistance from the United States and the stimulating and stiffening presence of American troops in the actual center of the invasion route from the north. Since 1953, the bill for American aid of all kinds to the Republic of Korea has amounted to well over $6 billion, including direct grants of about half that total. This is apart from the approximately $1 billion the United States has paid to maintain the two ROK divisions that have been fighting in South Vietnam.

In return for the withdrawal of 20,000 American troops in mid-1971, the South Korean government has been assured of a further U.S. expenditure of more than one billion dollars in new equipment for the regular ROK armed forces and with something left over for the 2,500,000 members of the Homeland Defense Reserve Force. The American military presence thus has been reduced from 300,000 at the end of the Korean War in 1953 to 40,000 in the early 1970s. Even this remaining "token" force could be dispensed with were it not for Korean insistence on retaining enough American troops to guarantee American involvement in the event of an attack.

Obviously, a difference of 20,000 American troops—and perhaps even more to come—will not work perceptibly to South Korea's disadvantage. As the situation was summed up by a former United States commander in South Korea, General Charles H. Bonesteel III, "When you realize the effectiveness of the ROK army, as it proved itself in Vietnam, it [the American troop reduction] will not change the basic security of the Republic, particularly if the ROK army is continuously modernized."[6]

The South Korean military establishment, therefore, is considered likely under normal circumstances to be strong enough to deter overt aggression from the north. For North Korea's 400,000 troops, backed up by a 1,300,000 Worker-Peasant Red Guard Militia, have neither the resources nor the support that are available in such lavish form to the South. In theory, Pyongyang can count on adequate supplies of war matériel and funds from both China and the Soviet Union. But in practice, it doesn't quite work out that way. Neither of the giant Communist rivals is very enthusiastic at present about encouraging the North Koreans to start another war. And Premier Kim Il Sung himself appears satisfied with a campaign of dirty tricks against the South in the form of infiltration and subversion.

Because of the historic American policy of retaining control of the larger part of available air power in the South, the ROK air force is not considered a match for the 600-odd fighters and bombers that are maintained in the North. Nor is the ROK navy as well equipped as North Korea's. While the modernization program is likely to reduce the disparity in the two armed forces by air and sea, South Korea has no real cause for concern. For it is on the ground that the difference between the two military establishments cancels out and creates what amounts to a military stalemate in the area.

Seoul's Economic Powerhouse

South Korea's great advantage over the North is in the field of economic development. True, North Korea has loudly claimed a high growth rate, too, and without doubt there has been progress. But the average North Korean still lives at a bare subsistence level and workers reportedly have a daily rice ration of 1.7 pounds, rounded out with other grains, and only half that amount goes to a dependent family.[7] Moreover, such deficiences are recognized among the top

[6] Cho Se-hyong, interview datelined Washington, in the *Korea Times*, July 5, 1970, p. 6.

[7] From the New York Times News Service, published in the Hong Kong *Standard*, October 31, 1970, p. 6.

leadership, one of whom was quoted as saying, "The problem is that leading cadres are irresponsible and unconcerned about the working peoples' problems of food, clothing and housing."[8]

Not that Seoul, for all its newfound economic power, is about to rival New York, Tokyo or even Bangkok. Totally flattened at the end of the Korean War, the capital city of the Republic of Korea is now a bustling, dusty, noisy metropolis of 5,000,000 people. While the array of miraculous statistics conjures up the image of a golden city to those who are willing to accept the undigested evidence of an IBM computer, that is scarcely what Seoul is like now. To the eye of the realistic observer, it is a place of stark, raw contrasts—unexampled prosperity at the gleaming new Chosun Hotel, put up by American Airlines with un-Korean lavishness, and a beggar boy asking for alms nearby; massive skyscrapers side by side with hovels, and little children with shoeshine boxes looking for work; a traffic jam of new American and Japanese automobiles on broad avenues in midtown, and peasants staggering in the byways under backbreaking loads on their rough A-frames.

There is a new superhighway between Seoul and the southern port of Pusan, now a city of 3,000,000, which shortens what was once an all-day trip to a mere three hours and ten minutes. Other expressways are in the planning stage to spread out the nation's industrial development. Yet, when it comes to human habitations, some of the long-promised modern housing is built of such flimsy materials that a flat has been known to cave in during an ordinary rainstorm with fatal consequences.

After one building collapsed in Seoul, the outcry against corrupt builders and officials was so great that a leading officeholder was forced to resign. But generally, Asian corruption takes its toll in South Korea, no less than in other lands, without a great deal of public to-do. For under the dictatorial regime of President Park Chung Hee, the press is under such control that its watchdog function cannot be maintained. And no one has ever pretended that there is free speech or free assembly in South Korea.

It is apparent to the most casual visitor that the country is still in a

[8] Burns, *op. cit.,* p. 11.

state of war—"semiwar," in President Park's phrase. Military aircraft, ranging from fighters to big cargo carriers, outnumber commercial planes at Seoul's big airport. On the busy eight-lane highway to Seoul, soldiers and police are highly visible. Along a popular drive that mounts into the awesome fringe of rocky hills ringing the capital city, soldiers often stop automobiles—even cruising taxis—and question every occupant in an apparently aimless manner. It was along this route that North Korean infiltrators traveled in their desperation effort to attack the Blue House and the South Korean military are not likely to forget it. Despite the 1971 Panmunjom conferences between the South and North Korean Red Cross to try to reunite long-divided families, watchfulness is always maintained in Seoul.

Progress in South Korea

The South Korean success story is based primarily on a large pool of cheap skilled and educated labor, which has induced foreign investors to set up new plants or enlarge old ones at an increasing rate. The per capita national income, while small by Western standards, bulks large in Asian eyes. From less than $100 after the Korean War, it has more than doubled to $220 in 1970. As for the GNP, it soared from $2 billion in the early 1960s to $6 billion in 1970. The increase in exports has been even more dramatic, jumping from $41 million in 1962 to $835 million in 1970.

However, South Korea still has its troubles. Its large trade imbalance (imports were $1.98 billion in 1970) forced a 13 per cent devaluation of the won in 1971, from 327 to 370 won to $1, and Washington's "dollar war" hurt the won still more. But the South Koreans are likely to lick their difficulties over a decade or so. For their third five-year plan, they are going into heavy industry, building a shipyard, stamping factory and heavy-industry workshop.

The toughest problem of all will be to make South Korea self-sufficient in food grain production by 1975. It will mean widespread reform in a primitive agricultural system and a lot more help from Japan, which the South Koreans are prepared to accept. By the end of this decade, they hope for an $18 billion GNP, a per capita income of nearly $500 and exports of $5 billion.[9] And they just might make it.

Of course, the South Koreans don't like to be so dependent on Japan. President Park Chung Hee is said to have sent word to Peking in 1971, after the beginning of the Chinese-American "thaw," that South Korea did not intend to enter into a military alliance with Japan even after the last American soldier leaves Seoul. Still, Park knows perfectly well that the time is fast approaching when the Japanese will replace the United States as the Korean Republic's chief trading partner. Can military aid be far behind?

It is symbolic of the Seoul government's position that in 1971, when it had to import 800,000 metric tons of rice because of a crop failure, half came from the United States and half from Japan. If the Japanese had been as easy to deal with as the United States, there would have been no problem. But for that year, Japan's trade advantage over Seoul was 5–1. It was with good reason that ex-Foreign Minister Tong-won Lee exclaimed that Koreans had a just grievance against the "selfish greed" of Japan.[10]

The Japanese relationship, however, hasn't been all that bad. Since normalizing relations with Japan in 1965, South Korea has received $300 million in Japanese wartime compensation funds and $200 million in economic aid. With the American military withdrawal, Seoul asked Tokyo for an additional $200 million credit and promptly got it. Japanese private capital, too, has flowed into South Korea, the total investment in 190 companies being estimated at $530 million since 1959. And a good many millions of Japanese money have flowed into South Korea's ailing agriculture, with much more still to come.

Outside the trade imbalance, what galls the South Koreans in particular is the continued Japanese trade with North Korea and the "Made in Japan" labels that show up on captured North Korean spy

[9] Reports in *Korea Herald*, July 1, 1970, and *Japan Times*, February 20, 1971. "Goals for Korea" in *Korea Herald*, July 2, 1970, p. 2.

[10] Tong-won Lee, in *Pacific Community*, October, 1970, p. 51. Lee says the trade imbalance actually was 7–1. See also "Made in Japan," *Asia Magazine*, October 4, 1970, pp. 12–13. The report of Park's message to Peking was in *The New York Times*, September 2, 1971, p. 1.

equipment. The protest against this "two Koreas" policy sometimes grows too hot for even the bland Japanese to handle, especially in times of crisis. "There has been evidence to show that the government in Tokyo is condoning—encouraging at times—secret and unofficial trade between North Korea and Japan," says Tong-won Lee. ". . . There have been instances in which some Japanese firms were permitted to initiate commercial deals to sell large-scale industrial plants to Communist North Korea."[11]

With American aid being phased out in 1971, the Koreans have turned to British and European commercial sources as a counterweight to the growing Japanese financial influence. The combined French and West German private capital invested in Korea at the outset of the 1970s was close to $400 million, about $100 million less than the capital provided by American firms. The British had loaned nearly $160 million and were building the first Korean nuclear power plant at Tongnae.[12]

Yet, the Japanese are still indispensable to the South Korean economy. As one Korean put it, "More than the Japanese need our market, we need their capital, know-how and even their market."

The Rites at Panmunjom

The confrontation between North and South Korea goes on at the tin huts in Panmunjom, day after day and week after week. The aimless charade, in which the United Nations side and the Communist side gather to insult each other and indulge in a grotesque display of ham acting, shows no sign of ending. The tourists come by the busload from Seoul—giggling schoolgirls from Korean institutions and fat American ladies in orange pants—to peek through the windows of the battered "conference hall" and see the two sides go through the meaningless rites that have grown up during the better part of two decades.

Here, in the center of the Joint Security Area, with a line bisecting the green felt conference table, is the hard reality of South Korea's position. With China in the United Nations, it is questionable whether

---

[11] Tong-won Lee, *ibid.*, p. 53.

[12] Siho Lee, report from Seoul in financial section of *South China Morning Post*, October 26, 1970.

the symbolic presence of the world organization on South Korea's side of the table will last much longer. Today, the American general who sits in the United Nations seat is emblematic only of dwindling forces, indifference and withdrawal. But North Korea, after a five-year hiatus, once again is strengthened by a Chinese representative, who returned July 9, 1971.

The truth is that the South Koreans are now very much on their own. The blue-and-white United Nations flag represents the forces that once were sent to Korea by sixteen member states. And with the pullout of 20,000 troops of the American Second Division from the middle of the front-line defenses along the DMZ, the South Korean army alone confronts the northern forces. The lone remaining American division, the Seventh, is twenty-five miles to the rear, and may not be around too long.

The American withdrawal has embittered many in the Republic of Korea. There are only a few like Korea's serene great lady, Louise Yim, who still have faith that the United States will defend her country in a crisis. For grim little Park Chung Hee, the secretive general who seized power on May 16, 1961, and has retained the presidency for three terms in successive elections, the situation calls for strengthening and modernizing his armed forces with American funds and American advice. But he also recognizes that great changes are coming in his country's relations with both Japan and China, and perhaps North Korea as well.

At his third inaugural, on July 1, 1971, in Seoul, he said: "A great change is taking place around us, as indicated by the rise of a so-called mood of thaw between east and west, and the initiation of efforts for rapprochement between the United States and Communist China. It is to be hoped that these changes may dispel the dark clouds of aggression that hang over Asia."

To South Koreans who are less careful of the niceties of political rhetoric, the future is stated in less ambiguous terms: "Whether we like it or not, we will have to depend now on the Japanese to help us. We have no other choice."

It is worth noting that on inauguration day President Park conferred anxiously with Prime Minister Sato, asking for more Japanese loans and 200,000 tons of much-needed Japanese rice.

A State of National Emergency

Although President Park will have ruled South Korea longer than Syngman Rhee by 1975, the three-time chief executive does not feel secure. On December 27, 1971, his party rammed a declaration of national emergency through the National Assembly which broadened his dictatorial powers. The pretext was fear of North Korean attack, which did not appear imminent at the time. The reality was probably closer to the charges of the opposition, which accused him of fearing his own people. The anti-government leaders pointed out that Park now could restrict strikes, ban demonstrations, completely censor the press and control wages and prices.

Certainly, in advance of the grant of emergency powers, Park's hold on the country was slipping. He had defeated his New Democratic Party opponent, Kim Dae Jung, by 920,000 votes in the 1971 elections, considerably less than the 1,200,000 the ruling Democratic Republican Party gave him in 1967. Subsequently, the DRP suffered a stiff reduction in its majority in the National Assembly, being cut from a margin of eighty to only twenty-four seats. While the DRP could outvote the New Democratic Party, it did not have a two-thirds majority to revise the Constitution. Moreover, the opposition was able to get through a vote of censure against Park's home minister.

Despite the national emergency, pressure is growing for a change in South Korea. Park has declared publicly that this is his last term in office; probably, he will back his nephew, Premier Kim Jong Pil, for the presidency in 1975. But the opposition will have a powerful case against the regime by that time if the Korean boom slackens, as is probable, and unemployment rises. While nobody believes that a deal with North Korea is possible, there is a great yearning for peace. As Kim Dae Jung put the position in an election valedictory:

"The Americans are withdrawing from Asia. It is a trend we cannot stop. Although we would like them to stay, eventually they will leave. Then it will be up to us to defend ourselves. We should maintain a strong defense but without a four-power guarantee [involving China, Japan, the Soviet Union and the United States], we cannot have peace."

There is no hope of such a four-power guarantee for the foreseeable future. South Korea, facing an implacable enemy, will have to play off her three great-power neighbors as best she can. It is not a very happy prospect for the "Land of the Morning Calm."

3. TAIWAN: PERENNIAL LOSER

For more than two decades, the United States practiced the diplomatic fiction that the government of Taiwan, with a population of two million Chinese and twelve million Taiwanese, was the true representative of the 800 million people of China. To sustain this illusion, presumably hard-headed American governments spent more than $4 billion—$1.5 billion in economic aid from 1951 to 1965, when the practice ended, and $2.5 billion in military assistance. Costly though this proved to be, it was small when measured against the incalculable damage that the "Taiwan First" policy inflicted on the prestige of the United States in Asia.

Yet, it was not until July 15, 1971, twenty-one years after Chiang Kai-shek's expulsion from the Chinese mainland, that the United States forced Taiwan to recognize the inevitable. It was then that President Nixon announced he would visit the People's Republic of China to "seek the normalization of relations" between Peking and Washington. Taiwan's expulsion from the United Nations soon followed, with Peking taking over the disputed seat.

Taiwan was shocked by the turning of the tide, but neither its outcries nor its protests moved Washington. For the United States at last was taking account of things as they are in the Pacific, not as the mythmakers of the American right wished them to be.

Actually, the change was not as abrupt as it seemed at the time, for the United States had been cutting its ties with Taiwan for at least six years. Economic aid ended in 1965. Four years later, some of the 12,000 American troops on the island were withdrawn. The Seventh Fleet's patrols in the Taiwan Strait had long since ended except for a token presence by a destroyer or two. Taiwan's importance as an American air base was also de-emphasized. And, despite continued though diminished support for the Nationalist Chinese forces, the

Americans let Chiang Kai-shek know in no uncertain terms that the Nationalists' hit-and-run raids on the mainland would have to end.

Chiang could not say that he had not been warned.

Chinese and Taiwanese

At the height of the American government's strange love affair with Taiwan, it was argued in Washington that the refugee government of Nationalist China represented "Free China" and therefore must be perpetuated as a symbol of resistance to Communism. Under this thesis, the American apologists for Chiang contended that life on Taiwan was not as rigidly authoritarian as life on the mainland. And while they reluctantly agreed that the one-party Kuomintang state was no model of democracy in action, they maintained it was preferable to the one-party Communist state dominated by Mao Tse-tung. They also saw nothing wrong with 2,000,000 Chinese refugees from the mainland imposing their will on the 12,000,000 Taiwanese.

I remember, on one visit to Taiwan, that an enthusiastic American embassy official assured me solemnly that there was no difference between Taiwanese and Chinese and that the people of the island should be described uniformly as Chinese.[13] It was a mild case of Foreign Service-itis, a congenital ailment that produces in the victim the illusion that he must be more loyal to the government to which he is accredited than to his own. While I didn't take it seriously, the Taiwanese very soon let me know of their injury and their outrage. They did not like their Chinese rulers then and they don't like them now, even if they have been able through persistence and sheer force of numbers to build up some influence at the local level in Taiwan.

There is always fear among the Chinese of a repetition of the bloody uprising of 1947 on Taiwan. They have, in consequence, permitted the Taiwanese to dominate the Taiwan Provincial Assembly and the Taipei City Council, as well as the governing bodies of other municipalities. Necessarily, the Kuomintang leadership tries to assure itself that Taiwanese candidates for office will be comparatively docile but it doesn't always work out that way. The most respected of Taiwanese leaders, Kuo Yu-shin, a member of the Taiwan

[13] This is also Chou En-lai's position.

Provincial Assembly since 1963, is usually followed by a police surveillance group. Lee Ao, a mainlander who sympathizes with the Taiwanese, was forced to close down his magazine in 1968 by the government and has been so harassed since that he has trouble making a living. It is common knowledge that several thousand political prisoners remain in custody in Taiwan, but little is heard of them unless they escape or have powerful friends abroad who intercede for them.

The escape of Professor Peng Ming-min, one of the most prominent victims of Taiwan's system of justice, centered world attention on the Taiwan independence movement despite its ineffectiveness. As a graduate of McGill University and the University of Paris, he had considerable standing as a teacher in Taiwan. When he fled from the island in 1970, after serving a thirteen-month sentence on conviction of trying to overthrow the government, he was invited to teach at the University of Michigan. The Taiwan regime protested to Washington, but without avail. Professor Peng was warmly received in the United States, still another sign of changing times.

The Illusions of Chiang Kai-shek

When President Chiang Kai-shek presided over the annual National Day celebration at the age of eighty-three on October 10, 1971—the "Double Tenth" anniversary of the Chinese Revolution of 1911—he called once more on his troops (many of them young Taiwanese) to prepare to reconquer the mainland. It was a garish scene in the center of Taipei, where 250,000 people had gathered for the festivities. Trim and erect despite the burden of his years, the indomitable Chiang wore his generalissimo's uniform, complete with gold-laced cap, rows of gleaming medals on his chest and five stars on each shoulder.

Once this annual rite was over, Taiwan returned to normal. There has, of course, never been any substance to the illusion that Chiang, on a white horse, would one day come prancing into Tienanmen Square in Peking at the head of his victorious army. Even when John Foster Dulles threatened to "unleash" Chiang, in a moment of sheer aberration, no sensible person took either of them seriously. The hero of the Kuomintang was a loser, no matter how he and the "China

Firsters" of the 1940s and 1950s tried to disguise it. He lost China through years of misrule and, at the end, military incompetence.

Bright as the Chinese performance has been on Taiwan in the economic field, Chiang has never been able to rehabilitate himself as the champion of a worthy cause, either in the United States or the United Nations. Few of his friends remain in power in Washington, and those who do, for the most part, are turning away from him. He leaves a troublesome heritage for his successors.

The View from the United Nations

The myth of Taiwan's permanence in the United Nations, too, has been shattered. It was just as much of an illusion as Chiang's dream of reconquering the mainland. For despite their theoretical status as one of the "Big Five" powers, the representatives of Nationalist China in reality led a sequestered existence in the green glass house beside the East River. They were seldom consulted, for they had little power and even less prestige. Very often, in major crises, they were ignored.

The extent to which Taiwan's position in the United Nations had eroded was dramatically demonstrated in the General Assembly's vote on November 20, 1970, which for the first time produced a majority for the annual resolution to admit Peking and expel Taiwan. Prolonged applause followed the announcement of the vote—51–49, with 25 abstentions. The only reason it didn't take effect then was that the United States had succeeded once again in its strategy of persuading the General Assembly to rule that a two-thirds majority was necessary for adoption of the resolution.

Even if the 1970 vote had no practical effect, its meaning could not be mistaken by anybody, not even the State Department in Washington or the Nationalist Chinese government in Taipei. China, the real China, was coming back to the United Nations after too long an absence. With the innovative Premier Chou En-lai directing a brilliant campaign from Peking, nation after nation switched sides during the ensuing year. Even Washington was obliged to take note of the shape of things to come, with President Nixon announcing his trip to Peking and twice dispatching his national security affairs adviser, Henry Kissinger, to consult with Chou in the Chinese capital.

Chiang fumed in Taipei and his representatives publicly denounced the Americans for stabbing them in the back. But actually, there was little that Washington could have done to avert the inevitable. Perhaps the Nixon-Kissinger moves did help to undermine Taipei's position in the United Nations, but it was so far gone that it would have collapsed anyway. Once the 1971 session of the General Assembly began, it was only a question of time before Taiwan was expelled and Peking was admitted. When the crucial vote was taken on the night of October 25, the 76–35 majority for the change in Chinese representation merely confirmed the realities of global power.

Taiwan might have been in diplomatic trouble long before had it not been for Mao Tse-tung's conviction that membership in the United Nations was an empty honor and one without meaning to a dedicated revolutionary. What changed Peking's mind? Undoubtedly, the tightened rivalry between the Soviet Union and China and the presence of an enormous Soviet military force on China's northern borders had something to do with it. The American withdrawal in Vietnam also was a factor. In any event, the Chinese saw that they had everything to lose and nothing to gain by continuing to isolate themselves from the world and permit Taiwan to continue to represent the Chinese people by default.

Peking's campaign hurt Taiwan in numerous ways. Outside the United Nations, countries that were friendly to Peking either reduced their representation in Taipei or simply closed down their diplomatic missions there. Such nations as Canada, Italy, Belgium and Austria straddled by merely "taking note" of Peking's claim to Taiwan—a nice diplomatic evasion. Nevertheless, their resumption of diplomatic relations with Peking was a blow to the Nationalist Chinese and it could not be disguised.

Taiwan's Status

The case against an independent Taiwan rests on its historic position as an integral part of China until it was ceded to Japan after the Sino-Japanese War of 1895. Then, in 1943, Chiang's Chinese government joined the United States and the United Kingdom in pledging at the Cairo Conference that "Formosa and the Pescadores shall be restored to the Republic of China." That position also appears in the

Potsdam Declaration of 1945, to which the Soviet Union adhered, but it can hardly be considered a legal transfer of title. Chiang's government took over *de facto* control of Taiwan and the Pescadores under General MacArthur's General Order No. 1 of August 15, 1945.

The real problem of Taiwan's legal status was raised in the Japanese Peace Treaty of April 28, 1952, when Japan was obliged to yield "all right, title and claim" to Taiwan and the Pescadores. But the treaty signatories did not decide who did own Taiwan because, at the time, Mao had taken over China. Neither in this treaty nor in any subsequent legal act of the victorious powers of World War II has there been any recognition of the contention by both Peking and Taipei that Taiwan belongs to China. That step was finally taken alone by the United States in the Shanghai communiqué of February 28, 1972, signed by Premier Chou En-lai and President Nixon, in which the American government held Taiwan to be part of China, left the solution of the problem to the Chinese, and agreed to begin removing all American troops.

Taiwan as a Going Concern

Two decades ago, Taiwan was an economic liability. Today, it is prosperous, regardless of what the future may bring. While it is about the size of Massachusetts and Connecticut combined, the land available for cultivation is considerably less than that of the two New England states because the whole eastern half of the island is mountainous. However, as an island 110 miles off the Chinese coast, it has many other assets.

While the Kuomintang never bothered with such elemental matters as land reform on the mainland, this was almost the first major change on which Chiang insisted when he came to Taiwan. Consequently, 90 per cent of Taiwan's farmers own the land they cultivate and have boosted their production by 100 per cent, even more in the case of food grains. Industry has tripled its output and is still expanding.

From a per capita income of $100 a year, Taiwan has boosted average individual earnings to $250 in 1970. The GNP has exceeded $3 billion annually and was booming at a $4 billion rate in 1971. Attracted by Taiwan's cheap labor and various financial advantages, both American and Japanese business firms have not hesitated to locate there. American investment in Taiwan now runs to $175 million, with the Japanese second at $70 million in investments and $300 million as credits for 1971.

The twists and turns of diplomacy have failed to deter tourists from seeking out Taiwan. From only 15,000 visitors a year, the tourist influx approached 500,000 in 1970, with a gain to the island's economy of $67 million annually. For the 1970s, it is not inconceivable that 1,000,000 visitors a year, many from Japan, will come to Taiwan, although it may never rival Hong Kong as a "shoppers' paradise."

In common with all developing countries that are hastening to industrialize, Taiwan has its problems. Its self-sufficiency in food, one of Chiang's achievements, is being threatened by a steady shift of the once predominantly agricultural population to the cities. At the beginning of the 1970s, rural living accounted for only 43 per cent of the island's population and by the end of the decade was expected to go down as low as 30 per cent. Worse still, the agricultural units are so small that many are uneconomical. The average is only about 2.5 acres and 37 per cent of Taiwan's farmers make do with only one acre.

The proposed Kuomintang solution has been the establishment of more than 600 voluntary farming cooperatives, but that is not likely to go far enough. The new American economic policy is hurting Taipei, although not as much as Japan, and the Taiwan government is not likely to have too much money for experimental agriculture.

Taiwan's Military Establishment

The dead weight that the Taiwanese economy has had to carry is a military establishment that is out of all proportion to the size of the island and its resources. While the United States was ladling out military aid in large amounts, Taiwan might have been able to afford such a luxury. But the golden flow from Washington, although it still continues, is not enough to keep 600,000 troops in the style to which Chiang's son and probable successor, Chiang Ching-kuo, has become accustomed. Nor can he count on American troop support, for when United States forces on the island go, they are unlikely to return.

What Washington has tried to do in this extremity is to urge Taiwan to help itself by reducing sharply the size of an army that is eating up about half the country's budget. This would make available some of the manpower that Taiwan's industry and farms so desperately need. It would also ease the strain of Taiwan's military spending.

To increase the firepower of a reduced armed force, the United States has donated about $200 million worth of F-104 fighter aircraft to Ching-kuo's air force on the convenient theory that they are obsolete and has also contributed some $30 million in military assistance for an army modernization program. But Washington has stopped short of supplying Taiwan with offensive weapons. The Kuomintang's generals could use them to create trouble.

Taiwan, in short, will have to decide on its priorities. If the military comes first, then the huge growth rate—a very important symbol of success for both government and people—will have to be sacrificed to maintain an army that may never fight a battle. And if trade is to come first, then it follows that so large a force cannot be maintained in so small a land. For the United States no longer can make up deficits for Taiwan and is far more interested in improving relations with Peking.

This is not to say that the United States is about to repudiate the Mutual Defense Treaty that was signed with Taiwan in 1955 and is still in effect. President Nixon, like his predecessors since the days of Franklin Roosevelt, has been generous with his assurances that the United States will keep its treaty commitments to Taiwan, even while mounting his diplomatic offensive toward Peking. But it surely has not escaped the attention either of Chiang or his son that the treaty makes military aid to Taiwan contingent on American "constitutional processes" in the event of unprovoked attack. Moreover, since Ching-kuo narrowly escaped assassination by Taiwanese gunmen at New York's Plaza Hotel on April 24, 1970, he retains a lively awareness of the existence of the Taiwan independence movement. And what the United States would do in the event of civil strife is an even bigger question mark than possible American action against foreign attack.

Taiwan has been hoping against hope that the Mutual Defense Treaty doesn't mean what it says. Until the United States began its overtures to Peking, perhaps there might have been some basis for Taiwan's lingering faith. But today, at last, there is a general appreciation of the bitter truth that, whatever American administrations of the past have promised, those of the present and future are unlikely to take any grave military risks in the defense of Taiwan.[14]

4. TROUBLE IN THE PHILIPPINES

The Republic of the Philippines is casting about restlessly for a new relationship with the United States.

Instead of being the mere custodian of past American glories and the docile recipient of American largess, the Filipino seeks greater assurance of his own security in a menacing and divisive era. He is through with being a comparatively helpless dependent of the United States in Asia. Out of tragic experience, he has learned what it means to be a small and virtually defenseless ally of the United States at a time when Washington is bent on disengagement from the violence of Asia.

When the Filipino sees an increasingly powerful Japan to the north, an unfriendly China to the west, an unpredictable Indonesia to the south and a retreating United States to the east, no one has to draw him any diagrams to illustrate the seriousness of his position. He is bound to strike the best bargain he can with any who will help him.

Relics of an Imperial Age

In the sentimental America of another day, there was always a warm feeling of comradeship for the Philippines. To soldiers and politicians, teachers and textbook writers in the United States, Filipinos were cast in the American image—a hard-working, righteous and God-fearing people. These were no distasteful polyglot Asians in

---

[14] For statistical material, I used American government records. The United Nations analysis is my own, based on my acquaintance with U.N. affairs. I found the following helpful: "China Isn't Chiang's," in *The Economist*, October 17, 1970, p. 13; "The Game Goes On," *Time*, October 26, 1970, p. 20; and articles in the *Far Eastern Economic Review*, October 31, 1970, p. 50, and March 6, 1971, p. 31.

the mass American view. They were little brown brothers, zealously guarding American interests in the Orient.

If few Americans had ever heard of José Rizal's passionate championship of independence or remembered the forceful repression of Emilio Aguinaldo's uprising, it didn't seem to matter. In the United States, the feeling was widespread that it was the God-given mission of Americans to overcome 350 years of Spanish misrule in the Philippines and transport the Filipino into the mainstream of Western civilization. To that end, the satraps sent from Washington to govern this new Asian colony strove mightily from 1898 on to encourage the merger of the American heritage with Filipino culture. It was a case of well-meant intentions, applied in the wrong place.

The results were curious, to say the least. Manila, founded as a gracious Spanish city beside a beautiful bay, was transformed into a roaring American metropolis, complete with everything from hot dogs to traffic jams. The trappings of American democracy were cast over age-old Asian governmental practices, with the worst features of each surviving. American movies, American bars, American clothes, American dances and American jazz music molded the social patterns of the rising generation. And at Clark Field, Subic Bay and Sangley Point, the important military bases, the Americans did pretty much as they pleased.

During the flowering of colonial rule, the Filipino meekly adapted himself to his ordained place in the new scheme of things. He was told constantly that he was independent, but of course he knew that he was not free. In the lovely islands, green jewels set in a sunlit sapphire sea, the American was king. Many a Filipino, his cheeks burning with shame, used to hear carousing American sailors roaring in Manila of a Saturday night:

> *Oh, the monkeys have no tails*
> *In Zamboanga . . .*

If this was bad, however, the Japanese conquest of the Philippines in 1941–42 made things infinitely worse. In the armed forces with the Americans who fought their way back from one island to another, in the hills of their native land as hunted refugees, and in the brutal Japanese prison camps, the Filipinos came to realize that there was no substitute for freedom, no course that was acceptable other than national independence. But when it came on July 4, 1946, by act of the Congress of the United States, the new Republic of the Philippines was not ready to assume its responsibilities. And the United States, all too anxious to be rid of a burden in the postwar era, did not help make the transition easier.

Most Americans, however, chose to believe that the grant of Philippine independence was a selfless act, a suitable reward for the sacrifices that had been made by a wartime ally. American sentiment continued to glorify the American experience in the Philippines. From the victory at Manila Bay in 1898 to the fanatical resistance at Corregidor in 1941 and 1942, and from the horrors of the death march from Bataan in 1942 to the thrill in 1945 of General MacArthur's return at the head of his armies, the pageant of wartime achievement in the Philippines overshadowed all else.

But to the newly independent Filipinos, all these belonged to history—the relics of an imperial age.

The Politics of Violence

There are two ways in which the United States looks at the Philippines.

The first is that the island republic has in truth demonstrated political stability as a practicing democracy in Asia. In two decades, six orderly transfers of power have taken place. And in 1970, a freely and peacefully elected constitutional convention was chosen to shape the future of the Philippines. On the basis of such evidence, it would seem that Asia could look up to the Filipino as an example of self-rule.

The trouble is that the second, and more prevalent, view of the Philippines nearly always blots out the more reasonable image. For despite a quarter century of self-government, the republic has a violent reputation for misrule, corruption, pillage and murder. Instead of revering the occupants of the Malacanang, the presidential palace in Manila, Asians regard them askance. And instead of accepting the good record the Filipino has made, most Americans are more likely to believe that bribery and rapine are a way of political life in the Philippines. Such is the result of the politics of violence.

Senator Emanuel Pelaez, an outstanding liberal, actually fears for the survival of Philippine democracy. Another senator, Benigno S. Aquino, Jr., warns, "This business of the elite being able to run things as they please has to go. The blow-up is coming." A columnist, Maximo V. Soliven, wrote in the Manila *Times* that the Philippines was a "fake democracy," that a state of anarchy existed throughout the country and that "land-grabbing has become our way of life." The editor of an intellectual weekly, Teodoro M. Locsin of the *Free Press*, concluded, "The government is generally considered by foreigners and Filipinos alike to be one of the most corrupt, most terroristic, most disgusting in the world. To contemplate it is to vomit."[15]

Within a very short period, this is what Filipinos read in their newspapers and heard in news broadcasts: Seven barrio officials and a driver were shot down in cold blood before a provincial governor and a number of other witnesses. A town mayor and thirteen other persons were massacred by an opposing faction. A congressman was shot to death as he knelt in a church to take Communion. Attempts were made on the lives of several other congressmen, causing fatalities among their friends or followers in some cases. And when instances involving violence did result in arrests and trials, key witnesses mysteriously disappeared or recanted damaging testimony, causing defendants to be freed.[16]

This has been typical of the quality of life in the Philippines for some time. Part of the climate of violence may be blamed on what Soliven has described as "land-grabbing," widely prevalent in the early 1970s, in which politically powerful property owners seized the lands of weak and defenseless minority factions or tribes. Sometimes they even were able to get the local constabulary to help them with their infamous schemes.

But that is only a part of the story. Shoot-outs in local political feuds, particularly at election time, are too numerous for even the

[15] I interviewed Pelaez July 9, 1970. Aquino's quotation is from the *Far Eastern Economic Review*, October 31, 1970, p. 14; Soliven wrote his comment in his Manila *Times* column, July 10, 1970, p. 5; Locsin was quoted in the *Far Eastern Economic Review*, September 19, 1970, p. 23.

[16] See the Manila *Times*, *Philippines Herald* and Manila *Chronicle* for the spring and summer of 1970.

diligent and free-swinging Manila papers to catalogue. Then, too, there is a vicious Filipino practice that enables the politically prominent to acquire their own retinue of gunslingers. While the government has protested against the activities of these tin-pot war lords, it is reputed to have its own unofficial army, known ingloriously in the headlines as "The Monkees."

Under such circumstances, it becomes an uphill battle for the Philippines to maintain its reputation as a practicing democracy in Asia, for the sensational headlines scream that violence is the hallmark of Filipino life. To cap the climax, the civilized world was shocked on November 27, 1970, when a Bolivian artist, wearing a priest's robe, tried to stab Pope Paul VI with a foot-long knife shortly after his arrival in Manila. It seemed to confirm all the suspicions that the Filipinos, indeed, were violence-prone.

The War Against the Huks

In addition to irresponsible politicians with private armies, the Philippines has had to contend with revived activity by roving bands of Communists known as the Huks—the remnants of the Hukbalahap rebels whose extinction has been proclaimed annually ever since the successful campaign that President Ramon Magsaysay waged against them. During the fall and winter of 1970–71, the government's drive against the Huks in Pampanga and Tarlac provinces was mounted in such strength as to cast doubt on the official estimate that the rebels amounted to only a few hundred poorly armed vagabonds.

It was a strange campaign. The Huks had suffered an ideological split in 1968, with Commander Dante, the name adopted by a thirty-year-old law student, Bernabe Buscayno, leading his faction into alliance with a small group of city-based Maoists. He thereupon proclaimed his leadership of a guerrilla movement known as the New People's Army. His chief associates, Pedro Taruc and Faustino del Mundo, alias Commander Sumulong, broke with him. In September 1970, Sumulong surrendered to the government—a leader without an army—and proclaimed that he had never been a Communist. Taruc, after twenty years as a freebooter, was shot and killed by government forces a month later.

The government jubilantly announced that only 300 Huks remained at large out of an organization that had once been estimated at 50,000 men.[17] But its credibility in this as in other matters has been so undermined that few have taken the claim at face value. Maximo Soliven has always believed that the Huks can muster a considerable force in central Luzon, ranging from a few thousand hard-core Communists to as many as 25,000 barrio sympathizers, depending on circumstances.[18] Eduardo Lachica of the *Philippines Herald* has estimated that the Huks, through their adherents, are able to control nearly 60 per cent of the almost 2,000 barrios in the five provinces of central Luzon's rice country.[19]

But large or small, the Huks still are the only group that could mount a guerrilla campaign against the government.

The Well-Publicized Revolution

These conditions, understandably, have led to widespread talk of revolution among Filipinos, almost daily discussion in the press of the possibility of an uprising, and the multiplication of foreign dispatches from Manila-based correspondents that the Philippines is tottering on the verge of insurrection. If a revolution does occur, it will certainly be the best-publicized uprising of the century. But the trouble with such predictions is that no one seems to know if revolt is more likely to come from the right or the left, if it occurs at all.

There is no question of the dissatisfaction of Filipinos, young and old. In a poll conducted for the Filipino publishers by the Asia Research Organization, 24 per cent of those questioned said that they believed governmental reforms could come about only through violent change. Among those in the 16–23 age bracket who responded to this question, 37 per cent were convinced that violence was necessary to insure better government.[20]

From the hippie-type Filipino Maoist students who daily circle the Malacanang with insulting red banners to the deeply religious young people in the Christian Social movement, the call for revolution is general. "Everybody," says a cynical student, "is for revolution these

---

[17] Reuters report, November 7, 1970, from Manila.
[18] In an interview with me.
[19] *Far Eastern Economic Review,* October 17, 1970, pp. 29–30.
[20] *Ibid.,* p. 23.

days." And Maximo Soliven, as usual, makes no effort to conceal his feelings. "I often feel like taking to the hills as a rebel," he says, "except that I know I would be the first to be executed if the Communists came to power."[21]

This is precisely the sticking point for many a generous and liberal-minded Filipino. In a country that is 83 per cent Catholic, and took the Pope to its heart on his 1970 visit, it is difficult to envision a mass movement under the red flag. The leader of the Philippine Communist Party, which is Maoist in sympathy, has to operate under a pseudonym, Amado Guerrero ("Beloved Warrior") and is a hunted man with a handful of leftist sympathizers.[22] Moreover, in a country where the Chinese never have been popular, a Chinese-supported revolution probably would alienate more people than it attracted. Not that there is any evidence of substance to show that the Peking government is putting any of its slender resources into so unpromising a project.

Any Filipino revolution of consequence would have to take its inspiration from Rizal and Aguinaldo and not from Mao's little red book. In the barrios, the seat of dissatisfaction, the foreigner is still looked upon with suspicion. And if the foreigner happens to be Chinese, he usually has his troubles. The Chinese-oriented direction of the new Huk People's Army is its weakness. Any government that undertook to right the many wrongs in the Philippines with vigor and determination could turn back a challenge from this or any other part of the left with very little trouble.

But the government has dawdled. And more than one of its opponents has suspected that if there is a take-over, it is likely to come from the right rather than the left, from within the government rather than from outside. This could be. If conditions continue to worsen, almost anything could happen in a land so seething with discontent. During a visit to the Philippines in 1970, I found increasingly tense situations developing in Manila between radical students and police and between government troops and Muslims fighting in defense of

[21] In an interview with me.

[22] According to O. E. Rojas in *Asia Magazine*, November 15, 1970, p. 3, he is reputed to be a former political science instructor at the University of the Philippines, José Sison.

their land in Mindanao. In the following year, these crises erupted. Student activists in Manila touched off a series of fatal riots, occupied several campuses and stirred up May Day violence in which three youngsters were killed. In Mindanao, meanwhile, there were nearly 200 fire fights between the beleaguered Muslims and the troopers.

The climax to all this fighting came at a midsummer eve's rally of the opposition Liberal Party on August 21, 1971, in Manila, when terrorists hurled grenades into the crowd, killing ten persons and wounding more than fifty. By that time, most Filipinos had lost all hope for reform through their constitutional convention, which was picketed and denounced as a sham and a failure.

There was no telling where such violence and discontent would lead.

Hard Times for the Philippines

Despite the Philippines' potential for growth and prosperity, it has never come close to realizing its promise. By contrast with the Republic of Korea and Taiwan, it has done poorly.

Today, the unemployment problem in the island republic is becoming critical. Of the Filipino labor force of about 13,000,000, more than 10 per cent are admittedly unemployed; even worse, the underemployed are estimated at nearly 50 per cent. Instead of easing, the problem grows worse each year with the addition of some 400,000 eighteen-year-olds to the labor force. As for the 65,000 college graduates, most of them hang out on street corners, for the economy can't absorb them.

To all outward appearances, the Philippines has thus become a land of the very rich (about 400 families are estimated to dominate the nation's economic and political life) and the very poor, of whom perhaps as many as 95 per cent earn less than $150 a year. Nobody can feel safe in the Philippines; in the cities, it is a familiar sight to find a guard with a loaded shotgun in an apartment-house lobby, and in the countryside it is always better to carry a weapon.

The once-thriving middle class, at one time so prosperous and still estimated to form at least 20 per cent of the 38,000,000 population, has been hard hit by the gyrations of the peso. It suffered a *de facto* devaluation of more than 50 per cent in less than a year, a calamity that caused most Filipinos to shrug off the added blow of the American "dollar war" of 1971 and its consequences to the Filipino economy.

With consumer prices rising by about 50 per cent in 1970 and a further increase of 7.5 per cent for 1971, the Filipinos were in real trouble. There was no certainty that even the modest 6 per cent growth rate of the late 1960s could be maintained. For one thing, the Filipino population is still increasing annually by 3.5 per cent, one of the highest rates in the world. For another, much foreign business is leaving the Philippines; in particular, more American firms are leaving than entering.[23]

The Apo

Without doubt, President Ferdinand Edralin Marcos must bear responsibility for some of his country's ills. It is true that he inherited many of the troubles that bedevil him today. But the Apo, so named after a dormant Filipino volcano, has not helped matters any by calling his principal opponents "Communists" and threatening to run his beautiful wife, Imelda, as his successor.

Marcos is an authentic World War II hero. As a guerrilla, he was wounded five times in combat with the Japanese and won twenty-two medals. In 1965 he campaigned for the presidency on some issues that are being used against him now—among them financial disorder and corruption. Upon his victory as the Nacionalista (conservative) candidate, he made a sensational opening presidential address. Before an enormous crowd under the palms in Manila's lovely Luneta Park, he exclaimed: "The Filipino has lost his soul and his courage! Our people have come to a point of despair. We have ceased to value order. Justice and security are as myths. Our government is gripped in the iron hand of venality, its treasury is barren, its resources are wasted, its civil service is slothful and indifferent, its armed forces demoralized and its councils sterile . . . Not one hero alone do I ask from you, but many—nay all."[24]

[23] Benigno S. Aquino, Jr., *Pacific Community*, October, 1970, pp. 188–189.
[24] For Marcos election result and sketch, see *The New York Times*, November 13, 1965, p. 2; for Marcos policies, *Time*, January 27, 1966, p. 26.

As it turned out, there were no heroes. After the passage of four years, the only things that Marcos had to show for his term in office were some new roads and the achievement of self-sufficiency in Filipino rice production. But the miracle of abundant rice within less than five years, from a time when the nation had been obliged to import 1,000,000 tons annually, was scarcely the Apo's doing. From 1962 on, the Ford Foundation and Rockefeller Foundation had sought to develop a new and more productive rice strain at Los Banos and their efforts had paid off in the new IR5 and IR8 varieties.[25] However, the Filipino electorate wasn't too fussy about investigating political claims. It still liked Marcos.

In most national elections in the Philippines, the national treasury suffers through the sometimes uninhibited expenditure of funds for pork barrel and other projects on the part of the party in power. But from all the evidence at hand, including Marcos' own testimony, the spending in the 1969 presidential campaign was so monumental that it almost bankrupted the treasury. Fortified by government funds that were allocated generously to both barrios and cities, the Nacionalistas put on a dazzling campaign to re-elect Marcos on a platform of industrialization, land reform and an end to the "special relationship" between the United States and the Philippines. He won overwhelmingly, but the consequences were appalling.

The *Free Press* disclosed at the end of 1969 that the Central Bank was at the end of its international reserves, that the dollar reserve was $150 million with debts of $151.1 million. "It is doubtful that the Central Bank coffer has ever been that empty before," wrote the *Free Press*. In his Four-Year Development Plan (1971–74), President Marcos himself authorized the following explanation: "About two-thirds of the estimated total expenditures for fiscal year 1970 was spent during the first semester [this was the campaign period]. Heavy current and capital spending during FY 1969 and the first half of FY 1970 necessitated a slowing down in expenditures for the entry FY 1971."

The consequences were not long in coming. The peso was unhinged and put on a floating rate, a thin disguise for devaluation. Inflation

[25] *Time*, July 13, 1970, p. 26.

rose steeply. The World Bank came to the rescue with much-needed funds on the basis of the new Development Plan, and the Rand Corporation, in a study for the United States Agency for International Development, called the country "politically stable." But neither kind words nor fine plans eased the financial plight of the nation. Things had gotten out of control.

From the height of his popularity at the time of his re-election, Marcos tumbled in a single year to such a low estate that he had to be carefully guarded wherever he went. He issued self-righteous statements: "Politics here is becoming too rough, becoming too dirty. It is corrupted. It is already the activity of the irresponsible, the almost insane." And again, on the issue of private armies: "I will not and cannot tolerate private war lords. Our peace-keeping agencies have standing orders to disband any armed clique maintained by politicians." He became rattled when the United States pulled out 6,000 troops from Clark Air Base, a loss of about $25 million annually to the Filipino economy.

The attacks against him increased. It wasn't so much the daily demonstrations outside the palace that hurt him. He was thrown on the defensive by such charges as the one in the 1970 *Pick's Currency Yearbook*, attributed to "well-informed insiders," that he had amassed a personal fortune exceeding the gold and foreign exchange reserves of the republic's Central Bank. While he denied it, a better answer was given at the end of 1970 by the Central Bank's governor, Gregorio S. Licaros, who said the country had accumulated a surplus of $35.7 million, wiping out a $141 million deficit incurred during the previous year. It was made possible, Mr. Licaros said, by a 20.4 per cent increase in export earnings and a 9.5 per cent decrease in import payments.[26]

[26] The *Free Press* analysis quoted in *Far Eastern Economic Review*, September 19, 1970, p. 53; the Four-Year Development Plan analyzed by Juan Mercado, Depth News dispatch in Hong Kong *Standard*, September 29, 1970, p. 11; the Rand Corporation report is "An Interdisciplinary Study of the Social, Political and Economic State of the Philippine Nation," 314 pp., 1970. *Pick's Currency Yearbook*'s charge was reported October 25, 1970, by UPI, Tokyo. The Licaros Central Bank report was carried in the AP file from Manila, December 9, 1970, and was published in the Hong Kong *Standard* the following day, p. 4, Sec. 2.

Marcos: The Legend and the Man

When I visited the Malacanang for my appointment with President Marcos on a hot summer's morning, the principal evidence of hostility to his rule consisted of several small circles of student pickets bearing red placards and banners. Occasionally, they chanted an uncomplimentary slogan. But for the most part, they were good-humored and orderly. Often, they are not. But the daily demonstrations had been going on so long that they had become part of the palace routine. Whatever ills there are in democracy as practiced in the Philippines, the suppression of unpopular sentiments is not one of them.

I was passed through the fenced-in grounds by armed guards at several checkpoints and wandered along the well-kept walks through the velvety green lawn, past gracious old trees and magnificent shrubbery, to the main entrance to the palace. I had been expected, so there was no problem. Within a few minutes, I was escorted to the glamorous and impressive second floor, with its glistening chandeliers and framed portraits of historic Filipinos, Imelda Marcos' being the most prominent of all. Presently, an obsequious secretary escorted me through a large inner room to the President's office—a rather dark, heavily furnished room with Filipino and presidential flags flanking a big ornate desk and six overstuffed chairs that were lined up in an L-shape beside it.

There was almost constant movement in the President's office from the time I entered it. Members of the secretariat and some bodyguards, judging from their size and general disposition, came and went from an inner room, stood about in corners conversing in low voices, or waited by the door for instructions. All were men. Except for one big fellow who dropped into a chair beside me for a brief greeting, nobody paid any attention to me. It was scarcely what I had expected, but it was fascinating to watch.

After about ten minutes of this maneuvering, President Marcos entered from the outside—a small, lithe, handsome figure in a light-colored suit, black hair gleaming, smooth face aglow with an ever-present smile. After a handshake and a word of greeting, he excused himself to receive two pilots who had helped him in World War II.

An embrace, a few warm words of gratitude, more handshaking, and he was back at his desk across from the chair in which I sat. Curiously, the movement of his people in and out of the room was uninterrupted; if anything, his presence seemed to increase the bustling, the murmured conferences in corners, the flitting to and from the inner room.

Marcos paid no attention to his henchmen and leaned across the desk, completely at ease, to adjust a small mike that recorded our conversation. We were duly photographed, a courtesy of the palace. But before I could get out my first question, which had to do with the state of the nation as he saw it, he blurted out: "What do you think of the prospects of war between Russia and China?" That, of course, had been farthest from my mind. I remarked that I wasn't a military man, that he was, and what did he think? He thought there might be war eventually, beginning on the ground. I gathered that he wasn't anxious to talk about matters much more immediate and closer to home.

He chattered along in good humor about the Nixon Doctrine ("What does it mean?") and the prospects of an American withdrawal. Evidently, he had changed his mind since making his celebrated statement about the Japanese replacing United States power in the Pacific, for he said, with a laugh, "You [the U.S.] couldn't withdraw from the Pacific if you wanted to—you are a Pacific power." He argued that the Americans had their commitments to keep, but repeated his claim to the American-occupied anti-submarine base at Sangley Point.[27]

After a time, he edged into the touchy domestic affairs of the Philippines with a reference to the campaign against the Huks. He defended his issuance of arms to the barrios. "I want to make the citizens themselves a bulwark against the Huks." He chuckled. "It drives the friends of the Communists crazy because I have done this—armed the barrios." As for his major domestic problems—inflation, unemployment, crime, land-grabbing and war lordism—he remarked airily that these things all were being tackled.

Abruptly, the President switched the conversation back to the

[27] The United States announced the return of Sangley Point to the Philippines in December 1970.

prospects of a Russian-Chinese war and wondered what the United States would do in the event of such massive hostilities. It was not, of course, a matter on which I was competent to talk (and I doubted if the Secretary of State could have satisfied him, either). But he chattered on about the dangers from mainland China and his suspicions of the Russians, who were, he said, "trying to put on an Asian face even though they aren't Asians."

This might have gone on indefinitely, with the secretariat buzzing in the background, but for the arrival of the Foreign Minister, Carlos Pena Romulo, who joined us briefly with a few pleasantries and ended forty-five minutes of rather aimless interviewing. I was sent off with more smiles and handclasps, but with rather less appreciation of Filipino policies for the future than when I had entered. Marcos the man had proved to be infinitely more of a pleasant and fallible human being rather than the awesome figure of Marcos the legend, the reputed genius of Filipino politics, the center of maneuver in a land in crisis. He is more like an old-timer out of a familiar American big-city tradition, a convivial spirit who would have felt at home in the little house on K Street of Harding's time.[28]

Dealing with the United States

Marcos, like any other Philippine president, has obvious limitations in dealing with the United States. He would like to revise the Laurel-Langley economic agreement, expiring in 1974, to do away with the parity principle under which American nationals and companies may own land and run wholly foreign-owned companies in the Philippines. But in response to proposals to force Americans to let 60 per cent of their companies' operations in the Philippines be owned by Filipinos, the United States has threatened to shift part of its sugar trade to Latin America.[29]

That is just one instance of what it means for a small nation to try to revise its commercial relationships with a retreating United States. There are others. In response to Filipino threats of tightened economic controls, American firms are selling out to local investors and removing badly needed foreign capital. The Philippines also is not in

[28] Interview, July 11, 1970.
[29] *South China Morning Post*, November 9, 1970, p. 1, Sec. 1.

a position to compete with increased American protectionism. Washington holds all the high cards.

Militarily, the 1971 revisions of the 1947 military bases agreement point to the probable removal of at least half the 30,000 American troops currently stationed in the Philippines within a few years. To make up for the blow to the Philippine economy, it is probable that American economic aid amounted to about $50 million for fiscal 1971 but there is no guarantee of continuance at that level. As for the major bases at Clark and Subic Bay, it is a good question whether the Philippines could afford to keep them up even if the United States should vacate them in time—and the Filipinos know it.

If they are able to put their economic house in order, and there is no reason why they should not, then their bargaining position will be much stronger, although the notion that Manila will ever be able to bring Washington to terms is an illusion. But an unfulfilled economic plan, such as the 1971–74 proposal, is only a snare; since 1945, there have been eleven such plans and all of them, as Juan Mercado has observed, have been honored more in the breach than in the practice.

The Philippine Congress therefore will have to update and improve its tax structure instead of taking the easy way out and borrowing. In an economy that is fundamentally sound, what is required here is an act of conscience and of will. True, the 400 families aren't going to like it. Still, the millionaire whom I visited in Forbes Park isn't likely to be obliged to give up one of his polo ponies, or his fleet of magnificent cars, ranging from Mercedes' to Cadillacs. And the moral effect in the barrios will be of greater benefit than another intrusion of "Monkees" in search of the elusive Huks.

If these necessary financial measures cannot be taken, then the peso cannot be stabilized, foreign assistance projects will vanish for lack of peso counterpart funds, and the unhappiness of the Filipino citizenry will increase beyond the point of acceptability on the part of the government. Instead of finding some new relationship with the United States that will augur well for the future, the old ties will deteriorate. And the long-predicted uprising in the cities and the countryside may well come to pass.

Many Filipinos have asked, more out of curiosity than anxiety, what the position of the United States would be under the Nixon

Doctrine if such a revolution threatened to boost an unfriendly regime into power in Manila. When I called on Senator Gil Puyat, the majority leader, in Makati, he said that as a last recourse, under current treaty arrangements, the Filipino government would have to appeal to the United States for armed assistance and the United States would then have to decide what to do. Neither of us bothered to speculate on what the answer would be.[30] For despite the close ties of the past between the Philippines and the United States, it stands to reason that no American President in the foreseeable future is likely to invite another Vietnam situation by intervening in the internal affairs of the island republic. And if by some chance a President were disposed to do so, he would surely encounter massive opposition from both the Congress and the people of the United States.

The policy of American disengagement in Asia, consequently, has placed the Filipino on his own to a greater extent than he ever has been before. With a GNP in the neighborhood of $4 billion and even a modest growth rate of 5 to 6 per cent annually in the early 1970s, this would be manageable for Manila were it not for its chaotic governmental affairs and a rising internal debt. Even if United States aid does not maintain its generous volume in years to come, Japan is still paying off on its $550 million twenty-year program of war reparations and making major loans to industry as well. And Filipino trade with the United States is still around $2 billion annually, with Japan coming up fast and accounting for about $1 billion a year.

What is desperately needed is a respite from politics as usual.

The Voice of Reason

There are, fortunately, a few voices of reason that can still be heard in the Philippines. The most important, by all odds, has been that of Carlos Pena Romulo, the greatest of living Filipinos. When he returned to the Foreign Ministry once again, in the twilight of his career, the septuagenarian statesman was in a position of unexampled strength to talk sense to his own people and to the Americans as well. He did not hesitate to do so.

As a veteran Cabinet member and adviser to presidents, ambassador to Washington and the United Nations, president of the United

[30] I saw Puyat July 11, 1970.

Nations General Assembly, president of the University of the Philippines, and a distinguished soldier and journalist, Romulo always occupied a unique position in Washington, Manila and the United Nations. Even when he opposed American policies, only the unthinking thought of him as being anti-American. For this little gray man with the solemn eyes, the crinkly smile and the thunderous voice won a Pulitzer Prize as a journalist, all manner of American decorations for his wartime service on General MacArthur's staff as the last man off Corregidor and one of the first to return to the Philippines, and the profound respect of every American government with which he dealt.

Sometimes, Romulo's very familiarity with Americans and their ways has created trouble for him. Once, at a United Nations meeting in Paris in 1948, he arranged a premature dinner in honor of John Foster Dulles as the next Secretary of State and gamely went through with the proceedings even when the Republicans lost the election. Four years later, however, when Dulles assumed office as President Eisenhower's Secretary of State, Romulo was called upon as the Filipino ambassador to give the first dinner in honor of the new appointee. He laughed about it later. "It cost me eight thousand dollars but it was worth it," he said.

At the old building of the Department of Foreign Affairs in the Padre Faura in Manila, where I saw him at eight thirty on a cool and refreshing July morning, he already had been working away for two hours. We had had a brief talk the day before about the difficulties that were arising to bedevil Filipino-American affairs. He had wanted to think things over before speaking his mind. When he began over coffee, sitting comfortably at his big desk with an admiring but unnecessary Foreign Ministry official as a silent auditor beside us, he said: "What we want from the United States is a commitment, not a military presence. With a real commitment from you, on which we can count, we will be well able to defend ourselves."

The first point he made was a familiar one to those who had followed his career over thirty years or more. It was the simple but essential matter of paying closer attention to Asian sensibilities. "You Americans," he said, "will have to show more consideration for Asian feelings than you have in the past. It is still true, unfortunately, that Asians pay close attention to American opinions, but the American public has little or no interest in Asian opinions. You don't care what Filipinos think."

The point was valid and beyond dispute. But with conditions as they existed in the Philippines, and even the Filipino press disclosing new excesses almost daily, what could be done to create greater mutual respect? As an old journalist, Romulo might with some justice have flung back the reproach, so often heard in the Philippines, that Filipinos acquired their bad habits from Americans. But he did not. He conceded that the problem was difficult for the news media.

"Still," he objected, "why do we always have to hear about the gun-toting Filipino and not the hard-working rice farmer of the barrios, the political wirepuller rather than the builder or teacher, the angry student with the red flag rather than the earnest majority seeking a better way of life? I say that we need equal loyalty between us. You ask loyalty of us. We have a right to ask you, in return, to be loyal to us."

Romulo had no quarrel with the American policy of disengagement. After all, he pointed out, the Seventh Fleet and the United States Air Force are remaining in Asia for the present as a deterrent to aggression from without. "You say that the United States has learned that it cannot be the world's policeman," he continued. "But it has never been the world's policeman. It has been a Samaritan—in Europe, Japan, India, in many other places. The point most Americans overlook is that there are no permanent friends or permanent enemies in international relations—there are only permanent national interests and each of us must act in accordance with those national interests."

The national interests of the Philippines, he maintained, must inevitably point the country toward a greater degree of independence in international affairs. "We cannot continue to hang on to America's coattails," he said. "We should seek self-reliance and self-respect. The United States makes a mistake in thinking that the democracy of an affluent society can be exported. For the long tomorrow, all of us must count on Asians working out their own problems."

But, I asked, is it possible for developing countries like the Philippines or Indonesia to be industrialized in twenty-five years so that they will be capable of working out their own destinies? Romulo agreed that the process of building an industrialized society would take a long time, particularly in countries like the Philippines, where people are not prone to accept sacrifices for the national good. But he argued that industrialization alone was not the answer—that policies of mutual cooperation would bring great benefits to both partners in a new Filipino-American relationship, once it was worked out.

To that end, he foresaw a limit to American disengagement in the Pacific as a matter of national interest. "I can't imagine a complete American withdrawal from the Pacific that would leave China and the Soviet Union and Japan to divide hegemony over more than one billion people," he concluded. "To do so would reduce the United States to a second-rate power, slash its standard of living and bring about more dangers in the Pacific than we presently face. The United States cannot give up power by default. Nor do I think that most Asians in non-Communist countries want that to happen."

It was, on the whole, an optimistic view but Romulo was, by nature, an optimist. He did not shrink from the unpleasantness of the domestic scene in the Philippines. And he remarked with a smile that he was prepared for fresh arguments with Washington. But as we parted, I noticed framed portraits of President Nixon and his Secretary of State, William P. Rogers, in positions of honor at the entrance to the office. I suppose it was Romulo's way of showing his colors.[31] Whether his successors in the Padre Faura will continue to do so is another question entirely, and one over which Romulo himself could have little control.

Tomorrow and Tomorrow . . .

The Philippines is heading into an era of change, in common with all Asian countries. The rising generation of Filipinos knows nothing at first hand of the heroic period of Filipino-American cooperation during World War II and cares less. The older generation, for that matter, is realistic enough to perceive that the onetime mother country has less interest in the Philippines today than at any time

[31] I talked with General Romulo July 9–10, 1970.

during this century. The days of sentimental association are at an end.

If a special relationship (always a fuzzy term) is to be maintained between the United States and the Philippines, it will have to be on an entirely different basis. The rising feeling of nationalism among Filipinos as well as the changed circumstances of the United States both bar a return to the old ways even if such a course were desirable. President Salvador P. Lopez of the University of the Philippines, a former foreign minister and United Nations ambassador, has written: "The real touchstone of Philippine-American relations is to be found in the degree to which their political and economic interests can be harmonized."[32]

In a practical sense, this is undoubtedly true. But both Romulo and Lopez would agree with the impatient young Filipinos of the cities that it is even more important for the Philippines to find a new sense of identity with Asia and for the Filipinos themselves to develop a greater sense of responsibility and self-reliance if their fragile democracy is to survive.

5. SHADOWS OVER HONG KONG

For most of the year in bustling Hong Kong, the square gray skyscraper of the Bank of China is just another dull, conservative business building in the great forest of stone and steel that reaches up toward Victoria Peak. But every October 1, on the anniversary of the completion of Mao Tse-tung's conquest of China and for some days thereafter, the seemingly stodgy bank is ablaze with a fierce glow of floodlights, monstrous red flags, revolutionary slogans in Chinese characters and, above all, a portrait of the old master of Peking. For here, set down in the very heart of Hong Kong's capitalist establishment, is Peking's chief agency for the receipt of its profits in the form of foreign exchange through Britain's Crown Colony.

As Hong Kong prospers despite its precarious situation on China's flank, the payments to its gigantic but less prosperous neighbor grow larger year by year. In the mid-1960s, it was estimated that Peking

---

[32] S. P. Lopez, "The Philippines in Search of a New Role," *Pacific Community*, July, 1970, p. 700.

was earning $500 million a year through the Crown Colony. In 1970, on the basis of the most conservative figures issued by the colonial financial secretary, net payments to China were running at the annual rate of $720 million.[33] Should Hong Kong's expansion continue, as seems likely, the time is not far distant when its business will mean $1 billion a year in much-needed foreign exchange for China.

The Perils of the Pearl

Except for the 1967 disturbances, which threatened for a time to wreck the colony's business affairs, the Chinese government has chosen to adopt an evenhanded policy toward its followers in Hong Kong, of whom there are many, and the rather shaky British colonial regime. Just how long Peking will maintain this coldly tolerant position depends very largely on how much satisfaction it derives from the triangular relationship of convenience with Britain and its remaining possession in Pacific Asia, the sometime Pearl of the Orient. The situation, as has often been pointed out in the Far East, resembles that of the Chinese household in which the husband and wife fall out occasionally in their quarrels over the behavior of the concubine, in this case, Hong Kong.

There is no question that China, if it desired, could seize Hong Kong as easily as India took Goa and there is precious little that anybody could do about it, least of all the weakened British. The argument against such rude conduct, as the British put it in the most hopeful terms, is that the conquest would defeat its own purpose. The brilliant white skyscrapers of Hong Kong island would turn into tombs. The busy market places of Kowloon, across the harbor, would become cemeteries. The frantic activity of one of the greatest ports in the world would be reduced to the lonely hooting of ferry whistles. And the fabulous golden flow of capitalist profits, which China so urgently requires to help finance its industrial expansion, would be choked off for good.

Nevertheless, the Chinese threat remains. The tiny British colony, with its 4,000,000 people crammed into 391 square miles, most of

[33] Estimate by Sir John Cowperthwaite, Hong Kong financial secretary, in an interview with *The Banker* magazine, July, 1970. All sums herein are given in American dollars.

them on the 35.5 square miles of Hong Kong island and the neighboring Kowloon peninsula, is living on borrowed time and knows it. In 1997, the 355 square miles of the New Territories, leased from China in 1898 for ninety-nine years, are scheduled to revert to Peking. It is a good question whether the intensely developed urban areas can survive without the thriving hinterland or, even if they can, whether China will permit them to continue as a capitalist outpost. Armed force, after all, isn't really needed. Since the colony gets nearly all its food and emergency water supplies from China, a long blockade of all travel, trade and communication could be fatal.

Once again, the British argue against what many Chinese believe to be inevitable. Some kind of an agreement may eventually be worked out, in the view of the last of the colonialists, through which Hong Kong will retain some special status or even achieve the rather nervous state of independence in which Singapore exists. In any event, Hong Kong isn't giving up and neither are the British. Like a village perched on the rocky slope of a live volcano, the colony goes about its business each day with little or no thought of the morrow. Sometimes, to an observant outsider, it seems as if nothing really matters in Hong Kong except the mindless devotion to larger sales and greater profits.

Maintaining the Balance

There is always tension in Hong Kong. Despite the undoubted watchfulness and efficiency of the police, a small incident can cause trouble and set people of opposing political sympathies at each other's throats. Fortunately, everybody knows the danger. Even so, it is not a simple matter to preserve the amenities and maintain a proper balance under such circumstances, but the British somehow have managed to do it for most of the years since they took back their colony from the Japanese at the end of World War II.

Hong Kong (from Heung Kong, meaning "Fragrant Harbor") is 99 per cent Chinese. There are only about 50,000 non-Chinese in the colony, mostly subjects of Commonwealth countries, with 5,000 Americans, 2,000 Japanese and a scattering of others. About half the 4,000,000 population consists of refugees or children of refugees who fled from China during the overthrow of 1949 and thereafter. They still come in at the rate of 400 to 600 a month, perhaps more; the British are reticent, for obvious reasons, and the Chinese do not advertise defections.

During the fall of 1970, in a particularly pathetic case, a Chinese girl swam across Deep Bay for nine hours while supporting the body of her weakened lover. But when they were picked up by Hong Kong police after reaching freedom, the boy was dead.[34]

The refugees have become an integral part of the life of Hong Kong and a major source of manpower for the colony's industrial expansion. There are few places, even in the Orient, where such an abundance of cheap, willing and docile labor exists; however, signs are multiplying that the available supply is running out and demands for higher pay and better living conditions cannot long be resisted. Even though some 28 per cent of 2,000,000 people in need of better housing have been moved into the government's new 500 low-cost resettlement estates, the majority still exist in miserable hovels—a reproach to the riches they see all about them. Skilled workmen who won't live under such conditions go to Singapore, Canada or the United States.

The politics of violence and protest is not popular in Hong Kong, which makes reform a sometime thing. Except for a campaign by Chinese students against Japanese seizure of the Tiao Yu Tai (or Senkaku) Islands and a movement for the adoption of Chinese as an official language coequal with English in the colony, there has been scant agitation for any cause. The 1967 fighting threw too much of a scare into the government and opposing factions alike. At that time, as the Cultural Revolution raged inside China, the Chinese Communists encouraged an uprising in Hong Kong against British authority. Border demonstrations took place in the New Territories. And in Kowloon and Hong Kong island itself, there were strikes, riots and bombings. Complicating everything, the Chinese deliberately closed down their deliveries of food and water to the colony for a time and charged that the British were maltreating Chinese subjects.

Eventually, order was restored but nothing was quite the same thereafter. The Communist press in Hong Kong continued to attack the British but there were no excesses and no calls for street demon-

[34] *South China Morning Post*, November 11, 1970, p. 1.

strations or strikes. The Communist labor unions, representing a substantial part of the work force although not a majority, were under instructions to be cooperative. As for the non-Communist unions, they didn't want to rock the boat and didn't protest too much, even though they had adequate cause, against the failure of wages to keep up with inflation.

The annual "Battle of the Flags" was eliminated by tacit consent as a possible incitement to violence. Instead of the riotous display of Chinese Nationalist and Communist banners during the October 1–10 rival patriotic celebrations, each side permits the other to show the flag of its choice in a kind of unofficial truce. Thus, on the Communist holiday of October 1, up go the red banners with their five gold stars and the gigantic portraits of Mao Tse-tung over the Chinese establishments that are either under Communist ownership or dominated by sympathizers. To the casual tourist, it appears as if the colony has thrown itself into the arms of Peking. But ten days later, on the "Double Tenth" anniversary of the Chinese Revolution of 1911, the red, white and blue of the Chinese Nationalist banner sprouts in such profusion that one wonders if the Kuomintang has replaced the authority of the Crown.

The Hong Kong Chinese accept the whole business with bland permissiveness. As long as there is no fighting, and business goes on as usual, they have no objections. It is a place where most Communists and non-Communists agree, at least for the time being, that what's good for trade is good for Hong Kong. A part of the social and political balance, in fact, is maintained by the Communist owners of industrial sweatshops, hotels and other establishments. They may quote ecstatically from Mao's little red book at their sumptuous monthly love feasts in Peking's honor, held at the Hilton Hotel under the auspices of the Marco Polo Club, but what they really believe in is the profit-and-loss sheet.

The Golden Record

For those who enjoy the heady gamble of facing risks for the sake of fat profits, Hong Kong is the place to operate. The Hong Kong dollar is so strong that it took in stride an 8.57 per cent revaluation against the American dollar at the end of 1971; moreover, the Chinese chose to keep their yuan at parity with the Hong Kong dollar while changing it from 2.4 to 2.25 in terms of the American dollar. At the time, imports were outrunning exports by $2.4 billion to $2.2 billion in American currency. But in the $5 billion-a-year trade era for the Crown Colony, the trade imbalance was offset by a number of factors, the most important of which was tourism, which rose from 765,000 in 1969 to almost 1,000,000 visitors in 1970, an estimated $300 million annually for Hong Kong's bulging coffers. It was the colony's second-largest source of revenue.

Hong Kong's 16,600 registered factories, 95 per cent of them with fewer than 200 employees, turned out clothing and textile fabrics, electronics, plastic toys, ships, machinery, footwear, wigs and hundreds of other products. In exports, Hong Kong's growth rate thus reached 25 per cent in 1970 and was reduced in 1971 only because of the American "dollar war" and temporary import restrictions. Despite fears of a slump induced by these American actions, an additional $18 million flowed into Hong Kong's industries in 1971. Clothes remained the main export item, 38 per cent of the total, but textiles and toys each accounted for more than $100 million a year and wigs, a new item, joined the $100 million class. The biggest foreign investment, however, was in electronics.

While Hong Kong did not issue official statistics on its gross national product, it was believed to be about $3 billion a year or more, with per capita income at the rate of $700 for 1971, very good for Asia.

Despite its efforts to right its balance-of-payments deficit, the United States remains Hong Kong's best customer. The colony in 1970 sent $715 million in clothing, textiles, wigs and other items to the American market and bought $300 million. The British, hard pressed by Japan and West Germany, were a distant second with about half the U.S. total, but retained $1.25 billion in Hong Kong reserves in London. Japan, with $600 million in sales, was Hong Kong's biggest supplier, but China was a close second with $500 million. Neither, however, bought as much from Hong Kong as West Germany and Canada.

The willingness of speculators to invest in Hong Kong land was just as important an index of confidence in the colony as trade. For

1970–75, it was estimated that construction would rise $300 million a year, double the 1970 rate. Government building included such gigantic projects as the Cross-Harbor Tunnel between Kowloon and Hong Kong island, the construction of a new reservoir on High Island, and a 2,780-foot extension to the great international Kai Tak Airport, one of the busiest and most valuable in the Orient. But, their builders encouraged by skyrocketing rents, high-rise apartments and big office buildings also were rushed to completion at an increasing rate. And new hotels were so numerous that even the incorrigible optimists in the colony wondered where all the additional tourists were coming from to fill them.

The uproar of construction in some of the central parts of the colony was deafening. It kept up unremittingly, day and night and weekends. Diners could enjoy sitting beside picture windows in a Kowloon rooftop restaurant one evening, watching the glittering lights of the most impressive skyline outside Manhattan island, but not long afterward the view would be blotted out by high-rise construction. Nor was there any escape in other areas. Around Repulse Bay and other fashionable areas, land values were so high that premium rents had to be paid and building speculators raced each other to seize the profits that seemed so easy to grasp. And as far away as Shatin, in the New Territories, the beautiful campus of the Chinese University of Hong Kong was rising on a rocky promontory because no other land parcel of sufficient size was available.

The business rule in Hong Kong for all investors was that they had to get back their money in five years or the project wasn't worth considering. Preferably, they wanted to get back their investment in three years. One Chinese millionaire, asked by a friend to explain why he plunged so heavily in real estate when Hong Kong's fate was so uncertain, laughed and said, "I can make a better profit here than I can anywhere else in the world. By the time the New Territories lease is up in 1997, I won't care. I'll be dead."

Hong Kong's role as an international financial center assured the entrepreneur of a ready flow of capital for well-conceived projects. Taxes were low, amounting in the early 1970s to a flat 15 per cent on business enterprises. As for personal taxes, they ranged from a 2.5 per cent minimum to a maximum of 15 per cent with a personal deduction of about $1,100. But whatever savings the average citizen was able to make on the ridiculously low tax structure were eaten up by the staggering rise in the cost of living, the high rents and the constant scurrying around that appeared to be a part of the routine of life and work in Hong Kong. As for the banker, real estate operator, factory owner and speculator, they didn't care as long as their profits continued to outrun their expenses.

The Communist Establishment

Almost everywhere else in the world outside Hong Kong, the dedicated Communist is a mindless creature of the state and accepts, without question, the zigs and zags, the advances and outright reversals of the contemporary party line. It is only in the Crown Colony, in Singapore and a few other Oriental centers of trade that the Chinese capitalist and Communist entrepreneurs compete on an equal basis. But in Hong Kong alone there exists a Communist Establishment that accepts, on the surface at least, the laws and governmental regulations of the "imperialists," as represented by the colonial regime.

It is difficult, of course, to define exactly which establishments are Communist-owned, Communist-controlled or under Communist discipline in such a rough-and-tumble commercialized society. But as nearly as can be determined, fourteen or fifteen of the approximately eighty banks in Hong Kong are Communist-owned or -controlled. It is through them that the enormous remittances from overseas Chinese flow to relatives on the mainland (although once the Chinese government began accepting food and clothing packages through Hong Kong, the remittance total was cut sharply). These banks also finance Communist enterprises in numerous ways but are reputed to be as conservative in their risk-taking as their more prudent capitalist contemporaries.

Mao's little red book and the sacred principles of Marxism-Leninism have not prevented the Communist banks from offering 7 per cent and more interest on savings or investments in private corporations, insurance companies and shopping centers. They are tough, too, on rent collections, whatever Lenin may have thought about that horrid capitalist practice.

In the retail field, there are at least thirty Communist department stores and smaller shops, the most glamorous and efficient being the establishments of Chinese Arts & Crafts, Ltd., with their helpful English-speaking sales force and varied stock. For the Americans in particular, with the relatively recent permission of their government to purchase goods of Chinese mainland origin, it is an experience to buy reasonably priced hand-embroidered tablecloths, precious or semi-precious stones, silks or art goods under the beaming portrait of Mao Tse-tung. Slogans of imperishable warfare against the imperialists, which are draped prominently on the walls of these emporiums, go unnoticed as American sailors in uniform vie with portly gray banker types from Peoria in sampling the latest bargains authorized by Peking with the blessings of the somewhat decimated Chinese Communist Party.

As for the press, the Communists invariably make certain that their presence is noticed. They neglect the daily English-language field, where the *South China Morning Post* and Hong Kong *Standard* are dominant, and concentrate heavily on the Chinese-language publications. In a recent survey, out of approximately fifty Chinese-language publications that were considered important enough to classify, it was found that three were Communist Party organs, two were Kuomintang papers, twelve were pro-Kuomintang, six were pro-Communist and the rest called themselves independent. But, of course, the advertising and the important readership still belonged to the big conservative dailies such as the *Sing Tao Wan Pao* (*Star Island Evening Post*) and the *Kung Sheung* (*Industrial and Commercial Daily*).

Even though the two official Communist organs have small circulations (about 10,000 each), they are closely watched by government agencies and by correspondents for indications of changing policies in Peking. *Ta Kung Pao* (*Impartial Daily*), all that is left of a once-great independent paper that was originally published in Peking, is the more important of the official papers, although occasionally *Wen Wei Pao* (*Literary Concourse Daily*), its companion publication, drops hints that are worth reflection. The most important pipeline to the fountainhead of Chinese Communist policy, however, is the Hong Kong branch of the Communist wire service, the New China News

Agency, one of the largest—and most secretive—news organizations in the world.

With mainland China's emergence from the confused isolation of the Cultural Revolution era, the Hong Kong border now is a busy place. Particularly during the Canton Fair period during the fall, business people by the thousands converge on China and many take the thriving Kowloon-Canton Railway, British section, from Kowloon station to Lo Wu, cross the Shum Chun River bridge, and continue on the railway's Chinese section to Canton. In 1971, for example, no less than 2,000 businessmen from Hong Kong were in Canton, more than even the bumper Japanese representation of 1,500. With the development of efficient air traffic and the slackening of annoying controls, it is probable that more flights will go from Kai Tak Airport in Hong Kong to various points in China as well.

While the Communist Establishment in the Crown Colony is not of major commercial importance, and accounts for a relatively small share of the trading in Chinese mainland goods, it is significant as a manifestation of Peking's good intentions. It is also a barometer that can be read with some degree of accuracy for short-term predictions on rising or slackening storm signals from the Chinese mainland.

What cannot be gauged for some time to come is the degree of influence that China exerts on the minds of the rising generation in Hong Kong—the troubled students in the universities and the far more numerous youngsters in the English and Chinese middle (high) schools. Although they are mainly the children of refugees, who have no cause to love the Communist regime in Peking, most of them are imbued with the same nationalistic fervor that is characteristic of their Asian contemporaries in other lands. They speak of China as "the fatherland," knowing perfectly well all the while that they would be among the first to be cast into prison or sent to work farms and camps if there ever was a Communist take-over in Hong Kong. They have no affection for Taiwan, and few feel any loyalty to the British, who have, after all, given them security and made possible a better life for many of them.

The mystic ties to China are stronger, regardless of what type of government is in power in Peking. If the United States, the Soviet Union and China all conduct atomic test explosions, as occurred in the fall of 1970, it is the Chinese blast that brings a thrill to Chinese youth in Hong Kong, Singapore and other centers of overseas Chinese life. And if the United States sends a rocket to circle the moon or even land on it, and the Chinese dispatch an airplane to photograph an eclipse of the sun at about the same time, the Chinese exploit is the one that arouses pride among young Chinese inside and outside the mainland.

This may be a monstrous inversion of values, but it is typically Chinese. For to those whose sympathies lie with "the fatherland," China is—and has been throughout its 6,000 years of recorded history—the center of the universe and Chinese life and Chinese thought are more important than those of other nations. True, the young Chinese of Hong Kong are in no position to demonstrate, much less to indulge in pointless rioting, to show their feelings. But if the government of the Chinese mainland should ever show a friendlier face toward those who have fled from its excesses, then the young people of Hong Kong may well throw off restraint and seek a different, if a less assured, future for the colony that has given them life, hope and shelter.

The United States and Hong Kong

To the average American visitor, Hong Kong is little more than a stopover on a two- or three-week package tour of the show places of Pacific Asia. It lies somewhere vaguely between Japan, Taiwan and the Philippines, heading southward; for those coming north from Saigon or Bangkok, it represents a break in the rather tiresome life of those who have an enforced commitment to existence in Asia. There may be some who find that Hong Kong really is, as it claims to be, a "shoppers' paradise." But many don't care. In the frantic world of tourism, the eternal and misleading promise is that tomorrow's stop will be more exciting than today's and this is particularly true of most Americans who visit Hong Kong.

Neither the casual American visitor nor the American citizen back home knows of the $1-billion-a-year trade between the colony and the United States, unless he is directly or indirectly involved. Nor do most Americans care very much that nearly 500 partly or wholly American-owned firms are doing business in Hong Kong. Yet, the position at the beginning of the 1970s was that these companies owned more than $800 million in assets in Hong Kong itself or controlled through the colony. Of the total, some $340 million was invested in Hong Kong, with the remainder as indirect investment. The total work force controlled by thees firms was more than 30,000 persons.

In the days of gunboat diplomacy, such an industrial stake would have made Hong Kong a vital interest of the United States that deserved the protection of American warships and United States Marines. It isn't true any longer. In order to avoid offending Chinese sensibilities and British relationships, the American warships that come into Hong Kong harbor are few in number and their visits are carefully spaced out. And despite much table-thumping in Parliament and harrumphing on the part of latter-day Colonel Blimps, the talk of Britain's return to a respectable role in the defense of the Far East can scarcely be taken at face value. The few British troops, plus the small assortment of aircraft and naval vessels, may be helpful for purposes of national identity and domestic policy in the colony; but in event of attack, the best they could do would be to hold off an aggressor for a few hours at most.

Hong Kong's security, therefore, cannot be seriously assigned either to British forces or to a combination of Commonwealth forces backed by the U.S. In the first place, there are no American responsibilities for Hong Kong; in the second, even if some injudicious mahatma of the Pentagon should try for covert intervention, he would be disavowed. Every American firm or citizen in Hong Kong knows of the business risks there, particularly since the American policies on import limitations have tightened. Hong Kong's well-being means a lot less to the United States than the restoration of health to the American economy.

The real value of the Crown Colony to Washington is that of a watchtower, a point of contact between peoples whose friendly relations over two centuries were seldom interrupted until Mao Tse-tung seized power in 1949. The slow return of Americans to China has been mainly through Hong Kong. And the presence of an impressive United States reporting machine on China, centered at the American consulate in Hong Kong, is further indication that the

United States and China mean to heal their generation-long rupture in one way or another.

Hong Kong, in consequence, is something more than a gateway to China for American journalists, businessmen, teachers and missionaries who patiently await admission. It represents, symbolically, the hope of a new three-way relationship between the United States, Britain and China, based on past friendships and mutual interests. Therein lies the best chance for the preservation of Hong Kong in years to come.[35]

6. THE TEST FOR WASHINGTON

The outposts of Pacific Asia are prepared for a reduced American presence in the Orient, but not for total American withdrawal, major protectionism and eventual isolation. That would be a calamity.

It is perfectly true, of course, that Japan and the border states have been among the major beneficiaries of the wars in Indochina. They have shared in the $2 billion American expenditures for military purposes in the Far East and the spillover from the $20 to $30 billion annual American war appropriations from 1965 on.

But Vietnam spending isn't the entire answer to the remarkable period of expansion and growth in Pacific Asia. The world-wide trade that has come to South Korea, Taiwan and Hong Kong is the best proof of that. As for Japan, the profits from the Vietnam War add up to less than 1 per cent of its gross national product.[36]

Nor have the "dollar war" and the temporary American import

[35] My chief source for current statistics on Hong Kong is the series of publications issued by the Hong Kong government for 1969, 1970 and thereafter, entitled "Hong Kong Monthly Digest of Statistics." Also helpful were numerous articles in the business sections of the *Japan Times, South China Morning Post* and Hong Kong *Standard*. In the *South China Morning Post*, useful reports were published September 25, 1970, p. 2, Sec. 2; September 28, 1970, p. 1, Sec. 2; October 28, 1970, p. 1, Sec. 2; and November 12, 1970, p. 3, Sec. 2. The *Standard*'s report on Hong Kong's growth rate, November 9, 1970, p. 3, Sec. 2, was illuminating. Statistical material on Communist business and other data are from my own sources. The farewell address of the outgoing governor, Sir David Trench, on October 1, 1971, summarizes progress in social affairs.

[36] *Far Eastern Economic Review*, October 31, 1970, p. 54.

barrier of 1971 made further expansion impossible in Pacific Asia. The outpost states can keep going despite the winding down of the Vietnam War and a period of economic adjustment to American needs. In fact, with the establishment of greater stability in Asia, if it is possible, the thriving economies of the region may find new outlets.

Although some American troops still remain in three of the four outpost states, they aren't required. Nor are other forms of American military assistance really necessary, despite the grant of "modernization funds" by the United States to soften the blow of American disengagement. All but the Philippines require little or no American economic aid any longer; for that matter, even the Filipinos could dispense with such assistance if they had the intestinal fortitude to submit to reasonable taxation instead of crying eternally for new loans and tapping the national treasury at election time.

What all the outposts *do* require over the next decade, at the very least, is some reasonable assurance of stabilized relationships with the United States. This they do not have. Time after time, Asian government leaders have told me privately that they cannot depend on Presidential assurances from Washington when they know that a hostile Congress can deny what the Executive branch has promised. Moreover, the public attitude in the United States toward smaller Asian lands is not reassuring.

What it all adds up to is fear of American intentions—fear that the assurances of protection under American treaties of long standing cannot now be taken at face value, fear that in a sticky situation the United States would nullify its most solemn pledges on the ground that they are subject to American Constitutional processes.

The outspoken Joaquin P. (Chino) Roces, publisher of the *Manila Times,* puts it this way: "We have to face many uncertainties, it is true. But what are we to think of the United States? We do not know what you will do from one day to the next and this creates the greatest uncertainty of all."[37]

Linked to the uncertainty of American defense policy in a period of disengagement is the likelihood that a reviving protectionist sentiment in the United States will damage the cause of free trade, which is basic to all the expanding non-Communist economies of Asia. That

[37] In an interview at the Press Foundation of Asia, July 9, 1970.

causes more concern among the border states than continued American troop withdrawals, for the American trade is the breath of life to South Korea, Taiwan and the Philippines and it is today the most important factor in the economy of Hong Kong.

The border states are prepared to do the best they can against Communist-directed campaigns of infiltration and subversion, regardless of their origin. With the exception of Hong Kong, they know they can count on continuing hostility from mainland China; as for the Soviet Union, none expect anything to their benefit from Moscow. If the United States fails them, in consequence, they can turn only to Japan in an extremity and hope for the best.

The test for Washington is whether the border states are to be dealt with fairly and justly over the next ten to fifteen years, or cut adrift to make their own way by whatever means come to hand.

IV. Divided Indochina

1. VISION AND REALITY

Indochina is a land of fabulous promise. Given a sufficient period of peace and stability, it could become one of the richest and most productive areas on earth. Its people—brave and tenacious and self-sacrificing beyond ordinary human capacity—could set an inspiring example of achievement and progress among developing nations.

The Vision

There are many possibilities for postwar development in Indochina. The $4 billion Mekong River development project, a grand-scale Asian TVA, could be brought to completion under the United Nations. A joint ten-year development plan, the dream of American and Vietnamese economists, could repair the ravages of war in other parts of Indochina as well. Offshore oil explorations give promise of new sources of energy and revenue. And through the Asian Development Bank and other agencies, an industrial complex of giant potential could take root in urban areas.

By air and sea, trade could flow into the port areas of a reconstructed Indochina from all parts of the Indo-Pacific and beyond.

And in the beautiful green countryside, with its crisscrossing network of brown rivers and canals, the farmers who have patiently worked the land through decades of internecine conflict and foreign invasion could provide enough food to banish the threat of famine over much of Asia.

This is the vision of men of good will who have witnessed at first hand the suffering and the agony of the people of Indochina through more than thirty years of conflict. But it is far from achievement. Neither pity nor stoic courage nor love of humankind will end the torture of tens of millions of helpless people in Indochina. Nor can any temporary settlement, of the kind that was achieved in Geneva in 1954 and 1962, restore stability throughout the area. It will take nothing less than concerted action by the United States, China and the Soviet Union to make possible a lasting Indochina peace.

The Reality

Having undertaken to retreat from Vietnam after ten years of war, the United States is not likely to relish serving as a guarantor of peace in any part of Indochina. Nor will the American public take kindly to anything less than a clear-cut disengagement from an area that has created so much turmoil and dissension at home. It is all very well for an impatient American citizenry to proclaim, as so many have in all sincerity, that the United States has no vital interest in Indochina. That was said about Europe, too, in Warren Gamaliel Harding's age of normalcy. And George Washington's Farewell Address was quoted at great length as an excellent eighteenth-century guide to the requirements of a great nation that is advancing toward the twenty-first century.

The trouble with the thesis of an advance consensus on what constitutes the national interest is that it does not lie solely in the power of the United States to determine where its interests lie. Certainly, the national interests of the United States in 1919 were not those of 1939. Had it been left to Americans alone, none would have chosen to go to battle during World War II at Guadalcanal, Tarawa, Kwajalein and Iwo Jima. Before December 7, 1941, any American who might have proclaimed a national interest in the Coral Sea would have evoked only incredulous laughter among his fellows. And before that peaceful Sunday of June 25, 1950, not many in the United States could have foreseen a vital national interest in the 38th parallel across Korea that was worth the sacrifice of more than 30,000 American lives in combat. It was something not even the Joint Chiefs of Staff anticipated.

What Is Peace?

Just as the decision on what constitutes the national interest can scarcely be determined by fiat for all eternity, it follows that the restoration of peace to a turbulent area such as Indochina cannot be unilaterally ordained. Peace, in essence, is a cooperative effort to restore tranquillity to the land and its often requires more patience, courage, skill and demonstrable initiative than war.

If the government of the United States has at last discovered that it cannot be the world's policeman, the people of the United States have yet to learn that they cannot bring about peace merely by backing out of a war. After ten years of fighting in Vietnam, the United States can't just quit, say it was all a big mistake, and forget it. For those who make war must also provide the necessities of peace. And this applies just as much to the Soviet Union and China, Hanoi's chief supporters and suppliers, as it does to the United States. An international conference, with official signatures grandiosely affixed on behalf of the high contracting parties, is not enough. Beyond that, the powers directly or indirectly involved in the war will determine— each in its own national interest—whether an enduring peace is possible in that part of the world.

It goes almost without saying that if such a peace is attainable, new ways will have to be found to deal with old Asian rivalries. This Asian thirty-year war can scarcely be concluded in terms of the old balance-of-power tradition that goes back to the end of the Thirty Years' War in Europe. The great powers are always willing to listen to fine speeches about the self-determination of small nations but seldom endorse the concept unless, by some chance, it coincides with policy. And even if one great power does happen to weary of the struggle and pull out, that does not necessarily mean that the rest will follow suit.

In consequence, the best that can be anticipated in Indochina for some time to come is a respite in the destruction of towns and villages and the wanton killing of civilian non-combatants. If the people of Indochina are lucky, they will live for years—as the people of Korea have—in a state of tension in which there is neither peace nor war. But if the great powers and their client states agree only on another temporary respite and then pursue their rivalry with reckless disregard of the consequences, then the Indochina wars can only be a horrible prelude, as was the Spanish Civil War, to a far greater disaster.

What Is Victory?

Victory in Indochina, the chimera that both Communist and non-Communist forces have sought to achieve for three decades, can scarcely be contemplated by either side now except as a kind of Hitlerian madness. If massive American intervention in Vietnam forestalled a Communist take-over between 1965 and 1970, it did not by any means knock North Vietnam out of the war. Nor can North Vietnam look forward to the crushing of its remaining enemies in Indochina without further interference from the United States. For one thing, South Vietnam's army of 1,000,000 troops, 600,000 of them Army regulars, will remain an obstacle to a take-over for the short run. For another, even if North Vietnam's weakened army of 400,000 could seize all of South Vietnam, Laos and Cambodia, the troops would be spread so thin over so vast a territory that they couldn't hold it, or even organize it.

The reality for the early 1970s is that Indochina has been divided between Communist and non-Communist regimes in the manner of Germany and Korea. And if the German and Korean precedents hold, then this is the shape of the future. It is a part of the diplomatic necromancy of our time to talk of running democratic elections in places where democracy has taken shallow root or withered and died and to propose coalition governments to the bitterest of enemies.

Such devices, if accepted, are merely face-saving formulae to avert an open concession of defeat. They have been scornfully rejected by both sides in Korea for almost two decades. They are certainly not regarded with any degree of trust, much less enthusiasm, by either North or South Vietnam or their native allies in Indochina.

I remember that in 1964, when I first went to Saigon, a young American correspondent burst out almost in despair: "Everybody talks of victory—victory. What in hell *is* victory?" The question is still unanswered. Probably there is no good answer. For years, the war in Indochina was one that neither side could win. If it cannot be finally settled by diplomatic means, then it will surely end in utter exhaustion.

The Asian Melting Pot

Indochina is a little larger than Texas, but with almost five times the population. Its long war has inevitably shaped the future of much of Southeast Asia, with 30 per cent more people than there are in the United States compressed into less than half the total area.[1] No region on earth is more turbulent and unstable; it is part of the conventional wisdom of our time that, with few exceptions, the nations of Southeast Asia are unlikely to achieve a real measure of stability for the remainder of this century and a part of the next.

Strife has been the heritage of Southeast Asia for more than 2,000 years. It has been Asia's dark and bloody ground—a prize that was contended for by peoples of many races and diverse beliefs. Here, the best and the worst of the ancient civilizations of China, India and the Malayo-Polynesians of the South Pacific took root. Here, too, Buddhist, Muslim and Christian rivaled each other for power and influence. And when the Asian empires and kingdoms collapsed, the Portuguese and the British, the Dutch and the French, established their colonies on the ruins of the old order only to be driven out at long last by the breaking waves of Japanese power on far distant shores.

In Cambodia are the visible remains of what was once the wondrous Khmer empire. And in central Vietnam will be found the scattered Cham peoples, the descendants of the Hindu Kingdom of Champa that lasted until the fifteenth century. To this day the Thais

[1] In addition to the two Vietnams, Laos and Cambodia, I include in Southeast Asia the countries of Burma, Indonesia, Malaysia, the Philippines, Singapore and Thailand, with a total area of 1,730,000 square miles and a population of 265,000,000. In Indochina alone there are 47,500,000 people in an area of 288,000 square miles—one of the most densely settled regions in the world.

have been able to preserve both their independence and their ancient monarchy, although they have always had to fend off far more powerful foes from the east, west and north. But the warlike Viets and the good-natured Lao, the Malays and Burmese, the Shans and Karens and many another people have not been as fortunate.

Beset by their own interminable feuds, they have weakened themselves. From within and without, their lands have seldom been secure. They have been accustomed to take up the gun as readily as the plow, to turn their hand against their neighbors, to suspect the worst of all foreign influences, and to rely for their lives and their frail fortunes primarily on their kinsmen, their tribes or regional partisans, and sometimes their coreligionists. Few have either known or understood the principles of nationhood; as for democracy, it has existed in the main as something between an affliction and a puzzlement.

The relatively new respect for national boundaries in Southeast Asia has been an additional trial to many of its peoples, for numerous tribal landholdings have extended on both sides of national boundaries and still do. It has complicated life for the Lao, who also live in both Vietnam and Thailand; for the Vietnamese in Cambodia; and for the strange grouping of peoples in the Union of Burma who have never submitted to Burmese sovereignty. Moreover, it has exacerbated the traditional rivalry between the peoples of the valleys and lowlands and the minority groups in the mountains from the hills of western Burma to the lovely sandy beaches of South Vietnam.

While governments in the region have concluded alliances of convenience with neighboring or nearby powers from time to time, these have not in essence changed the way diverse peoples regard each other. The Cambodian has always been fearful of the Thai on the west and the Vietnamese on the east. The Thai have never had much regard for the Burmese. The Lao have feared all their neighbors, and with good reason. During the Sukarno regime, Indonesia waged an undeclared war against Malaysia and the Filipinos seized the occasion to lay claim to Malaysian Sabah (North Borneo).

In every country of Southeast Asia, moreover, the presence of millions of indigenous Chinese (misnamed as "Overseas Chinese") has been another divisive factor. This was the primary reason for the split between Malaysia and Singapore, for Singapore is for all practical purposes a Chinese city; despite that, the numbers of Chinese and Malays in Malaysia today are almost evenly divided and the Chinese may yet become a majority. In Burma, Thailand and the Philippines, the Chinese have also been resented and sometimes mistreated. And in Indonesia, since the abortive Communist coup of 1965 that sought to make Djakarta the southern part of an axis with Peking, the Chinese have been suspect.

With so many conflicts, past and present, there is scant reason for hope of rapid progress toward stability in Southeast Asia. It remains a gigantic melting pot of peoples who, for the most part, cannot easily be fused with one another. During the time when China was encouraging national wars of liberation with ferocious blasts of propaganda from Peking, such a situation was made to order for infiltration and subversion through the use of indigenous forces after the Vietnam pattern. There is nothing to stop China from resuming the pattern at any time.

Outside Indochina, Thailand and Burma are still feeling the effects of Chinese-supported insurgencies. And other nations could well be affected, particularly after the American withdrawal. Such movements are far more effective, and better suited to Peking's purposes, than any bullheaded invasion by swarms of Chinese troops. Such an incursion is just about the last thing that may be expected in Southeast Asia in the foreseeable future.

2. VIETNAM: THE ANATOMY OF RETREAT

Whatever else may be said of the American retreat from South Vietnam, it was well planned, thoroughly organized and effectively conducted. It gave the South Vietnamese ample opportunity to take over the main responsibility for the defense of their country, whether they were able to take advantage of it or not. Without doubt, many American lives were saved. And while the main objective of extricating the United States from its excessive commitments in Asia could not be easily achieved, the ground troop withdrawal represented a beginning even though the air war escalated again in early 1972.

Yet, for all these favorable factors, no American is ever likely to consider this massive pullout as a particularly glorious moment in the history of his country. The retreat in itself cannot, by any means, be regarded as a national disgrace. The American Army was not, after all, defeated in the field and it retired from its mission with a demonstration of soldierly skill. It was not the first time that American troops had fallen back before a resolute foe and it will not be the last. But always, in the past, every withdrawal carried with it the implicit promise of an eventual triumph—a Yorktown for every evacuation of New York City, a Gettysburg for every Bull Run, a victorious crossing of the Rhine for every Bastogne.

. Such prospects never existed in Vietnam because it was a different kind of war—a conflict with a hundred battlefields but no front lines, no solicitude for the international conventions applying to warfare, no immunity for civilians or war correspondents, and no heroes. Every village was a target, every farm a potential strong point, every road a salient that could be used as a mine trap or ambush. It was greatly to the credit of young and untried American soldiers that they proved themselves able to fight such a war on better than equal terms. But it must also be said that not since the War of 1812, and the burning of Washington, D.C., were American troops obliged to withdraw before a foreign foe amid so deep and bitter a division among the American people.

Whose Fault?

Two successive American governments representing each of the major political parties—the Johnson and Nixon Administrations—have laid the blame for the withdrawal primarily on an intransigent and hateful segment of public opinion in the United States. The partisans of peace, in turn, have not hesitated to belabor their government for getting the nation into the Indochina wars and have regarded themselves as public benefactors for insisting on withdrawal. All sides, regardless of their position on the war, have looked askance on the war makers in the Pentagon for deciding in the first instance that it would be practical to escalate the war and then being unable to break the fighting spirit of a tiny country. The military tacticians, to complete the deadly circle, have in a number of individual instances privately blamed the President of the United States for giving in to domestic political pressures instead of supporting the Pentagon in an ever-mounting cycle of war demands. Yet, had either President Johnson or Nixon given in to ill-judged proposals for a national mobilization, American involvement in Vietnam would have been prolonged indefinitely for no good end.

General Matthew B. Ridgway, certainly no dove, wrote at the height of the American withdrawal: "It should not have taken great vision to perceive that a mountainous, jungled area such as Vietnam, devoid of the territorial and electrical communications essential for the operations of a modern army, and with a population bitterly divided and in large part existing under near primitive conditions, would be a morass into which we could endlessly and futilely pour our human and material resources."[2]

Regardless of what the verdict of history eventually will be, the United States as a whole has had to bear the consequences both of defeat and an unfavorable world opinion. As always, the sympathies of the non-combatants have gone to the small nation that has somehow become involved in a conflict with a great power. And this is as true of the publics in nations closely allied with the United States, such as Britain and Japan, as it is of the rival powers in the Communist world, the Soviet Union and China. In the so-called Third World, represented by such nations as India, Yugoslavia, Egypt and the developing lands in sub-Saharan Africa and Latin America, the prestige of the United States has never been so low.

Although the Soviet Union has played a role of unexampled duplicity as Hanoi's chief supplier of war matériel while serving as cochairman with Britain of the Geneva conference that was supposed to guarantee peace in Indochina, Moscow has suffered less blame for the continuation of the war than the United States. This is no miracle of Moscow's propaganda. The Soviet Union has merely taken advantage of a world climate in which everything Hanoi did was right and almost everything Washington did was wrong. Thus, by acting as Hanoi's benefactor, Moscow wrapped about itself the capacious cloak of the good Samaritan, a rather unlikely image for a great power that ruthlessly crushed the Hungarian uprising of 1956 and the bold

[2] *Foreign Affairs*, July, 1971.

"Czech spring" of 1968. But this has been the Soviet Union's good fortune and it has not bothered to look this international gift horse in the mouth.

At a time when all efforts to promote peace in Indochina seemed to be going nowhere, the Soviet government evidently felt so confident of the strength of its position that some of its best-known diplomats did not bother to conceal their pleasure over the American predicament. Thus, when Hubert Horatio Humphrey traveled to Moscow with a United Nations exchange mission in 1969 and implored the editor of *Pravda* to ask his government to end the war, gleeful Soviet journalists circulated the tale all over Moscow. One diplomatic commentator, always in the good graces of the Kremlin, told me with a broad grin, "Mr. Humphrey should have addressed himself to Hanoi, not to the editor of *Pravda*. *Pravda* does not control North Vietnam."

It was a typical Soviet attitude. Two years before China sent up signals for an international conference on the war, the Soviet ambassador to the United Nations, Jacob A. Malik, briefly raised that possibility but quickly dropped it. Evidently, Moscow didn't like the notion. Thereafter, for a long time, the only answer that Moscow gave to pleas for its intercession as a mediator in the Vietnam War was to direct them to the Paris peace talks. It was no part of Soviet policy to help the United States out of its Vietnam predicament. The upshot was the American decision to turn to China, then also annoyed by Soviet intransigence on common problems, in the hope of doing better.

The Lessons of Paris

To those who have had some contact with the Vietnam War, it seems sometimes as if an age had passed since the start of the long discussions between the North Vietnamese and the United States in Paris beginning May 10, 1968. How great hope then was, in the atmosphere of Lyndon Johnson's renunciation of the Presidency and his order to end the bombing over most of North Vietnam! If months were frittered away in aimless discussion, it didn't seem to matter. People of good will assured each other that the main thing was accomplished—the negotiators were in place and were meeting face to face. If anything, the hope for a quick peace increased with the cessation of bombing over all North Vietnam on November 1, 1968, and Richard Nixon's election. For in 1969, the peace talks were expanded to include South Vietnam and the National Liberation Front, the political arm of the Vietcong.

After the passage of three years, however, the American public began to realize at long last that hope alone was not enough to bring peace to a sorely beset land. It became clear that North Vietnam and the Vietcong were holding out resolutely at the conference table for the victory that they could not attain by warlike means. No great diplomatic perspicacity was required to see that Hanoi and the Vietcong aimed first of all at getting American troops out of Vietnam, then taking over the Saigon government by one means or another.

From the interminable arguments over the shape of the negotiating table in Paris to the timetable for American withdrawal and the release of American prisoners of war, nothing gave the United States any reason to believe in the good faith of the other side. At length, after China indicated it would take a more significant role in the proceedings, the deadlock finally showed signs of loosening. But the procedures of Paris taught the United States once again that it could never negotiate successfully from weakness, only from strength. And in Vietnam, American strength long since had been dissipated.

A visit to the Hotel Majestic in Paris during the American pullout was an exercise in futility and disillusionment. Where once the delegates had had to fight their way past eager platoons of reporters and photographers from the world press, few except curiosity seekers came to watch them enter and leave the staid old gray stone conference salon for all of 1970 and much of 1971. The press briefings were static most of the time; where nothing happens, there is nothing to say. Ambassadors and other functionaries came and went without a change in the position of either side for weeks on end. And when a change was announced, it was at that period more shadow than substance. For the emphasis in Paris, from the beginning, was not on peace but on an American capitulation.

This kind of war was the bequest of Ho Chi Minh to his tenacious and confident successors in Hanoi. It was the pattern of conflict he had ordained—the adaptation of Mao Tse-tung's alternate practice of fighting and talking until the enemy's will could be broken. In Ho's lexicon of combat, as in Mao's, there was no middle way; each of them was prepared to go to any length to attain his goal. It was the way Ho had beaten the French. It was the way his successors determined they would beat the Americans.

High Tide for the Vietcong

I remember flying north to the Kontum area in the summer of 1964 with General William C. Westmoreland, then the American commander in South Vietnam, to see what the condition of the country was at first hand. It was a time when Washington's once-confident predictions of victory were being muted, when one incapable government after another was being tried in Saigon after the overthrow and assassination of Ngo Dinh Diem.

Near Kontum, we saw a well-fortified South Vietnamese base that had been abandoned by its defenders and overrun by the Vietcong. A young American officer, one of the 16,000 advisers the United States was then maintaining in Vietnam, told simply and unemotionally how he had tried to rally his men. But only a handful of Montagnards—hard-fighting tribesmen from the mountains—had helped him hold off the enemy. In less than an hour, outmatched and outfought, they also had been obliged to give up the unequal battle; with their American adviser, they had just been able to save themselves.

This kind of thing was then going on all over South Vietnam. For a proud soldier, Westmoreland's hallmark as a commander, such experiences were difficult to bear; at that time, he was calling repeatedly on the Pentagon for massive American reinforcements. It was obvious to him, as to those with much less military knowledge, that the South Vietnamese Army was no match for either the Vietcong or the North Vietnamese regulars who then were just beginning to come south.

The countryside, in large part, already belonged to the Vietcong. Most of the major highways and all the smaller roads were under enemy control. No one could guarantee the safety of military convoys that moved along the ground; for insurance, supplies to hard-pressed outposts had to be sent by air. Desertions from the South Vietnamese Army were rising daily under these dolorous circumstances. It was apparent that the end was not far distant unless the United States decided to intervene in force. And that being the period of the 1964 Presidential campaign, Lyndon Johnson could not make up his mind to the insistent demands of the Pentagon.

The air of impending crisis enveloped even Saigon, still a pleasant and rather leisurely city then, with its tree-lined streets and red-roofed villas in the tradition of the French provincial towns it so greatly resembled. By night, the Vietcong were able to roam the city with very little trouble. It was a rare South Vietnamese soldier or Saigon policeman who challenged them, even when they were identified, which wasn't too often. A considerable share of the populace in South Vietnam's capital city was pretty well convinced by this time of the eventual triumph of Ho Chi Minh. If he had been able to defeat the French in an eight-year war between 1946 and 1954, he also seemed to have a pretty good chance of beating the Americans, who had intervened in 1961. For most South Vietnamese, in any event, it didn't pay to incur the ill will of the Vietcong. Their retribution could be sudden and swift.

Disgruntled Americans in Saigon often asked each other, "Why is it that Ho's Vietnamese fight and ours don't?" Obviously, it wasn't for lack of fighting ability. The two millennia of Vietnamese history were sufficient evidence of that. A people who had been able to free themselves of nearly 1,000 years of Chinese domination and had defeated the legions of Kublai Khan could scarcely be accused, in whole or in part, of lack of courage or martial spirit.

But being an eminently practical people as well, the Vietnamese saw no point in siding with a losing government in Saigon. Nor did the regime itself do anything at that period to persuade them to the contrary. Its position had deteriorated to such an extent that it had to pay demonstrators to take part in its thinly attended anti-Communist rallies. There was mass evasion of military service in the South Vietnamese Army through corruption, desertion and sheer neglect. The government could not summon up enough gumption to order a general mobilization. It also side-stepped the imposition of every other necessary but unpopular war measure for fear that its rule would be totally discredited.

This, then, was the disorganized and well-nigh chaotic land that the

United States military leadership had determined to save from Communist domination. The enormity of the self-deception that was practiced by so many patriotic and well-meaning American officials at the time came through clearly to any disinterested observer who chanced to be in Saigon. For this was the period when a covert war was being waged at American direction against North Vietnam, when the provocative destroyer patrols already were under way in Tonkin Gulf that resulted in the attacks of August 2–4 in Tonkin Gulf and the passage by Congress of a prefabricated resolution authorizing retaliatory action.

No great nation has ever constructed such a gigantic booby trap for itself and jumped in with such a triumphant whoop.

New Times in Saigon

If the massive American intervention of 1965 and 1966 frustrated a Communist take-over of South Vietnam at that period, it contributed very little to the process of nation-building. This was something the South Vietnamese had to do for themselves and they had little stomach for it. While American bombers dropped their lethal loads over North Vietnam and American ground troops came pouring into Southeast Asia, the governmental process in Saigon remained well-nigh paralyzed. It was not a happy augury, but the American genius for avoiding unpleasant realities evaded the issue. The bombing statistics and the enemy body counts, both heavily influenced by military mythology, were put out at regular intervals for the news media, as if to show once again that victory in Vietnam was just around the corner.

It wasn't. From 16,000 military personnel in 1964, the American troop total went to 184,000 in 1965 and 385,000 in 1966, with 33,000 additional troops taking over the supposedly secret bases in Thailand from which the big B-52 bombers operated against North Vietnam. It was in 1966 that Ho Chi Minh rejected a secret peace feeler from the United States, more than sufficient testimony to North Vietnam's staying power.

By 1967, both President Johnson and his Secretary of Defense, Robert Strange McNamara, developed serious private misgivings about the course on which they had so enthusiastically put their country. On April 27, the President pathetically demanded of his advisers, "When we add divisions, can't the enemy add divisions? If so, where does it all end?" And McNamara wrote on May 19, "The picture of the world's greatest super power killing or seriously injuring 1,000 noncombatants a week, while trying to pound a tiny backward nation into submission on an issue whose merits are hotly disputed, is not a pretty one. It could conceivably produce a costly distortion in the American national consciousness and in the world image of the United States—especially if the damage to North Vietnam is complete enough to be 'successful.' "

The damage was bad enough, as eyewitnesses such as Harrison Salisbury of *The New York Times* were able to report from Hanoi, but the prospects of American success—if that is what it could be called—were as far off as they had been in 1961. At the end of 1967, American combat troops in South Vietnam totaled nearly 475,000— more than the American forces that had fought in Korea. American casualties since 1961 in this "crummy war" had been 15,000 killed in action and 110,000 wounded. The material cost, as President Johnson himself admitted in his State of the Union message of January 17, 1968, was $25 billion a year.

But there still was no South Vietnamese nation of substance, the only real bulwark against absorption by the North. At that stage, the Saigon government had had almost three years to train an effective army and build a better country, one that its people would want to fight to defend. There was appallingly little to show for all the sacrifices the United States had made. The flashy and voluble Air Force commander, Nguyen Cao Ky, had become premier on June 19, 1965, supported by a National Directorate of military leaders under the chairmanship of General Nguyen Van Thieu. It was the ninth government since the assassination of Diem and the only one that had shown any sign of staying power. Amid the most profound skepticism by both the populace and the foreign correspondents, the Ky government held elections on September 11, 1966, for an Assembly that was to draw up a new constitution for a civilian government. Of the 117 members elected, 35 were regarded as Catholic representatives, 34 were Buddhists, 10 were adherents of a native sect, Hoa Hao, and 5 of another sect, Cao Dai, with the rest scattered among smaller groups. By nationality, the majority turned out to be ethnic Vietnamese, 104 out of 117, the rest being Montagnards, Khmer and Cham. The only people who really were disenfranchised were the indigenous 1,000,000 Chinese, some 600,000 of them in Cholon, Saigon's twin city. They prudently preferred not to protest.

This Constitutional Assembly, admittedly an American experiment in exporting Western civilization to an Oriental land that wasn't ready for it, had a tremendous task. It was a forum, first of all, for the airing of differences between the religious, political and ethnic groups in South Vietnam. It also was the only democratically chosen body that could conceivably tackle the confusing—even overwhelming—issues of war and peace.

More than sixty registered political parties were then in existence in South Vietnam and at least thirty that were unregistered—a testimonial to the complexity of the nation-building process for these 17,500,000 people. Old feuds had to be resolved, old differences had to be dissipated. And confidence had to be created in a new and untried national government.

The Buddhists Go Along

The position of the Buddhists, as everyone realized, was critical; through their opposition, they had been the key to Diem's downfall. Their refusal to cooperate also had caused the collapse of most of the governments that had followed him. The Buddhist power base was concentrated on the 35 per cent of the Vietnamese population south of the 17th parallel that actively practiced Buddhism and heeded its leadership.[3] These 6,000,000 people constituted a majority of the electorate.

In the absence of a census or any other authoritative calculation, the best available data divided the remainder of the South Vietnamese approximately as follows: Catholics and the native sects, Hoa Hao and Cao Dai, about 1,500,000 each; Montagnards and Chinese, about 1,000,000 each; Nationalist Party (Vietnam Quoc Dan Dang) and

---

[3] The usual statistic is that 80 per cent of South Vietnam is Buddhist, which may be true, but the practicing Buddhists are closer to 35 per cent. The dominant religion, Cult of the Ancestors, is also practiced by numerous Buddhists but it is generally thought of as non-political in character.

Khmer, about 500,000 each; Confederation of Vietnamese Workers, 400,000 to 500,000 (with some duplication in the others); Greater Nationalist Party (Dai Viet Quoc Dan Dang), 200,000; Cham, 50,000; and the rest scattered.

On the basis of the new constitution that this Assembly produced, the first national South Vietnamese election on September 3, 1967, made General Nguyen Van Thieu the president and Marshal Ky the vice-president of the country. These results were expected. What was not anticipated was the rather lopsided constitution of the upper house of the National Legislature, or Senate, in which Catholics took 29 of 60 seats and Buddhists received only an estimated 15. It wasn't a very promising start, but the October elections for the 137-seat lower house appeared to be more representative, with a choice of about 65 Buddhists, 35 Catholics, 13 Hoa Hao and the rest scattered.

In any event, the Buddhists decided to go along. The wearisome but necessary democratic processes of coalition and trading began among the various blocs. President Thieu, who had at first been looked upon as a potential military dictator, began to show a little evidence of political responsibility. But of charisma, the magic human touch that had always been the strength of Ho Chi Minh, he had none. Cheering crowds could not be expected to go swarming through the streets of Saigon to hail Nguyen Van Thieu; nor, for that matter, would women fight to touch the hem of his coat. This small, taciturn military careerist had too much to answer for. His power base, such as it was, rested primarily on his support by the Americans and his own military associates, plus his trading strength with the various blocs in the National Assembly. As time went on, he raised up powerful enemies against his continued rule, one being his own vice-president, Nguyen Cao Ky, and the other the leader of the uprising against Diem, General Duong Van Minh, better known as "Big Minh."

South Vietnam after Tet

All the latent hostility between the disparate groups in South Vietnam intensified after Ho Chi Minh's devastating Tet offensive— the attack on Saigon and thirty provincial capitals in South Vietnam that coincided with the Tet (or New Year's holiday) truce beginning the night of January 30–31, 1968. And the United States, at last, had to face up to the fact that it was supporting a weak, corrupt, ineffective and unpopular regime. The upshot was increased American pressure on the Thieu government to take a greater share in the fighting of the war, something that had never aroused much enthusiasm among the warriors of Saigon. National mobilization resulted, leading to the creation of an army that added up on paper to 1,000,000 troops, 600,000 regulars and the rest militia. True, it could not be developed overnight into a fearsome fighting force, but its divided leadership now saw that they would have to make something of their army or go down before the Communist onslaught.

If South Vietnam reeled under the shock of Tet, the United States was absolutely stunned. On American television, the home front saw Ho's bold invaders storming the American embassy in Saigon and shooting their way past both American and South Vietnamese defenders. It was almost unbelievable that this could happen to the greatest military power on earth, with a large army in combat and a massive air force bombing the northern enemy night and day. But there it was, for all the United States and all the world to see.

President Johnson's capitulation on March 31, 1968, when he signaled the end of the bombing campaign and called for peace talks, was something more than a personal tragedy. For by bowing out simultaneously as a candidate for re-election, he showed how greatly the American government had forfeited the trust of the American people in the conduct of the Vietnam War. Hanoi had taken terrible losses during the Tet offensive, it is true, but the psychological result had been worth the risk. The American campaign in South Vietnam had been blunted. From then on, the United States role in the war would be winding down.

It was, Hanoi perceived, only a matter of time before South Vietnam would have to fight alone.

The Pacification Program

After Tet, the always thin covering of South Vietnamese agents in the countryside was ripped to shreds and had to be rewoven in an entirely new and more effective pattern. For here, eventually, was where the fate of South Vietnam would finally be determined.

The essential South Vietnamese program for this movement was called Pacification and Development, noble terms that had often been used before in its publicity. This time, there was a difference. Both the Regional Forces in the provinces and the Popular Forces in the village areas, which had been indifferently manned on a part-time basis, now became the responsibility of full-time combat troops. The soldiers were given modern arms, including M-16 rifles, uniforms, tactical training by American teams, and major support from regular Vietnamese Army units. For the first time, the Vietcong village and provincial forces were being given more than mere paper opposition.

For the United States, this was the crucial part of the post-Tet campaign. More than 10,000 key military personnel and about 1,000 civilians were assigned to work in the districts and provinces in active cooperation with South Vietnamese troops. Mobile advisory teams were set to move up wherever they were needed. Village and provincial development funds were placed at the disposal of local councils, whether elected or appointed, to show they that they had a stake in the success of the Saigon government and to stimulate the spread of local projects, from school building to irrigation. In 1970 alone, $44.2 million was expended on such work by the United States through an agency known as Civil Operations and Rural Development Support (CORDS). It was only a small part, however, of the CORDS total mission, which cost in excess of $1.5 billion for 1970.

The Undercover War

The Vietcong Infrastructure (VCI) in the provinces and villages, through which the guerrillas had been protected, fed, housed and supplied for many years, soon came under attack from the hamlets of the delta to the northermost provinces. Where it had once been impossible to obtain the cooperation of any but a handful of local people, the new dispensation brought about a change. The reversal was not dramatic. Far from it. After a quarter century of almost unimpeded occupation, the Vietcong could not be chased into the mountains and across the border quickly, despite optimistic claims to the contrary.

Some roads, long closed, began to open up. More schools functioned. Village market days were better attended. And a few more community leaders began offering to serve as village chiefs, appointed or elected, although Vietcong harassment, attack and even assassination continued at a reduced rate.

If more of the South Vietnamese countryside was now safer by day, it still was a gamble to be very venturesome at night. The Vietcong still threatened numerous villages. And the North Vietnamese Army units were still in action. In 1969, for example, more than 6,000 people were killed in terrorist attacks and 15,000 were wounded. The dead included 90 village chiefs and other officials, 240 hamlet chiefs and officials, 229 refugees and 4,350 of the general populace. The rate continued at that level for the next two years, with a total of 2,143 persons reported killed, wounded or abducted by terrorists in May 1971.

Still, CORDS tried to put a good face on the pacification program, contending that 95 per cent of the 2,151 villages and 94 per cent of the 10,522 hamlets in South Vietnam had popularly elected governments. What the Vietcong did to them was something else again.

Whatever improvement the South Vietnamese regime was able to make in the southern and coastal regions, the vast central highlands remained a happy hunting ground for the Vietcong. In mid-1971, the United States conceded that fewer than half the 3,000 hamlets in these 12 provinces and only 62 per cent of the 3,000,000 people were regarded as securely under control of the Saigon regime.

John Paul Vann, a veteran American adviser, said of the area: "We don't have pacification here. What we have is military occupation . . . The government of South Vietnam is not admired or respected by the people. But it is hated less than the enemy."

After the withdrawal of 65,000 American troops from the highlands, it was obvious that South Vietnamese forces would have trouble going it alone. With rising Vietcong assaults, the evidence showed that Saigon's problem of finding courageous and responsible leaders for its provincial forces in the highlands would become the most critical of all.

Operation Phoenix

One of the most controversial parts of the pacification program was known as Operation Phoenix, an anti-subversion campaign that

was aimed at rooting out the Vietcong's Infrastructure in the countryside. There had been rumors for years that the Vietcong's assassination tactics had been used with the knowledge of CORDS officials.
But until such admissions were made before a House subcommittee
by William E. Colby, an ex-CIA operative who directed CORDS
operations from 1968 to 1971, the American public knew nothing of
this particular cloak-and-dagger venture.

In his testimony on July 19, 1971, in Washington, Colby conceded
that there had been "occasional" political assassinations and killings
of suspected Vietcong agents in South Vietnam, but he argued that
Operation Phoenix was not a cover for a program of general assassination. He said unjustifiable abuses had been halted but added,
"There are some other things that are not ideal that we are associated
with in Vietnam." He testified that the death total under Operation
Phoenix was 20,587, of whom 3,560 were killed in 1971 and 8,191 in
1970. In Saigon, the unofficial totals were higher.

This, in the phrasing of the American government, was the nature
of the operation that was "designed to protect the Vietnamese people
from terrorism and political, paramilitary, economic and subversive
pressure from the Communist clandestine organization in Vietnam."
It was not very pretty, but then not much of what went on in South
Vietnam was very satisfying to the American people as the war
wound down.

Would the South Vietnamese government be able to hold the
countryside? It was still an enormous gamble. In the words of one
official in mid-1971: "We are holding our own on the Vietcong
Infrastructure. But the other side is still better at improving and
expanding it than we are at whittling it down."

A New Phase in the War

The brief but effective American-led strike into enemy sanctuaries
in Cambodia in the spring of 1970, which created such revulsion
among peace groups and in the universities of the United States,
actually enhanced the pacification drive in South Vietnam. For one
thing, it deprived both the North Vietnamese Army and the Vietcong
of an immune shelter and supply area that had sustained them for
many years. For another, it closed—for the time being—the water

supply route through Cambodian territory from the port of Kompong Som (Sihanoukville), obliging Hanoi to channel both troops and matériel along the much-bombed overland network of roads known as the Ho Chi Minh Trail. As enemy forces had to be shifted to meet new circumstances, pressures eased on Saigon and the Mekong Delta area. The centers of warfare moved northward toward the 17th parallel and westward into Cambodia.

Then came the South Vietnamese offensive against the Ho Chi Minh Trail itself in what should have been a crippling blow to the enemy supply line. In the United States, the Laos invasion in early 1971 was represented at the beginning as a master stroke by Saigon's underrated fighting forces. It turned out to be considerably less than that, for after forty-four days the South Vietnamese Army was lucky to escape from Laos without being cut to pieces. Had not United States air power held off the North Vietnamese, the affair might have turned into a disaster. It was a less than brilliant manifestation of President Nguyen Van Thieu's military planning and leadership. Worse still, it caused even the most optimistic of American military planners to see that the Nixon Vietnamization program—the waging of the war by the South Vietnamese themselves—was in a lot more trouble than Washington was willing to admit.

Taken together, the military drives into Cambodia and Laos should have disrupted enemy communications and supplies for at least a year and made possible a more rapid withdrawal of American troops. As it turned out, the North Vietnamese Army probably was not seriously inconvenienced for more than a few months at most. The threat to Cambodia, Laos and the northern portions of South Vietnam was far from eased, as North Vietnam's spring offensive in 1972 soon established. Thieu was in deep trouble.

Throughout South Vietnam, the truth had always been difficult to come by. As the American pullout intensified, neither Washington nor Saigon made it any easier to arrive at a reasonable evaluation of South Vietnam's position. Far from encouraging an outburst of candor among those in authority, the publication of the Pentagon Papers, with their record of evasion and deceit, created an almost conspiratorial atmosphere in Saigon.

For those who were willing to accept the theory of a computerized war, the American Hamlet Evaluation System provided an endless belt of statistics that could be used in any number of ways. For example, the HES statistic for 1967 was that 62.1 per cent of the people of South Vietnam lived "under government protection" while toward the end of 1970 that figure went to 92.8 per cent. However, any tyro at war reporting could have punctured that soggy balloon of a phrase, "under government protection." What it really meant was that a village or hamlet could be counted as "secure" for as long as government forces remained in it; once they moved out, the Vietcong could and did come back.

There was no doubt that things had improved in the great rice basket of South Vietnam, in which one-third of its people lived, the Mekong Delta area. For years, it had been a rallying place of the Vietcong. As late as 1968, Highway 4 from Saigon had been under enemy control, with mines and ambushes imperiling South Vietnamese Army truck movements. The Vietcong tax collectors could impose their levies on the delta farmers with impunity at that time. And the delta's youth were impressed into the enemy's service by the thousands.

All that changed after the Cambodian invasion of 1970, but only for a limited time. By July 1971, an American survey disclosed both the Vietcong and the North Vietnamese Army again were active in the delta following the American pullout and the South Vietnamese pacification effort there was slumping. There was considerable question, therefore, not only over the Saigon government's claim of controlling 80 per cent of the delta area but also over the effectiveness of the entire Vietnamization program. After all, between 200,000 and 250,000 North Vietnamese troops and their Vietcong allies were still in action south of the 17th parallel and the infiltration rate was still running at a pace of 50,000 to 70,000 troops a year. Hanoi still packed a punch.

In general, in the early part of 1972, the Communist side still held the scantily populated and less accessible mountain areas in large part and seemed to have a fair chance as well of detaching some of the northern provinces of South Vietnam. The South Vietnamese held the heavily populated Region III around Saigon and the coastal areas, but even here security was dropping off in the wake of the

American evacuation. Despite claims of over-all progress for the pacification program, the evidence didn't substantiate it.

Change Comes to Saigon

The changes of war were disheartening in Saigon. Returning to that once-pleasant city for the first time in six years during the summer of 1970, my wife and I could not help but notice that if security was up, civility was down and the quality of life was best symbolized by a cat clawing through a garbage heap.

Except for the soldiers who aimlessly wandered the streets and the fleets of madly spluttering Vietnamese motorbikes, the center of Saigon was much as we remembered it—only filthier and shabbier. Tu Do and Le Loi, the main streets, were so ripped up that it was difficult to use the sidewalks. On these and other main thoroughfares, the little "blue bullets"—the old French Renault taxis—were even more decrepit than we had remembered, but the drivers were just as reckless as ever.

In this war capital of 2,000,000 people, there was no society worthy of the name. A kind of glum anarchy seemed to have taken hold. The sidewalk shops were loaded with contraband, from cigarettes to watches, cameras and even more expensive items. The food was very high (for those who chose to stay out of the black market and live at the legal rate of exchange) in the most modest restaurants. For our first two meals after arriving from Tan Son Nhut Airport, my wife and I had a small omelet for lunch and a very tough bit of steak for dinner and the two meals—without cocktails or wine—cost more than $25.

The American troop withdrawal program had already taken effect at the time and the local newspapers were full of accounts of Saigon bars and brothels falling on hard times. However, many were still open. The prostitutes were thick in the Tu Do bars and also worked the side streets. Boys and little street girls peddled everything from black market piastres to marijuana and, so we were told, heroin. The Saigon police were seldom to be seen. Nor did they appear to have much authority when they did show up. They were bored by the black market, somewhat amused by the prostitutes and indifferent to the drug peddlers. It was a part of Saigon's way of life.

Outside the Joint United States Public Affairs Office (JUSPAO), just off Le Loi, there were bales of rolled-up barbed wire and long rows of very heavy cement castings three feet each in circumference and three feet high—a buffer zone for riot control. Inside, a yawning GI guard was shining his shoes.

On the terrace of the old Continental Hotel, not a very safe place six years before, the apéritif, tea and Coke drinkers were crowded together in uncomfortable and joyless disarray while little children sidled and crawled among them, begging with outstretched hands. The waiters were morose misanthropes, clearly considering the customers to be unmitigated nuisances, and perhaps some of them were. But it was difficult to sit in such a place and talk, let alone think, for the roar of the motorbikes was continual and hammered against the brain. As we departed, we were told by a solitary good-natured soul to keep away from the river, particularly after dark, because no one was safe there any longer.

We were staying at the Hotel Caravelle, a Vietcong bombers' target in 1964 but now perfectly safe, shabby, dull and—like everything else in Saigon—run-down and expensive. There, we met a young American correspondent, a friend for some years, who showed us bruises where he had been beaten up by Vietnamese police while watching an anti-war demonstration the previous week. It was the first time he had been hurt in three years as a war correspondent both here and in the Middle East. At the American embassy, when I casually mentioned the incident, I was told that a lot more of such bestiality could be expected as the American presence lessened. It was the kind of special resentment that Americans encountered toward the end of the Korean War in Seoul, which they had also liberated.

Up the tree-lined Tu Do, the Vietnamese military were guarding one of their headquarters, clad in helmets, flak jackets and combat boots, rifles held at the ready, behind bale after bale of barbed wire. It is a good question whether they feared anti-war demonstrators or the Vietcong; certainly, in all the time I was in Saigon, there wasn't even a whisper to indicate a Vietcong presence. The main action had shifted to Cambodia for the time being, with Saigon receiving only an occasional rocket or small street attack spaced at a considerable interval from each other.

Yet, outwardly, Saigon still resembled a city in a state of siege. Despite all the official talk about the war "moving west" and the appearance of confidence in the South Vietnamese Army, neither the South Vietnamese government nor the retreating United States forces let down their guard. One Tet surprise attack was enough. Extreme caution was still the rule. From President Nguyen Van Thieu's palace to the American embassy, and from Tan Son Nhut Airport to MAC-V Headquarters, the military presence was overwhelming; in many places, the sidewalks were so jammed with barbed wire that people had to walk in the streets and take their chances with the charging motorcycles.

Just about the only place in central Saigon that got along without its complement of military police and their surveillance of all visitors was the old red brick French cathedral. Two solitary beggars squatted outside, hands outstretched. In the gloomy interior, four worshipers and a nun knelt in silent devotion. A few candles flickered on the altar. A priest walked by slowly, his head bent and his eyes half-closed. It was a small and solitary island of peace in Saigon. Once outside again, the roar from the motorbike exhausts was deafening.

A Defiant Regime

All about the official quarters of General Tran Thien Khiem, who had become prime minister effective September 1, 1969, troops, machine guns and barbed wire were massed in such a jumbled array that a single well-placed enemy rocket would have taken a heavy toll. It was a reminder, if any were needed, of the military character of President Thieu's regime and the emphasis that he and his chief associate, the Prime Minister, put on their personal security. Vice-President Ky already had split with his chief about the oncoming presidential election, and was not in evidence in the upper echelons of the government. Nor was the other prominent military rebel, General Duong Van Minh—"Big Minh"—any more popular with his erst-while colleagues.

Defiance was the hallmark of the Thieu regime. It was perfectly apparent that the men around the President were more interested in strengthening their position than in participating in a search for some form of coalition with the Vietcong. Syngman Rhee had never compromised in Korea. Why should they?

Naturally, as Prime Minister Khiem told me during a rather extensive discussion, the South Vietnamese government realized it would have to put its own house in order with the speed-up of the American withdrawal. But in almost the same breath he insisted that massive economic help from the United States was urgently needed and that American military support in one form or another would have to continue for the foreseeable future. A precipitous American pullout, he said, would have the effect of turning Southeast Asia over to the Communists.

It was a position that his chief, the President, frequently took in public. In private conversation, the appeal for continued American assistance was even more strenuous and insistent, based, as it was, on a kind of unwavering anti-Communist posture that had been so welcome in the United States of the early 1950s. The Saigon leadership seemed to be aware that the American public no longer responded automatically to such a stimulus and the American government was similarly disenchanted. But both Thieu and Khiem continued to gamble on the favorable disposition of the United States to shore up their government. It was not a policy that was calculated to pay dividends much longer for either the United States or South Vietnam.

The Declining Economy

The weakest point in South Vietnam's position at the outset of the 1970s was its economy, which was based on an artificial valuation of the piastre at 118 for $1 while the black market rate was no less than 400 to $1. It was an open invitation to corruption, a plague in almost every Asian land, and particularly in South Vietnam. From the moment of arrival at Tan Son Nhut Airport, a smugglers' paradise, the traveler noticed all kinds of illegal transactions that casehardened Vietnamese didn't bother to conceal. It was the way they chose to do business and they didn't care who knew it. As for their attitude toward Americans, it was a rather sordid mixture of indifference and contempt.

Basically, the trouble with the Vietnamese economy was that the war-paralyzed land could produce very little—a mere $15 million in exports to the United States in fiscal 1970 as compared with $600 million in American imports. Over all, the adverse trade balance ran as high as $800 million, according to conservative unofficial estimates, and it would have surprised nobody in 1971 if it had gone over $1 billion.

In consequence, the cost of living soared all over South Vietnam, but worse in Saigon than anywhere else. In a single year, living costs in the land went up almost 50 per cent, canceling out a 20 per cent general pay increase for the government's civil servants and troops. Visitors found that a cab ride from the airport to town cost $8; a shorter ride, $2; tea or coffee, 90 cents a cup; Coca-Cola, 60 cents a small bottle; a tough piece of bony chicken, $4; a glass of canned orange juice, tasting of tin, $1; a cup of watered consommé, $1.25; a badly printed Vietnamese newspaper, 25 cents; a glass of badly brewed and tepid local beer, 45 cents; a motorized bicycle, more than $700.

President Thieu tried to help matters in October 1970 by instituting what he called a partial devaluation of the piastre to 275 for $1, but at the same time he retained the 118-for-$1 rate for what he called intergovernmental transactions and Defense Department funds spent in Vietnam. It was typical of him and his administration that he gave the appearance of yielding a little ground but still tried to preserve his own advantage. On the black market, after this shadow devaluation, the piastre went up and was headed for even greater heights of inflation. The Saigon government, ever dilatory, could not summon the will to take prompt and drastic measures to clamp on higher taxes, assure more stringent tax collections and mount a real attack on black market operations.

What the Thieu regime did do in March 1971 was to increase the price of imported rice by 40 per cent; imported sugar, 100 per cent; wheat flour and cement, 40 per cent; and boost the cost of all other imported commodities in general by applying the 275-to-$1 piastre rate to all foreign freight. Treasury bond rates were raised 100 per cent and government subsidies to all public enterprises were abolished. Instead of increasing income taxes to give the government more revenue, President Thieu exempted all civil servants and members of the armed forces from the levy for the duration of the war. It was a prelude to mounting inflation in South Vietnam, which caused the government to devalue the piastre to more than 400 to $1 at the end of 1971.

For the average South Vietnamese who had a few piastres, the objective was to buy something—almost anything—for he knew his money was bound to depreciate still further in value. Despite all palliatives, it was a situation that was bound to continue for as long as the South Vietnamese economy remained flat on its back.

Had it not been for massive American financial support in the face of the troop withdrawal, there is no doubt whatever that the South Vietnamese government would have collapsed in the summer of 1971. It was for this reason that the American embassy continually predicted that more American money would have to be poured into the stricken land even after the last American combat soldier went home.

If the Saigon government's land reform program had been as effective as the claims that were made for it, the rural areas could have made considerable progress and would have been in much better shape than the cities. But the blessings of land reform, up to the end of 1971, were not equally spread throughout the land. For one thing, the bureaucracy was painfully slow about distributing new titles to farms once the reforms were instituted. For another, the old prejudice of the plainsmen against the hill people, so prevalent in Vietnam, was very much in evidence. The Montagnards, the mountain people, received on the whole nowhere near the benefits that were given to the Vietnamese in the valleys.

But benefits, one way or the other, didn't mean much to any Vietnamese. Fertilizer costs had gone up 50 per cent between 1970 and 1971; agricultural machinery, 150 per cent; industrial fuel, 40 per cent, when it could be obtained; and gasoline, 10 per cent. It would have taken the yield of at least twenty acres of rice paddy if a farmer had wanted to buy a medium-sized tractor, reason enough for continued reliance on the age-old backbreaking methods of farming with primitive implements.

Under such circumstances, it was a mockery to predict, as well-fed pro-government economists did from time to time, that South Vietnam could be put on its feet very quickly once the fighting ended. As far as the average Vietnamese was concerned, whether he lived in the city or the countryside, it was a triumph merely to be alive.

The Heroin Plague

Disillusion came with disengagement for Americans and Vietnamese in South Vietnam. If most Americans were pretty well fed up with Vietnamese incompetence and the Vietnamese were hard hit by the American withdrawal, both were at each other's throats over the indiscriminate peddling of heroin to American troops. It was the single most divisive conflict between the allies in the latter stages of this ever unfortunate war. For the plague of heroin deeply affected governments as well as users, the home front in the United States as well as the troop centers where the remaining Americans were waiting impatiently to leave a country for which few had either affection or even respect. Some high officials and military commanders in both the South Vietnamese and Laotian regimes were accused of complicity in the heroin traffic, but proving such charges was manifestly difficult. The upshot was increasing resentment and bitterness against the Americans in both Saigon and Vientiane.

President Thieu was importuned by the American embassy and the American military to do something to cut the mounting flow of hard drugs to American troops. He appointed a task force, which was about as effective as throwing a bag of sand on a levee to check a raging flood. President Nixon in mid-1971 then ordered what he called a "national offensive" to deal with the heroin epidemic, but that turned out to be a long-term proposition of choking off the supply at the source. For the addicted soldiers, what it amounted to was an offer of treatment for those who were found to be habitual users.

The measure of the high-level response indicated the extent of public shock in the United States. To a nation that had so freely and gaily violated the law to nullify a Constitutional prohibition against liquor, the use of habit-forming drugs somehow had always seemed to be obscene. That was why, when the first reports were printed and broadcast in the United States of the use of marijuana by newly arrived American combat soldiers in Vietnam, the first public response was disbelief, then indignation. But the younger generation of Americans seemed to enjoy experimenting with marijuana and not many saw anything wrong with it; the smoking of pot, in consequence, became fairly widespread in the American armed forces because the weed was so cheap and so easily obtained in Vietnam.

From that beginning, the plague of heroin—called scag in Vietnam—took hold with devastating effect beginning in 1968. In 1969, there were 250 arrests of American servicemen charged with use or possession of heroin; in 1970, 1,146 arrests; and in the first quarter of 1971 alone, 1,084 arrests. As for the death toll, it went up, too, from 26 heroin fatalities for each quarter of 1970 to 35 in the first quarter of 1971. The estimates of addiction ranged from 4.5 per cent of 22,000 departing American troops, or 990 cases, determined from urine tests reported in mid-July 1971, to a high of 25 per cent of the troops then remaining in South Vietnam, or about 60,000 cases. The most commonly reported figure at the time was 10 per cent, or about 24,000 cases. Any way the heroin plague was considered, it was very bad—and it could not be wished out of existence.

Amnesty was offered to American soldiers who would come forward and submit to voluntary treatment to break the heroin habit, resulting in almost 4,000 patients during a limited period of 1971. Rehabilitation was offered to those who already had been discharged and were suffering from the habit in the United States, although Army centers were too small to handle the demand and the Veterans Administration had to help. Drastic punishments were devised under the military code of justice for soldiers who persisted in pushing or using heroin and were caught. The Vietnamese were told to crack down on their own peddlers and sources of supply, as well. But the program looked better in the headlines than it did on the ground in South Vietnam.

Representative Robert H. Steele of Connecticut, a Congressional investigator, reported to the House, "The soldier going to Vietnam today runs a far greater risk of becoming a heroin addict than a combat casualty." He also made the familiar charge of connivance by some Vietnamese officials in the flow of heroin to the Americans and accused the American command of laxity in moving against the plague. Nor was he alone in his opinion.

The worst of the problem for the individual American soldier who was hooked on heroin in Vietnam was that it made a normal life impossible for him once he came home. For in Vietnam, he could buy 95 per cent pure heroin for as little as $3 or $4 at a time and sniff it or smoke it; in the United States, the price was much higher for heroin that was only 5 per cent pure and had to be injected intra-venously—"mainlined," the junkie jargon—for maximum effect. It meant that many a Vietnam veteran, in need of heroin, would have to turn to housebreaking, armed robbery and worse for the money to sustain his deadly habit.

Heroin has always been in plentiful supply in Indochina in general and Vietnam in particular. American intelligence sources have pin-pointed at least twenty-one opium refineries in the so-called "golden triangle" border areas of Laos, Burma and Thailand, the source of perhaps as much as half the world's supply. With production for 1971 in that region alone estimated at 1,000 tons of opium, the refineries will be going at full blast, for the demand is steady and the price is going up—$800 a pound for 95 per cent pure heroin at the source and many times that amount when it is cut and sold on the American market.

The heroin traffic moves in numerous ways, from Mekong River trawlers and overland smugglers to private aircraft. For a time, until they attracted too much attention, the small carrier known as Air Opium operated aircraft out of both Vientiane and Saigon. Much of the opium traffic from Burma and Thailand passes through Vientiane and a large part of the refined heroin is sent directly to Saigon for distribution and sale to the American market.

The American government's efforts to enlist the aid of the Laotian government, as well as that of the regime in Saigon, have had only qualified success. In response to threats of a cutoff of American economic aid, the regime in Vientiane has pleaded that it will take time to phase out the profitable opium crop and persuade farmers to raise something more acceptable to the United States. That, too, has been the case in Turkey, another major opium producer. From all outward indications, therefore, the problem of the service-connected heroin addict will not be solved for the present in Indochina. Like so many other consequences of the Vietnam War, it will have to be handled in the United States.

The Pace of the Retreat

In its victorious wars of this century, it has been the usual practice of the United States to remove the bulk of its troops from the field almost as soon as the last shot is fired. In Vietnam, however, American troops were outward bound long before the end of hostilities. Far from being crushed by the notion of a retreat in the face of a still active enemy, the American public was all for speeding up the movement. For the way to a realistic peace, as North Vietnam and China insisted, could only be opened with the removal of all American forces from South Vietnam.

The pressure on President Nixon to get the American armed forces out of Vietnam thus was far greater than the Pentagon's demands on President Johnson to put them in. But Nixon tried, as best he could, to use the pace of the pullout as a means of bargaining with the enemy for the release of American war prisoners and for additional time to build up South Vietnam's forces. From a top figure of 543,400 when the Nixon Administration took office on January 1, 1969, American field strength declined to 184,000 at the end of 1971 and, except for a residual force of uncertain size, was headed for an end to American involvement on the ground during 1972. That being an American presidential election year, an impatient public was holding the President to his pledges of disengagement.

Even if American involvement in the ground war was winding down, however, the United States Air Force remained very much a part of the action. At the end of 1971, a major five-day air attack involving 350 aircraft was conducted over North Vietnamese territory. North Vietnam, unexpectedly, had come up with a small but effective force of Russian-built fighter aircraft that was taking a heavy toll over Laos. True to the confusing rhetoric with which Washington had fought the war from the outset, the air action was billed as "defensive."

The South Vietnamese Election

At the outset of the great retreat, Nixon had asked his ambassador to Saigon, Ellsworth Bunker, if his plan would work. The lean, silver-haired New Englander, a septuagenarian, replied, "Yes, if you keep to your timetable and we increase our economic aid as we withdraw."

Nixon tried to do both, being well aware of the fate of American presidents who champion losing causes. For fiscal 1972, he proposed to give $765.5 million in economic aid to South Vietnam, Cambodia, Laos and Thailand, of which $565 million was for the Saigon regime. He also exempted these countries from a 10 per cent cut in foreign aid to help the American economy. As for the troop withdrawals, they came even faster than originally planned.

Where both the President and his ambassador failed was in trying to produce a fair presidential election for South Vietnam on October 3, 1971. President Thieu was so afraid of losing that he first amended the electoral law to require any opposition candidate to win the endorsement of either 40 of the 195 members of the National Assembly or 100 provincial and city councilors. Next, he broke with his chief rivals, Vice President Ky and General Duong Van Minh. Both accused him of rigging the election, withdrew from the race despite appeals from Bunker, and forced Thieu to run against himself in a sham election. He claimed to have won 93 per cent of the vote, but nobody checked up. If Thieu looked bad, the United States looked a lot worse.

The split in American public opinion over the war was thus reproduced in measurable scale in South Vietnam, and none could know how far-reaching the consequences would be. Marshal Ky encouraged reports that he was planning a coup to overthrow his former boss. "Big Minh," who had run one successful coup against Diem, was closely watched to make sure that he would not pull off another.

Thieu, from his post in Saigon as virtual dictator of the ravaged land, permitted the election of a new lower house from among 1,240 candidates on August 29, 1971, in which his opposition made significant gains but not enough to threaten the government's rubber-stamp majority. It was just a sop to the embarrassed Americans, however, and didn't mean much. The dignified Bunker turned out in the end to be little more than a discouraged messenger boy, shuttling between Thieu and the White House and unable to please either.

The White House, meanwhile, was told by the CIA that some 30,000 Communist agents had been able to infiltrate the South Vietnam government. Another report, this one from Sir Robert Thompson, the British guerrilla warfare expert, confirmed the comeback of the Vietcong and the failure of the South Vietnamese government to maintain suitable progress in its pacification program.

Just how South Vietnam would fare without the full military support of the United States was something that only time would determine. Thieu's forces took a battering in the spring of 1972 despite all his brave talk. And in view of the bitterness that developed in the South Vietnamese presidential campaign, his usefulness was clearly near an end and the country's prospects for maintaining itself within its 1954 borders became increasingly dubious.

The Position of North Vietnam

If South Vietnam's position was precarious, North Vietnam's wasn't much better after the punishment it had taken during a decade of war. Outwardly, the regime in Hanoi was united behind its ruling trinity of Le Duan, first secretary of the central committee of the Lao Dong (Communist Workers' Party); Premier Pham Van Dong, and Truong Chinh, chairman of the National Assembly's Standing Committee, with the octogenarian Ton Duc Thang serving as president. However, no one had really been able to replace President Ho Chi Minh, who at his death in 1969 also held the posts of chairman of the National Defense Council and Lao Dong chairman. And no one had the military competence of Ho Chi Minh in collaborating with North Vietnam's brilliant strategist, General Vo Nguyen Giap.

There was a facade of popular representation in North Vietnam. Much was made of the elections of April 11, 1971, during which 420 representatives were elected to the National Assembly—one for every 50,000 people—but none were chosen this time for South Vietnam as had been the previous custom. The point was that North Vietnam did not want to interfere with the Provisional Revolutionary Government it had set up for South Vietnam. Other than that the new National Assembly in Hanoi was pretty much the same and it acted as its predecessors had in faithful reflection of the policies of its leaders. Its task was, in the words of President Ton Duc Thang, to "achieve victory over the American aggressors and take a further basic stride in building the material and technical bases of socialism, bringing peace, independence, liberty and happiness to the Vietnamese people."

That was quite a big order for a small, poor military state of 21,000,000 people with a per capita income of about $100, chronic food shortages, an almost desperate shortage of labor and a disrupted economy. To some, it seemed totally dependent on its quarreling Communist suppliers, the Soviet Union and China; however, in celebrating the twenty-fifth year of its Communist regime and the fortieth anniversary of its Communist Party, North Vietnam left no doubt at the outset of the 1970s that it meant to maintain its independence of maneuver at all costs. That was its strong point, and more than anything else accounted for its remarkable will to survive.

North Vietnam's food problem antedated the American bombing campaign that hit its industry so hard. As early as 1962, appeals were broadcast from Hanoi to conserve food and substitute such things as maize and sweet potatoes for the standard rice diet. Le Duan put on a land reclamation campaign in that year, calling for a 2 per cent increase each year thereafter for the cultivatable area. But the American bombing wrecked that project. In 1964, the year before the attack, North Vietnam had 6,200,000 acres under cultivation; in 1970, the total was down to 6,000,000, indicating that some land had been abandoned.. It was only after the bombing halt that Premier Pham Van Dong was able to go before the National Assembly with a report for 1970 that agricultural production had progressed. For 1971, he said, the plan Hanoi put forward was to "settle the question of food." Without continued large contributions of rice and other food grains from China, however, it was evident that North Vietnam would go hungry.

The attack on the labor shortage was more productive. While the American bombing campaign was under way in October 1965, Hanoi conceded that its labor problem was "very grave" because of both military needs and the many emergency calls for labor to keep essential services going. North Vietnam had to call on its women, who accounted in the following year for 35 per cent of its production brigades and a majority of its irrigation force. By 1967, women formed 70 per cent of the farm labor force, 58 per cent of government workers, 48 per cent of light industry, 30 per cent of heavy industry, and 45 per cent of physicians, pharmacists and public health workers.

For an Asian land, women also were accorded more political recognition, for they received 14 per cent of the deputies' offices in the National Assembly, 20 per cent of village council memberships and 26 per cent of the total of provincial council members. In militia and home guard units, women formed 14 per cent of the total force. The system worked. While the manpower shortage was not solved, women helped close the gap and kept the nation's economy going.

Like the Saigon government, North Vietnam had its troubles with the black market and its official actions were replete with attacks on Communist Party members who "become selfish and corrupt and violate party principles or who abuse their power." The difference was that Hanoi tried to take effective action, decreeing punishment that included the death sentence for those who tried to profit from the war. But it was doubtful that the tired and war-weary population of North Vietnam was any more reassured than their fellow Vietnamese to the south. Patriotic rallying cries weren't going very far in any part of Vietnam in the latter period of the war. What the people clearly wanted was an end to the fighting.

The cost of the war in North Vietnam has been enormous. While no one has ever placed much trust in the fanciful body-count figures issued in Saigon at the old "Five o'Clock Follies" briefings (latterly 4:15 P.M. and earlier), Hanoi has absorbed serious casualties. General Giap publicly conceded in 1969 that the North Vietnamese Army had sustained 500,000 war deaths—a figure that almost certainly reached 700,000 by mid-1971. The wounded, the captured and the deserters together equaled several times that figure, indicating the extent to which North Vietnam already had sacrificed its youth to the cause of protracted war. The consequences of such losses for the future in North Vietnam are incalculable; without doubt, the heart of the younger generation has been torn out and can never be replaced.

Economically, despite all the propaganda blasts from Hanoi, the havoc wrought by the American bombing campaign has not been overcome; nor will industry be restored to normal until the pressures of war are lifted from the land. Foreign sources calculate that North Vietnam's gross national product for 1965, estimated at $1.6 billion, was higher than the GNP for 1970, which makes a mockery of exaggerated claims of growth rates for the country. The effect on its industry is scarcely a secret. In a match factory, for example, the controlled Hanoi press conceded that the 1971 production target was only 81 per cent of that for 1965. No wonder the North Vietnamese trade deficit with the Soviet Union and the countries of the East Europe bloc increased sixfold, from $50 million in 1965 to $300 million at the beginning of the 1970s!

Necessarily, such strains produced differences within North Vietnam's ruling group. The doves, among them Truong Chinh, were believed to be agitating for a reduction in the scale of the fighting in South Vietnam in order to relieve the domestic manpower shortage. The hawks, said to be under the leadership of Le Duan, always tried to put the conduct of the war first. These differences, of course, seldom surfaced but all the signs of conflict were there. In one instance, Truong Chinh demanded the abandonment of a government policy of permitting private farming of collectivized land and Le Duan apparently opposed it but lost. In a disapproving speech early in 1970, the Communist Party boss then clothed himself in the mantle of Lenin, who lectured his colleagues on the need for an unorthodox New Economic Policy to guarantee the survival of socialism.

What the hawks in North Vietnam wanted to do was to keep up their three-front war in South Vietnam, Laos and Cambodia despite their setbacks in Cambodia in 1970 and the Laotian invasion of 1971. For a minor military power that already had been strained to the limit, it was a bold gamble. The available evidence suggests that North Vietnam's daring troubled both Moscow and Peking. For from March 5–8, 1971, Chou En-lai himself paid a visit to Hanoi and referred to the war in notably less belligerent terms than his hosts. Very soon thereafter, Le Duan took off for Moscow and was gone for six weeks. On his way home, he was the guest of honor at one of Chou's ceremonial banquets on May 11 but it couldn't have made him feel any better when he learned of Peking's new approaches to

Washington. Nor was the Shanghai communiqué of 1972 any more reassuring.

For Hanoi, as for Saigon, the war was near a climax. The North Vietnamese and the National Liberation Front of South Vietnam made new offers in Paris, which Washington at the time was in no position to dignify. More fighting and a lot more talking lay ahead as the North's 1972 spring offensive rocked the Saigon regime and raised anti-war sentiment in the United States.

The War in Retrospect

Four successive American administrations for almost twenty years waged war in Vietnam, directly or indirectly, on the dubious premise that South Vietnam could be preserved as an anti-Communist base and that Laos and Cambodia thereby could be prevented from falling under the domination of either Hanoi or Peking. It was a war that cost the United States about 50,000 combat deaths, more than 300,000 wounded, tens of thousands of service-connected drug addictions and an estimated expenditure of $150 billion. It was the least successful and most wasteful war in which the United States ever participated, with more bombing tonnage being dropped on tiny North Vietnam than all of Europe absorbed in World War II. It was also fought for a sham cause, the professed right of the South Vietnamese to determine their own government, something President Thieu roundly denied to them in 1971.

Whatever the damage to Vietnam, and it has been so great in human sacrifice and suffering that those now living will be affected for the rest of their lives, the cost to the United States has been incalculably greater. A divided country, a disaffected and disillusioned younger generation and a discredited military establishment are among the intangible costs that may have the most serious consequences for the American future.

Years before this lamentable outcome of the conflict shaped up for the United States, it was clearly anticipated by some of those who were leaders in waging war. On October 14, 1966, Secretary of Defense Robert Strange McNamara wrote to President Johnson: ". . . I see no reasonable way to bring the war to an end soon. Enemy morale has not broken—he apparently has adjusted to our stopping his drive for military victory and has adopted a strategy of keeping us busy and waiting us out (a strategy of attriting our national will). He knows that we have not been, and he believes we probably will not be, able to translate our military successes into the 'end products'—broken enemy morale and political achievements by the government of South Vietnam."

Yet, blindly and stubbornly, the American political and military leadership kept on fighting for more than five years thereafter. And that, more than anything else, compounded the American tragedy.[4]

3. LAOS: THE MYTH OF NEUTRALITY

The Lao are among the most pleasant and peaceful of peoples. Yet, surrounded as they are by often quarrelsome and frequently aggressive neighbors, they have known far more of war than peace. In this generation, the 2,800,000 Lao, locked off from the sea in a primitive

[4] Much of the background of the Vietnam War is drawn from *The Pentagon Papers*, the unabridged *New York Times* articles and documents published by Bantam Books in 1971, and additional Pentagon historical material published in the Washington *Post*, Boston *Globe* and St. Louis *Post-Dispatch*. I am grateful to Ambassador Ellsworth Bunker and Ambassador Samuel Berger for their private discussions with me in Saigon during 1970, to General W. B. Rosson for his explanations of the military position, and to General William C. Westmoreland for his many courtesies shown to me during my 1964 visit. I also wish to acknowledge the usefulness of William E. Colby's private discussion with me of the CORDS program while he was its director in South Vietnam. The reports on the South Vietnam economy are drawn from numerous sources, including a *Japan Times* special section of November 1, 1970; an article by Philip Dion in the *Far Eastern Economic Review*, May 1, 1971, pp. 19–21; and an article by P. J. Honey in the quarterly *Pacific Community*, July, 1971, pp. 754–766. Material on the pacification program also comes from many sources, including Gerald C. Hickey's report for the Rand Corporation, "Accommodation and Coalition in South Vietnam," issued in 1970; *The Economist*, October 17, 1970, p. 26; *Newsweek*, October 26, 1970, p. 11; *Time*, October 26, 1970, p. 27; George Esper's report from Saigon in the Associated Press file for October 8, 1970; and an editorial in the *Japan Times*, April 10, 1970, p. 14. Material analyzing the strategy of the war on both sides is derived from sources including *The Economist*, April 17, 1971, p. 21, and June 26, 1971, pp. 15–16; *Far Eastern Economic Review*, June 12, 1971, pp. 15–16, and June 26, 1971, pp. 5–6; Max Frankel's summary article on the Pentagon Papers in *The New York Times*, July 6, 1971, p. 1; and Harrison Salisbury's book *Behind the Lines—Hanoi*, published in 1967 by Harper & Row, and based on his *New York Times* articles.

mountainous kingdom smaller than Colorado, have suffered almost continuous strife.

It is not their fault. They have professed to be neutral. Being 95 per cent rural and composed mostly of mountain tribes without interest in the outside world, it is difficult to see how Laos could be anything else. The great powers, and neighboring lands as well, have pledged themselves to uphold Laotian neutrality. But war, nevertheless, has been the kingdom's lot for two decades. The practical result has been dismemberment.

Like Belgium in World War I and Belgium, the Netherlands and Luxembourg in World War II, the Laotian neutrality treaty of 1962 received no more respect than a Teutonic scrap of paper when it suited the purposes of an aggressor. The world, however, did not react against the repeated violations of Laotian sovereignty with the shock and horror that accompanied the German invasion of the Low Countries. Few in the West wept over bleeding Laos, not having a very good idea in the first place of where Laos is. Nor has there been any noble talk about Laotian rights in the case of this suffering and divided land.

The Lao are doubly unfortunate in this respect. They are Asian and they are poor.

For a thousand years their land has served as a battleground for more powerful peoples—the Viets, Burmans, Khmer, Thai and Chinese among others. The Lao have never really known what nationhood is, although they have been allotted national boundaries; however, more of them live outside Laos—in Cambodia, Thailand and Vietnam—than inside. Indeed, some in Laos have never heard of its dual capitals, Vientiane and Luang Prabang, the literacy rate being appallingly low and the sources of information minimal. There is, as one French journalist remarked after a visit, total freedom of the press because there is no press, only radio, and no public opinion worth mentioning.[5] The highways are few. There isn't even a railroad, although military airfields are all over the place. But the rivers are great highways for everything from the shipment of rice and military supplies to the smuggling of gold bars and the abundant yield in narcotics of Laos' perfectly legal and abundant poppy fields.

[5] Jacques Champagne, IPI Report, XII, No. 7 (November 1963), pp. 2, 4.

The law in Laos, as once was true of Tombstone, Arizona, is what each person makes it.

All the Lao peasant knows of the modern world is that it possesses terrifying weapons of war. To such a people, most of whom earn less than $75 a year, little matters except self-preservation. Their fellow farmers in Asia may be lucky enough to be knee-deep in new brands of miracle rice and wheat and surrounded by massive road, irrigation, public health and school projects. But the Lao account it almost routine to see, instead, North Vietnamese regiments defend themselves against the bombing runs of American jet aircraft. And north, near the Chinese border, a great road is being built by Chinese engineers across Lao territory, one branch going into Vietnam and another toward Thailand, without so much as a by-your-leave. That is the kind of a place Laos is. If you want the land and are strong enough, you take it.

This is the land into which the United States has poured almost $400 million a year for what is theoretically known as Laotian security but actually amounts to long-term undercover warfare planned and directed in large part by the United States Central Intelligence Agency.

The Partition of Laos

Laos lies divided, for all practical purposes, between the rightist-neutralist government of Prince Souvanna Phouma, which is supported by the United States, and the forces of the Communist Pathet Lao, directed by his half brother, Prince Souphanouvong, which are backed by the North Vietnamese Army.

About two-thirds of the land is held by the Pathet Lao, from the 6,000-mile network of the Ho Chi Minh Trail in the south to the Plain of Jars and the northern provinces along the North Vietnamese and Chinese borders. The Mekong River Valley and the principal centers of population, clustered closer to Thailand, have been mainly in government hands for much of the war. Vientiane, the administrative capital, with its 150,000 people, could have been taken at almost any time by the North Vietnamese if it had suited their strategic purpose to do so.

But North Vietnam's main interest in Laos throughout the war steadfastly remained the build-up and protection of the Ho Chi Minh Trail between its own border and South Vietnam, for this was—and is—a matter of life or death for Hanoi. During the years when North Vietnam was able to use the Cambodian sanctuaries through the cooperation of Prince Norodom Sihanouk, water-borne transportation of troops and supplies was much more feasible than the long, hard overland route. But once the Cambodian invasion of 1970 enabled the American and South Vietnamese forces to deny sea transport to Hanoi, the Ho Chi Minh Trail became the lifeline for North Vietnam. Without it, continuation of the war would have been impossible. For this reason, the American bombers concentrated on the network from their Thai bases from 1965 on. For this reason, too, the South Vietnamese hurled 20,000 of their best troops, with American air support, at the heart of the trail in the winter and spring of 1971 for forty-four days. But North Vietnam, with a force of 75,000 troops and 50,000 Laotian laborers, proved able to repulse attacks from every quarter and keep the network in reasonable repair.

This strategy, in effect, set the course of the long war in Laos. On another level, the Pathet Lao and the forces supporting the Laotian government fought a curious war in an entirely different manner. From 1965 on, when the Americans escalated the conflict in Laos as well as in South Vietnam, the Laotian war developed into a kind of martial quadrille. During the dry season, the Communists advanced across the Plain of Jars; during the wet season, they generally retreated and government forces then announced a triumphant counterattack during which they temporarily occupied the contested area. This went on as late as the summer of 1971, when Meo tribesmen under the command of General Vang Pao, trained, equipped and paid for by the Central Intelligence Agency, took the Plain of Jars once again, almost without opposition. They were certain of control until the beginning of the dry season in late autumn, but it didn't really mean very much.

The trouble with this rather stylistic brand of warfare was that the government troops, year after year, usually had to give up more territory than they were able to recapture. Consequently, the American government, with the consent of Premier Souvanna Phouma, stepped up its bombing campaign against the Ho Chi Minh Trail until Laos became one of the most bombed countries in the world. Nothing like it had ever been seen before in Asia. But it didn't stop the flow of Hanoi's troops and matériel southward into the theater of war. And it did far more harm than good for the United States in Asian eyes.

From their Thai bases, American B-52 bombers flew as many as 400 sorties a day against the Ho Chi Minh Trail and the two passes into South Vietnam through which all trail traffic eventually had to pass. Other types of aircraft used the 300 fields scattered throughout Laos, many of them airstrips, for interdictory forays here and elsewhere in the country. The best this effort produced was a reduction in the volume of North Vietnamese military traffic; some observers believed that the 600 to 800 trucks that used the trail each week suffered bombing losses of no more than 20 per cent. Even when the South Vietnamese temporarily cut the trail in 1971 and ripped apart the big oil pipeline that serviced North Vietnamese vehicles, the southbound traffic merely shifted farther to the west and kept pushing ahead.

Naturally, the North Vietnamese encouraged the Pathet Lao to seek some kind of a limited truce, the key to which always was a demand for the cessation of American bombing of the Ho Chi Minh Trail. And such overtures, in turn, gave rise to frequent reports that Souvanna Phouma and his talented and militant half brother would make a separate peace. But for the long run, it was evident that any settlement in Laos would be temporary unless it was made a part of an over-all arrangement for the rest of Indochina.

The Peace That Failed

One of the miracles of Asia is the manner in which the Lao managed to survive as an independent entity for as long as they did. In 1893, at just about the time Thailand was preparing for a quiet annexation of the country, the French stepped in and made Laos a protectorate. Six years later, the Laotians were granted the inestimable privilege of acceding to the French Indochina Union but not on the basis of liberty, equality and fraternity. These were not for ignorant Asian peoples, but for those who more truly deserved to bask in the grandeur of France.

Until the Japanese struck off the French colonial shackles, Laos remained obediently in the Indochina Union with Vietnam and Cambodia. But after World War II, when Ho Chi Minh already had begun his long battle for Vietnamese independence, the Lao seized the opportunity to set up a parliamentary government and a limited monarchy in 1947. The French obligingly recognized Laos as an independent state within the French Union two years later, but that didn't satisfy the Communist elements that had been cooperating with Ho Chi Minh.

In 1950, at a secret conference in northern Laos, the Pathet Lao (meaning "Land of the Lao") was organized as a Communist resistance movement with Prince Souphanouvong as its most prominent member.[6] By the time France was expelled from Indochina under the 1954 Geneva agreements and Laos gained its freedom, with Cambodia and the two Vietnams, the Pathet Lao had a strong base in northeastern Laos and a formidable following.

Within six years, it was apparent that Laos had become a battleground once more. Rightists, neutralists and leftists all were maneuvering for power; frequently, two of the factions would unite temporarily against the third—an old Asian scenario. Events in Laos, never very clear to the outside world, became monumentally confusing. The situation had deteriorated to such an extent in 1961 that both President Kennedy and Soviet Premier Nikita S. Khrushchev agreed in Vienna to do something about it.

The 1962 Geneva conference was the result, with its guarantee of respect for Laotian neutrality. Prince Souvanna Phouma frequently has said since that if the Geneva agreements had been faithfully executed, there would be no problem in Laos today. That was the trouble. Just as had been the case with the 1954 agreements on Indochina, the 1962 compact on Laos was violated one step at a time, first by one party, then by others, until nothing at all was left except a smaller version of the protracted warfare that was being waged in Vietnam.

Externally, the 1962 treaty prohibited the introduction into Laos of "foreign regular and irregular troops, foreign para-military forma-

[6] "Prince Who Leads the Pathet Lao," *The New York Times*, March 11, 1970, p. 4.

tions and foreign military personnel." Moreover, all signatories undertook to forbid shipment into Laos of armaments, munitions and war materials in general, except where the Royal Government of Laos had requirements for national defense.

Internally, the 1962 pact set up a coalition government that included representatives of the neutralists, the right and the Pathet Lao. In a Provisional Government of National Union, there were eight neutralists headed by Prince Souvanna Phouma, four from the right and four from the Pathet Lao, including Prince Souphanouvong. It should be noted that Prince Souvanna Phouma, who then was pro-leftist and anti-American, had asked for and received assistance from both the Soviet Union and China. Yet, he could not gain the necessary support of the Pathet Lao and the Laotian Communist Party, the Neo Lao Haksat, for the organization of what was termed a "free and democratic" election.

Within a year, Prince Souphanouvong departed from Vientiane, although he was thoughtful enough to leave a Pathet Lao representative behind him in the immemorial Laotian tradition. The Pathet Lao once again took up arms, with the support of North Vietnam. In preparation for the final assault on South Vietnam, North Vietnamese armies began moving south along the Ho Chi Minh Trail with their supplies in 1964. This was the final chance to do something to insure the neutrality of Laos, but no effective protest came from the principal signatories to the 1962 agreements—Cambodia, France, India, North Vietnam, People's Republic of China, U.S.S.R., United Kingdom, United States and South Vietnam.

The United States and Laos

The United States has usually sought to conceal its military operations in Laos, where secrets are seldom kept and the human condition is notably frail. In spite of vast amounts that have been poured from the United States Treasury into a land that couldn't absorb such generous funding, the United States public has not often been given a very penetrating view of its government's activities. In fact, the story of American intervention in Laos over the years has frequently been told with greater frankness and accuracy by itinerant foreign correspondents than by the governments directly concerned.

One reason for this unsatisfactory state of affairs has been a rather touching concern in Washington for the 1962 Geneva agreements, which most of the signatories, including the United States, have violated for years. Another has been the ever-suspicious United States Senate, which early on took a position against committing American ground troops to combat in either Laos, Cambodia or Thailand and assumed it had the right to forbid the President to make a commitment to any land without prior Senate approval.

This large assumption, based on the Constitution of the United States, was not borne out in practice. For the American presence in Laos has always bulked large, being represented by American air power, the forces of the Central Intelligence Agency, various American government economic agencies and a large and hustling embassy staff. It became almost a standing joke that Americans assigned to "temporary duty" in Laos found that their mission could be stretched out for quite a long time and that other Americans were busy with mysterious activities in the land without actually being listed among those present. The United States, in fact, always tried to act like the big man who wasn't there.

While the main American effort in Laos was directed against North Vietnam's movements over the Ho Chi Minh Trail, a monumental exercise of American air power, the United States also became involved in the support and even the direction of operations by three pro-government armies and two air lines. There was, first of all, the Royal Laotian Army of about 60,000 troops that had to be paid for and equipped, even if they couldn't or wouldn't use the weapons. Then, as a secondary force, the Neutralist Army of about 6,000 troops also had to be fitted out in a style to which it had never been accustomed. And finally, the swarm of active CIA agents in Laos formed the so-called "Secret Army," which wasn't secret at all, of Meo tribesmen headed by General Vang Pao.

This "Secret Army" eventually turned out to be one of the most publicized outfits in Indochina because it was about the only pro-American force in Laos that showed any ability at all to fight in the field. It was the subject of special attention from the Pentagon, the State Department, the Senate Foreign Relations Committee and every wandering foreign correspondent who found his way a few miles out of Vientiane. At one time, Vang Pao's troops numbered at least 30,000 men, half of them regulars, but its effective fighting strength varied widely. By the end of 1971, it was believed to have no more than 8,000 to 10,000 effective troops in action.

As for the two air lines, both of them hush-hush outfits at the outset of their history but famous throughout Indochina long since, they formed the basis for American logistic support of the Laotian government forces. The pilots of Air America and Continental Services flew all kinds of aircraft, from the old work-horse DC-3s to the latest models of transport planes. Far from being secret, shady figures, the veterans in particular were well known and most of them were rather garrulous adventurers instead of thin-lipped cloak-and-dagger types. There was only one set of clandestine air line operatives who were more talked about during their heyday in Indochina—the swaggering French pilots of Air Opium, which for several years helped transport the plentiful yield of the Laotian poppy fields to various Far Eastern centers for processing and sale to the West. Their job was to avoid sharing the burdens of war while making a fat profit from it.

One other major element on the Laotian government side was the participation of Thailand in a supporting role. Although American authorities in the 1960s tried to pretend that the United States bases in Thailand were secret, no informed person was ever in the dark about the Thai war effort in Laos. Put quite bluntly, the Thais sponsored and supported the use of their bases by American B-52s and smaller bombing aircraft in the war on the Communist enemy in Laos. At least 5,000 Thai troops operated in Laos up to the border areas along the Ho Chi Minh Trail and acted as training instructors for the Laotian government forces.[7] It cannot be said with any degree of accuracy how many Lao in Thailand participated in Thai operations in their homeland, but certainly there were more than a mere handful. All this, of course, was denied by Bangkok just as fervently and continuously as Hanoi denied that there were North Vietnamese troops in Laos, Cambodia or even South Vietnam.

Against the government's forces, the Communists were able to

[7] Max Coiffait, "Laotian Leaders Search for Peace," *Pacific Community,* October, 1970, p. 186.

throw an increasingly effective combination of Pathet Lao, Vietcong and North Vietnamese regular troops. These varied widely in both numbers and assignment, depending on the season of the year and the type of operations in which they were involved, so that the estimates of enemy strength were often unrealistic. But at the peak of the Communist effort, the 75,000 North Vietnamese and Vietcong troops in Laos also had the assistance of anywhere from 12,000 to 20,000 Pathet Lao. At the beginning of 1972, these forces were strong enough to hold much of southern Laos.

Compared with Vietnam, Laos' war was smaller in scope but it took an increasing toll of life and added daily to the numbers of homeless refugees, of which there were perhaps as many as 800,000. In all, this war cost the United States well in excess of $1 billion from 1965 on, and that did not include the massive cost of bombing the Ho Chi Minh Trail. Until the Senate Foreign Relations Committee produced a report from the CIA in 1971, few knew how American funds were spent. Then only was it learned that the "partial cost" of the war for fiscal 1970 was $284 million in American funds, of which $162 million was for military aid, and for the 1971 fiscal year American spending soared to $374 million. There were many who believed that on a per capita basis, Laos received more American aid than any other country in the world—and there was precious little to show for it.

The Laotian economy was a disaster, regardless of how it was considered. The United States organized a five-nation stabilization fund to support the Laotian kip (at about 500 to $1, and sometimes more). For 1969, despite American efforts, Laos' exports (mainly of timber and tin) amounted to only $3 million while imports were $42 million. The Economic Commission for Asia and the Far East reported that over a recent three-year period, foreign aid to Laos amounted to more than 200 per cent of the value of imports into Laos. The bizarre little kingdom was thus the most successful mendicant nation in all Asia.[8]

[8] The first CIA figures on the Laos war were disclosed August 2, 1971, through a Senate Foreign Relations Subcommittee staff report, *The New York Times*, August 3, 1971, p. 1. Other details of CIA activities in Laos from *Far Eastern Economic Review*, May 15, 1971, p. 70.

On Morality and Peace

The morality of the covert CIA operations in Laos became increasingly difficult to defend, particularly with the coming of stepped-up efforts for peace in Indochina. For neither the American Congress nor the American public had the slightest idea of what new shenanigans the CIA would dream up in Laos to try to keep the Communist side off balance. For the United States to conduct serious negotiations for peace under such circumstances was difficult, to say the least; and yet, this was the way the scenario was set up for Laos.

Senator J. William Fulbright, the chairman of the Senate Foreign Relations Committee, took a grave view of such CIA operations. While he conceded that the organization was following its orders, he also argued that its role as defined in the National Security Act had "never contemplated this function." In concluding his committee hearings on this aspect of the war in 1970, he said: "If it is in the national security to do this, it seems to me it ought to be done by regular United States army forces and not by an intelligence-gathering agency."

By that time, the contending factions in Laos were close to exhaustion. The government forces had been losing on the average of 4,000 killed in action in a year; the enemy, having been obliged to absorb punishment from the air as well as a severe cholera epidemic, had an even higher toll. Moreover, as events unfolded through the period of the Cambodian invasion and the South Vietnamese push against the Ho Chi Minh Trail in early 1971, both Vietnams began to look at Laos in an entirely different way.

The opening passages in the orchestration for the Laotian peace had begun early in 1970 with Prince Souvanna Phouma's proposal for a cease-fire except over the Ho Chi Minh Trail. That wasn't to North Vietnam's liking, so the Pathet Lao rejected the overture. Next came a five-point peace plan from Prince Souphanouvong, which insisted mainly on an unconditional halt in American bombing of the Ho Chi Minh Trail. It was no more serious than his half brother's bid and also led nowhere. Prince Souvanna Phouma moved next for the opening of peace talks in Laos without conditions. To this, Souphanouvong said yes, but only after a bombing halt. There was some maneuvering between the government and the Pathet Lao thereafter, which resulted in an agreement to send representatives to Khangkhai, on the edge of the Plain of Jars. But during the summer and early fall of 1970, Souvanna Phouma made a leisurely tour of sympathetic world capitals, putting the peace talks in a deep freeze. Upon his return, Souphanouvong apparently dropped his insistence on an American bombing pause as a precondition. But typically enough, just when there was a slight hope for a Laotian settlement in 1971, the American-supported South Vietnamese thrust was made against the Ho Chi Minh Trail. And both sides had to start all over again to try to move, sidewise and with averted gaze, toward the conference table.

It was proof, if proof were needed, that the great powers would finally decide if there was to be peace, war or an uneasy and indefinite truce in Laos. With North Vietnam in possession of so much Laotian territory and the Chinese building roads through its northern areas, the tiny land faced a desperately uncertain future.

4. THE PARTITION OF CAMBODIA

During a skirmish in the early days of the Cambodian war outside Pnom Penh, when a small Cambodian unit was pinned down by Communist fire, a young soldier suddenly advanced toward the enemy waving a Cambodian flag. Before he had gone very far, the Communists killed him. But his comrades, inspired by his valor, charged past his fallen banner, for which he had given his life, and routed the enemy.

To the handful of war correspondents and television cameramen who witnessed the incident, it was unbelievable heroism—something they hadn't seen from Asian troops in all the weary years of fighting in Indochina. Telling about it some weeks later, Paul Brinkley-Rogers of *Newsweek* said, "It was like something out of an old war movie— a boy giving his life for the sake of a brave gesture. I can't get it out of my mind."[9] Nor can many another, far removed from Cambodian

[9] Told to me in Tokyo when I saw him there June 12, 1970.

battlefields, for through repetition in print and film and word of mouth, the young soldier's sacrifice became a matchless legend in the history of an ancient land.

This, however, was not the kind of war that was generally fought in Cambodia from then on. It sometimes took government troops weeks to clear a handful of Communists from a mountain pass to permit supplies to flow into their embattled capital. And the Communists, too, sometimes found it prudent to fall back in the face of repeated sweeps by South Vietnamese troops. The government, hurling back a threadbare slogan at the Communists who had coined it, called the struggle a "People's War."

It was more than that. In a very real sense, it became a war for national survival. No less than Greece in 1947–49 and South Korea in 1950–53, Cambodia was unprepared and well-nigh defenseless when North Vietnamese troops struck in the spring of 1970, shortly after the overthrow of Prince Norodom Sihanouk in Pnom Penh. Despite the build-up of the Cambodian Army with the support of the United States and South Vietnam, the Communist side held more than half of the countryside within a year. True, it was a part of the land that was sparsely inhabited and didn't amount to much; moreover, in places like the marshy bottoms only ten miles or so from Pnom Penh or the ancient monuments of the Angkor Wat at Siem Reap, the government deliberately chose not to give battle. But whatever the rationalization, it had to be admitted that the net effect was the partition of Cambodia.

To try to appear in the guise of liberators, the North Vietnamese waged a vigorous campaign to build up the local Communist fighting arm, the Khmer Rouge, but at best it didn't amount to more than 5,000 troops and not very good ones at that. This only added to the ancient enmity between the Cambodians and the marauding Viets, who had never been trusted outside their own territory. In the struggle for the loyalty of 6,500,000 Cambodians in a land close to the size of the state of Michigan, the Communists appeared to be the losers even when they were able to roam at will over much of the eastern portion of the country.

Cambodia and Communism

There is a sense of history about Cambodia. On the base of the earliest kingdoms that flourished in the area more than 2,000 years ago, the Khmer people built a magnificent civilization that was distinguished for its massive architecture, great cities and beautiful temples. For 500 years, from the ninth century onward, the Khmer "God-Kings" ruled with an openhanded lavishness that has never since been matched in Indochina, as the ruins of Angkor Wat so eloquently testify. And if their splendor was forgotten by the outside world, it remained as a conscious race memory that was passed on to their less fortunate successors.

The Cambodia of today may be very largely underdeveloped. Its people may be poor. But they are better off, for the most part, than their neighbors. Land reform is not an issue here, for perhaps as many as 90 per cent of Cambodia's farmers own their own land. Nor are there striking extremes of wealth and poverty, as may be seen in the Philippines. The most recent census has shown that out of 806,000 landowners, only about 1,200 hold more than fifty acres and together control less than 5 per cent of usable land.[10] It is also true that no one goes hungry in Cambodia. The per capita consumption of rice, except in wartime emergencies, usually is calculated at 1.5 pounds a day, seasoned with generous helpings of fish and vegetables and sometimes a little meat as well.

It was not strange, therefore, that North Vietnam found Cambodia unprepared to accept the glowing promises of deliverance through Communism. The fact is that most Cambodians already had more than a systematic communization of the land could have given them; if anything, being such arrant individualists, they stood to lose more than they could have gained through a collective economy. This explained why the Khmer Rouge never made much headway as an indigenous radical movement before the Communist drive began from North Vietnam.

An equally important bulwark against the spread of Communism within Cambodia was the strength of the Buddhist movement, no small matter in the lands of Southeast Asia. Both the Mohanikay and

---

[10] "Cambodia at War," *The Economist*, November 21, 1970, p. 39.

Thommayuth orders of Theravada Buddhism maintained a steadfast alliance with the new government of Cambodia following the overthrow of Prince Sihanouk. It was a force that the invaders found difficult to combat and became one of the underlying reasons for the initial Cambodian resistance to enemy incursions. Unlike the South Vietnamese, who had to be drafted into their Army, Cambodians rushed to the colors with valorous spirit once they realized that their country was fighting for its life.

No people in Asia displayed more unity of spirit in a time of extreme adversity.

The Latter Days of Sihanouk

It is fairly obvious that the Communists counted in large part on Prince Sihanouk's leadership to win Cambodia for them. No doubt, the mercurial ex-ruler, too, hoped that his support of the invading North Vietnamese would quickly put him back in power in Pnom Penh. But both were wrong.

However shaky the new Cambodian government proved to be, and there was a great deal of initial doubt that it could survive, the first year's fighting was sufficient indication that any eventual Communist triumph would be costly. As for Prince Sihanouk, his celebrated charisma did not work too well from far-off Peking. Too late, he learned that his identification with the Communist invader and his refugee status in China had cost him the trust and affection of his people.

Even when the Prince held power in Pnom Penh, there was a general disposition in the West to regard him as a kind of musical comedy character, perennially youthful and high-spirited and given to colorful conduct. He was much more important than that in Southeast Asia. His experience as a national leader extended over three decades. His long balancing act between the United States and South Vietnam on the one side and China and North Vietnam on the other kept his country at peace while the rest of Indochina was being torn apart. He was no mere Marxist playboy. Whether he was known as Son Altesse Royale or Snooks, he was a force that had to be reckoned with.

Had there been no Sihanouk, the course of events in Indochina might have taken a far different direction. At only nineteen years of age, ten months after the fall of France, he became King of Cambodia during the Japanese occupation. He changed sides with alacrity when the French returned after the war, creating a parliamentary government and drafting a new constitution for his country. Unfortunately, this first—and last—princely experiment with democracy in Cambodia died before birth. First of all, the French didn't like it. And even if they had, the Cambodians weren't ready for self-government at that stage in their history.

But Sihanouk persisted. Before the French collapse at Dienbienphu and the 1954 Geneva conference that followed, the Prince won independence for his country on November 8, 1953, and proceeded to install himself as an authoritarian ruler. But when he saw how much opposition he had aroused, he gave way; upon his abdication on March 2, 1955, he installed his father in the royal palace and went into voluntary exile. Five years later, upon his father's death, he resumed power—this time as Chief of State.

Such a man was not to be taken aback when he saw that all Indochina was threatened with war once again. He knew perfectly well that the Vietcong were using Cambodian territory as a refuge and regroupment area in their earliest attacks on South Vietnam, but he shouted his denials from the housetops. For quite a long time, he convinced the peace-at-any-price faction in the United States that he was a pure and undefiled neutralist, seeking to keep his country aloof from combat. But in fact, he had made a careful calculation and decided that this was not a war that the United States could win. He may not have been overly impressed with the North Vietnamese; yet, he felt he had to come to terms with Hanoi and Peking.

Therefore, when the crunch came and he had to make a choice, he turned his back on the United States. It cost him a lot, for he had received $366 million in American military and economic assistance between 1954 and November 20, 1963, when he charged the United States with intervening in Cambodian affairs and rejected further financial aid. To make up for the deficiency, he hustled off to Peking to collect $10 million, took an unspecified amount from Moscow and other Communist capitals, and graciously accepted a French offer of $32.6 million in gifts, loans and suppliers' credits. At the beginning of 1965, when the United States escalated the war in Vietnam, Sihanouk appeared to be sitting pretty. He had $95 million in foreign exchange reserves in his treasury and he was sure that he had chosen the winning side. All over the world, he became the darling of anti-American factions; he had tweaked Uncle Sam's nose and was the very devil of a fellow. Accordingly, it was no surprise when he broke diplomatic relations with the United States in the spring of 1965 after South Vietnamese aircraft had attacked the Vietcong sanctuaries in Cambodia.

He felt he had nothing to lose, everything to gain.

The Cambodian Sanctuaries

The North Vietnamese Army already had moved into the Cambodian sanctuaries—the Parrot's Beak and other border areas—that had been prepared by the Vietcong. These were now used for forays in strength into tottering South Vietnam. It was a frustrating time for the Americans and their South Vietnamese allies. For from Cambodia, it was simplicity itself for the Communists to dominate the Mekong Delta and supply their troops by sea. Through the port of Kompong Som (Sihanoukville, as it was then called), it was much easier to keep up a steady flow of war matériel than it was to pack it down the Ho Chi Minh Trail.

Until the spring of 1969, Prince Sihanouk maintained his policy of loudly and fiercely denying that the North Vietnamese were fighting from Cambodian bases. Once, when American correspondents in Cambodia were able to locate and photograph an abandoned shelter, the Prince called their articles lies and their pictures a fraud. No ruler in Asia displayed more consummate gall.

Had it not been for General Lon Nol, Sihanouk might have remained unchallenged in his own country. But the popular and powerful chief of the Cambodian Army argued with his Chief of State early in 1969, pointing out that the North Vietnamese and the Vietcong had in effect annexed the Cambodian border territory they had occupied for the better part of five years either individually or together. To appease Lon Nol, the Prince finally made a public protest.[11] But the North Vietnamese merely continued to deny that their troops were fighting in Cambodia or even using the Ho Chi Minh Trail. Sihanouk let it go at that. His reproaches to the side he supported were only for the sake of appearances. The Communists knew perfectly well that he would do nothing to embarrass them, if he could avoid it, and conducted themselves accordingly. Their attacks on South Vietnam intensified.

It was not the first time that the Communists had set up such a third-country base for attacking a small nation on which they had designs, and it would not be the last. By lending himself quite willingly to the campaign that had been planned in Hanoi with the support of Peking, Sihanouk made it possible for North Vietnam and the Vietcong to dominate the South Vietnamese countryside. Only massive American intervention frustrated a Communist victory at that time.

In Sihanouk's defense, it could be argued that he had no other choice than to go along with the designs of Hanoi and Peking. He himself forecast at the time of his break with the United States that Cambodia was marked for eventual Communist domination. That being taken for granted, he adopted the position that he wanted to make the transition as pleasant as possible for himself and for his people. "When the inevitable moment comes," he wrote, "I want my country to meet its fate with the least possible loss of life and destruction."[12]

Sihanouk and Tito

Prince Sihanouk gave every evidence in the latter part of the 1960s of preparing himself for the role of an Asian Tito. He fancied the part. With greater frequency as time went on, he took to lecturing all the great powers from Pnom Penh, the Communists in a more respectful manner than the West, and was gratified at the amount of attention he received. He was an inordinately vain man but, unlike Tito, he had no iron in his soul.

[11] Sim Var, "Restoring Peace to Cambodia," *Pacific Community*, October, 1970, p. 157.
[12] *Atlas*, August, 1965, p. 97, translated from *Réalités Cambodgiennes* (Pnom Penh).

There were, of course, certain surface similarities between the position of the Prince and the far tougher and more durable Yugoslav leader. Like Yugoslavia, which was used by General Markos Vafiades as a sanctuary for Communist guerrillas in the attack on Greece in the late 1940s, Cambodia served as the base for the Communist assault on the Saigon government. Both thereby opposed the designs of the United States. And both, up to a point, gambled on the eventual victory of the Communist side.

It was at this stage that the similarity between Yugoslavia and Cambodia ended. For in 1948, at the height of the Communist struggle to take over Greece, Tito's long-smoldering differences with Moscow burst into flames that threatened to consume the heretic in the Communist camp. But he marshaled his armed forces, refused to give in, and prepared for the worst. In the process, he closed Yugoslavia's borders to Communist incursions against Greece. With the enunciation of the Truman Doctrine, Washington's bold answer to the threat to Greece, Yugoslavia found itself on the same side as the United States but Tito did not seem to be in the least inconvenienced. In the long run, he became the first Communist leader to defy Moscow's power and survive.

Sihanouk, being outside the Communist camp while he was in power, had a better basis in principle for resisting the demands of Hanoi and Peking in the Vietnam War, had he chosen to do so. He had an Army of 28,000 troops, which despite lack of training and equipment could have been used as a rallying point for resistance to the Communist side. But he had long since given up on the Army, holding it to be of little use either to his country or to himself, and had contemptuously turned his soldiers into a road-building force. He felt that he did not need the Army. He fancied himself as a kind of Southeast Asian Machiavelli who could accomplish by guile what he could not attain by force.

In the end, it was his disregard of the Army that cost him his power.

Revolt in Cambodia

The leaders of the despised Cambodian Army had been concerned for some time over Prince Sihanouk's alliance with Hanoi and

Peking, his overweening pride in his own abilities as a diplomat, and his refusal to prepare his armed forces for the defense of his country. For military men, it was no small matter to see an important and strategic part of the country used by foreign troops as a base for war against a neighboring land.

At first, the Cambodian military had been complaisant about the presence of the North Vietnamese Army and the Vietcong in border areas west of the Mekong River. But as time went on, and the long-anticipated Communist victory did not materialize, Lon Nol and his fellow officers suspected that the Prince had miscalculated. After five years, the Communist presence in Cambodia had become nothing more nor less than an armed occupation and was likely to remain so unless some firm action could be taken.

It was hopeless to expect that Prince Sihanouk would deal firmly with Hanoi and Peking. He had, in effect, made his country their protectorate; not even he could pretend, at least to his own people, that Cambodia could preserve her independence for very much longer with large contingents of foreign troops on her soil. Dissatisfaction with the Prince's position arose in Pnom Penh, spreading from the military to the National Assembly, which had been used as a royal rubber stamp for years. But if Sihanouk knew, he did not care. He was so confident of the strength of his position that he took off for another of his periodic visits to European capitals, Moscow and Peking in the late winter of 1970. While he was in Moscow on March 18, Lon Nol led an uprising against him and the National Assembly deposed him as Chief of State.

In furious haste, the Prince flew to Peking in the hope that his Chinese allies would deal quickly with the upstarts who had taken over in Pnom Penh. But the Chinese, although polite and full of regrets, were unwilling to do anything rash for a puppet who had inconsiderately let himself be overthrown. They helped him set up a government-in-exile, distributed his press releases and maintained him in approximately the style to which he had been accustomed. But they couldn't restore him at once to the power that formerly had been his. Worse still, his government-in-exile was not recognized initially by much of the world, including Great Britain, France and even the Soviet Union.

Cambodia Fights Back

Before the Lon Nol government was a month old, the North Vietnamese struck in force at the strong point of Saang in Cambodia. Few believed that Cambodia would be able to hold out for very long. In Pnom Penh, foreign embassies made emergency preparations to move, for the capital city seemed as good as gone. As for Lon Nol, the most popular forecast was that he would be flying into exile soon and Sihanouk would once again be the master of the land.

The tiny Cambodian Army, with little training and few modern weapons of any kind, abandoned its road-building chores and responded to the emergency with an astounding show of courage and *élan*. The troops mounted up for combat in Pepsi-Cola trucks and ancient taxicabs. And when they met the enemy, they did not run but bravely stood their ground for as long as their slender supplies of ammunition held out. Of communications, there were none. More than one field commander had to leave his troops at this critical time to search for a public telephone in the nearest town and ask for directions from the high command in Pnom Penh. But for all their handicaps, in much the same manner as the Israeli Army stood off the encircling Arabs in 1948, the Cambodians frustrated the first enemy drive to crush them.

Had it not been for the intervention of American and South Vietnamese forces, however, there is no doubt that the Cambodians would have been overwhelmed after their narrow initial victory. But once the combined American-South Vietnamese incursion had destroyed the Communist border sanctuaries, the Lon Nol government found it had time to build up its armed forces. Within six months, mainly through a surge of volunteers, the tiny Army became a fighting force of 150,000 troops, and military supplies came in by sea, air and overland at the rate of thirty tons a day, mainly from the United States.

This did not mean, of course, that either the government or its capital was safe. More often than not, the enemy was able to cut off Pnom Penh from most other parts of the country for long periods by attacking the principal highways. And the route to the key port of Kompong Som was cut so often that it became more feasible to send in much-needed supplies of gasoline and oil by way of the Mekong River to Pnom Penh. It was the chief responsibility of South Vietnamese troops, who operated in Cambodia after the American pullout, to insure that the enemy would be kept sufficiently off balance to permit supplies to get through to Pnom Penh and other centers.

Cambodia did not become a major theater of warfare in Indochina chiefly because the North Vietnamese were already spread very thinly across South Vietnam and Laos. During 1971, they kept 40,000 to 50,000 troops inside Cambodia with the assistance of perhaps 10,000 Vietcong and 5,000 Khmer Rouge. But it was seldom that the Communist side committed more than 5,000 troops to battle at any one time; frequently, their forays were confined to much smaller tactical units. It was their strategy, as in South Vietnam and Laos, to wear down their enemies through persistent guerrilla warfare instead of the frontal attacks with which they opened the Cambodian war.

Against this invading force, the Cambodians hoped to create a well-equipped army of 200,000 and were training their recruits in Laos and South Vietnam as well as in their own country. They also brought into being a 2,000-man air force that flew anything that came to hand, including a few American T-28s, French Fougas and Russian MIGs. In the air, as on the ground, the Cambodian forces lived from hand to mouth and constantly looked to neighboring South Vietnam for support. It was fortunate for both that the South Vietnamese Army, so long in the making and so often an undependable force in the past, seemed to find itself in the first weeks in which it was able to fight the enemy on foreign soil. Had it not been for the excesses of South Vietnamese troops, which angered the Cambodian peasantry almost as much as the presence of the North Vietnamese invaders, everything would have gone much better. As the first year's fighting indicated, however, the outcome in Cambodia was largely dependent on what happened in Laos and South Vietnam. And that is how the Cambodian government read its own fate.

The Ills of Pnom Penh

For almost a year, Premier Lon Nol carried the heavy burden of running the government, directing the Army as defense minister and maintaining a firm working partnership with the United States and

South Vietnam. But in the end, the task proved to be too much for him. He suffered a stroke that incapacitated him on February 8, 1971, just at a point when Cambodia's fledgling government seemed to be rounding the corner in a time of the gravest national crisis. His deputy, Lieutenant General Sisowath Sirik Matak, held the principal executive power in his absence, and after two weeks of indecision following Lon Nol's return, Sirik Matak agreed to stay on in that capacity. But it was clear enough that Lon Nol was so incapacitated that he could be premier in name only of the Cambodian republic he had created in October 1970.

The Cambodian Establishment, however, was not as badly split as its counterpart in Saigon. In Pnom Penh, no matter how great the disagreement between the various factions over the way power should be allotted in the next phase of Cambodia's struggle for national survival, an effort was made to preserve the amenities. Just how long the political truce would last remained a problem for all sides, and for the United States and South Vietnam as well. For everybody realized that a Cambodian collapse could well be the end of the whole rickety anti-Communist front that the United States had patched together.

There was no doubt that Sirik Matak was by far the most competent administrator in the government. The Chief of State, Cheng Heng, and the president of the National Assembly, General In Tam, joined with him in carrying on their tasks and giving the Cambodian regime a sense of stability. The balance of military power apparently had been inherited by the Premier's younger brother, Colonel Lon Non, commander of the 15th Brigade. And waiting in the wings for a chance to go to the top was an old Cambodian hero, Son Ngoc Thanh, one-time head of Cambodia's Democratic Party and the long-time leader of the anti-Sihanouk guerrillas, the Khmer Serai.[13]

Thanh advocated national elections to solve the dilemma of the Cambodian succession, which seemed logical enough. But in a country so divided by war, it was a good question whether elections might not raise more problems than they resolved. Accordingly, Sirik Matak faced up to a monumental task in the latter part of 1971 when his government abolished the democratic system. As an Asian com-

[13] *The Economist*, June 5, 1971, p. 40.

mentator put it: "Hardly another political leader in the world faces such formidable problems and dangers, and we can only hope that what must appear to be a very frail unity will coalesce into a force that will continue to maintain the independence and freedom of the Khmer Republic."[14]

There was, in other words, more hope than faith in Cambodia's future among sympathetic Asians elsewhere.

The United States and Cambodia

The United States did not exactly leap into the breach when Cambodia faced up to its desperate situation. After the public uproar over the American-South Vietnamese intervention that blocked the 1970 Communist take-over, Washington's attitude toward the Cambodians was compounded of extreme caution and great doubt. As President Nixon kept assuring the unruly American peace faction, the sole American interest in Cambodia was to insure the success of the Vietnamization program. It wasn't calculated to make Pnom Penh very enthusiastic about the staying power of Cambodia's noble American ally.

Initially, the Pentagon rushed in ammunition and 50,000 automatic rifles from a stock of American-made and captured Communist weapons in South Vietnam. American C-119 transports, an old-fashioned aircraft, served as air support for Cambodian ground troops; later, when the Cambodians showed they were not about to collapse immediately, American fighter aircraft intervened when needed, although most of the combat support missions for normal military operations were flown by the South Vietnamese. The State Department, which had only three officials in Pnom Penh at the time of Sihanouk's removal, built up its forces to about one hundred operatives of all kinds. And the CIA, too, came in with its mixed bag of spooks who created more confusion than support during the initial emergency.

But when the total American military effort for the first eighteen months of the new Cambodian government was added up, it amounted to much less than the backing that was given to the

[14] *Japan Times*, editorial, May 11, 1971, p. 14.

government of South Vietnam or even the neutralist-rightist regime in Laos. Indeed, sentiment against further American involvement in Indochina continued to be so abrasive that Congressional approval of the Defense Department appropriations bill for 1971 was hinged to a refusal to finance operations by American ground combat forces in Laos, Cambodia or Thailand.

Despite its gratitude to the Lon Nol regime for its resistance to North Vietnam, which helped buy time for the Americans elsewhere in Indochina, the American government was obliged to be extremely careful about its participation in the war. The first six months of American aid amounted to about $90 million and for the entire year Congress reluctantly granted $185 million, mainly for military aid. The 1971 total was about the same, $165 million for military aid and $20 million extra for road repairing and bridgebuilding to insure improved military movement. For 1972, the Cambodians received a slight increase, to $200 million. The United States, of course, also had to stand the bulk of the cost of the South Vietnamese support operations in Cambodia, which drew off anywhere from 10,000 to 30,000 troops, depending on the situation.

Cambodia did not lack for individual supporters in Washington, regardless of the government's attitude. One enthusiastic official, after a visit to Pnom Penh, was aglow over Cambodian enterprise and remarked, "If you give one hundred dollars to the Vietnamese, you generally get ten dollars' value. If you give the same amount to the Cambodians, you get one hundred and ten dollars' value." However, in very precise terms, the prize in the war in Indochina was South Vietnam, not Cambodia, and this more than anything else determined the position of the United States.

Cambodia's Economic Crisis

Even before the Communist invasion, Cambodia was not exactly bursting with prosperity. Its gross national product, based mainly on rubber and rice, ran to about $430 million a year, which meant that per capita earnings were only about $70. The total was about half of what it had been in the prosperous year of 1966, indicating the extent to which the war had hurt the country's economy. In all the land, there were only about 1,500 tractors and 25,000 automobiles, all but about 5,000 of the latter being in Pnom Penh. Less than 12,000 tons of fertilizer was sold each year.

While there was peace, such things didn't matter much to the Cambodians; in a land so richly endowed, they were always able to get along. But once the war tore apart the economy, destroying nearly all the rubber plantations and cutting heavily into the rice crop, it was inevitable that a crisis would follow. And this was as much of a danger to the new Cambodian government as any Communist thrust.

All that Cambodia was able to export in 1970 was 1,000 tons of rubber, as against 16,000 tons in 1969. For 1971, the outlook was even less promising. As for rice, the Cambodians had to depend on military convoys to distribute the domestic crop; whereas 180,000 tons were exported before the war, the country had barely enough to feed its people thereafter. Hoarding boosted prices from about $12 a 220-pound sack at the official rate of exchange to almost $40. And the official rate of 54 riels to the dollar was boosted to 140 late in 1971; on the black market the rate was as high as 250 riels to the dollar.[15]

The United States asked for help to prop up the Cambodian economy and received some assistance from Japan and Australia, among others. But it didn't solve the problem for Pnom Penh. It had to find ways of meeting its mounting military payrolls, financing aid for some 500,000 Cambodian refugees and getting a commodity import program going. There was only one place where assistance of such magnitude was available and that was Washington.

Cambodia had survived the American military pullout. Given sufficient South Vietnamese support, the Khmer republic had at least a fighting chance against the North Vietnamese. But it was problematical that it could surmount the virtual collapse of its economy without a massive infusion of American economic assistance.

5. THE UNITED STATES AND INDOCHINA

To a disillusioned and embittered American public, the extent of the American commitment in Indochina today, even with the pullout of

---

[15] Kim Willenson, UPI economic report filed October 3, 1970; *Far Eastern Economic Review*, June 5, 1971, pp. 20–22; *The New York Times*, June 28, 1971, p. 3.

American combat troops, remains far too dangerous and too costly to an economy that is not running with all its accustomed smoothness. The dour mood is understandable after a decade of war without victory, the sacrifice of so many young lives and so much treasure, the disgrace of the My Lai massacre and the subsequent conviction of Lieutenant William L. Calley, Jr., as the perpetrator, the disclosure of widespread heroin addiction among American fighting men and the agony of American war prisoners in confinement in North Vietnam. One hears on every side, "What business have we in Indochina anyway? We should never have become involved."

A good case could have been made out for such a position at one time. Unhappily, it is an academic matter now.

No matter how much it may be denied by men of good faith and good will, an American interest does exist in Indochina and it will last beyond the withdrawal of the American military and the end of combat. It was established, not by political guile or mercantile ventures, but by the Americans who died by the tens of thousands in the rice paddies, jungles and mountains of Indochina. If they could not win a victory, they purchased at the very least the right of the United States to help decide what kind of peace will be established in Indochina and what measures will be taken to see that it is observed. They fought in the same tradition as the British seamen who, in Winston Churchill's phrase, established Britain's stake in the freedom of the seas with their white bones, scattered across the bottom of the ocean.

As a participant in the Indochina conflict, the United States is thus committed to stay the course in seeking and maintaining peace. And this means, much as many in the United States may regret it or oppose it, that there is a continuing American commitment to the people of South Vietnam, Laos and Cambodia. It may not be fashionable these days to refer to such things as national honor but it exists; once it perishes, the country first forfeits respect, then power and finally its very identity as a nation.

Few in the United States, however, will ever again delude themselves into the belief that an American military presence on the mainland of Asia is either practical or desirable. Nor can there be any false hopes for the erection of a bulwark of states along the Southeast Asian perimeter that will "contain" China. The long-deferred

American approach to Peking, and the warmth with which the American public initially received Washington's change in policy, are at least an indication that the United States is going to continue to play an important role in Asian affairs.

What effect will a normalization of relations between Peking and Washington have on the future of Indochina? Certainly, such a rapprochement, if carried out in good faith, will dissipate some of the hostility that was produced by a quarter century of strife. If it makes impossible an American dream world in Indochina cast in the image of Thomas Jefferson, it also nullifies hope in Peking and Hanoi that the peoples of Indochina will turn as one to worship at the shrine of Mao Tse-tung. The best that the United States and China can do, under prevailing circumstances, is to seek stability in a reconstituted postwar Indochina, which will at last permit the Vietnamese, the Lao and the Cambodians to work out their own destinies.

That, of course, is the ideal and it is probably unattainable in an imperfect world. But it remains the goal toward which the great powers must move if they seriously intend to build a peaceful Indochina.

V. Trouble on the Flank

1. THE DISCONTENTED

There are comparatively few national leaders in non-Communist Asia today who would willingly trust their lives, their fortunes and their sacred honor to the United States in the next decade.

What has happened to the committed ones in Indochina, despite the vast outpouring of American military support and economic assistance, has not been very reassuring elsewhere in Southeast Asia. Outside the areas of conflict, therefore, doubt of American intentions and disaffection with American policies are the melancholy order of the day. And this is as true in the lands of an ally of the United States, such as Thailand, as it is of more or less neutral powers, such as Burma, Indonesia, Malaysia and the city-state of Singapore.

The Bouncing Dominoes

It is now almost two decades since President Dwight David Eisenhower likened these nations unflatteringly to a row of falling dominoes, toppling before the forces of Communism. In his press conference of April 7, 1954, when the French were about to be ejected from their Indochina empire, he said: "You have a row of dominoes set up and you knock over the first one and what will happen to the last one is the certainty that it will go over very quickly. So you have the beginning of a disintegration that would have the most profound influence."

Just to make certain that there could be no mistake about his meaning, President Eisenhower named Thailand, Burma, Malaya[1] and Indonesia as the domino states that would collapse once the Communist forces overwhelmed Indochina. Although few Americans realized it, what their President was talking about was an area as large as the eleven westernmost states in the United States, populated by almost 200,000,000 inhabitants. He predicted, as well, that once Communism dominated the region, the United States would be expelled from the Indo-Pacific.[2]

Except for dedicated anti-Communists, the domino theory never attracted many adherents. Not even the Joint Chiefs of Staff were particularly pleased with the analogy. It is obviously out of date today, with the United States turning about to seek improved relations with China and removing its ground forces from the Asian mainland. Even U.S. atomic bombs, withdrawn from Okinawa, won't be placed in South Korea or Taiwan for fear of offending Peking. And the flights over China by U.S. spying aircraft have been halted.

Instead of falling, therefore, the dominoes have taken to bouncing around. The slide toward Communism is not now so much to be feared as a slide toward chaos. For most of the national leaders who have depended on the United States, in whole or in part, are bound to be in deep trouble with their own people over the quick American turnabout. Some are furious and can't be blamed for their hurt feelings. Others either are taking it philosophically or trying, in one way or another, to make sure that some of the benefits of their association with Washington are retained for the time being.

But like leaders of the outpost states of Asia to the north, the

[1] It became the Federation of Malaysia in 1963.
[2] Robert J. Donovan, *Eisenhower: The Inside Story* (New York: Harper, 1956), p. 261.

statesmen of Southeast Asia are all thoughtfully surveying their foreign policies in the light of unpleasant realities. In consequence, some governments may fall. Others may change front, and still others may very well try to arrange for the best terms they can with more powerful Communist neighbors.

A Star-Spangled Gulliver

What this means, quite bluntly put, is that many a disillusioned non-Communist Asian leader cannot now consider the United States as a dependable ally. Its image, particularly in Southeast Asia, no longer is that of an all-conquering Western colossus but rather resembles a star-spangled Gulliver trapped by the voracious pygmies from Hanoi. Such neutrals as Prime Minister Lee Kuan Yew of Singapore, too, have lost confidence in Washington's sweet assurances. Upon returning home after an American visit late in 1970, the blunt-spoken Lee let his colleagues know how unfavorably impressed he was with both a wavering American government and an increasingly divided American public opinion.

Yet, neither the neutrals nor the erstwhile American client states think very much of the proposition of abasing themselves before the high altars of Communism in Moscow, Peking or Hanoi. Out of long experience with resistance to power centers in Asia, regardless of political orientation, most non-Communist leaders of Southeast Asia are well aware of the dangers of an abrupt change of front. Almost certainly, it would mean giving up their independence at one stroke, following the somewhat less than inspiring example of Prince Norodom Sihanouk of Cambodia. And if there is one issue on which these often quarrelsome statesmen agree, it is the necessity of maintaining their national integrity, each in his own land.

They may be discontented with things as they are. But they do not want to do anything that will imperil the future of their countries at a critical time in Asian history. The deliberate pace of the American withdrawal is giving them time to consider their options. The extent of American protectionism and the shifting values of their currencies against the dollar, now cut off from its gold base, will make them more cautious than ever. But before long—a few years at most—the time of decision will be at hand for each of the non-Communist nations of Southeast Asia.

2. THE FLEXIBLE THAIS

During the Bandung conference of 1955 in Indonesia, Prince Wan Waithayakorn of Thailand asked Premier Chou En-lai why China was setting up a "free" Thai state. It was a worrisome matter to the Thais because a former premier, Pridi Phanomyong, was then residing quite comfortably in Peking.

The ever-courteous Chou was soothing. As Prince Wan recalled, "He said the new state was being established in accordance with his government's policy of giving more freedom to various states, but it had nothing to do with the Thai government. He also said that Mr. Pridi Phanomyong was merely a political refugee."[3]

The Chinese-supported insurgency is still going on along Thailand's northern and northeastern frontiers, but Pridi Phanomyong no longer is a political refugee in Peking. Since 1970, he has been residing even more comfortably in Paris on the pension, with back pay, that the Thai government is reported to have granted him. Although he was once anathema to Bangkok, where he was branded rightly or wrongly as the head of a Communist conspiracy, he has his Thai passport today. He also regularly receives visits, reputedly far more than mere courtesy calls, from Thai officials in the French capital. Without doubt, he is one of the principal Thai channels to Peking—a useful man to have around in changing times.[4]

The rehabilitation of Pridi is just one aspect of the Thai return to a more flexible foreign policy in the wake of the American decision to seek better relations with Peking and pull back from an over-extended posture in Asia. Having preserved their freedom for more than 1,000 years through the most intricate dealings with their far more powerful neighbors, the Thais are doing what comes naturally to them. Their very name means "free." And through whatever

[3] Interview with Prince Wan in the Bangkok *Post*, July 26, 1970, pp. 13–15.
[4] Stanley Karnow, *Japan Times*, March 10, 1971, p. 14.

means are necessary, they may be counted on to try to maintain their independence.

How the Thais Have Changed

It is one of the commonplaces of diplomatic discourse in Southeast Asia (and a number of great foreign capitals, as well) to stress the coming changes in Thailand. The Thai watchers have their work cut out for them. For this prosperous nation of 36,000,000, about the size of Colorado and Wyoming, with fourteen times their population, may well be able to tip the balance of power in Southeast Asia in any one of a number of ways. And their leaders know it.

What the outside world has come to believe of Thailand has very little to do with reality. Its potential cannot be measured by the Westernized veneer and artificial glamour of crowded Bangkok, once a mini-Tokyo to the weary American serviceman. Nor is Thailand in any sense the dreamy musical-comedy kingdom that Richard Rodgers and Oscar Hammerstein II created for the amusement of an older generation of Americans. Behind the facade of what is presented as a democratic government, the Thai Establishment operates with subtlety, skill and, usually, a well-ordered secrecy. To those who would read its intentions in time of crisis, it masks its meaning with the small gestures and movements of the charming native dances.

Such Oriental graces serve to soften, but scarcely conceal, the essentially practical nature of the Thais. When they found their long reign of absolute monarchs to be irksome, they changed quietly and bloodlessly to rule by constitutional monarchy in an orderly military coup on June 24, 1932. It was completely in the Thai manner for the reigning king, Prachathipok, to support the new order by publishing articles about democracy in his newspaper, *Nangsuepim Thai*, and to forbid members of the Royal Group from participating in politics lest they be unfairly attacked.

When the Japanese overran Southeast Asia and occupied Thailand in 1941, the Thais signed up as Japanese allies because there was nothing else they could do under the circumstances. But they made sure that someone, the useful Pridi Phanomyong, as it turned out, led a more or less effective resistance movement against the time that the

Japanese would have to leave. When that happy day came, Pridi was given the premiership as a reward, but only briefly, for he proved to be too radical for the times. The Thais saw that it was to their national interest to face toward the United States and away from a war-ravaged China that had just been seized by the forces of Mao Tse-tung.

The American era, for however brief a time it may last, has brought great benefits to Thailand but it has also created new dangers for an Asian land that associated itself so closely with the shifting fortunes of the West. With Pakistan and the Philippines, Thailand became one of the Asian members of the Southeast Asia Treaty Organization in 1955, joined in the fateful pledge to help defend the successor states of French Indochina from Communist aggression, and made Bangkok the seat of the new organization.

Thailand's vague democratic practices were ill-suited to the needs of its leadership, however. In another of the nation's celebrated bloodless coups, the old field marshal Sarit Thanarat seized power as a dictator in 1957, outlawed the Communist Party, and set out to modernize the country by every means at his command. He enriched himself in the process, for when he died, on December 8, 1963, he was disclosed to have amassed $140 million. But after authorizing publication of the news in the usually cooperative Thai press, the new Premier, Marshal Thanom Kittikachorn, warned the editors to refrain from publishing anything "prejudicial to peace and public order." The damper was put on the scandal.

In any event, the Thais had more important things to worry about. In little more than a year, the United States was sinking ever deeper into the mire of the Vietnam War, the secret Thai bases were being built to mount the massive B-52 bombing campaigns against North Vietnam, and American ground troops were pouring into the Asian mainland by the hundreds of thousands. Nobody had to tell the Thai watchers that Thailand had made—and received—enormous commitments involving the United States. The evidence was clearly visible in the form of 50,000 American troops massed about the B-52s at the new bases. The secret, the most poorly kept of the Vietnam War, was out.

United States Arms and Thailand

Next to American expenditures in Indochina, the funds that have been pumped into Thailand for military purposes are the largest in Asia. Beginning in 1965, with net expenditures of about $35 million, the American military construction program reached a high of $215 million in 1967 and was duplicated in 1968. The decline began in 1969, with spending at $171 million, and was less in 1970.

In addition, American military assistance to Thailand in 1968–70 totaled $75 million in each year while economic grant aid and loan programs came to $87 million more. Resources worth more than $100 million each year were thus put into the Thai economy through such programs.

The most controversial part of the whole operation was the $50 million a year that the United States paid to have 12,000 Thai troops sent to the war centers of South Vietnam, beginning in 1967. It wasn't worth all the excitement and bitter feeling, once the deal was exposed by a Senatorial investigating committee in Washington. For the Thais, only a small part of the American-armed 125,000 troops that were deployed on the home front, took comparatively little part in the fighting. And their presence, largely symbolic, did not do very much to support the fiction that an international alliance, and not merely the United States and South Vietnam, was resisting Communist encroachments. It seemed to many Americans, once the Thais began pulling out in 1971, that the whole sad business had done more harm than good to relations between the United States and Thailand.

For many reasons, the Nixon Doctrine meant different things in the various countries in Asia to which it applied. In Thailand, without any doubt, it continued to denote large American contributions to the Thai military even after the first 6,000 American troops had been pulled out of Thai bases. During his 1969 visit to Thailand, President Nixon had gone beyond the scope of his doctrine, as it was then understood, in promising support to the Thais. Two years later, the American Secretary of Defense, Melvin Laird, went even further by assuring the Thai leadership during a visit to Bangkok that American military aid would actually increase during the ensuing decade. Since it was running at the rate of $75 million a year in 1971, the pledged total could be calculated in the range of close to $1 billion. But the cautious Thais, like everyone else, realized that it was one thing for the Nixon Administration to make promises and quite another for a Democratic-controlled Congress and subsequent administrations to insure delivery as guaranteed.

Boomtime Comes to Thailand

While the requirements of American defense have turned out to be of major benefit to Thailand in the broadest sense, the Thais have not done as well as they had expected in their commercial bargaining with the United States. From the time that King Mongkut offered to send two Siamese war elephants to President Abraham Lincoln during the American Civil War, the Thais have been interested in promoting a modest kind of dealing with the far-off Americans. But in their most elaborate fantasies, the members of the Thai Establishment scarcely anticipated what a booming two-way commerce with the United States would do to their country.

What happened in Japan, and to a lesser extent in Hong Kong and Singapore, was duplicated in Thailand in many respects, except that the Thais could not keep their profits. From 1965, when American-Thai trade amounted to $162 million, commercial exchanges between the two countries jumped to almost $400 million at the outset of the 1970s. At their most expansive period, the Thais were importing goods from the United States, mainly machinery and other equipment, at the rate of nearly $200 million a year and sending back less than half that amount in tin, rubber and fibers.

The Thais soon found that, even with the Americans picking up the bill for much of their national defense, that kind of trading didn't pay. Despite $30 million annually spent by American troops in Thailand and an additional $15 million from 125,000 American tourists in a year, the Thai trade deficit with the United States mounted steadily. In 1967, it was $78 million; in 1968, $130 million; and in 1969 it exceeded $150 million.[5]

---

[5] Most of the statistics on American trade with Thailand and American military expenditures there are from an address by the American ambassador to Thailand, Leonard Unger, before the American Chamber of Commerce in

What made the Thais even more sensitive was the annual imbalance in their trade with Japan, which was mounting at the same time to almost $100 million a year in Japan's favor. The tough-trading Japanese, by 1970, had taken over a very large share of the Thai trade in textiles, electrical goods and automobiles, all of them luxuries in the Thai agriculture-oriented economy. The Japanese were selling Thailand 90 per cent of its synthetic yarn, 50 per cent of its textiles, 70 per cent of its electrical equipment and goods, and 55 per cent of its automobiles and allied products. But the Thais couldn't sell the Japanese much of anything, a usual complaint among Japan's Asian trading partners.[6]

The Thais Tighten Their Belts

Some of Thailand's neighbors scornfully suggested that the Thais had been going on wild buying sprees and bringing into the country far more than they could afford. Others called them improvident wastrels. Tales of graft and corruption, too, abounded but that was usual in almost any Asian country. Very possibly, there was something to each of these complaints, even though they were often grounded in envy, but the main reason for Thailand's tightening economic situation was a slump in the rice market, the nation's main resource in foreign trade.

Before Asia's rice bowls began to be filled by the "green revolution" wrought by miracle strains of rice, Thailand had maintained close to a monopoly of the Asian rice market. At its peak in 1964, it was exporting 1,900,0000 metric tons of rice; by 1969, that total had fallen to 986,000 metric tons, and in 1970 it was still less. As if that weren't bad enough, the price of rice began declining. And worst of all, Thailand's two biggest trading partners, the United States and Japan, began undercutting the rice market. The Japanese, with more

Bangkok on January 21, 1970, and from a paper, "Economic Trends in Thailand," prepared by the American embassy in Bangkok March 30, 1970. The secret 1967 agreement between Thailand and the U.S. to send a Thai combat division to Vietnam for $50 million a year was disclosed in U.S. Senate testimony June 7, 1970. Additional trade statistics are from the *Far Eastern Economic Review*, July 2, 1970, p. 40.

[6] *Asia Magazine*, October 4, 1970, p. 21.

rice than they knew what to do with, began giving it away to some of Thailand's customers. The United States began selling rice in Asia at non-commercial prices, primarily in South Vietnam and South Korea, under the "Food for Peace" program, more formally known as Public Law 480.[7]

For all the benefits that the American arms bonanza had brought them, the Thais were in trouble and they knew it. What good was their expanding GNP of more than $5 billion a year at the outset of the 1970s, and their anticipated growth rate of 6 to 8 per cent annually, if they couldn't earn their way? Their foreign exchange reserves, which stood at nearly $1 billion in 1968, had declined to $850 million two years later. Their total imbalance of trade reached $1 billion for the two-year period of 1968–69, and some Thais predicted it would continue to drain away $250 to $300 million a year unless some drastic changes were made.

Having embarked on an ambitious system of dam building and all-weather roads to develop the countryside, the Thais decided on a program of belt tightening at home and a search for markets abroad. They boosted import duties and sales taxes in 1970 to try to curb the Thai passion for buying foreign luxury goods, but succeeded only in raising prices. A pending tax bill stirred up a crisis.

The fragile Thai democratic system, rooted in the new Constitution of June 20, 1968, and revived the following year with the first general elections in more than a decade, was threatened by an angry uprising in Bangkok. The Army had to be called out. But in spite of political pressures and a show of force by the government, the 219-seat Assembly proved unexpectedly stubborn. It passed the tax bill by only one vote, 102–101.

The government of Marshal Kittikachorn was severely shaken—so much so that the new Thai strong man, General Praphas Charusathien, the Minister of the Interior, felt it necessary to offer a public pledge of his continued support. Nevertheless, it was clear enough that the days of the Thai democratic system were numbered. Thanom became annoyed by rising criticism of his regime in the Parliament and the press. He resented threats among legislators to cut the defense

[7] *The New York Times*, January 18, 1971, p. 53; *Far Eastern Economic Review*, January 23, 1971, p. 8.

costs and their prolonged refusal to adopt a budget. When neighboring Cambodia disposed of the last vestiges of its weak experiment with a democratic regime, it seemed almost like a signal to the Thais.

The admission of China to the United Nations provided what amounted to a convenient excuse for an authoritarian take-over. Playing on the fears of the Thais of the millions of indigenous Chinese in the land, Thanom and General Praphas seized power on November 17, 1971, at the head of a military junta. They clamped martial law on the country, did away with Parliament, set aside the 1968 Constitution, dissolved the Cabinet and even abolished the ruling United Thai People's Party. This was done in the name of protecting King Phumiphol Aduldet and the Thai people from rather vaguely defined dangers.

The scenario was sickeningly familiar. In the manner of the military dictators of South Vietnam and Cambodia, the new bosses of Thailand called upon the American ambassador, Leonard Unger, to explain the situation to him. Without doubt, the ambassador being among the most knowledgeable diplomats in Asia, few explanations had to be made. After paying their respects to the United States, that guardian of democratic rights in non-Communist Asia, the new military rulers then broke the news to their king. The people were informed last of all, in menacing official communiqués broadcast over the state radio. What it all really meant was that General Praphas, for so long the power behind the government, now had become the real force in Thailand.

The Thais and the Communists

The new government professed to be as anti-Communist and pro-American as its predecessor, and no doubt it intended to be. For it had to depend on continued financial support from the American government to pay its way. And yet, in their own devious way, the Thais continued to seek room for maneuver. It was a part of their historic heritage.

In addition to their pressing internal problems, the new masters of Thailand had to face up to the serious prospect of a heightened border warfare against the Communist guerrillas. This was no shadow play despite the apparent indifference of the Peking govern-

298 : New Era in the Pacific

ment to the efforts of the Thai insurgents. Having survived for so
long and earned the respect of at least a part of the dissatisfied
borderland peoples, the Communists could scarcely be disregarded.

Thailand found that it had to deal with Communist regimes. On
Christmas Day, 1970, it signed a trade agreement with the Soviet
Union. It also broadened commercial relations with Czechoslovakia,
Poland and Rumania and exchanged a good-will mission with Yugoslavia. Even the unthinkable, the restoration of diplomatic and trade
relations with China, now became possible. After all, the abolition of
the Chinese trade in 1959 had cost Thailand benefits of $3.5 million
annually and this was not the kind of money the Thais could shrug
off now, regardless of their anti-Communist posture beside the United
States.

Soon, Bangkok became the scene of a strange spectacle—the visit
of a mission from North Vietnam, with whom the Thais were fighting
in Laos and South Vietnam. On the surface, the people from Hanoi
were interested in negotiating with the Thais over the future of some
30,000 North Vietnamese refugees who were living in northeast Thailand. But in reality, the mission was testing the temperature of Thailand's fealty to the United States. It was tepid.

And yet, there were changes. Thanat Khoman, the resolutely anti-
Communist foreign minister who lost his post in the 1971 coup,
conceded that the country was "not as concerned about North
Vietnam and China" as it once had been. It was a signal to Washington that the Thais might not maintain their ties to the United States if
the expected advantages of such an association turned out not to be
as great as advertised.

A Problem of Internal Security

The nagging question remains: Could Thailand go Communist in
time?

If the Thais do not have to contend with a major Chinese-
supported insurgency movement in the foreseeable future, the answer
is clearly in the negative. The people of Thailand are remarkably
homogeneous and for the most part tolerant of their minorities—the
4,000,000 indigenous Chinese, 1,000,000 Malay-speaking Muslims to

the south, and about 300,000 hill tribesmen. They share a common language, practice a gentle form of Buddhism and have enjoyed a far higher standard of living than their $165 a year per capita income indicates. Some 82 per cent of the people live outside the cities and, of this total, 75 per cent of the tillers own their own farms, the average size being ten acres.

Such a people would scarcely be likely to support a guerrilla movement as long as they maintain confidence in their government. But with the world rice market in a slump and the program of agricultural diversification only beginning, the Thai government is well aware that it will have to do something more for its farmers. This is as much a problem of internal security as it is of maintaining export earnings, 90 per cent of which come from agricultural products.

There was good reason for Kukrit Pramoj, editor of *Thai Rath*, to cry out editorially: "What is happening to our country? The people are becoming steadily poorer and suffering increasing hardships . . . Crime and banditry are widespread and political bandits seem to be springing up everywhere . . . I am loyal to our king, but when I consider the conditions in the present day, I cannot help but feel that our country will not be able to avoid having a leftist policy."[8]

The Insurgents

For years it has been the practice of every Thai government to deny that any insurgency of consequence exists on its borders. In this respect, the Thais resemble the Filipinos, who regularly announce the extinction of the last Hukbalahap fighter, and then go on looking for more. The Royal Thai Army has been similarly engaged for years in the hill country to the north and northeast as well as to the south, where sporadic fighting continues.

The Chinese Communists have never been very diligent about creating a major guerrilla force on Thailand's borders. Probably, while support of North Vietnam and the Vietcong preoccupied Peking, there was no good reason to do so. Yet, no more than a few

[8] *Thai Rath*, December 12, 1970.

thousand guerrillas have been able at times to create a menacing impression in northern Thailand, where the hill people are more amenable to support of the insurgents. They call themselves the Thai Patriotic Front and they have a radio behind the Bamboo Curtain that broadcasts as the "Voice of the Thai People."

Just what China's eventual intentions are, no one knows. But the progress of road building by Chinese Army engineers from Yunnan Province toward the Thai border is bound to create a certain amount of nervousness in Bangkok. Air surveys have shown that the sturdy two-lane, all-weather highway is completed from Mengla, in Yunnan Province, to Muong Sai, in northern Laos, where one branch goes northeast toward Dienbienphu and the other stretches southwest as far as Muong Houn, only twenty miles from the Mekong River village of Pak Beng, on the Thai border. The final stretch of the road has been surveyed and could be completed at any time the Chinese choose to do so.[9]

Of equal importance is the disaffection of a few thousand Malay-speaking Muslims along the Malaysian border to the south who have been building up a separatist movement. Mingling with them are the remaining few hundred hard-core guerrillas of the old Malayan Communist Party who were driven out of Malaysia after a ten-year struggle. The problem for the Thais is to distinguish between the Muslim separatists, who have a certain amount of sympathy among their coreligionists in Malaysia, and the Communist guerrillas.

Since March 1970, Thailand and Malaysia have been participating in an anti-terrorist agreement that permits troops of either side to cross the border of the other in "hot pursuit" of guerrillas. It is quite a step in cooperation among the non-Communist powers in Southeast Asia, for it permits pursuing troops to go up to five miles across their borders and remain in foreign territory for up to seventy-two hours. Yet, the southern guerrillas, like their allies to the north, continue to present the Thai government with a problem.

The future of the slender ring of guerrillas around Thailand depends to a very large extent on the turn of events in Indochina. For

[9] Hong Kong *Standard*, October 26, 1970, p. 3; *The New York Times*, February 15, 1971, p. 4.

if North Vietnam continues at war, its attention is not likely to be diverted to troubled areas elsewhere. It is on this basis that Thailand feels itself strong enough to press Hanoi to repatriate the refugee Vietnamese, who are believed to provide a certain amount of support for the Thai guerrilla movement in the north and northeast. But the Thai Establishment isn't likely to present any challenge either to Hanoi or Peking in the foreseeable future. In the light of a diminished American presence in Indochina and the rest of Southeast Asia as well, that would be the height of foolishness.

The Glamour of Bangkok

None of the slippery uncertainties of the present and the painful choices that must be made in the future are reflected in the proud center of Thailand's national life, Bangkok. In this glamorous Westernized city of almost 3,000,000 people, new office buildings, factories and hotels are rising everywhere among the ancient monuments of Asian culture—the walled monasteries, gilded temples, shrines and palaces. Along the wide thoroughfares of the main business district, gleaming new automobiles and taxicabs—mostly Japanese—weave in and out of traffic with reckless abandon and often end up in a snarl of their own making. The shops are jammed with attractive merchandise in the Hong Kong manner, the markets with a dazzling variety of foods. For this is a country in which no one goes hungry and in which a beggar is seldom if ever seen.

A half-million tourists a year come to Bangkok. Most of them live in beautiful new Western-style hotels and consume huge portions of Western-style foods, just as if they had never left home. And that is a part of the artificial pleasure of visiting Thailand. Even the colorful old klongs, the canals that meant so much to Bangkok's trade, are gradually being filled in. Along the broad and muddy Chao Phraya, as it winds through the center of the city, water buses race between their stations and the casual citizenry, like the Parisians on the old 73 bus, jump on and off the rear at the landing stages with magnificent aplomb. There are also speedy river taxis with powerful engines that roar past long lines of teakwood boats towed by panting tugs, the local method of loading and unloading ocean-borne freight.

But Bangkok has its unattractive side, too—its dark alleys and hovels to which the poor are confined, its primitive factory chimneys belching clouds of evil black smoke in the heart of the city, its open sewers and uncollected refuse. The once-attractive floating market, which tourists were advised to visit in the early morning hours, is now so crowded with tour launches that there is little place for the farmers' produce-laden small boats and the air is foul with the stench of gas-engine exhaust pipes.

A little of old Bangkok is still to be seen, here and there. The strong-armed Thai women in their great broad-brimmed straw hats still ferry the school children across the Chao Phraya, skillfully catching the current and steering their fragile craft with one long oar. The Thai men still cluster about their favorite eating places in small out-of-the-way sections of Bangkok, enjoying the kind of food that only their skilled cooks can prepare. In the few remaining klongs, the kids still dive into the filthy brown water of a summer's morning and emerge with dripping bare bodies and happy smiles. In the heat of the afternoon, the bonzes in their saffron robes may be seeen at prayer in the temples, ignoring the stares of the tourists and the inevitable clicking of the cameras. And twice a year, King Phumiphol, in his crisp white officer's uniform, visits the Temple of the Emerald Buddha and sprinkles the kneeling school children who line his path with holy water from a silvery flask.

A Sign from the People

Except for such sights, Bangkok is changing even faster than the surrounding Thai countryside—and it is not always for the better. With the increasing movement of people to the cities, all the familiar Western problems, from urban sprawl to pollution, are developing at an appalling rate. Many of the cherished old Oriental values are being smothered in the rush to Westernize almost everything.

Usually, the people passively accept the new trends that are portrayed for them over their national television and elaborated on in their lively and developing press. But here and there, quite unexpectedly, a flash of anger may break suddenly from a complaisant citizenry or a brief and obviously unplanned demonstration may sweep through a side street. It is then that the true feelings of the Thais show through the mask of their habitual reserve.

I remember riding in a big black American automobile one midsummer's day through a crowded network of narrow streets in outer Bangkok on the way to the Thai Foreign Ministry. At one point, we were held up for some time by a long line of Thai military trucks, each bearing a complement of fine-looking Thai youngsters in their neat tan Army uniforms. My Thai driver told me that they were replacement troops, bound for Vietnam. Long lines of women and girls, some with babies in their arms and others guiding small children, passed by us silently and sadly. Some were crying as they moved away from the trucks.

There were a few men in the crowd that had gathered to see the soldiers leave for the war zone. Like their womenfolk, they walked quietly past us, too. Occasionally, one turned to look back toward the trucks and wave at some distant figure. It was a bitter and deeply affecting scene to any onlooker.

I was conscious, presently, that the people walking past me had taken notice of the chauffeur-driven American car. Almost insensibly, the crowd spilled over from the narrow sidewalk into the street and slowed our progress. Soon, the driver wisely decided to stop. People surged all about us then, and many gave me angry looks. Almost any European type in Bangkok is likely to be taken for an American, particularly in an American automobile, and this time the herd instinct could not be mistaken. Perhaps I showed my concern. I can't be sure. But all at once a man hammered angrily with his fists on the body of the car—a gesture of mingled rage and impotence. He glared at me as if I personified the United States, that distant power that was drawing the young men of Thailand into a war they had done nothing to bring about. For a moment, I thought he was about to summon the crowd to overturn the car; then, irresolutely, he banged on the car once more and moved on.

The sad-eyed women and the weeping girls flowed past us on either side for some minutes. Then, as the crowd thinned out, my driver took the car slowly past the line of Thai Army trucks. The uniformed youngsters looked at me curiously. One pointed and laughed unpleasantly. And I wished mightily that the senators who had spoken so glibly back home of the Thais as paid mercenaries for the United States in South Vietnam had been with me that midsummer's day.

Which Way for Thailand?

Thanat Khoman, a stout and dignified Thai with a flair for theatrical gestures and emphatic rhetoric, received me at the Foreign Office that day without any of the small talk reserved for such occasions.[10] Undeniably, he felt himself on the defensive. For as the architect of Thailand's decade-long pro-American, anti-Communist policy, he now had to face up to the unsavory prospect of a diminished American presence in Asia, a subtle turning to the left for Thailand, and a whole series of contingencies that circumstances would help to create.

It was difficult to determine, during the dialogue of an hour or more at the Foreign Office, whether Thanat's opinions reflected the policies over which he had presided for so long or the framing of a newer and more independent posture for the Thais. Certainly, regardless of his bravado on other occasions, he had no illusions that day about the manner in which China and the Soviet Union regarded the Thai position.

"China," he said, "has given ample warning of continued 'wars of national liberation' and has given aid to the insurgents on our northern borders. Everyone knows that. But we are containing that insurgency by our own efforts, and we will continue to do so. We don't need American help. We can do the job ourselves."

As for the Soviet Union, with which Thailand even then was preparing to sign a trade agreement, he remarked with a wry gesture that he was sure the Russians would keep their commitments to supply Hanoi and the Vietcong. "There will be no question of any pullout by the Russians," he said.

Toward Japan, Thailand's biggest trading partner, Thanat took a cautious attitude. "It seems unrealistic," he began, "for the world's third-largest economic power not to be able to play a larger role in the defense of the Pacific." Did that mean the Thais were willing to entrust themselves to the Japanese once more after their experiences in World War II? Thanat didn't say. He limited himself to the predic-

[10] The interview was on July 24, 1970.

tion that Japan would do more to arm itself in the foreseeable future.

He turned then to the United States, still, in his mind, the strongest reliance for Thailand and the rest of non-Communist Southeast Asia. "I can't understand how the world's foremost military power can entertain the notion of a complete military pullout in Southeast Asia because of political pressures at home," he said. "I don't believe it will happen. I think that certain bases may be retained and a sufficient military presence will remain in the Pacific to make credible all American commitments in the region. We would welcome that although," and here he measured his words carefully, "what the small and medium-sized powers of Asia really want is to be let alone to do their own job of self-defense. If we continue to receive sufficient American arms and military funds, we can do it. We have never asked for American ground troops and we don't need them for our defense."

Thanat went to some trouble to make it clear that he did not blame Thailand's recent guests, President Nixon and Vice-President Agnew, for the American decision to reduce its commitments in Asia. Rather, he had a wide assortment of villains—liberal senators, leaders of the peace movement, television commentators and, as always, the eastern American press. "It is a pity," he went on, "that certain senators and academic leaders have been able to cast such doubt on the ability of the United States to carry out its commitments. To some in Asia, there is now a very real doubt that the Senate will permit your President to do what he thinks is necessary in the military field. That may not hurt Thailand so much, but it is bound to hurt the United States by weakening faith in its judgments, purposes and pledges." He added, almost as an afterthought, "Personally, I think American commitments will be kept."

It was noteworthy that the optimistic Thanat, even though he was the architect of Thailand's pro-American policy, was the first to go when the Thanom-Praphas junta took over in the 1971 coup. Certainly, the Thai regime appeared to be far from resigned to living with a vastly reduced American military presence in Southeast Asia and, despite all the pledges made under the Guam Doctrine, the prospect of undependable American military assistance in the form of funds and matériel.

Thailand's Prospects

Pote Sarasin, the Thai deputy premier who joined the 1971 ruling junta as its most prominent civilian member, put his country's case very sharply in two questions to me:

"How can we develop our country if we do not enjoy national security? And if the United States does not help us, who will?"

To Pote, there is only one real answer to Thailand's problem and that is self-sufficiency. He is pushing ahead, as best he can, with the creation of an infrastructure for national development—roads, dams, homes and power stations (the latter up 32 per cent in a single year). But as a world diplomat of long experience, he would be the first to concede that Thailand must continue to have help. True, the Thais are going in heavily for offshore oil exploration with American and British firms, but few believe in get-rich-quick miracles. Thailand also hopes to share in the eventual development of the Mekong River Valley but that, too, is a far-off prospect.

Facing the realities of the present is a good deal grimmer. What all the interviews and opinions in Thailand add up to is that the Thais, for all their insistence on a more independent policy and a greater area for maneuver, actually have very few options. To throw themselves into the arms of Peking or Moscow, even if anybody in Bangkok seriously entertained the notion, would be suicidal for the current leadership. To strike an acceptable bargain with Hanoi on the assumption that Communism represents the wave of the future in Southeast Asia would be both dangerous and difficult. Nor would it be particularly practical, from the Thai point of view, to be tightly linked with an anti-Communist alliance that included South Vietnam and Taiwan. The Thais have been disillusioned enough about their membership in the Southeast Asia Treaty Organization.

For action by the international community, Thailand has no hope. As Thanat put it to me, "The Soviet Union wouldn't let the United Nations Security Council act and, once the Chinese get in, they will be even tougher." The Thais continue, however, to maintain an active interest in the United Nations and in such organizations as the Asian and Pacific Council (ASPAC) and the United Nations Economic Commission for Asia and the Far East (ECAFE). But none of these can be considered a major reliance in Thailand's current position.

The Thais may tinker with their government and their political orientation in the foreseeable future, shifting left or right for whatever advantage they fancy it may give them. But it seems probable that they will have to continue to strike the best bargain they can with the United States, Japan and their other trading partners if they intend to maintain control of their own development as an independent land. They also must come to terms with China. The Thais have always dreamed of becoming the Switzerland of Asia. It is, sad to say, an impossible dream in these turbulent times.

3 . ISOLATED BURMA

Among all the developing countries of Asia, few have been as blessed as Burma with bountiful natural resources and an industrious citizenry, a glamorous tradition, and an ancient heritage of resistance to the will of more powerful neighbors.

Before Burma achieved independence from Britain, it was the largest rice supplier in the world. And after its long struggle for freedom, first against the British and during World War II against the Japanese, it advanced toward self-government as the Union of Burma in 1948 with great expectations of a brilliant future.

Unfortunately, the Burmese dream—like those of its neighbors in Southeast Asia—has been cruelly shattered.

A Nation Divided Against Itself

Across two-thirds of this lush and beautiful land, which is almost the size of Texas, a confusing array of insurgencies has spread death, chaos and desolation among its 28,000,000 people. The rebel Karens and Mons, the Kachins and the Shans, two brands of native Communists and various combinations of these and other groups have placed an increasing strain on Burma's 200,000-man army. The economy, hard hit by the plummeting world market for rice, has stagnated. And the exile of some 300,000 Indian and Chinese business people and managers has taken away at one stroke most of the business and industrial leadership that Burma so desperately needs.

Thus, toward the conclusion of a decade of harsh military rule that has isolated Burma from the world, the dictatorship of General Ne Win is approaching the end of its resources. In his sixty-first year, the Burmese strong man can scarcely keep going much longer. By every sign and portent, his version of the Burmese "Way to Socialism" is doomed. He himself is not well, having suffered a heart attack in 1970, and now is said to rely more and more on his chief of staff, Brigadier San Yu. Moreover, in the familiar manner of dictators whose reign is winding down, Ne Win has thriftily taken heed of his future by acquiring a town house in London, a nine-hole golf course in Surrey and a villa in Austria.

The general's most articulate opponent, former premier U Nu, has said of him in a broadcast heard in Burma: "We are fighting Ne Win and his crowd because they are a bad lot and, as thieves, robbers, black market operators and self-seekers, are using the army for their benefit and have no business to be governing a country like Burma."[11]

The Chinese Influence

Ne Win's answer to the plague of troubles that has beset him is to resume diplomatic relations with the People's Republic of China after engaging in three years of border warfare with the People's Liberation Army and fending off guerrilla attacks inside Burma by the China-dominated Burmese Communist Party, the so-called "White Flag" Communists.[12]

The dictator clearly has lost his appetite for what was almost certainly a losing effort to defend his 1,000-mile frontier with China. He had been bold enough in 1967, with the appearance of Maoist badges and Mao's little red book of quotations in Rangoon among enthusiastic Chinese. At that time, with the benign approval of the government, Burmese street crowds rioted against China and brought about a rupture in diplomatic relations. In return, China stepped up anti-Burmese broadcasts and placed the Burmese Army under a very real disadvantage by giving aid to the China-supported Burmese Communists.

At first, Ne Win resisted. While he purged some of his close

[11] *Far Eastern Economic Review*, December 12, 1970, p. 22.
[12] UPI and AFP file from Rangoon, October 12, 1970.

associates in the government, he permitted a slow infiltration of his regime by members of the Moscow-oriented "Red Flag" Communists who joined his Masala Party. Peking's response was to call Ne Win a "greedy Fascist bloodsucker." The unequal contest continued for more than two years without a break until Ne Win sent up his first distress signal. He freed all Chinese Communist nationals who had been sent to jail during the 1967 riots. The Peking government was agreeable to a truce. It dampened its anti-Burma campaign. Nevertheless, it continued to supply the native Burmese Communists with arms that enabled them to fight at least nine pitched battles with Ne Win's Army between 1969 and late 1970.

Since the resumption of diplomatic relations between Rangoon and Peking, the Burmese Communist guerrillas have been at such a disadvantage that Ne Win has been able to divert his Army's main effort to attempt to subdue the rebellious Karens in southern and eastern Burma. There are many inside and outside Rangoon who believe he must have paid a steep Chinese price to relieve pressure on his northern flank. Among his probable concessions are an agreement to recognize Chinese rule in border areas that Chinese troops have long controlled, including the rich Kokang opium-producing area, and willingness to increase Burma's two-way trade with China.

Certainly, the Chinese would not have let Ne Win off very easily after the crude manner of his challenge.

The United States and Burma

Except for a comparatively large and active embassy in Rangoon, the United States has paid little attention to Burma's troubles and has accepted Ne Win as a "neutralist" who was trying, by every possible means, to maintain his country's independence. Ever since Burma in 1959 accused the United States of supporting the so-called "opium army" of Chinese Nationalist troops[13] who still fend for themselves in the Shan States, the American tendency has been to be wary of involvement in Burma. And with good reason. For in 1962, when Ne Win took over the Rangoon government in a coup, one of his excuses

[13] These are two remaining brigades of Chiang Kai-shek's defeated army that crossed into Burma from Yunnan in 1949 and still remain there, subsisting mainly on illicit trade of various kinds.

was that the Central Intelligence Agency and the entire SEATO alliance were secretly backing a Shan-Karen rebel take-over. Nine years after spreading this unlikely story, Ne Win was accusing the Shans and Karens of being Communist agencies.

In a bumbling diplomatic effort to establish his evenhanded ways before the world, the general has ventured from Rangoon now and then to present himself in the contending capitals of East and West as a stalwart leader who is able to resist pressure from all sides. Such missions have made little impression, even in Burma. In 1966, for example, he rushed to both Peking and Moscow and then, as a kind of afterthought, came to Washington to pay a call on President Johnson. All he had to show for his efforts was a rather effusive salute from *The New York Times*, which called him a "Cromwellian military chief of state."[14]

For all his pretensions, Ne Win in a very real sense shapes his policies to conform with the hard facts of geography and the long years of disorganization of Burmese life. He wasted no time after his 1962 take-over in appeasing Peking by cutting off a program of American foreign aid that had brought Burma $89 million in loans and grants from the end of World War II. He also got rid of the Ford and Asia foundations and the Fulbright educational program, but at the same time encouraged the Chinese by accepting $85 million in credits from Peking.

During the rupture of Burma-China relations between 1967 and 1970, Washington made little effort to take advantage of the situation, being otherwise occupied in Vietnam. But Ne Win tried to warm up the Americans in his crude way by opening up a program of seven-day tourist trips to Burma. His biggest coup was a visit of twenty-five tourists from Fresno, California.

During the same three-year period, there was a modest improvement in the never very robust trade between the United States and Burma (Burmese teak and non-ferrous metals for America, American electrical machinery, pharmaceuticals and dairy products for Burma). Burma's sales to the United States doubled, reaching about 10 per cent of total exports, while its purchases from American firms remained at about 11 per cent of total imports. Actually, the Ameri-

[14] Harrison Salisbury in *The New York Times*, June 20, 1966, p. 1.

can impact on the Burmese economy, with an estimated gross national product of about $2 billion annually, was quite small and is likely to remain so.[15]

The most ambitious venture the Burmese have entered into with the United States since resuming diplomatic relations with China is to charter two Boeing 727s at $2 million each annually to try to beef up the tourist trade. But few American tourists find Burma worth the trouble, bother and thumping expense of a short and highly regimented visit.

The Decline of Rangoon

To Americans of an older era, Burma conjured up a pleasant intermingling of visions of gleaming pagodas, hardy boatmen bent over their paddles, sloe-eyed Burmese beauties, a snatch of half-remembered verse from Rudyard Kipling and the magnificent voice of Reinald Werrenrath booming out "On the Road to Mandalay." That was the Burma of long ago, governed by Britain and largely run by thrifty and efficient Indian civil servants and Chinese shopkeepers. During World War II, the heroics of American pilots flying in the China-Burma-India theater and the tortuous missions along the Burma Road to Kunming added a new and different dimension to the pictures in American heads. But it was still a romantic Burma, and Rangoon was its fabled capital.

Today, Rangoon is a weary and dirty city, impoverished and undernourished. Its old buildings are neglected, some being little more than crumbling shells. Many of its once-prosperous shops are shuttered. Beggars can squat in the streets and small boys can play wherever they wish in the center of the city because there is so little traffic. Almost everything from food to machinery is in short supply. At the slightest hint of new shipments of almost anything, but food in particular, long lines of hopeful Burmese form as if by magic. For those who still have the resources, the black market is the only other place to go. If Ne Win has ousted the capitalist exploiters, as he so

[15] *Far Eastern Economic Review*, July 2, 1970, pp. 59–60. See also *Far Eastern Economic Review*, July 9, 1964, p. 86, and Dennis Bloodworth in the *Straits Times*, Singapore, June 15, 1964, p. 10.

312 : New Era in the Pacific

frequently boasts, he hasn't been able to do much about the domineering home-grown Socialist black marketeers, reputedly because they are most punctilious about paying protection to the right people.

For a city of 1,700,000 people, Rangoon seems more like a discouraged backwater than the capital of an independent nation. The heavy hand of the military is felt everywhere. All newspapers and other publications are strictly controlled. No opposition to the will of the Revolutionary Council is tolerated. Despite all the promises of the government, there is no progress and there is no hope. By comparison with neighboring Bangkok, Rangoon has the air of a mortuary. And Mandalay, Burma's second city, is little better. Except for an occasional movie, the citizenry find little diversion outside the ancient pagodas that still manage somehow to maintain an impressive appearance in an era of general neglect.

In the Economic Doldrums

One of the main indicators of Burma's slumping economy is the decline of both foreign exchange reserves and gold. At the outset of 1971, only $85 million remained of the $214 million in reserves that Burma had accumulated in 1964. The kyat, nominally valued at 4.76 to $1, was worth only 25 per cent of that amount on the black market and there wasn't much demand for Burmese currency.

The decline in Burma's rice trade has had a lot to do with these economic doldrums. The Burmese produced nearly 3,000,000 tons of rice annually for export in the years immediately before World War II, about 38 per cent of the world's total. While the Japanese occupation era and the rebellions thereafter hit the rice industry hard, it did come back to a bumper export of 1,800,000 tons in 1961–62. Since then, however, there has been another major decline, with an export of only 630,000 tons for 1969–70 and the most optimistic estimates at 800,000 to 900,000 tons for 1971. Thus, income from the rice trade has shrunk from $181 million in 1961–62 to only $59 million in 1969–70, and the export market is still declining.

Several factors account for the drastic change in Burma's fortunes. Being against anything foreign, General Ne Win has also failed to appreciate the value of growing the so-called "miracle rice" that has been introduced successfully by most of Burma's former customers in

Asia. Moreover, the general has only belatedly realized that such things as fertilizer plants and irrigation works were needed to maintain a thriving agricultural economy. So Burmese rice gives comparatively low yields. Finally, the people of Burma, having increased in numbers from 16,000,000 to 28,000,000 in a little more than two decades, also are eating much more of their rice crop. Less than one-third of the pre-World War II total is now available for export.

In the face of such appalling conditions, the government naturally is trying to diversify by urging its largely agricultural population— 83 per cent live on the land—to raise long-staple cotton, jute and sugar cane. But in a country that suffers so much from insurgencies of various kinds, the tilling of the land and the gathering of crops become difficult in some areas, almost impossible in others. Like the export of teak, another major foreign exchange earner for Burma, the distribution of the newer agricultural products is bound to suffer when transportation is disrupted by the comings and goings of marauding bands of soldiers, whatever their degree of loyalty or disloyalty to the government. In consequence, Burma's total exports from 1963 to the outset of the 1970s were cut in half, dropping from $270 million to less than $130 million.

Domestically, the nationalization of almost everything has been an unmitigated disaster as well. Ne Win's decision to take over all shops from private ownership in 1963–64 resulted in the creation of 10,000 people's shops that were supposed to distribute the products of twenty-two trade groups. It didn't work. For lack of decent transport, some commodities rotted in warehouses and others disappeared into the black market. Bureaucrats didn't care whether the shops were stocked or not. Even rationing didn't help, and the bare shelves soon became a bad joke. Ne Win finally gave up on the plan and put in a system of cooperatives, ruled by localities, but the main result to date seems to have been higher prices and not much to sell at any price.[16]

[16] Sources of the economic data on Burma are two articles by David Baird, *Far Eastern Economic Review*, April 17, 1971, pp. 19–22, and May 1, 1971, pp. 47–50; two articles by Henry Kamm of *The New York Times* in the Hong Kong *Standard*, September 28, 1970, p. 7, and September 29, 1970, p. 7; the *South China Morning Post*, October 2, 1970, p. 2, business news, and October 7, 1970, p. 2, business news. Also, some private estimates given to me by American, British and Japanese authorities.

With such economic crises taking hold both at home and abroad, the government has had to seek outside help despite all of Ne Win's xenophobia. He tried the British, but it was reported that he couldn't provide the kind of collateral that was required. Both the Japanese and the West Germans have proved more amenable, but neither is risking too much on Burma, for the revolution that is sweeping over Asia has taken hold in the Burmese uplands and the end is not in sight. Nor can the Burmese Way to Socialism long survive the combined weight of inefficiency, sloth and massive corruption that is crushing it.

U Nu's Crusade

Burma has existed under autocratic governments for almost 1,000 years. The periods of comparative freedom for the land have been brief and few. For the great bulk of the population, therefore, the cause of individual liberty—so sacred in the West—has had little meaning and even less relevance to their daily lives. To have food, to be sheltered and clothed, to enjoy the homely pleasures of family life and to worship after the manner of the Buddhist faith—these have been the key objectives of the majority of Burma's people. While their per capita income has been only about $60 a year, life has been tolerable in all but the areas of insurgency. In so incredibly fruitful a land, no one starves and farming people always seem to be able to make do somehow.

The framework for much of Burmese tradition was set during the eight centuries of absolute monarchies that preceded the annexation of the land by the British in 1885. It was Burma's misfortune to be doubly colonized—first by the British and eventually by the Indians to whom so much of the government was delegated by the British raj. The Burmese, in consequence, never did develop much of a feel for, or even understanding of, the principles of self-government. And when the Japanese came in World War II, adding the indignities of their own particular brand of tyranny to all that had gone before, the people of Burma suffered even greater degradation.

Under such terrible pressures, the easygoing Burmese finally took to armed resistance under the leadership of Aung San, the leader of the Anti-Fascist People's Freedom League. With the defeat of Japan, the league continued its struggles against the British but the vigorous Aung San did not live to witness the independence of his country in January 1948. On July 19, 1947, he and six of his associates were shot to death by political rivals. U Nu, a onetime student rebel leader at the University of Rangoon who later became a novelist and playwright, became the nation's first prime minister and ruled continuously, except for a two-year interregnum in 1958–60, until he was overthrown in Ne Win's military coup of 1962.

In spite of the facade of democratic practices that Burma adopted with the coming of independence, it should not be imagined that the soft-voiced and visionary U Nu was able to govern his country in the manner of a parliamentary executive of the Western stripe. The sufferings of the people had been too great. Almost as soon as the Burmans took control of the country, having 75 per cent of the population, the restive minorities rose against them. Then as now, the redoubtable Karens, consisting of about 10 per cent of the people merged into the Union of Burma, were the chief opponents of the Burmans. But the Shans and Kachins, the Chins and Arakans and Mons, and even the indigenous Chinese, all had their grievances and took to arms in small groups. It was U Nu's good fortune that they could not unite against him, being divided by their own internal quarrels.

Nevertheless, in 1958, he found it so difficult to govern that he raised comparatively little fuss when General Ne Win took over at the head of a military government. Two years later, when Burma's electorate went to the polls, U Nu was returned to office with a four-fifths majority in his favor in the Chamber of Deputies. The military, however, remained unconvinced that his easygoing ways could rescue Burma from chaos; in two years he was out and Ne Win was back in power to stay. The first result was the suspension of all the forms of democratic government, including free speech and a free press; the next, imprisonment of some 4,000 enemies of the regime, headed by U Nu, most of his Cabinet associates and virtually every independent-minded editor of Burma's vigorous and independent press.

The Revolutionary Council did not release U Nu until 1967 and refused to permit him to leave Burma until 1969, when he took up residence in a suburb of Bangkok with one of his closest associates,

Edward Law Yone, the editor of the *Nation* of Rangoon and a Magsaysay Prize laureate, who had been imprisoned with him. In October 1970, the former premier slipped across the Thai border into lower Burma and proclaimed himself the leader of the Burmese resistance with the support of the combined rebellious minorities.

There were a few clandestine radio speeches that were beamed into Burma, a little student rioting in Rangoon, and a flurry of headlines in the world press. Then, silence. U Nu's friends argued that he had gone underground and was biding his time. But for a less than robust Burmese politician in his sixties, such a position was scarcely credible. It appeared that U Nu's effort to mold the restive minorities into a solid revolutionary phalanx had been less than successful and that considerably more work was required.

Nevertheless, the Burmese freedom crusade took shape along the Thai border. Several thousand recruits to U Nu's cause were drilling for some months in early 1971 north of the Thai village of Mae Seriang. Weapons, too, were being smuggled in but few believed that U Nu could go very far without the support of a sympathetic government. The indulgent Thai attitude toward his efforts was scarcely enough to help him.

As one jaundiced observer put it: "U Nu is not going to be able to win, as in a Burmese legend, with a great white bird swooping down and letting him ride off to the royal palace to take over the kingdom."[17]

Is Burma Worth Fighting For?

There is little doubt that the fight for Burma, far from being at an end, is just beginning. Whether Ne Win is overthrown eventually by someone in his own palace guard or is replaced by U Nu or one of his younger deputies, Burma is very far from self-government, stability and peace. Whoever takes power in Rangoon will have to come to terms with Peking or Moscow, and probably both for at least a limited time. But over the long haul, there is little doubt now that China will exercise an ever-increasing role in the calculations of whatever government is in authority in Burma. This may cause great

[17] *The New York Times*, January 27, 1971, p. 6.

anguish in India, but there is precious little that the Indians can do about it. The Chinese have the power. The Indians do not. And the Russians are so far away, except for their "show-the-flag" Indian Ocean fleet, that their "Red Flag" Burmese adherents can scarcely hope to exert much leverage for very long.

In the days of John Foster Dulles, such prospects as these would have stirred up a minor storm among the dedicated anti-Communists in Washington. There would have been talk of stiff countermeasures to "save" Burma. But in the fading light of the Vietnam War, the cause of Burmese independence is seen very dimly—if at all—by the watchmen in Foggy Bottom. And in the daily comings and goings at the Pentagon, neither the military requirements of the Burmese government nor its rebellious foemen form any part of the major calculations of generals or budget makers.

It is not beyond the bounds of possibility that when an openly pro-Communist government takes over in Burma, the White House will have some mournful words to utter. But clearly, in the third decade of the atomic era, the United States has come to a decision that Burma is not worth fighting for. If the Japanese do not feel that it is worth their while to try to make an economic colony out of Burma, then China will have no other remaining rival in the area for influence over the 28,000,000 people of Burma. It will scarcely be a surprise to the Burmese, or even a new experience in their history. For in 1287, the mighty Kublai Khan conquered Burma and he, his descendants and his Shan allies ruled the land for almost 300 years. The Chinese have never forgotten it.

4. MALAYSIA PLUS OR MINUS SINGAPORE

Malaysia and Singapore are a prosperous and constantly bickering pair of divorcees who can't live without each other.

Their bill of divorcement in 1965, for all its good intentions, has merely complicated their lives. And yet, although they complement each other in so many ways and must in great measure depend on each other, there is little chance that they will join in a glorious reunion in the foreseeable future.

The Perils of Racism

At the root of their trouble is the turbulent, ever-shifting multiracial society of which both are a part. The Muslim Malay, who often considers himself the forgotten man in his immensely rich and fruitful peninsula and its appendages, is almost constantly embittered by the wealth and prosperity of the Chinese communities of Malaysia and Singapore, which place their faith in Buddhism and Confucianism. Twice there have been fatal racial riots—in Singapore on July 21–25, 1964, and in Kuala Lumpur on May 13–16, 1969—that could have destroyed what is, after all, a very fragile experiment in multiracial democracy.

The old Tunku (Prince), Abdul Rahman, the founder and first prime minister of Malaysia, wept before his television set during the Kuala Lumpur outbreak and prayed for his people.[18] His close associate Tun Dr. Ismail, the gentle-voiced but hardheaded home minister in charge of internal security, said: "Democracy is dead in Malaysia." And it was, for the time being.

What continues to upset the Malays, who for better or worse regard themselves as the successors to the British raj in this part of the world, is the increasing political and economic influence of the indigenous Chinese. It doesn't matter to the radical Malay leadership that these Chinese profess for the most part to be anti-Communist; to them, Chinese of whatever political affiliation are not to be trusted. They see, moreover, that in the city of the lion, Singapore, the Chinese constitute 80 per cent of the population of 2,100,000 and feel themselves so strong that a venturesome minority dares to oppose the stern and self-righteous government of Prime Minister Lee Kuan Yew. And in their own land, Malaysia, the country of the tiger, the Malay activists cannot feel secure any longer. For although the authorized figures give the Chinese only about 35 per cent of the population of nearly 11,000,000, at least one high official—granting me an interview on the understanding that his identity would not be revealed—concedes privately that they actually are very close to 50

[18] After Tunku, or Prince, there is no exact translation of the other honorifics in Malaysia such as (in descending order of importance) Tun, Tan Sri and Dato.

per cent. The talk of a Chinese prime minister in Malaysia some day no longer can be regarded as an empty theory put forward by die-hard Malays in an effort to whip their cohorts into a frenzy. But the Chinese, of course, profess no such ambitions.

It must have given the Malays quite a turn, nevertheless, when the Chinese Silver Star performing troupe from Hong Kong filled the 40,000-seat national stadium in Kuala Lumpur for a program of dances in which red flags were flourished and sickles defiantly held aloft. Ostensibly, it was a benefit performance for a Chinese national disaster fund for flood victims. Actually, it was a part of a campaign being conducted by a Chinese leader in Malaysia, Tun Tan Siew Sin, to bring a greater degree of unity to the nation's Chinese community.[19] But the Malays got the message. Chinese dominance of the commercial life of Malaysia is so great today, from small shops to giant national branches of international combines, that it is a familiar Malay saying that "you might as well go to Hong Kong as to Kuala Lumpur."

Estimates of non-Malay ownership (Chinese, Indians and others) of Malaysian commercial enterprises run as high as 95 per cent and top Malay business executives are usually put at only about 10 per cent of the total. It is for this reason that Tun Dr. Ismail wants to see Malays brought into control of at least 25 per cent of the nation's commercial establishments. Just how this is to be done in a country that professes fealty to parliamentary democracy is a puzzler, but both Dr. Ismail and his Cabinet associate, the strong-minded Tan Sri Ghazali Shafie, the minister for information, believe it is possible.

"The main trouble between the races is economic," Dr. Ismail argues with great conviction, "and I am convinced that the way to handle it best is to introduce more Malays into commerce, now dominated by the Chinese and the Indians. If we could get twenty-five per cent Malay participation, I believe hard feelings would subside. Our task is to develop our economy and increase the well-being of all our citizens."[20]

Actually, there is a lot more to the Malaysian story than that, as Dr. Ismail would agree.

[19] *Far Eastern Economic Review,* April 3, 1971, p. 17.
[20] In an interview with me, August 20, 1970, in Kuala Lumpur.

The Survival of Malaysia

During the first decade of its existence, Malaysia has managed to survive many trials. With British help, it was able to put down a long and dangerous Communist insurrection. It expelled its leading city, Singapore, and forfeited the revenue that went with the fourth-largest port in the world. For three years, it withstood both the pressures of Sukarno's Indonesian propaganda and a swarm of "nuisance" invasions by small bands of Indonesian soldiers in a "confrontasi," as Sukarno called it, that was intended to break up the Malay federation. And finally, for all the bad feeling between Malays and Chinese and the rioting, the form if not much of the substance of a parliamentary democracy was preserved.

Very little of this could have been foreseen in 1963 when, with the blessings of the withdrawing British, the Federation of Malaysia was created out of the Malayan Union on the Malay Peninsula (now called West Malaysia), the colonies of Sabah (North Borneo) and Sarawak on the island of Borneo, and the city of Singapore. The oil-rich Borneo colony of Brunei decided at the last minute to stay out of the Federation and remain a British protectorate, guarded by a battalion of Gurkhas and the small native police force.

What led the Malayan Union to enter into so risky a compact, considering the ethnic problems that were involved? One of the most authentic accounts heard in Kuala Lumpur, from those who were around at the time, was that the Tunku calculated that the addition of the Malays in Sabah and Sarawak would provide the new Federation with a ready-made Malay majority and insure an all-Malay government, or at the very least one dominated by Malays. If this was indeed his rationale, he soon found out that he was wrong.

Under the dynamic Lee Kuan Yew, the overwhelming and well-disciplined Chinese majority in Singapore showed that it could work well with the upcountry Malayan Chinese. In fact, the combination was so impressive that the Malays raised serious questions about the political status of the ethnic Chinese. Unable to deny the Chinese claims to citizenship, the government of Malaysia saw that it would have to adopt sterner measures to protect itself from eventual domination by Lee Kuan Yew's followers in Singapore.

The tough and truculent Lee, great-grandson of an emigrant Chinese peasant, had gone up the ladder of politics rapidly as a graduate of Cambridge, a fluent and forceful speaker and a political figure with a formidable record of accomplishment. His People's Action Party (PAP), with its Socialist orientation, defeated the opposing pro-Communist Barisan Sosialis and became the dominating force in Singapore. Next, he openly challenged the Alliance Party, the most powerful in the rest of Malaysia, with its component United Malay National Organization (UMNO), the Malayan Chinese Association, and the Malayan Indian Congress. The fanatical secretary general of the UMNO, Syed Ja'afar bin Albar, and his fighting Malay Ultra-Nationalists surged to the attack.

At this juncture, the 1964 race riots exploded in Singapore, with a toll of 24 dead, 460 others injured, and 2,000 thrown into jail. In the aftermath of the fighting, Syed Albar demanded Lee's arrest as a Malaysian enemy and a pro-Communist. Whatever faults the pugnacious Lee had shown, pro-Communism at this stage wasn't one of them; to achieve his leadership he had had to fight Communist factions in the labor unions, at Nanyang University and in the Barisan Sosialis.[21] Nevertheless, it became increasingly clear that both Lee Kuan Yew and Singapore were too powerful by far for the Malays in Malaysia.

Lee continued to hope for an agreeable solution. But on August 9, 1965, the Malay Ultras triumphed when Tunku Abdul Rahman announced the Malaysian decision, taken in secret, to expel Singapore from the Federation. Lee protested. Going before Singapore television, he charged that the Tunku's fear of another racial confrontation had led to the illogical separation. But there was nothing Lee could do about it. From that day on, Malaysia and Singapore went their separate but parallel ways, pursuing an announced policy of anti-Communist neutralism that led them into all kinds of contradictions. Their real position, of necessity, had to take account of the American withdrawal from Vietnam and new approaches to China, the rise of Chinese power and authority in Southeast Asia, the

[21] Seymour Topping, *The New York Times Magazine*, October 31, 1965, p. 67; Willard Hanna, American Universities Field Service Reports, Jeamia Series, Vol. XIII, No. 21 (September 1965).

presence of Soviet warships in the Indian Ocean and even the Strait of Malacca, and the return of Indonesia to a more rational government after the overthrow of Sukarno.

Friends or Foes?

Both Malaysia and Singapore soon found themselves sitting side by side in a number of joint enterprises. With Indonesia, Thailand and the Philippines, they became members of the Association of Southeast Asian Nations, a "crawling baby" of a non-military alliance—in Filipino terms—that could develop aspects of a common-market philosophy. They also joined in a rather weak five-power defense group with Britain, Australia and New Zealand, with air defense headquarters in West Malaysia and support from a 4,500-man contingent of Commonwealth military forces. On an informal basis, they exchanged information and set up joint arrangements with neighboring states to cut down subversive elements and infiltration. And they attended, together with others from Southeast Asia, the Djakarta conference of 1970 that attempted to mediate the conflict in Cambodia after the fall of Norodom Sihanouk.

But Singapore nevertheless felt it necessary to demonstrate that it could fight its partner on the Malay Peninsula. At the express invitation of the Singapore government, a party of Israeli military experts came to the thriving city-state in the late 1960s for training purposes and were obliged, much to their own amusement, to call themselves visiting businessmen. Singapore also equipped itself with a few tanks, mainly from Israeli sources, and some dated fighter aircraft.[22] The foreign business community in Singapore was as amused as the Israelis but Lee Kuan Yew and his followers were both earnest and grim about their small military venture. It was meant as a gesture of warning toward Kuala Lumpur.

Just how touchy relations could be between Singapore and Malaysia was demonstrated on August 18, 1970, when Singapore's police seized three Malaysian hippies who were coming across the Johore Causeway, cut off their hair, and then charged them one Singapore dollar each (33 cents) for the indignity. The influential

[22] Malaysia had about 50,000 men under arms in 1971, mainly for chasing subversives in border areas. Singapore had about half that number.

Malay-language newspaper in Kuala Lumpur, *Utusan Melayu,* picked up the story and made such an issue out of it that the press and electronic media of both states inflated the incident into an international issue. Tun Dr. Ismail made a formal protest to the Singapore government, upon which Singapore stiffly apologized "if these three men have been wrongly and poorly treated." In a fit of temper, Lee Kuan Yew canceled a state visit to Kuala Lumpur on August 20 to bid farewell to Tunku Abdul Rahman, who was at that point drafting a speech announcing his retirement in favor of his long-time deputy Tun Abdul Razak.[23]

Such shadow plays, of course, cannot be taken seriously when it is considered that more than $20 million of Singapore capital is invested in Malaysia, that Singapore is the third-largest backer of Malaysian pioneer industries, that much of Singapore's entrepôt (warehousing) trade is based on West Malaysian rubber, tin and other products, and that Malaysia has no port facilities to match those of Singapore.[24] Without Singapore, Malaysia would be a body without a head.

Melan Abdullah, editor of *Utusan Melayu,* says of Malaysian foreign affairs: "Our policy is to have more friends than enemies." That, too, would be a good definition of Singapore's position. For both, regardless of all other considerations, such a policy begins at home.

The Uses of Prosperity

Malaysia and Singapore have a great deal to defend. They have the highest growth rate and standard of living in Southeast Asia and rank with Hong Kong and Taiwan as Japan's economic rivals in the Far East. Not even the U.S. "dollar war" nor temporary American import barriers can hurt them very much.[25]

Singapore is a miracle in itself. In the 150 years since its settle-

[23] The Tunku described the incident to me with a flourish that day, announcing that I had been given the time allotted to Lee Kuan Yew.

[24] *The Economist,* January 30, 1971, p. xlii.

[25] China, Japan, the Soviet Union and the Commonwealth nations all are interested in boosting relations with Singapore and Malaysia, and the European Common Market isn't at all indifferent.

ment by Stamford Raffles, this island of only 225 square miles has become a dominant world trade center with miles of gleaming new warehouses fringing its busy waterfront. It is now a container port, one of the most modern to be found, with the latest machinery and a well-trained work force that operates twenty-four hours a day.

Attracted by both tax breaks and a good supply of dependable cheap labor, foreign enterprises have gone into Singapore in a big way. Textiles, electronics and petrochemicals have all been important. But in the new industrial complex in Jurong, even newer industries have been booming. The discovery of oil offshore has brought representatives of almost one hundred companies, including some of the world's leaders, into the waters around Singapore, Indonesia and Malaysia. As the hub of the area, Singapore has assumed a commanding position in the rush for Asian oil, with a resultant increase in such industries as shipbuilding, drilling equipment and even food processing. Refineries are being built and still more are on the way.

Nor has Singapore been backward in taking advantage of the mounting flow of tourists in the Far East. With more than a score of big hotels presently available or under construction, about 14,000 rooms were slated for tourists by the end of 1972 as compared with only 3,000 at the end of 1969. Even in 1970, many of the available rooms were empty, old hotels were giving up and going out of business, and complaints were widespread that Singapore had overbuilt. Perhaps so. But it isn't to Americans that the new Asian tourism will principally appeal; actually, Asian tourism will be more for Asians, particularly the restless and fast-traveling Japanese. And it is to them that Singapore has directed much of its attention.

On the basis of all this frantic activity, plus the attraction of one of the few relatively stable governments in Asia, Singapore has been able to show a growth rate of more than 12 per cent annually since 1965. During the early 1970s, it was approaching an annual gross national product of $2 billion and a per capita annual earning of close to $1,000. Its foreign reserves exceeded $850 million at the beginning of 1970, with its exports exceeding $1.5 billion and its imports in excess of $2 billion.

West Malaysia, as might have been expected, continued to be Singapore's major trading partner, accounting for 17 per cent, or

$600 million, of the city-state's total trade at the beginning of the 1970s, but Japan was a strong second, with $450 million, and Britain and the United States accounted for about $200 million each. Every major industrial country of Europe and Asia was increasing its commercial commitments to Singapore, and with good reason. As in Hong Kong, there was every prospect of a quick and mounting return on most investments.

For the Malaysian Federation, with its greater dependence on agriculture, the outlook was not as bright but it was still far ahead of most of the countries of the Far East. For one thing, its industrialization program was just beginning to develop in such key fields as electronics. For another, foreign investment has been slower to come into Malaysia than Singapore, for understandable reasons. But the biggest concern for Malaysia by all odds is the weakening position of its two traditional foreign exchange earners, rubber and tin, which have accounted in the past for 60 per cent of export revenues.

Natural rubber, under heavy competition from synthetics, accounted for only about 40 per cent of the world market in the early 1970s, and one major corporation, Firestone, was using as little as 25 per cent in its tires. The Malaysian rubber plantations' answer has been to boost natural rubber production and standardize its packaging. Through the use of a chemical stimulant known as ethrel, claims have been made that the yield of an acre of rubber can be boosted from 2,000 to 5,000 pounds annually at a cost of about $12 an acre. If the substance does not eventually harm rubber trees, it is estimated that Malaysian rubber production could be doubled, to 2,000,000 tons, by the middle of the 1970s. But if rubber prices continue to slump, not even so massive an increase in production is going to save the industry over the long run.

As for tin, the plain fact of the matter is that the reserves that can easily be worked without major new investment appear to be running out. Just what can be done about it, nobody knows. In any event, being realists, the Malaysians are not placing their entire dependence on their traditional exports any longer. Instead, they are turning to boosts in timber, palm oil, cocoa and dehydrated food products, mainly fruit and fish.

It should not be imagined that Malaysia is in a bad way, however.

For all its troubles, its foreign exchange reserves amounted to $620 million at the outset of 1970, its annual gross national product was approaching $4 billion and its annual per capita earnings were in excess of $350. While its prosperity could not be equated with that of Japan, Hong Kong or Singapore, it was doing just about as well as Taiwan and a great deal better than China or India. With continued progress toward industrialization on a broadened agricultural base, and with a stroke of luck in the incessant exploration for oil, Malaysia should do very well over the next decade or so.

Like Singapore, it enjoys a rising and highly diversified clientele in foreign trade, which amounted to a turnover of $2.9 billion at the beginning of the 1970s, $1.2 billion in imports and $1.7 billion in exports. The big four patrons of the Malaysian export market were Singapore, with $358 million; Japan, $309 million; the U.S., $250 million; and Britain, $90 million. For its imports, Malaysia had a far different order of priority, with Japan first, at $190 million; followed by Britain, $157 million; Singapore, $96 million; Australia and China, $80 million each; and the U.S. as a distant sixth with $76 million. As Malaysian needs and products change, that list is likely to be drastically altered, with a probable rise in trade with both China and Australia and perhaps a further drop with the U.S. China already is proving to be a good market for Malaysian rubber.

The end of the fighting in Vietnam is, of course, going to affect both Singapore and Malaysia but neither has been particularly dependent on making a profit out of military supplying. Barring an upset in their foreign relations, the uncongenial neighbors of the Malay Peninsula expect—together or separately—to be more than a match for Hong Kong in the foreseeable future.[26]

The Long View: Malaysia

The accident of geography has made both Singapore and Malaysia far more important to the development of Southeast Asia than their

[26] For the economic analysis of Singapore and Malaysia, I depended on the *Annual Bulletin of Statistics, Malaysia, 1969* and *Singapore, Facts and Pictures, 1970*, both government publications; "A Survey of Malaysia and Singapore," in *The Economist*, January 30, 1971; and interviews with members of both governments on estimates and prospects for the future.

size and economic prospects would indicate. Neither has military ambitions. Neither cares to dabble in distant foreign subversion after the manner of North Korea. Both have everything to gain and nothing to lose through the restoration of peace in their part of the world. But because of their strategic importance, both also are painfully aware that they could be used as pawns in a developing greatpower struggle over Asia. It is for this reason that realists in both Singapore and Kuala Lumpur, for all their caterwauling about the undependability of the United States, are genuinely concerned about the extent of the American retreat from Asia in the post-Vietnam War world and the degree to which Chinese power may be expected to increase. While there seems to be no particular desire to turn to the Soviet Union or Japan for aid, for there is no guarantee that either would be very helpful to two small and distant lands in time of need, the leaders of Malaysia and Singapore make noises from time to time about using either or both powers as a counterweight to Chinese pressure. As if the Soviet Union or Japan would easily permit itself to be so used!

The dilemma of what to do, and how to prepare for it, is greater in Malaysia than in Singapore if only because the Federation is closer to the seat of possible aggression and has a longer and far more exposed border. But as the Japanese demonstrated in World War II, the conquest of Malaysia almost automatically brings about the collapse of Singapore. And the equation has not changed. All over Asia, the wise men may scoff at Dwight David Eisenhower's "domino theory" but it still means something, in vastly more sophisticated form, to the divorced partners on the Malay Peninsula.

It is not unnatural that the leaders of Malaysia react very much in the manner of their father figure, Tunku Abdul Rahman. For it was under his firm guidance that the young nation emerged from colonial rule by the British and occupation by Japan and survived its earliest trials. To the students and the voracious liberals of Kuala Lumpur, the Tunku is an antediluvian figure out of a distant past that has no meaning for them. But to Tun Razak, the Prime Minister, and to his deputy, Tun Dr. Ismail, the Tunku's wisdom still has an enormous appeal.

To outsiders, it may seem quaint that the Tunku did much of the nation's business on the golf course and almost obliged the members of his Cabinet to play golf daily. But the men about the Tunku came to believe, with him, that golf would maintain their health and increase their tolerance of their fellows. As the Tunku put it: "You can't play golf every day without becoming tolerant." Accordingly, the hours of work for the chief ministers of the government in Kuala Lumpur still are from 8 A.M. to 4 P.M., which gives them time to get out on the golf course by 4:30 every afternoon. And some still manage to play at least nine holes before breakfast.

My wife and I talked with the Tunku just after he had reached his office in the hills fringing central Kuala Lumpur on a pleasant summer's morning. It was just before the announcement of his retirement in 1970 and he went over his speech with us, point by point, not so much to obtain our approval as to seek our understanding. No one could help but be impressed by the father of Malaysia—a tall, broad-shouldered sixty-eight-year-old giant in a flowing gray robe and jacket, and a tall black hat, who sat in the center of a large office decorated with dolls in the costumes of all the countries he had visited.

The Tunku had planned the transfer of power to Tun Razak so well that there was not a tremor in the government of Malaysia. To that extent, his gospel of tolerance had worked—and worked well—and he knew it. But when it came to a discussion of foreign affairs and the future role of Malaysia, all his tolerance vanished. His mistrust of the Japanese was great and his fear of the Chinese was even greater.

"China," he said, "is the source of the danger to Southeast Asia and the Chinese way is to practice subversion and infiltration. I see no end to China's war against us in Southeast Asia. As for the Japanese, they are not to be trusted and I have told them so. Whatever they do, they do for trade and their own benefit, so I do not see that they will play a vital defense role at any time in Southeast Asia. I think that the countries of Southeast Asia will have to rely more on their own efforts."

The Tunku was well aware that every dollar spent on the national defense would have to be taken from national development. And since he also was convinced that the best defense against Communist subversion was an increase in national development, he saw that large-scale military planning for a small country such as his own would be self-defeating. So he still hoped for a protected spot under the United States nuclear umbrella to ward off. major threats from the other great powers, and for substantial American economic support.

"But," I said, "the United States is withdrawing from Southeast Asia."

"Militarily, yes," he replied, "but in every other way, no. You are a great power and you can't withdraw. You Americans should realize that we don't want your troops and we certainly see little hope for SEATO. It is sufficient, for our purposes, if the Seventh Fleet stays in Asian waters because that gives us assurance that the United States will carry out its commitments. We also like the idea of a continued British presence in this part of the world, however small the British military commitment may be, and that is why we are going into the new defense agreement with them."

The Tunku had his reservations about other regional arrangements, however. He liked ASEAN only because the Indonesians were interested in the organization. And as for the unity of Islam, he thought of that as sheer poetry and counted on no help from his fellow Muslims merely because of the religious link between them. What he hoped to do with the rest of his life was to play golf, lead the good life and work for peace—and to these engaging prospects he cheerfully devoted the remainder of our interview.

That afternoon,[27] Tun Razak was waiting for us at his magnificent estate, Sri Taman, on a hilltop outside Kuala Lumpur, with the fine new Malaysian Parliament building bulking large in the distance. It had been six years since I'd last seen him, but he hadn't changed. At forty-eight years of age, he was still slim and serene, his dark eyes clear and challenging behind their black-rimmed glasses, his hair black with only a few traces of gray, his strong face unlined.

Like the Tunku, he argued that Malaysia was well able to contain internal threats of subversion but needed help from outside for its external defense. That, he said, meant military matériel, for one thing; even more important, it meant dependable partners in the event of outside attack. For that reason, he welcomed the limited

[27] We were fortunate enough to be able to talk with the Tunku, Tun Razak and Tun Dr. Ismail on the same day, August 20, 1970.

military agreement with Britain, Australia and New Zealand in addition to Singapore. And while he did hope for American military matériel to bolster Malaysia's defenses, he, too, saw no reason to seek a continued American military presence on the Asian mainland.

"Americans should not be asked to police the world," he said, "and certainly they should not have to fight without substantial help from other powers. But I don't think the United States by itself can ever hope to guarantee peace in this part of the world."

It was then for the first time that he sketched out his plan for neutralizing Southeast Asia through mutual agreement by the great powers, a proposal he has since put forward on a number of occasions. As a political realist, the new prime minister of Malaysia knew perfectly well how much difficulty there would be in getting the United States, the Soviet Union, China and Japan to agree on anything. And yet, he contended that it was in their own best interests, as well as those of the countries of Southeast Asia, to neutralize Southeast Asia. He saw it as the best hope, perhaps the only hope, of peace in the area in the foreseeable future. To continue a senseless great-power rivalry in so vital a region, he warned, was to risk drifting into an escalating war that could end in a nuclear holocaust.

"What I ask the great powers to do," he said, "is to guarantee the national borders of the countries of Southeast Asia and leave us to work out our own problems. We can do it."

Tun Razak was hesitant, on the whole, about the prospect of improved relations between Malaysia and China, although he was committed to make the attempt early in his term as prime minister. Like so many of his associates, he doubted that the Chinese would ever quit the dangerous game of subversion until it was made unprofitable for them to continue. But even at that very early stage in the efforts to achieve an American-Soviet détente, he saw a very real chance of an agreement to limit nuclear arms and to scale down the other aspects of the Cold War. As for the Vietnam War, he had never really changed his opinion that it would end only when Hanoi tired of a generation of fighting.

As for relations between Malaysia and the United States, the usual plea for greater American understanding of a small nation's problems meant something more when Tun Razak made it. He had had a somewhat unfortunate experience with Vice-President Spiro Agnew, which I learned about from other sources. It appears that when Agnew came to Kuala Lumpur, he spent the better part of an hour lecturing Tun Razak and others on the problems of being the mayor of a small city in Maryland and showed no interest whatever in discussing the concerns of Malaysia.

What, then, can the United States do for Malaysia? For one thing, a realistic discussion of rubber prices, on which so much of the Malaysian economy depends. For another, support for international backing of the Malaysian government's program of strengthening the rural economy by engaging in small but necessary projects such as dam building and electrification. Such things, the new prime minister said, mean a great deal more to a small country than the building of foreign air bases and the stationing of foreign troops on its soil. "You Americans must understand," he said, "that our great need is for national unity and this is something that nobody can accomplish for us except by giving us the strength to help ourselves."

When Tun Razak took over the government from the Tunku on September 22, 1970, he issued his call for a guarantee of the neutrality of Southeast Asia by the United States, the Soviet Union and China (but he omitted Japan). He also made his first bid to improve relations with the Soviet Union, despite Malaysia's bitter ten-year war against Communist guerrillas, as a gesture to balance the great-power scales against China. As one of his associates put it, Malaysia had begun so far to the right that it had to move to the left in order to reach a desirable center position—the goal of all the governments of Southeast Asia outside warring Indochina today.

There is, of course, little hope for Tun Razak's scheme of a great-power guarantee of Asian neutrality. And even less for American support for Malaysia or Singapore if either one or both explode into racial warfare that could bring about foreign intervention. As a realistic matter, the token forces of the British, Australians and New Zealanders could not hope to contain so dangerous a situation—and that is the very real danger of Malaysia for the rest of the world.

As Arnold Toynbee put it: "On a long view, Malaysia, not Vietnam, is the danger point in Southeast Asia . . . Would China wish to hold aloof if Malaysia did fall into a race war? And would China be able to keep clear of this, even if she wished to? This is the question that looms up when we look into Southeast Asia's prospect for the day after tomorrow."[28]

The Long View: Singapore

There isn't anything very gracious or engaging about Singapore. It is, even by Asian standards, a dull city. Whatever cultural interests it has are in the main a heritage of its unmourned British era. Under Lee Kuan Yew's dictatorial rule, it is run as a strictly commercial proposition.

True, the Prime Minister's adherents do not like to be classed with the Japanese as economic animals and perhaps, judged by their own lights, they are not. Certainly, no comparable area in Asia has built so much public housing in so short a time—more than 100,000 dwelling units for some 600,000 people in a decade at subsidized low-cost rentals ranging from $20 to $30 a month for three-room flats.[29] Standards of public health have been increased to such an extent that Singapore now boasts that its tap water can be safely consumed and guarantees hospital costs for any illnesses that can be traced to it. Urban renewal is so active a concept that Singapore's old Chinatown is marked for extinction. And more than 500,000 children are being educated in its 500 government or government-aided schools.

There is one other aspect of life in Singapore that is greatly to the credit of its leadership. While no government can be free of corruption, both diplomats and business people generally agree that there is less of it in Singapore than in any other big city in Asia—a verdict in which even chronically suspicious foreign correspondents are inclined to concur.

But for all its accomplishments, the government of Singapore can scarcely be considered an ornament to self-government after the Western fashion, even though it displays all the trappings of a Western-style democratic state. Unhappily, such institutions are window dressing in the main, for in practice it is Lee Kuan Yew who

[28] Arnold Toynbee, for Observer Foreign News Service, in the *Sunday Post-Herald*, Hong Kong, September 20, 1970, p. 10.
[29] *First Decade in Public Housing*, Housing & Development Board, 1969.

decides what can or cannot be done in Singapore. He was utterly ruthless in his offensive against the Singapore press in 1971, closing down the Singapore *Herald* by forcing its bankers to call in loans to the paper's backers, destroying the *Eastern Sun* with charges that it had received a subsidy of $1.35 million from Chinese Communist agents, and detaining four senior members of the staff of a Chinese newspaper, *Nanyang Siang Pau,* on charges of "Chinese chauvinism."[30] In the 1970–71 academic year, a number of faculty members resigned from the University of Singapore and one of them accused the government of authoritarian tendencies.[31] Lee Kuan Yew's lighthearted reply was that they were just "birds of passage."

It was not civil liberties, however, but inflation that finally produced signs of opposition to the Prime Minister's tightfisted rule for the first time in seven years. The People's Front, a leftist group that included some defectors from Lee's own People's Action Party, was formed in 1971 by Lui Boon Poh, a thirty-four-year-old lawyer. It appeared to be the first serious effort to attack Lee's regime, which came to power in 1959, but even his critics were doubtful that the People's Front would last very long if the Prime Minister decided to move against it.[32] He was, of course, fully capable of doing it.

What Lee Kuan Yew could not do, however, was to control the rise in inflation. No less than Japan and Hong Kong, Singapore was paying the price for its sudden prosperity and the government's efforts to protect its people were too little and, for the most part, too late. While low-income groups were affected to a greater extent than the 1 per cent cost-of-living rise admitted to by the government during 1970, it was the middle class that was really caught in the economic squeeze. Flats that had rented for $135–$165 a month soared to $400–$500 a month. Luxury apartments were being sold for $35,000 to $100,000 and land-grabbers were jubilantly reporting profits of up to 30 per cent within a week on land sales.[33] Other living costs were going up as well.

[30] The Singapore *Herald's* May 19, 1971, issue said it was being closed down because it "dared to take on the government."
[31] An American, Prof. Roland Pucetti, quoted in *The New York Times,* January 5, 1971, p. 6.
[32] *The New York Times,* April 4, 1971, p. 8.
[33] *Asia Magazine,* October 11, 1970, pp. 18–22.

While it was easy for the government to blame the American industrial influx for the onset of inflation, that was scarcely the entire story. For despite a seemingly chronic unemployment problem of 50,000 unskilled laborers, and sometimes more, Singapore was confronted with a continual need for more skilled people. The Finance Minister, Dr. Goh Keng Swee, predicted that the industrial work force would increase by 1974 to nearly 250,000 from its present 110,000, and most of these of necessity would be skilled technicians. To get such people to come to Singapore, the government was paying an average of $1,700 to bring a worker and his family from Hong Kong, provide him with a home, put his children in school and assure him of a monthly salary of not less than $400. This kind of recruitment was being conducted on a large scale with the help of the Singapore Manufacturers Association, which in 1970 alone represented more than one hundred firms interested in hiring skilled foreign labor.[34] The impact of such a drive on the economy could not help but boost both wages and prices in the disastrous inflationary spiral.

But the government, while bidding for a rise in foreign investment of all kinds, continued to attach most of the blame for its inflationary woes on American, British and Japanese capital. The Americans, as always, were in the forefront because of their characteristically high visibility on the foreign scene. In a decade in Singapore, their numbers had increased tenfold, from a mere 500 to 5,000, and more than 250 American firms were registered in Singapore in 1971, as compared with only 60 four years before. It was difficult to estimate the size of American investments in the city-state, with so much oil money pouring in, but one American government source put the stake of American firms at $200 million, with three times that amount committed to joint ventures.[35] Moreover, despite Singapore's disappointment over not receiving more American tourists from Expo 70, it still counted on American tourists to help put its annual total of visitors over the 500,000 mark.

[34] *Ibid.*, October 25, 1970, p. 3.
[35] An estimate made during my visit to Singapore August 21–28, 1970.

Singapore and the United States

All this may have something to do with Lee Kuan Yew's ambivalent attitude toward the United States. Actually, he is neither happy nor even comfortable with most Americans and he has only scorn for American permissiveness with demonstrators at home. He has had his troubles with the CIA and once disclosed that an American CIA agent had been arrested in 1960 in "an apparent attempt to bribe and subvert Singapore intelligence authorities." When Washington denied it, the angry Lee made public a letter of apology from Secretary of State Dean Rusk because American officials had engaged in "improper activities" in Singapore. The Prime Minister was so incensed that he thrust the letter in the face of an American correspondent and said, "The Americans stupidly deny the undeniable."[36]

Since then, Lee has swung his policies toward the United States in pendulum fashion, depending on what was in the best interests of Singapore. When I saw him briefly in Singapore just before he departed on one of his grandiose tours of world capitals, for example, he was about as pro-American as he ever gets. For while he agreed that American military withdrawal from the Asian mainland was inevitable, he cautioned against letting down the South Vietnamese and the Thais in such a way that they could not effectively defend themselves. But when he returned from his travels, including two weeks at a Harvard seminar, he could not contain his impatience over fuzzy-minded American education, rebellious students and a government that seemed incapable of dealing with a serious domestic crisis.[37]

His foreign minister, S. Rajaratnam, still uses the familiar old Communist bogeyman approach in dealing with Americans. With a perfectly straight face, he told me one morning that the Russians were likely to take over in Southeast Asia if the United States moves out, that Thailand could turn to Peking and that the United States in any case has such a big investment in Singapore that American

[36] New York *Daily News*, September 2, 1965, p. 1; *The New York Times*, April 25, 1966, p. 1.
[37] I saw Lee Kuan Yew for only a few minutes on August 25, 1970.

businessmen should be protected. It was, all told, not a very impressive or even believable performance.[38] The Russian take-over to date has consisted of a few warships passing through the Strait of Malacca.

What Singapore is trying to do, without notable success to date, is to develop a greater mutual commercial interest with the Soviet Union in order to counterbalance the undoubted attraction of mainland China for many younger Singapore Chinese. Here is Lee Kuan Yew's most serious challenge from abroad and he fully realizes it. It was for this reason that he put some pro-Chinese or anti-government papers out of business and still uses the threat of his licensing authority to control the rest of the press. Very possibly, this also is the reason for his lack of sympathy with Tun Razak's scheme for a three- or four-power guarantee of the neutrality of Southeast Asia. Seen from Singapore, the proposal doesn't seem very practical.

Even if it were, one of the world's largest and most important naval bases has just been bequeathed by the retreating British to Lee's government, which is somewhat of an embarrassment for a professed neutralist like the Prime Minister. At Lusaka and at other gatherings of the statesmen of the Third World, it is he who talks the loudest for independence of the great powers and an end to military domination. But at the same time, he either is going to have to see that the Singapore naval base is fully used or he will be obliged to close it up, put its 15,000 employees on the public rolls or add them to the ranks of the jobless, and then suffer a steep loss in revenue. The latter possibility, for a strictly dollars-and-cents place like Singapore, is the most horrendous of all.

Lee has tried to promote new business against the time of the final British withdrawal at the end of 1971. He has had a high level naval inspection mission from the United States and another from the Soviet Union looking over the dockyards. He also is trying to sell Australia and New Zealand on a ship-repairing proposition. Then,

[38] The Rajaratnam interview was on August 26, 1970. Lee's attitude toward the United States was reported by mutual acquaintances. His swing back toward anti-Americanism may have had something to do with U.S. coolness to a British move to boost him for Secretary General of the United Nations to succeed U Thant. He lost out to Kurt Waldheim of Austria.

too, there is the prospect of commercial ship repairs for the great powers. During 1970, for example, more than 500 Russian vessels, mostly fishing boats and freighters, called at Singapore. There also were about fifty American naval vessels that gave shore leave to 18,000 American sailors who are estimated to have spent nearly $3 million in Singapore.[39] It is going to be hard for Lee's government to lose that kind of business, whether it is neutralist or not.

Consequently, Singapore is clearly headed for a larger effort in shipbuilding and ship repair, with the Singapore naval base as a nucleus. Without doubt, the city of the lion also is going to make a determined bid for a part of the developing aerospace industry, using the former RAF bases at Changi, Seletar and Tengah to handle such sophisticated business. And in this respect, there is going to be increasing competition with both Japan and Australia.

Despite the growth of American business in Singapore, what rankles most at the old City Hall building where Lee Kuan Yew maintains offices is the unpleasant truth that the United States can get along without Singapore, but Singapore can't very easily get along without the United States. It is common knowledge that relatively few Americans know anything about the prosperous city-state, or even care that they don't know. The story is still told at diplomatic gatherings of the great American news executive who didn't know, until he arrived in Singapore, that the city no longer was a part of Malaysia. And there are sad and understanding smiles among foreign correspondents over the plight of one of their colleagues whose home office addresses mail to him at Singapore, China; Singapore, Malaysia; and even Singapore, Thailand.[40] Ignorance remains the greatest foe of an advancement in international understanding.

Singapore continues to be one of the few important places in the world that are not covered by one of the numerous American joint or multination defense treaties. Although a few advanced thinkers in international relations may dispute it, the United States does not have

[39] *Far Eastern Economic Review*, March 27, 1971, p. 73.

[40] This sad state of affairs works both ways. I remember talking with an intelligent young Malay from Sarawak, who knew all about cameras but remarked brightly when I said I was from New York City: "Oh, yes, where the cowboys come from." I had to explain that we saw cowboys only on television.

even a moral commitment to come to the defense of Singapore in the event of attack. Nor could the special nature of the American-British relationship, now undergoing such a profound change with Britain's advance into the European Common Market, be said to provide a basis for American intervention in the city of the lion. Whatever may happen in Singapore during the foreseeable future, the landing of an American fighting force in full battle dress is not among the more disagreeable prospects. Nor is there any real possibility that the Russian hammer and sickle on its traditional red banner will float from the flagstaff atop City Hall. But Chinese subversion is something else again, and it is with this threat that the government of Singapore will have to come to grips sooner rather than later.

5. INDONESIA COMES BACK

Flying in over the red tile roofs of Djakarta's palm-fringed outskirts, everything seems the same as it was during the days of the unlamented Sukarno. It is almost as if time has stood still.

The monuments of the Bung's overweening folly jut out of the Indonesian urban sprawl in silent reproach—the great sports stadium that is seldom used, the short but massive modern highways that lead nowhere, the towering memorial statuary to a less than heroic age. Such evidence of wastefulness is bound to be depressing in a land of 120,000,000 people that has so little and needs so much.

Once the airliner touches down at Djakarta's expanding airport, however, it becomes quickly apparent to the arriving traveler that some things have changed for the better. The formalities of health inspection, passport control and customs take only a few minutes, whereas hours were once required in the unhappy concluding years of Sukarno's reign.[41] The suddenly tour-conscious Indonesians also go out of their way to let a foreigner know that he is welcome, which is a pleasant and harmless courtesy. And while this is not a haven of unfettered freedom in the style of Western-type democracies, it also

---

[41] My wife and I were held up for hours on a hot night in the summer of 1964 with a planeload of other passengers at Djakarta airport while Sukarno's soldiers puzzled over our passports and made us fight to get them back. Six years later, this nonsense was dispensed with.

has shed many of the harsh trappings of the Asian-type police state. The interests of national security, still a matter of the utmost concern in Indonesia, are not usually extended to cover the harassment of travelers in general and journalists in particular. There is no uneasy sense of having to look over one's shoulder—the Sukarno glance— before making a critical remark about the state of affairs. And the once-common red posters and hammer-and-sickle streamers are no longer to be seen in Djakarta or the surrounding countryside.

These surface evidences of change, so apparent to anyone returning to Indonesia after a prolonged absence, reflect the difference between Sukarno and his less flamboyant and far more responsible successors. It is scarcely true, as some enthusiasts have proclaimed, that President Suharto has succeeded in leading Indonesia completely out of the political, economic and social morass in which he found it when he took over. But his military-supported regime, whatever other criticisms may be made of it, has at least made a beginning —and a promising one to date.

The View from Djakarta

When Sukarno was reproached for his profligacy by well-wishers from abroad and told that he must economize, he used to laugh and say, "Economics makes my head ache."[42] Today, with massive help from foreign nations, including the United States, a young and hard-working group of American-trained Indonesian economists[43] is trying to restore Indonesia to economic well-being. Its members have the trust and the support of President Suharto, without which they could not function, but their progress, of necessity, has been painfully slow. In view of the difficulties they inherited, the wonder is not that Sukarno was able to last so long in Indonesia, but that Indonesia was able to survive this incredible man, its founding father.

The Indonesian dream, like that in other developing lands, is of an exhilarating economic take-off that will capitalize on the fantastically rich resources of the country and bring prosperity to all its inhabi-

---

[42] Bernard Krisher, *Newsweek*, October 5, 1964, p. 84.

[43] Most of them come from the University of California and are known locally, with some degree of pride, as "the Berkeley school."

tants. Beyond that, Indonesia wants in time to become the military leader of a great Southeast Asian defense grouping of nations and a respected rival of Japan. Even with wise and trusted leadership at home and continued help from abroad, economic well-being can scarcely be created overnight, however, and the notion of a mighty military machine based on the island of Java is something left over from the hallucinations of the Sukarno era.

The uncomfortable reality is that Indonesia remains a poor country and, despite gains, both its political and economic systems are weak. Its main task, in the view of its knowledgeable and experienced foreign minister, Adam Malik, the 1971 President of the United Nations General Assembly, is to strengthen itself internally against the twin forces of Communist infiltration and subversion.[44] And that means, first of all, a strengthened economy, the main defense against another attempted Communist take-over at some future time. President Suharto, Malik, the Berkeley school of economists and the military are all pretty well agreed on this kind of priority in the national effort. For a nation in which the Army is the dominating element, it speaks well for the military that they recognize they must not divert funds from more necessary purposes, such as self-sufficiency in rice production.

Of course, there is always a chance for an economic miracle in Indonesia. But the kind of massive infusion of capital that would be required to sustain an economic take-off there could come only from the development of its latent oil resources and the adoption, at the same time, of efficient birth control methods. There is oil in Indonesia. No one can doubt it. In 1971, the country was producing almost 1,000,000 barrels of oil a day from onshore wells and had just gone into offshore drilling that could double oil production within two years. More than forty foreign oil companies were interested.

Indonesia also gained from substantial foreign capital that went into mining, forestry, construction and fisheries. With oil money, the total was approaching $1.5 billion by the end of 1971. As for the goal of self-sufficient rice production, that was within reach. It amounted to 12,000,000 tons in 1970, even more the following year.

[44] In an interview with me, September 1, 1970.

However, with the nation's birth rate still out of control and population growth hitting a rate of 2.6 to 3 per cent a year, the Indonesians had to face up to a less prolific existence if they really intended to enjoy an economic revival. From 1958 to 1967, in fact, the Indonesian GNP actually declined on a per capita basis because of the population explosion and in 1970 stood at only about $9 billion, or about $75 per capita. The rate of inflation in 1971 was still around 10 per cent annually, and the monetary crisis caused by the United States forced still another devaluation of the much-battered rupiah, this time by 10 per cent. (The new rate was 414 rupiahs to the dollar, from 378.) And, in response to the temporary 10 per cent American import surtax, Indonesia actually reduced its own taxes on items for export.

The saving grace for the Suharto government remained the wonderfully fertile and productive land that was so energetically cultivated by the native farmers with their primitive implements, for the most part, and with very little help in the form of fertilizer and modern agricultural methods. It has been said that a stick could be thrust into the Indonesian earth and made in time to blossom. Whether that is true or not, the Indonesians continue to be blessed with more than enough food to go around, regardless of the precarious state of the economy. It was wretched mismanagement in the Sukarno era that deprived Indonesia of its traditional ability to raise enough rice to feed its people, not any failure of the land and its tillers.

The Challenge to Indonesia

There is nothing small about either Indonesia or its problems. Its 3,000 islands extend for 3,200 miles from east to west, the five largest—Java, Sumatra, Kalimantan (Borneo), Sulawesi (Celebes) and West Irian—being among the most densely populated in the world. In land size, its 735,000-square-mile area is about 20 per cent larger than that of Alaska but its population is more than 400 times larger. Its sea area is almost four times the size of Texas.

Having been a link between Asia and Australia from its earliest history and a strategic area commanding passage between the Indian and Pacific oceans, these ancient Spice Islands—as they were once known—have always been a rich prize for foreign imperial adventure. For 300 years, the archipelago was owned by the Dutch and the story is still told of the Dutchman who, upon viewing the glories of an Indonesian sunrise, cried, "It was better under Dutch rule." As was the case with so many of Asia's emerging nations, the relatively brief period of Japanese occupation during World War II led directly to independence, the abortive Dutch attempt at a "police action" to return to power, and the proclamation of the Republic of Indonesia by Sukarno in 1950.

Under Sukarno's "Guided Democracy," a holy faith that was almost impossible to challenge in Indonesia, he thought of himself as the leader of the NEFOS (New Emerging Forces) doing battle with the OLDEFOS (Old Established Forces). He lurched from one disaster to another, sustained by his palace clique, the military and his devoted Communist allies. The economy broke down. The government degenerated into near-anarchy. And in the summer of 1964, Sukarno reached the end of a golden stream of American aid estimated at more than $1 billion, knew he could get no more, and publicly shouted at the gentle American ambassador, Howard P. Jones, "To hell with your aid!" A few months later, he took Indonesia out of the United Nations in a fit of anger because the Federation of Malaysia, with which he was conducting a small but nasty war, was elected to the Security Council.

It was predictable that Sukarno, having terminated all hope of substantial financial assistance from the West, would turn to China for help. The canny Chinese agreed, dispatching the veteran Marshal Chen Yi to Djakarta at the end of 1964 to seal the compact, but their price proved to be very high. Step by step, the PKI, the Communist Party of Indonesia, became bolder in its bid for power behind the protective shield of Sukarno's approval. Its membership reputedly soared to 4,000,000, with some 1,500,000 being indigenous Chinese, and it also boasted of commanding the sympathies, some open and some in secret, of numerous leaders of the Indonesian Army. One sign of things to come was the seizure or closing of most of the once-vigorous Indonesian press, of which only eleven dailies remained, six of them Communist propaganda organs. Another was the despair of the Western diplomatic community, with one senior diplomat saying, "What can anyone do? It's like the tide coming in."

The Peking-Djakarta Axis was being formed openly before the gaze of the world. The Communist Party was flaunting its authority in numerous ways, almost daring the Indonesian Army, with its $1 billion in Russian arms and equipment, to intervene. But nothing happened until the attempted Communist take-over began on the night of September 30–October 1, 1965, with the murder of six generals. Suharto, the commander of the elite Strategic Reserve in Djakarta, was so lightly regarded that he had not been marked for extinction. And that was the Communists' mistake. For within a few hours, he had led his troops against both the dissident Army regulars and the palace guard and was master of Djakarta, with Sukarno as his prisoner.

In the slaughter that followed, somewhere between 300,000 and 400,000 people perished as victims of the vengeful Army. Just how many actually died, and what proportion really were Communists who participated in the effort to take power, may never be known. Nor does the government of President Suharto worry very much about it nowadays. But clearly, the Communist uprising that failed is the great modern watershed of Indonesian history. For while Indonesia has not come down openly on the side of the West and still maintains a kind of theoretical neutralism, the leaders of its government leave no doubt that they still consider China to be their enemy and the revival of the China-supported PKI to be their greatest domestic danger.

It has often been said in the West, particularly by the neo-isolationists in Washington, D.C., that Indonesia is an example of how a nation can resist Communist power successfully by its own efforts without the use of a single American soldier, warship or aircraft. Judged solely by the results, that is so; but to the Indonesians who lived through the abortive revolt, it was a very narrow thing. The plot came within a few minutes of success. Had General Abdul Haris Nasution, the minister of defense and security, not received warning in time to be able to scramble over a back fence at his home just ahead of his would-be Communist executioners, perhaps General Suharto might not have been able to move to the rescue quite as expeditiously.

The State of Internal Security

The PKI still leads a precarious underground existence in Indonesia. Most of the new chieftains who replaced the massacred leadership in 1965 have themselves been clapped into prison, so that the Suharto regime seems to have the situation well under control for the immediate future. But because of the vast numerical strength of the PKI before 1965 and the influence it exerted over a very large part of the country, it cannot be disregarded as a potential force for the long term. Undoubtedly, there is still resentment in the old Sukarno stronghold in East Java over the massive killings of 1965. Furthermore, some 150,000 political prisoners still remain in detention camps and are unlikely to be released in the foreseeable future.

As for the frightened Chinese community of Indonesia, which numbers about 3,000,000, many are now adopting Indonesian surnames and trying to mix with Indonesian society. Regardless of the success or failure of this assimilation process, and it is not going too well, the Chinese remain an important economic factor in the country, but they have almost no political influence. The younger Chinese, particularly those educated in China, are still suspect.

The most disaffected part of the populace, as far as the government is concerned, is the religious Muslim faction, especially the young people, who now and then agitate for change. They feel, for the most part, that they played a major role in the overthrow of Sukarno but have not been properly rewarded. It would be difficult to estimate the number of activists at this level of Indonesian society, but by most accounts the group is comparatively small. However, they are an elite of sorts, and they do have access to the Indonesian communications media, so they can kick up a fuss. They have a potential for trouble, therefore, if they become so disaffected that they are able to provoke the government into extreme repressive action. So far, Suharto has kept his cool.[45]

[45] When Bandung students broke loose in a wild protest against the death of a student from a police beating after a soccer match between Bandung

But on the whole, the once-impressive student movement in Indonesia, so feared in the last days of Sukarno, is fragmented and no longer has the support of the military. They do not constitute a New Left in any sense. They are very far from it. By the private admissions of some of their leaders, most young Indonesians in the universities are more interested in getting ahead and becoming a part of the Establishment than in overthrowing the government. They do not seem to be a part of the middle-to-upper-class rebellion among students that was so remarkable a feature of higher education in Japan, Western Europe and the United States during the late 1960s and early 1970s.

Primarily, this is because students in Indonesia are usually poor. What they seek to do is to stimulate their government into faster action to solve the nation's problems, most of which cannot be tackled by speed alone. But by military estimates, they have so little potential for major political action that their demonstrations are viewed with a charitable eye and are seldom interfered with. At times, particularly when they cry out against corruption, the students actually reinforce President Suharto's hand and are welcomed as allies. He feels, in any event, that he has little to fear from them for the time being.[46]

Elections in Indonesia

Through an intricate series of devices and limitations, the Indonesian Army has pretty well assured itself of remaining the effective power in the land at least until 1975, and perhaps for three years thereafter. Thus, when President Suharto permitted the first general elections in sixteen years to be held on July 3, 1971, he wasn't taking too many chances and the resultant government majority in the House of Representatives vindicated his judgment. In the first place, one hundred of the seats were held by the military on government appointment. In the second, more than 25 per cent of the 3,000

Institute and the Police Academy on October 5, 1970, President Suharto condemned the incident but warned the students not to judge the police or the armed forces by such an event.

[46] The material on Indonesia's internal economic and political problems and the position with regard to internal security was gathered from a number of authoritative sources in Djakarta and elsewhere.

candidates for public office were removed from the lists by the government because they were unacceptable on one ground or another. Finally, the government in effect organized its own political party to oppose the seven already in the field. It was called Golongon Karya, or Golkar, the secretariat of such functional groups as government employees, teachers, pro-government journalists and others, and it represented President Suharto's main strength in his successful campaign. Over the next decade, his supporters hoped to make it dominant over the present Nationalist Party, the PNI, and the four strong Muslim parties, eliminating the rest.

With the support of the Suharto-dominated House, the government could look forward with confidence to control of the larger People's Consultative Congress, which was assigned to pick a new president in 1973. Few doubted that he would again be Suharto and that his Army adherents, plus Golkar, would widen his power over the country.

The Army on the March

Like the People's Liberation Army of China, the Indonesian Army is no ordinary fighting force that concerns itself with purely military duties. As the single most responsible and stabilizing force in the country, the 450,000-member Army extends its influence to almost every phase of the country's life. It is even in business for itself, operating its own factories, import-export operations, banks and night clubs, and apparently is able to make a profit on its conglomerate dealings. With these funds, it helps itself first of all by increasing the traditionally low military pay. And it also finances some civic improvements, including road and school construction, bridges and canals.

Soldiers may also be found in various industries, fulfilling various roles ranging in importance from a kind of political commissar to Western-style trouble shooter and efficiency man. But of course, in such a setup there are inevitably drones and there are also mounting tales of pay-offs and other forms of graft and corruption, never far below the surface in the life-style of any Oriental land. One of the accused has been Ibnu Sutowo, a lieutenant general who is the director of the state oil monopoly, Pertamina, which accounts for almost 40 per cent of Indonesia's exports. After an investigation, his absolute power over the enterprise was curbed but he remained in office. Other targets in the anti-corruption campaign have been Major Generals Achmad Tirtusudiro and Surjo, the latter being a private assistant (*aspri*) of President Suharto's. He has supported both of them loyally.[47] Such accusations have not perceptibly undermined the Army's dominant role in the country because there is no substitute for it.

The leading economists of the National Planning Board—Widjojo Nitisastro and Emil Salim—are actually dependent on the Army to maintain the national balance so necessary to the completion of the current five-year development plan. Without public order, they could scarcely hope to achieve economic stabilization, improvement of the country's infrastructure and a strong beginning toward the modernization of agriculture. The farthest Suharto has gone toward placating the liberal anti-military sentiment is to pledge that the Army will be reduced by at least 200,000 troops by 1975. But no realistic Indonesian believes that the Army will voluntarily give up its power by then, or for the succeeding decade as well.

The International Rescue Mission

If it were not for a rare parallel cooperation between the West plus Japan and the Soviet Union, Indonesia would be far worse off today than ever before. For in June 1970, the Indonesian external debt—mostly inherited from Sukarno—stood at $3.2 billion,[48] of which the Soviet bloc countries accounted for $1.3 billion and the United States $200 million. Since 1967, a ten-nation international group, including the United States, Japan and West European countries, has been supporting Indonesia with loans and grants while rescheduling payment of the principal of the debt over a thirty-year period ending in 1999. The Soviet Union, after some delay, has initiated similar action, but on less generous terms.

The end result for the West to date has been a heavy investment in

[47] *Pacific Community*, April, 1971, pp. 536–540.

[48] "Indonesia and U.S. Assistance," issued by Program Office, U.S. Agency for International Development, June 19, 1970, p. 2. For Soviet arrangements, see *Far Eastern Economic Review*, March 20, 1971, p. 30.

Indonesia. For example, the Inter-Governmental Group on Indonesia (IGGI) supplied $330 million in aid for Indonesia in 1969, the first year of the Repelita, or five-year plan. For 1970, that went up to $540 million, and for 1971, $660 million. This kind of commitment has encouraged private investment in Indonesia as well, with more than 200 foreign companies—led by the Americans and the Japanese—pumping more than $1 billion into the economy.

What everybody is betting on is a massive revival of Indonesian agriculture and industry. Even with the modest gains that the five-year plan has achieved, one of the most knowledgeable foreign experts in Indonesia estimates the unemployed and underemployed in the land at "tens of millions."[49] If the foreign rescue operation is to get anywhere, that problem will have to be resolved first of all. The key areas of attack are agriculture, forestry and fisheries, which together account for 50 per cent of the national income, employ 70 per cent of the work force and earn 80 per cent of the land's foreign exchange. Next come petroleum and rubber, both of which bulk ever larger in the Indonesian economy.

The goals are ambitious: a 90 per cent increase in industrial production, a 64 per cent increase in electric power, the rehabilitation of 10,000 miles of roads and the construction of new highways, the expansion of docking and dredging facilities in Indonesian ports and the broadening of both foreign and domestic air traffic.[50] All this is a very large order for a country that was tottering on the verge of bankruptcy not long ago. Despite favorable foreign investment laws and guarantees against expropriation of American investments in particular, the nature of the financial risk here is clear. Nor do wise ambassadors in Djakarta try to disguise it.

There is, nevertheless, a school of thought among the Indonesian elite that does not view the advent of Western risk capital as an unmitigated blessing. The influential daily *Merdeka* (*Independence*) was the first to attack the country's Western-oriented economists and editorially demanded that Indonesians should "determine the way of

[49] In most Asian countries, the euphemism "unemployed and underemployed" is used to try to soften the impact of the high rate of joblessness. There are few reliable statistics on unemployment as a result.

[50] "Indonesia and U.S. Assistance," issued by Program Office, U.S. Agency for International Development, June 19, 1970, pp. 3–4.

spending the amount of credit received from the foreign countries and not be dictated to by them."[51] These patriotic sentiments were prudently softened some days later by the paper's owner, B. M. Diah, a former information minister, when he bade godspeed to the Indonesian economists who were on their way to a meeting with the Western consortium. It had become known that President Suharto did not take kindly to such criticism of his policies.

But another and more redoubtable Indonesian journalist, the irrepressible Mochtar Lubis, did not hold back his doubts, regardless of consequences. He had spent nine years in Sukarno's prisons, half in solitary confinement in East Java, for speaking out against the old dictator; and, while he favored the new government, he would not let himself be silenced. In his revived newspaper, *Indonesia Raya*, he argued that "economics is too important to be left to the economists," that too much attention was being paid to economic theory and too little to practice, and that sufficient fertilizer and machinery—though on order—was not reaching the hard-pressed Indonesian farmer. There was merit to Lubis' position, which he documented both in his paper and in interviews.[52]

Still another leading journalist, Rosihan Anwar, editor of *Pedoman*, was more resigned to the growth of foreign influence in Indonesia. While he made no secret of his dislike of the trend, he said that Indonesia had no choice but to support an "open door policy" and invite American, Japanese, West German and other foreign capital into the country.[53]

The government's Minister of Information, Major General Budiarjo, had to walk a rather narrow line between insistence on a decent respect for President Suharto's policies and a large degree of tolerance for dissenting opinions. Certainly, the horrible days of Sukarno's outright suppression of the press were over and unlikely to return as long as Indonesia courted the favor of more liberal-minded Western opinion. The hundred-odd Indonesian dailies, with a total circulation of less than a million copies, recognized their ambivalent position for the most part. But those leaders who were not bound

[51] *Merdeka*, December 5, 1970.
[52] Interview with Lubis, September 2, 1970, one of many.
[53] Interview, August 30, 1970.

hand and foot to the government took the risk of indulging in editorial criticism when they felt it necessary, both as a matter of self-respect and as a demonstration to their readers that they were independent.

The trouble with the press was that, like the country, it was poor and not often able to support itself. *Merdeka,* flagship of the Diah publications, was an exception. So was *Indonesia Raya,* which published Mochtar Lubis' *Prison Diary* in daily installments for more than a year. Once when he was asked how he was able to make a newspaper successful in Indonesia, Lubis smiled reflectively and replied, "One way to do it is to go to jail for nine years." Not many were willing to follow his example.

The Indonesian press may not be at one with the press of the West in its devotion to the principle of philosophical anarchy, but for all its poverty and its technical and ideological hang-ups, it is a good deal more independent and more courageous than that of many another Asian country. It is all very well to acclaim the exercise of the vote by 57,000,000 Indonesians as an example of democracy in action in Southeast Asia if the various restrictions are conveniently overlooked. A better barometer of the state of individual liberty in Indonesia is the government's treatment of its press, which has vastly improved.

Living in Indonesia

There are improvements, too, in the life-style of the cities of Indonesia, from the once-chaotic atmosphere of Djakarta, with its more than 4,000,000 people, to Bandung, the lively capital of West Java, and from the university city of Jogjakarta to the tourist paradise of Bali. There is a new and altogether pleasing air of vitality about them all, something Sukarno strove to create but somehow couldn't.

Thanks to the strenuous efforts of the governor of Djakarta, Ali Sadikin, this once-drab metropolis is beginning to resemble a world capital, with tall buildings lining broad, clean thoroughfares in the expanding modern part of the city. It still isn't very easy to move around, for the ancient buses are always crowded and there are no taxis, only a few autos around the hotels that can be hired by the hour or the day ($12 to $16, if you can find one). But new hotels are being added to the once exclusive Hotel Indonesia, where payment still must be made in American dollars with a 21 per cent tax on all rooms and food. And the energetic Sadikin is trying by every means to persuade shopkeepers to give up their old-fashioned bazaars and install bright, modern storefronts after the manner of the Rue de la Paix, Regent Street, Fifth Avenue and the Ginza.

Some of the mistakes of the Sukarno era are disappearing, such as the ruin of the burned-out British embassy that has been replaced by a splendid new building. And the neon-lighted signs of many a Western and Japanese commercial giant flare in the tropical twilight, giving the illusion of a luxurious modernity to a thin, anxious and poorly clothed people who must struggle homeward by any means available to them at the end of their long working day. Although the noisy Honda motorcycles are coming in rapidly, Djakarta's work force still must rely to a greater extent on the humble bicycles that weave through the largely foreign automobile traffic at a near-suicidal rate. As for Sukarno's monuments, including the one in Merdeka Square that had to be taller than the Washington Monument, they are in danger of becoming mere traffic hazards.

It is manifestly true that today's annual rate of 9 to 10 per cent inflation is an improvement over the 60 to 100 per cent of the Sukarno years. Just how the Indonesian people manage to keep going in the cities in the face of such conditions remains a mystery. To the foreigners, inflation becomes a problem from the moment they arrive in Indonesia and almost everybody has a pet horror story. One American agency was lucky enough to be able to rent a house for an employee at $400 a month, but had to pay three years in advance. But an American oilman, less fortunate, was about to sign a lease on another house for $600 a month when a Japanese rival stepped in with a successful bid of $1,000. In that kind of an economy, the Indonesian rupiah is about as useful as a Yo-Yo.

Under the twin stimuli of the foreign industrial influx and tourism, Djakarta nevertheless is rebuilding its central area and expanding into the suburbs. Eight hotels with 2,000 rooms were completed in 1971 alone, more than there were at that time in the few other first-class hotels in the country. From 25,000 foreign visitors in 1967, including both tourists and business people, Indonesia hopes to attract as many as 350,000 by 1974 and is planning on another 6,000 first-class hotel rooms to accommodate them.

While efforts are being made to develop tourist attractions in the "Great Smokies" volcano region of central Java, Sumatra and the Celebes, there is still nothing in the land to touch the undoubted attractions of Bali, where 35 per cent of arriving foreigners go first. The trouble is that Bali has only 300 first-class hotel rooms, mostly in the luxury-type Bali Beach Hotel, and by the most conservative estimates will need at least 2,000 additional rooms by 1974.[54]

Pinned between the understandable desire to grab the tourist's dollar and the painful necessity of providing tax advantages and other costly stimuli to hotel builders, the Indonesian government is caught in an unhappy dilemma. Its people, too, have a developing problem; for, while it is pleasant to contemplate the added employment that will flow from tourism, no one likes to think of a shrinking supply of food and consumer goods that must be given up to encourage more foreigners to spend freely.

Nothing comes very easily in Indonesia. And nothing can be done quickly to everybody's satisfaction, now or in the decade to come. The land will pass through many trials before it is able to achieve even a modicum of stability.

The Defense of Indonesia

Like the other non-Communist and anti-Communist nations of Asia, Indonesia likes to believe that it will automatically come under the protection of the American nuclear umbrella in the event of big-power aggression. Sadly, there is nothing automatic any longer about any aspect of American defense policy in the Pacific. The Vietnam War changed all that and changed it for many years to come. As the case is put by senior American officials conversant with Asian policy, the United States has no responsibility of any kind—legal or moral— for the defense of Indonesia. Despite the eagerness of Washington to cultivate improved relations with Indonesia and the commitment of more than $1 billion in American aid funds to the Djakarta govern-

[54] *South China Morning Post*, September 8, 1970, p. 2, business section.

ment since 1966, no American of consequence is advocating responsibility for the defense of Indonesia. The most the United States has committed itself to do is to supply the Suharto regime with arms— $5.8 million in 1969, $18 million in 1970 and $25 million in 1971.

The Indonesians, for that matter, are disenchanted with pacts of all kinds, beginning with SEATO. In the view of Adam Malik, the quick-witted and cheerful Indonesian foreign minister, the defense of the nation rests first of all on close union and cooperation between the Army and the people. Next in importance he places bilateral defense plans among the nations with which Indonesia has common borders. Like Thanat Khoman of Thailand and Lee Kuan Yew of Singapore, Malik frequently cautions the United States not to withdraw from Asia too quickly. And he also has his doubts about the Sino-American rapprochement.

Even though Indonesians have never relied on the United States to defend them, most of their military planners argue for an American military presence in the area. They believe American forces should remain in Thailand and South Vietnam. For the rest of the area, the American Seventh Fleet and a string of air bases are considered to be a part of its necessary defenses. Some Indonesians even hope that the United States will facilitate the adoption of joint military training and joint weapons supply and equipment among the nations of the region—something that would surprise Congress in Washington and dismay the entire peace movement.

When Adam Malik was asked if these hopes were at all realistic, he replied, "I can't believe that the American public will turn so blindly and purposelessly isolationist as to shrug off its responsibilities in the Pacific."[55]

The Indonesians, of course, know better than to rely blindly on any single foreign power, regardless of their need. And, despite their very real fears of foreign support for their indigenous Communists of whatever persuasion, they do look to the Soviet Union for a certain amount of help other than financial to counterbalance the continuing danger from China. For example, the Soviet Union has pledged its assistance in the building of an Indonesian atomic reactor—a small

[55] From my interview with Mr. Malik at his home in Djakarta on September 1, 1970.

first step in the development of atomic energy for peaceful uses. Without doubt, Malik's excursions to Moscow will produce further results.

Both President Suharto and his foreign minister have made cautious overtures to the Chinese in the hope of normalizing relations and perhaps opening up the Chinese market to Indonesian rubber and other products. But Peking is not likely to let down the bars quickly as long as Djakarta attaches so many conditions to a renewal of diplomatic relations. What the Indonesians seek from China is recognition of the Suharto government first of all, followed by a pledge of non-interference in Indonesia's internal affairs and an immediate halt to the Indonesian-language broadcasts that denounce the Suharto regime as a "Fascist military clique."[56]

Behind all the fulminations between the two governments is the reality of geography and their interdependence as nations. For example, about $1 million a month worth of Chinese goods flow through Hong Kong to Indonesia and Indonesian shops find little difficulty in disposing of them. In fact, despite the lack of diplomatic relations between Djakarta and Peking, China ranks as the seventh-largest exporter to Indonesia, following Japan, the United States, West Germany, Singapore, the Netherlands and Taiwan.

The renewed Indonesian interest in improved relations with China is indicative of the belief that the PKI is not strong enough to attempt a comeback now, with or without Chinese support. The Suharto regime also appears confident that it can handle restless areas elsewhere, notably in the Moluccas, the home of the rebellious Amboinese who attacked the Indonesian embassy in The Hague in 1970 and forced a brief postponement of the President's state visit. For the long term, Indonesia is more assured of being able to maintain internal security, therefore, than of preventing the spread of Chinese influence elsewhere in Southeast Asia.

Where, then, can Indonesia turn for help?

On his trip to Washington, President Suharto pointedly told President Nixon in 1970: "The restoration of peace and stability in this region will require the combined endeavors of all countries in the

[56] *The New York Times*, May 18, 1971, p. 8.

area as well as of those external powers having a responsibility in the maintenance of world peace."[57]

This is no mere exercise of political rhetoric. Nor is it a poetic expression of Indonesian aspirations toward a better world order. For Indonesia, the sixth-largest nation in the world, is a ward of the international community in a very real sense. It was born through the intervention of the United Nations against the Dutch "police action" just as truly as the United Nations created the state of Israel. And significantly, the first major policy to which President Suharto returned after acceding to power was to send an Indonesian delegation back to the United Nations. Indonesia, for all its discouragement about mutual defense treaties, does have confidence in a regional consultative body such as ASEAN. But most important of all, Indonesia will continue for at least a generation to be the economic beneficiary of the so-called "Paris Club"—the international consortium of the West—and the separate beneficial arrangements it has made with the Soviet Union.

To many another nation, this would seem weakness. But to Indonesia, it is the main source of its strength as it struggles back toward a better place in the world.

6. TOWARD NEW TIMES

The extravagant notion that the United States could guarantee a collective security arrangement for Southeast Asia is dead, a casualty of the Vietnam War. It is just about as outdated today as the containment of the Soviet Union and China by the United States plus numerous allies, most of them either reluctant or undependable, and sometimes both. For its continued independence and safety from both internal subversion and external aggression, non-Communist Southeast Asia must look elsewhere.

It is all very well for Washington to proclaim, under one president or another, that Asian nations must now do a great deal more to defend themselves. The trouble with such a concept is that, as has been shown in both Thailand and Indonesia, the build-up of indi-

[57] *Ibid.*, May 27, 1970, p. 1.

vidual or collective regional defenses is likely to strip bare the national resources that should go into expanding agricultural and industrial development. Thus, by plumping for a policy of stronger external defense, non-Communist Southeast Asia critically weakens itself at the very point where it is most vulnerable to subversion—its internal well-being, the bulwark against Communist attack.

Despite this obvious drawback to the expansion of non-Communist military forces in Southeast Asia, there are still military planners in Washington who tend to think of Indonesia as the southern anchor of an American-supported line of big-island defenses in the Western Pacific, or, in terms of Fourth of July oratory, a Bastion of the Free World. This is sheer self-deception. Indonesia may have survived a Communist uprising and the profligacy of a wasteful and incompetent government, but that doesn't make it a bastion of anything except its own indebtedness.

Similarly, the proposition that Thailand, South Vietnam, Taiwan and the Philippines are going to support American bases on their territory indefinitely (given American Congressional approval, which is dubious) deserves a very close and skeptical examination. If the Japanese are moving rapidly toward the conclusion of the American Occupation and its offshoots, there is no reason to believe that any Asian countries—with the exception of South Vietnam and South Korea—will feel any differently over the next generation. Nor is the American public likely to tolerate continued foreign military ventures during that period, barring some cataclysmic event.

Plainly, as the overtures between Washington and Peking indicate, both the United States and its client states in non-Communist Southeast Asia are moving toward new times and new arrangements. There is no reason to believe that a comparatively weak and militarily futile gesture, such as the Singapore-Malaysia defense arrangements with Britain, Australia and New Zealand, suggests the shape of the future. Nor can it be said that the states flanking embattled Indochina are ready to give up to the Chinese-North Vietnamese alliance and sue for terms, regardless of what happens to South Vietnam, Laos and Cambodia.

There is a chance for stabilization of the area over the next two decades, but it depends almost entirely on the slow and uncertain processes of international action. The one factor that supports the admittedly slender hopes for international agreement in Southeast Asia is the feeling on all sides that nothing further can be gained by war. To this end, the Indonesian initiative in calling for a conference of neighboring states to limit the fighting in Cambodia may form the outlines of a pattern that could eventually be applied to all Southeast Asia. It is by no means foreordained that such a conference would end in failure, as the Cambodian meeting did, or that it would be as futile and unobserved as the Geneva agreements of 1954 and 1962. An exhausted Europe finally did agree to the Peace of Westphalia after its Thirty Years' War. And exhaustion clearly is a factor that is moving a considerable part of Asia toward a better accommodation and peace today.

Much, of course, will depend on the willingness of both China and the Soviet Union to participate constructively in the rebuilding of Southeast Asia. Broadened Chinese trade with some of the lands on its southern border and increased Soviet economic aid for Indonesia both are encouraging signs. Japan, too, will be important in helping to bring about a more stable Southeast Asia.

As for the United States, a thorough overhaul of its major policies for Southeast Asia is strongly indicated. The disastrous era of American military intervention on the Asian mainland has destroyed militarism as a policy for Washington and foreclosed further American political tinkering in the area. American economic policies, in addition, have hurt some thriving Asian economies and made things more difficult for less fortunate lands.

Constructive American initiatives for Southeast Asia, therefore, are more likely to come through the international community than by some unilateral, and generally ill-considered, act of an American President. If efforts toward a Sino-American rapprochement help stimulate such action, millions upon millions of desolate people in Southeast Asia will be the grateful beneficiaries.

VI. The Ills of the Subcontinent

1. AN OVERVIEW

Every disaster that can befall humankind has stricken the Indian subcontinent since its 700,000,000 people achieved independence. War, famine and pestilence have brought death to many millions; storms, floods and terrible times of drought have also taken their toll. Overpopulated, undernourished, insecure at home and abroad, India, Pakistan and neighboring Ceylon have become the sick men of Asia.

In the wake of India's fifteen-day conquest of East Pakistan, ending with the creation of Bangladesh toward the end of 1971, there are many who fear with good reason that stability and order will not be restored to the subcontinent for years to come. Primarily, this is because the forces that have torn its peoples apart threaten today to fragment them still more into warring regions, factions and sects. If Pakistan can be split, so can India.

To hardheaded realists, such as the Japanese, the fault lies mainly with the chronic refusal of the largest part of the subcontinent to let itself be governed. To anguished liberals, especially in the United States, the whole answer is the abysmal poverty that is the curse of one of the wildest and most beautiful parts of the earth.

Both, perhaps, have divined a part of the root cause. But surely,

359

intolerance, ignorance and superstition and the senseless passions they ignite have had as much as anything else to do with the pitiable state of the subcontinent. Here, the hand of man is raised against his neighbor with devastating consequences in the form of war, communal rioting between Muslim and Hindu, civil strife between Punjabi and Bengali, hatred of the untouchables, the fanaticism of people who speak one language and attack those whose tongues are different, the ruthlessness of political extremists who terrorize whole cities with arson and murder to gain some ill-conceived end. From the conflict over Kashmir to the war that dismembered Pakistan, this has been the tragedy of Indians and Pakistanis—and to a lesser extent the Sinhalese and Tamils of Ceylon. It has been truly said that every misfortune to which man is heir will be found on the subcontinent in exaggerated proportion.

No one can benefit through such appalling disorder, least of all the great powers that contend for primacy over Asia. For if neither India nor Pakistan can have any major effect on the power equation in the Indo-Pacific, they could nevertheless have a catastrophic negative impact on neighboring countries by plunging into chaos. The fact of a truncated Pakistan already has sent tremors of apprehension far beyond South Asia. India cannot really glory in her victory and temporary sense of unity, achieved mainly with Russian arms, for secessionist movements like that of Bangladesh could easily spring up in West Bengal, Kerala and even Tamil Nadu. The consequences of two Indias—or three or four—would be incalculable.

What Price Power?

In the heyday of the British raj, when a comparatively small force of British soldiers held these diverse and headstrong peoples in thrall, the Indian subcontinent was a power center in Asia. For two centuries of British rule, neither imperial Russia nor its Communist successor could influence the course of events in India. A Kiplingesque society held sway, diverting the wealth of the land for the benefit of the British crown and its adherents. And the impotent masses of brown people and their leaders aroused little feeling in their masters except an amused condescension in time of peace and an awful and unreasoning wrath in time of trouble.

To the imperial British, it seemed that India would lie forever prostrate at their feet.

Mohandas Karamchand Gandhi—the Mahatma—changed all that. He was mightier than guns and troops, warders and prisons, although he never fired a shot in anger in his entire life. By leading a massive campaign of civil disobedience from Amritsar in 1919 until independence on August 15, 1947, he showed how vast was the power of the Indian people when it was given rein and how irresistible their striving for freedom. And yet, not even Gandhi could control the tremendous force he had been able to release. Not by appeal and not by threat of a fast unto death was he able to hold Hindu and Muslim together.

Thus, as the day of deliverance came, the subcontinent was divided three ways between a turbulent India and the two parts of an unruly and resentful Pakistan that flanked it on the east and west. When Gandhi was assassinated in the peaceful greenery of the Birla garden in New Delhi during the following year, it was a portent of still worse things to come. No one will ever know how many people died in the frantic flight of millions of Muslims from India and other millions of Hindus from Pakistan. Nor can the consequences of India's seizure of the best part of Jammu and Kashmir be easily assessed. But such turmoil, almost certainly, helped to undermine whatever hope there was in the beginning for a self-sufficient and viable Pakistan.

Nehru as a Moral Force

The cool and intellectual Jawaharlal Nehru, India's first prime minister, remained unyielding on Kashmir and merciless to his Pakistani opponents. To the world at large, he was the great moral force of the United Nations, and he made India respected and even feared by other nations large and small through the strength of his dominant personality. Like Gandhi, he was able to reach the true source of Indian power and he used it, sometimes with remarkable effect, in issues that really did not concern India at all. Somehow, he was always able to impress world opinion with the rightness of India's position.

The net result was that Nehru's awesome prestige as a world leader was reflected back upon his people in such a manner as to place him beyond challenge. Without using repressive legislation, he stifled his querulous press opposition; as for the political alternatives to his almost monolithic Congress Party, they were so small as to be well-nigh helpless. He held himself above the battle and became almost as revered as the saintly Gandhi.

Just as the British were able to hold India together by military force, Nehru did it by moral persuasion; unlike the British, however, he did not interfere with the processes of parliamentary self-government. Except in emergencies, he never found it necessary to do so. His strength was so great that he could squander public funds on massive projects without arousing much criticism and he could orient his foreign policy toward the Soviet Union, rather than the traditional Indian alignment with the West, contending all the while that India was practicing non-alignment. To bitter policy makers in Washington, he was being, as they said, "non-aligned against us."

The Decline of Pakistan

The greater India's prestige in the world, the worse it was for Pakistan. While the Pakistanis on the whole made greater progress than the Indians in solving their economic problems, they received scant credit for it. In fact, the constant complaint of the Bengalis of East Pakistan was that they were both underrepresented and discriminated against because they did not share in whatever benefits came to the Punjabis of West Pakistan.

There were some who said Pakistan was doomed from birth, that it could never survive as a nation because it was divided by more than 1,000 miles of Indian territory, that the Bengalis and Punjabis would never get along. Yet, for all the tensions, both internal and external, Pakistan did manage to get along for a time. True, after the assassination of Liaquat Ali Khan in 1951, the leadership of the divided nation devolved on a series of generals who practiced arbitrary personal rule. But that did not prevent the United States from embracing the Pakistanis in the SEATO pact. However, not being overly impressed with Washington's maneuvers, they proceeded to improve relations with China in order to offset India's reliance on the Soviet Union.

Despite these devious moves, affairs in Pakistan turned steadily downward, first under General Iskander Mirza, then under General Mohammad Ayub Khan, and finally to disaster under General Agha Mohammad Yahya Khan. As one calamity followed another, from the 1965 war with India over Kashmir to the cyclone that devastated East Pakistan in 1970, the anger of the Bengalis increased and their separatist forces gained strength. When the Bengalis' Awami League triumphed in the first national election in Pakistan's 23-year history on December 7, 1970, and demanded almost full autonomy from West Pakistan, the crisis broke with shocking swiftness. Yahya Khan tried to repress the Bengalis with an army of 93,000, causing more than 10 million refugees to flee from East Pakistan to India. But he could not break the back of the Mukti Bahini, the Bengali liberation force. And when India's armed forces intervened with the support of the Soviet Union on December 3, 1971, Yahya Khan's occupation army crumpled and surrendered in 15 days. It was in this bloody manner that the new nation of Bangladesh (Bengal Nation) was born in East Pakistan as an appendage of India, and Pakistan itself was dismembered.

The Maoist rising in Ceylon against the rule of Mrs. Sirimavo Bandaranaike, who had barely settled in office after being reelected as prime minister, confirmed that the fragility of the political process on the subcontinent is not restricted to any one country or any particular region. For despite the Bandaranaike government's survival, it was far from safe. Nor could India, despite its triumph over Pakistan, look with certainty to the future.

The March to Nowhere

The continual crises of the subcontinent have exacted a high price in human suffering that would be unacceptable anywhere else on earth. And yet, ironically, its population has continued to grow at a rate that almost cancels out the hard-won economic gains of the 1960s and early 1970s—an average annual real growth rate for India of between 3 and 4 per cent, about the same for Ceylon, and a bit more than 5 per cent for Pakistan. The worst indicator of the continued plight of all three nations is the per capita national income of about $80 a year for India, about $100 for Pakistan and almost $150 for Ceylon—among the smallest in the world.[1]

Under such circumstances, there has been comparatively little progress toward closing the cesspool of ignorance that contaminates every part of the subcontinent. At least 75 to 80 per cent of the population remains illiterate, somewhat more than that in India.[2] And the fetishes of caste and religion condemn hundreds of millions of people to lifelong misery. For in India, the sacred cow and the monkey continue to be the greatest destroyers of badly needed food grains. And in Pakistan, the mere rumor that the hair of the Prophet had been stolen from a Kashmir mosque in 1963 was sufficient to set off fatal riots a thousand miles away.

It is understandable that no political leadership worthy of the name will stand still for very long when faced with such abysmal conditions. In India, Pakistan and Ceylon, a kind of political magic has been attached to the term "Socialism," although few in the three countries have read Karl Marx or Lenin and even fewer could give a rational explanation of what it means. I know that I have frequently asked people of all classes in India what Socialism means to them, from the literate and more sophisticated urban dweller to the simple villager. The less sophisticated usually answer without hesitation, "Socialism means brotherhood," which would have been a surprise to Joseph Stalin. The more educated, particularly the young people, more often think of Socialism as the ill-defined alternative to everything they abhor in a shadow world exclusively peopled by bloodsucking capitalists, economic imperialists and soul-destroying military leaders.

It is no wonder, therefore, that so brilliant and forceful a personality as Indira Gandhi has been able to attract the enthusiastic support of India's electorate with her summons for a "March Toward Socialism." And yet, the implication that power and profit are to be

---

[1] Statistics on growth rates and per capita incomes for the subcontinent are not very reliable, as a rule. These are the best that I have been able to come by from Indian, Pakistani, Ceylonese, British and American sources.

[2] This is less than the governments claim.

snatched away from the hated foreigner and the bloated domestic employer and distributed broadcast to the people is a cruel delusion. For in India there are an estimated 24,000,000 unemployed and the number is said to be increasing at the rate of 1,000,000 a year.[3] For such people, the "March Toward Socialism" is a march to nowhere.

Nor is Socialism in all cases a philosopher's stone for the aspiring politician. Sirimavo Bandaranaike, one of the outspoken proponents among Third World leaders of a rapid conversion of the state to Socialism, discovered in Ceylon that it wasn't enough to preserve public order. The 1971 revolt of Maoist-inspired revolutionary youth came close to overthrowing her government. As for Pakistan, the preservation of the state has bulked larger in the policies of the military leadership than mere ideology. Visionary Socialism is far off in Islamabad, even farther in Dacca.

The Free and the Not So Free

It is a part of the conventional wisdom of the West that the tenets of parliamentary democracy and the practices of self-government cannot easily be exported to the developing and less-favored nations of the earth. The peoples are too ignorant, say the superior voices from the West, and democracy is too cumbersome and blundering a system. Yet, within a twelvemonth in 1970–71, India, Pakistan and Ceylon all held elections on which governments and peoples staked their future. To be sure, neither the campaigning nor the electoral process was carried on in the Western manner; the X scrawled under a party symbol was the order of the day,[4] and such devices as voting machines were unheard of.

For Western observers who almost automatically assume that Oriental governments can return themselves to power if they control the electoral machinery, the results must have provoked a good deal of thought. In India, Prime Minister Gandhi was believed to have so

[3] Another difficult statistic to verify, for generally the "unemployed and underemployed" are lumped together, something Indira Gandhi invariably does. Eric da Costa, the director of the Indian Institute of Public Opinion, who made this estimate, said it was the best that he could offer. Some foreign statistics are higher, the government's are lower.

[4] In New York City, in non-English-speaking areas, word is still passed to "vote the chicken," the Republican balloting symbol being an eagle.

little hold on her people that she was given a bare chance of retaining power; yet, she won in a landslide. In Ceylon, Prime Minister Bandaranaike overturned her conservative opposition and made a rare comeback. And in Pakistan, it was not the election that failed; had the results been followed in good faith by Yahya Khan, there would have been at least a chance of averting civil war, Indian intervention and a crushing defeat.

Great as the risks of freedom may be for the subcontinent, most of its people appear to have determined for the time being that the penalties of authoritarian government are greater. But unhappily, they have not been—and still cannot be—the masters of their fate. For India is now a client state of the Soviet Union. Truncated Pakistan is at the mercy of the United States and China. And little Ceylon is scrambling everywhere for whatever help she can get.

2. THE TIDE TURNS IN INDIA

There have been many perceptions of India, each stranger than the other, but all have had one factor in common. Whether the beholder was Curzon or Gandhi, Disraeli or Nehru, Kipling or E. M. Forster, India has always seemed to beckon for world attention in one form or another.

Indira Gandhi's India is different. No longer does it pose as a great moral force in the world, as it did in Nehru's time. Its appeals for justice and righteousness in world affairs have been stilled. For the India of today, encouraged and supported by the Soviet Union, is the dominant military power in South Asia with almost a million men under arms, a modern force of more than 600 aircraft and at least 1,500 tanks. Even before the stunning Indian victory over Pakistan at the end of 1971, three-quarters of the Indian people who were consulted in a poll favored "going atomic."[5]

And yet, despite India's pride in its new-found position as an Asian counterweight to China, the world's largest democracy has far more compelling needs for its funds and its energies. What Indira Gandhi wants for her India, first of all, is a better life for her people and she knows full well that international posturing isn't going to get

[5] Poll by the Indian Institute of Public Opinion, reported August 7, 1970.

her very far; although, in mink coat, jewels and expensive sari, she can posture with experts in the field. In any conversation with her, her attention focuses invariably on domestic affairs. Except in extraordinary circumstances, such as India's crusade for Bangladesh, it is difficult to persuade her to philosophize about foreign policy, a favorite pastime of her illustrious father.

This shift in emphasis in India has been reflected in the new attention the world has devoted to New Delhi since the debacle in East Pakistan. Where only a half-dozen correspondents from the United States and perhaps a few more from other countries used to cover India, the war brought in 300 to 400 others and many have taken to shuttling in and out of the major Indian cities. And yet, it is not too long ago that a discouraged young foreign correspondent told me: "I wonder if anybody really cares any more what India does."[6]

This tougher and far more aggressive India still cares very much about world opinion and does want to play a major role in global affairs. But Indira Gandhi is the first to realize that India, as a client state of the Soviet Union, cannot exert much leverage on the United States, China and Japan. It will take an India with far more independence of the great powers, a much stronger economy and a keener sense of internal unity to aspire to world leadership. No, that is not for India now. The time for international daydreaming is over.

The Lean Years

India lives or dies by the fortunes of the monsoon rains, which make possible good crops or poor ones. Fortunately, during the first half of the 1969–74 five-year plan, on which the Indian government has based so much of its hope, the monsoons have been kind. From 80,000,000 tons of food grains in 1965, the Indian farmer boosted his yield to 95,000,000 tons in 1969, 108,000,000 tons in 1970, and hoped to achieve self-sufficiency thereafter.

For a nation that has always had to import food grains since 1920, this is heartening progress. Since 1967, the United States has contributed 14,000,000 tons of food grains to India and from 1946 to

[6] I counted only six American full-time correspondents in New Delhi in the summer of 1970.

1970 the total of American aid for India in all categories reached $9.3 billion, 80 per cent on a loan basis repayable in dollars or rupees. Under India's new alignment, it is one of the government's major goals to work itself free of dependence on American food grains, for the United States, as a champion of Pakistan, is unpopular in New Delhi. Given continued good fortune with monsoons and increased yields, that goal could be achieved, provided India hangs together. But it will also take a social revolution at the lower levels of Indian society to introduce effective family planning and keep the increasing population from outrunning production.

In contrast with the striking gains in farm production, India has not done very well industrially. Its planners aimed at a growth rate of 7 per cent a year and have achieved about half of that. The annual gross national product was still bogged down in the range of $48 to $50 billion in 1971 and seemed unlikely to rise very fast. With Indira Gandhi heavily favoring expansion of the public sector of the Indian economy and sternly lecturing Indian private interests on their failure to do more for their country, Indian industry was beginning to look elsewhere for opportunities. The great Tata combine, the most progressive employer in India, was surveying the field in places like Australia, Canada and even the United States.

The tighter the Indian government drew its regulations over private capital, the less enthusiasm there was among private investors for sending funds into the country. Total foreign investment in India for 1970–71 was estimated at only $1.8 billion, with Britain accounting for $1.3 billion, the United States for $300 million and West Germany for $200 million. American investments were centered in oil, $100 million (Caltex and Esso); drugs, $50 million; and a substantial amount in fertilizers. The major British oil investment was by Burmah-Shell. The Indians were bidding for more Japanese business, but the Japanese complained of Indian methods and erratic fulfillment of contracts; all things considered, not much help could be expected from that direction.

Still, there has been progress after a fashion. Through loans and other financing from international sources, India had almost $1.2 billion in foreign exchange reserves in 1971, $243 million in gold and the rest in SDRs (paper gold) from the World Bank. In addition to

American aid, the Soviet Union had provided funds estimated at about $1 billion.[7] But all signs indicated that both American and Soviet aid would be reduced in the foreseeable future and that India would have to do a great deal more to fend for itself. It could not continue to be what its outraged intellectuals call a "mendicant nation."

A Matter of Attitude

Whenever anything goes wrong in India, as frequently happens, critics at home and abroad are likely to blame the government first of all. Actually, the government's day-to-day performance is not nearly as inefficient as its detractors make out. The Indian Civil Service, with its heritage of British training, does more to hold the country together than any political organization. True, there are Indian red-tape horror stories that visitors delight to repeat, but such experiences are not by any means confined to India. Among developing lands, Indian government services are generally better than many others.

If it were not so, the vast program of small, even humble, measures to benefit the Indian countryside could not have been carried through to a measure of success. This concept of dam building, well drilling and fertilizer production was adopted by Lal Bahadur Shastri almost as soon as he became prime minister in 1964 after Nehru's death. It was a welcome change from Nehru's grandiose projects that really didn't do much for the Indian economy. When Mrs. Gandhi came to power after Shastri's untimely death in 1966 following the peace of Tashkent, ending the brief Kashmir war, she maintained and even accelerated the Shastri program. It became a part of her "March Toward Socialism."

In other areas of the Indian economy, the Gandhian concept of Socialism turned out to be quite pragmatic. For example, she readily accepted American financing of large fertilizer plants but national-ized fourteen domestic banks. Although the government-owned rail-

[7] It is a difficult and time-consuming business to gather and check statistics on the Indian economy and Indian industry in particular. These figures are from Indian and American public and private sources and are the most reliable that I can present.

ways, Indian Air Lines and the government steel plants all wound up in the red in 1970, Mrs. Gandhi decided to nationalize the insurance industry in 1971.[8] If she intended by such tactics to spur the private sector to greater support of the government, it didn't turn out that way. Instead, she only spread uncertainty and pessimism among those with invested capital and frightened off others who might have been inclined to take a risk on the Indian economy.

It hasn't deterred Mrs. Gandhi in the slightest. On matters of principle, she can be as unyielding as her father.

India's great industrial employers, who are among her principal targets, do not have a very good case to present when they violently oppose some of Mrs. Gandhi's more practical progressive measures. With the exception of Tata and perhaps a few smaller companies here and there, India's captains of industry are still in the stone age of industrial progress. It is widely recognized that Indian labor's low rate of production is due mainly to primitive methods and tools and lack of adequate instruction rather than to any failing in effort or intelligence on the part of the Indian workman. Despite miserable wages and outrageous working conditions, he puts in longer hours as a rule than labor in the West.

The Prime Minister draws her support from such people in the cities. To an even greater extent, she commands the loyalty of rural India—the 500,000 villages where 80 per cent of the population lives—for the policies she inherited from Shastri have done much to make life a little better for those who are bound to the land. In this, India's foreign aid consortium has played a very large part, as was evidenced by the $700 million for non-project aid and $400 million for specific projects for 1970–71.[9] The consortium members—the United States, United Kingdom, Canada, Japan, Australia and the World Bank—made proportionate contributions.

The Battle for Family Planning

To maintain its current precarious economic equilibrium and broaden its supporting base, India fully realizes the gravity of the

---

[8] India nationalized life insurance in 1956. Mrs. Gandhi, in 1971, called for nationalization of general insurance as well.

[9] Press Trust of India news file, August 2, 1970.

continual battle for better family planning. The best proof of Indian earnestness in this regard is the allotment of $400 million for the family planning campaign alone over the 1969–74 period. This is almost as much as the country's entire health budget. The objective is to force down the growth rate of India's population between 1966–70 to less than 2.4 per cent in 1971–75 and less than 2 per cent in 1976–80.

Lest these figures seem excessively modest, the enormity of the problem should be considered in all its complexity. India has only 2.4 per cent of the world's available land but 14 per cent of the world's population. In one-third the area of the United States is crowded 2.5 times the American population. Every year, for the decade ending in 1970, there has been an annual increase of 13,000,000 people, more than the population of New York City and Paris combined. Nor is this entirely due to the celebrated Indian fertility. Modern medicine and improved living have played their part, too, for from 1960 to 1970, infant mortality rates dropped from 146 to 113 per thousand, and the expectation of life at birth during the same period rose from 41.2 to 56.6 years.[10]

It is much easier to indoctrinate a highly literate population with the need for family planning, as the Japanese experience demonstrates, than the minimally literate Indians, who showed a total literacy rate of 27.8 per cent in the 1961 census. There has, of course, been some improvement since then but it has been mainly in the cities. One of the principal blocks to progress is the relatively poor Indian communications system, in which the daily press of all languages circulates only 7,000,000 copies and the weeklies and all others contribute no more than 15,000,000 additional copies.

As for All-India Radio, with its fourteen-language broadcasts, the lack of receivers has kept the audience relatively low, with the result that it generally reaches no more than 10 per cent of the population. Television, the best hope for close communication between government and people under current circumstances, will be slow to develop, for in 1970 there still were only 15,000 sets in the New Delhi area

[10] All family planning statistics are from "Family Planning in India, Programme Information, 1970–71," published by the Ministry of Family Planning, Health and Urban Development, Government of India.

and service to Bombay, Calcutta and other areas remained in the planning stage. With American help, India was counting on two satellites to improve television communication over the entire country. However, among a people too poor to buy many newspapers, it could not be expected that there would be a great rush to invest in television sets. Even for an entire village, it was quite an investment.

The Indian family planning effort, therefore, has had to depend in large part on word-of-mouth publicity and the work of devoted teams of government servants throughout the country. The main reliance is still on the conventional contraceptives—condoms, diaphragms, jelly/cream tubes and foam tablets—many of which are given away, but they account for less than 10 of every 1,000 people. Sterilizations rank next in importance, with a rate of about 5 of every 1,000 people. The loop, about which there has been so much unfavorable publicity, has the lowest rate of use, less than 2 out of every 1,000 people.[11]

In family planning, as in everything else concerning India, there is a lot of thoroughly discreditable politics. The Muslim League and the fanatical Hindu right, the Jan Sangh, deadly opponents on every other issue, stand together against birth control as a desecration of the nation. They can and do spread both prejudice and fear throughout the land, among both their adherents and their enemies. If India is to make any progress at all, it will have to be done in spite of extremist politicians and the disinclination of most rural people to try anything new. That progress can be made was noted in the results of the Indian 1971 census, in which the population was put at 547,000,-000, or 14,000,000 fewer than the previous official estimate. The government also announced that an estimated 1,300,000 births had been prevented annually since 1967. For India, that was the most cheerful kind of news.

The Defense of India

There is one other major drain on India's resources—the military. In Nehru's time, it was the fashion to pretend that everybody on earth except Pakistan loved India, so that military needs could be restricted to the defense of Kashmir and other border areas. The old

[11] *Ibid.*

Pandit even tried to play off Peking against Moscow with his little rhymed slogan of Chinese-Indian friendship: "Hindi Chini Bhai Bhai," meaning that Indians and Chinese are brothers. The 1962 border war, in which the Chinese shattered the Indian Army at one stroke, disposed of that myth. The 1965 Kashmir war made it clear that defense would have to be a major concern of the Indian regime for years to come.

Ever since 1962, India has been maintaining some 300,000 of its troops along the China frontier, facing an estimated Chinese force of 150,000. Even when there is no fighting, an additional half-million Indian troops are kept under arms at all times; in periods of fighting with Pakistan, that total jumps up sharply.[12] This is an insupportable drain on a poor country, particularly when foreign military aid is doled out from a single source, the Soviet Union. Just how much the Russians have put into the Indian armed forces is, of course, a state secret, but it probably runs to $500 million plus unspecified sums for the use of advisers and other technical personnel in Indian arms plants. A Russian-supported factory for the development of MIG fighters for the Indian Air Force is a part of this defense complex, which has been strengthened by the twenty-year Indian-Soviet mutual defense pact of 1971.

The United States, never much of a supplier for the Indian armed forces, has long since put a deep freeze on military aid for New Delhi. With Britain, the Americans were the first to help the routed Indian Army when the Chinese struck in 1962. But after the brief Kashmir war three years later, the United States was so malevolently criticized by both sides for supplying the "enemy" that Washington refused to provide arms for either nation for five years.

In 1970, that policy cracked wide open—and it was not for India's benefit. The United States sold Pakistan 18 Starfighters, 7 Canberra bombers and 300 armored personnel carriers. What made New Delhi even more angry was that the deal was pulled off at a 30 per cent discount bargain rate for Pakistan. Then, in 1971, just before the India-Pakistan 15-day war, the United States sent covert shipments of arms to Pakistan, which the State Department admitted finally to be

[12] This is an authoritative estimate, given to me by an Indian Cabinet minister familiar with military matters.

in the range of $6.2 million. Some other American authorities calculated the deal was closer to $35 million.[13]

With the United States and China pulling together to aid Pakistan, the Indians suddenly threw themselves into the arms of the surprised Russians and signed the twenty-year friendship pact on August 9, 1971. Although Prime Minister Gandhi proclaimed that India still held to nonalignment, nobody believed her—particularly in Washington. The Russians put out the story that they had made their deal to support India in order to persuade New Delhi not to attack Pakistan. The Indians, seeing the bottom dropping out of their relations with the United States, could think of nothing better than to send Mrs. Gandhi on still another futile mission to Washington. In any event, Indian nonalignment was dead and buried, without ceremony.

India and the Soviet Union

How dependent is India on the Soviet Union?

Militarily, through equipment and training, the Russians have acquired more influence over the Indian armed forces than any other nation. This was true even before the signing of the mutual defense treaty. As long ago as 1963, when a small United States Air Force contingent visited New Delhi, American intelligence sources believed that the Russians had deeply penetrated the Indian Air Force. Whether this was true or not, the United States has never given nor sold India any of its latest and most sensitive air components. That was why India bought Russian MIG aircraft.

As for American military missions, there have been none in New Delhi for years. The joint USAF-RAF-IAF training exercise of 1963, a few months after the India-China border war, was never repeated and a 120-member U.S. military supply mission was sent home a year later. In 1970, only five American military supply people remained in India and they had practically nothing to do in the supply field.[14] The Russians had taken over that function long before.

[13] *The Economist*, November 21, 1970, pp. 28–31; *The New York Times*, July 24, 1971, p. 1; August 10, 1971, p. 1; August 13, 1971, p. 1; September 6, 1971, p. 3.

[14] I have consulted numerous private sources, Indian as well as foreign, in preparing this estimate.

Not everybody in the Indian Establishment has been overjoyed by the long love affair with Moscow, particularly in the military field. The rightist opposition in Parliament, which isn't very powerful, has frequently tried to work up a sense of public outrage over India's dependence on Russian arms. As the issue was phrased by K. Subrahmanyam, director of the Indian Institute for Defense Studies and Analysis, in the *Times of India:* "Prominent members of the opposition have . . . publicly expressed the fear that the Centre's [government's] dependence on Soviet supplies is so heavy and spread over such a wide range that it can ground our air force and stop the functioning of other armed forces in the event of war."[15] In defense of the Indian government, he argued that it had little choice because of the United States arms embargo and that, in any case, India had little to fear from the Soviet Union.

"North Vietnam, Cuba and Rumania rely on Soviet defense supplies to a much greater extent than this country," he wrote, "and they have all managed to pursue an independent foreign policy. The Prime Minister has rightly said that there are no political bills to be paid to the Soviet Union."[16]

The opposition is not so sure. They have made much of Mrs. Gandhi's alliance of necessity with the Moscow-oriented Communist Party of India, whose votes she needed in the Lok Sabha, the lower house of the Parliament, before her great electoral victory of 1971. Such old hands as Morarji Desai and Asoka Mehta, conservative members of her father's Cabinet, have attacked her repeatedly as Communist-influenced, although they have been careful not to say or even imply that she herself is a Communist.[17]

The first journalist of India, Frank Moraes, has taxed Mrs. Gandhi's government with a dangerous lassitude toward the Naxalites, the violence-prone Communists of the Mao stripe who have conducted a reign of terror in West Bengal (Calcutta) and infiltrated southern Kerala and the border regions. In the *Indian Express*, which

[15] *Times of India,* August 3, 1970, p. 6.

[16] *Ibid.,* August 4, 1970, p. 6.

[17] I interviewed Mehta, the former planning minister, on August 5, 1970, and Desai, then seventy-four years old, the former finance minister, on August 7, 1970.

he edits, Moraes wrote: "A government's first duty is to govern. In this, Mrs. Gandhi's government has lamentably failed. Its tenderness for Communists, fellow-travelers and leftist lawmakers has cost and is costing the country a heavy price. Politicians are expected to do everything to keep themselves entrenched in power. But even in the shoddy game of politics, power can never be an end in itself. What matters is what one does with it for the good of the people and not of oneself."[18]

To this Sham Lal, the editor of the *Times of India,* added the warning that the country was "slowly sliding toward anarchy" because of a Communist-supported land-grabbing movement. "If the present system breaks down," he wrote, "and the country is plunged into chaos, the members of the ruling party who indulge in waffling cant and humbug will be as much to blame as the opposition groups which think that red hot rhetoric can be a substitute for clear thinking and planning."[19]

Evidently, Mrs. Gandhi felt at the time that she could do little for lack of a clear majority in the Lok Sabha and with the additional handicap of a Congress Party that she had deliberately split to identify and isolate her opponents. Even in little things, she would not risk criticism of the Soviet Union. For example, when it was disclosed that an official Soviet map had shown large chunks of Indian border territory in the north to be Chinese, Foreign Minister Swaran Singh pleaded with the opposition "not to be unduly exercised" over a matter that had no political significance. Almost the entire opposition walked out of the Rajya Sabha, the Parliament's upper house, in protest.[20]

Regardless of Mrs. Gandhi's contentions that she was being even-handed in her relations with the Soviet Union and the United States, nobody really believed her. Some of her own Cabinet ministers, in fact, agreed during my 1970 visit that Indian foreign policy had veered sharply in favor of the Soviet Union and that American influence was minimal.[21] This did not still the private appeals for

[18] *Indian Express,* August 3, 1970, p. 6.
[19] *Times of India,* August 11, 1970, p. 8.
[20] *Hindustan Times,* August 7, 1970, p. 1.
[21] Some ministers were brutally frank about this.

continued American economic aid and more private American capital to help build up Indian industry. But publicly the Indian government's position was best expressed by the rather arrogant finance minister, Y. B. Chavan, who held that American capital investment "had to be for India's own benefit and India wasn't soliciting it."[22] Nor did India get it.

Once the mutual defense treaty with the Soviet Union was signed, the Indians went on an anti-American rampage. Almost all elements of Indian opinion blasted American support of Pakistan, American moves toward China, American denunciation of India as the aggressor in Bangladesh and President Nixon's show of friendship for Zulfikar Ali Bhutto at the White House just before he was called home to take over from Yahya Khan. Even the usually pro-American Frank Moraes, in his *Indian Express*, attacked American policy as "deliberate cynicism in the face of a massive human tragedy."

If there were elements in the Indian government that had second thoughts about New Delhi's pro-Moscow alignment, they kept a stiff upper lip. I remember in particular one influential minister who told me, before the treaty with Moscow was signed, that he favored a continued American military presence in the western Pacific. His point had been that an isolationist America would hurt Asia as well as itself.[23] Needless to say, that point of view made no impression, then or later, on Mrs. Gandhi. She didn't care much for the United States and seldom bothered to conceal her attitude.

"The Lady"

To nearly everyone who refers to her in private conversation, the Prime Minister of India is "the Lady." This is as true of foreigners as it is of Indians. It is almost as if they were speaking of a queen— and in a sense they are. For while there is quite a difference in India between the Victorian and Indiran eras, one point of similarity is striking—the power that a dedicated woman exercises over a land with the second-largest population on earth. Whatever her enemies may think of her, they respect her political acumen and her force of

---

[22] The Chavan interview was on August 5, 1970.

[23] The minister asked me to safeguard his identity.

character. As for her friends, they are comparatively few. She conducts her life quietly, and with strict propriety, at the lonely summit of leadership.

Indira Gandhi is a born leader, although her style is quite different from that of her adored father, who did so much to imbue her with the tenets of leadership. Almost from the time of her birth in Allahabad in 1917, her destiny was marked out for her. In hundreds of letters addressed to her from prison while she was a child, her father wrote to her of the history of her land, of its relations with its neighbors, and of the responsibilities of power. Once, on her thirtieth birthday, he wrote to her: "What presents can I give you? They can only be of the air and the mind and spirit, such as a good fairy might have bestowed on you." It was he who named her Indira Priyadarshini (the one pleasing to look at)—and she still is.

Throughout her father's lifetime, she was his close associate and his confidante but she never ran for public office. Some thought her a typical and rather retiring Indian widow; her husband, Feroze Gandhi, a Parsee lawyer (and no relation to the Mahatma) had died, leaving her with two young sons to bring up. But the gifts of mind and spirit that Jawaharlal Nehru had bestowed on her assured her of high office soon after his death. She entered Lal Bahadur Shastri's government as minister of information and broadcasting—India's chief propagandist, in effect. However, her succession to the prime ministry following his death was scarcely automatic. Kumaraswami Kamaraj, the Madras leader who became president of the Congress Party, had to work day and night on his associates in the Syndicate (the old-line regional party bosses) to insure her election over the perennial challenger, Morarji Desai. After it was all over, the embittered Morarji exclaimed: "How could I have defeated her when God was on her side?"[24]

The Syndicate was confident that the new prime minister would be pliable. She wasn't. Instead of going along with the old-line party bosses, Mrs. Gandhi put up a determined show of strength against them. For "the Lady," there was to be no politics as usual. It seemed to her that what India needed was new leadership divorced from

[24] Kuldip Nayar, *Between the Lines* (Bombay: Allied Publishers, 1969), pp. 1–29.

party considerations. She felt very deeply that the country would reject a Congress Party grown old in power. The general elections of 1967 proved that she was right, for India's monolithic governing structure broke down under voter disapproval in state after state.

The Syndicate, however, seemed not to believe that anything was wrong. When President Zakir Husain died in 1969, the old bosses did not take seriously the Prime Minister's nomination of V. V. Giri to succeed him. But in the ensuing power struggle, Giri won, the party was split, "the Lady" took over leadership of her "New Congress" and left the Syndicate with the ruins of the old. But her hold on Parliament was so precarious because of her minority support that she had to put together a curious alliance between her Congress adherents, the Muslim League and the Moscow-oriented Communist Party of India.

It was under such circumstances that she called the elections of 1971, a stroke of political genius as it turned out. For seven weeks she campaigned tirelessly throughout the land, pleading for support for her government and her program. Massive crowds turned out to hear her and to applaud her wherever she went, for she had become a personage with a charisma all her own. Her aunt, Vijaya Lakshmi Pandit, had doubted that she could stand the strain of the prime ministry. But at fifty-three, "the Lady" not only confounded her foes. She astonished even her friends.

She had to take abuse. The furious leaders of the Syndicate called her a dictator, a fascist, a woman crazed by power. Someone in a crowd along the campaign trail threw a shoe at her. An opposition orator screamed, "What sort of a Socialist is she? She has seven hundred saris in her wardrobe when most women go around naked in the countryside." Still another cried out that the Prime Minister's agents had tried to bribe him. She was called petty, arrogant, autocratic, domineering, faithless and unprincipled. Her two sons, Rajiv, an Indian Air Lines pilot, and Sanjay, an automotive engineer, both in their twenties, received a certain amount of political battering as well.

But as the returns came in after the ten days of voting in March, it became clear that "the Lady" had won a stupendous victory—the greatest in Indian history since the 1952 triumph of her father. She piled up a two-thirds majority in the Lok Sabha, the lower house of the Indian Parliament, and virtually wiped out the Syndicate. Of all the old-line political leaders, only the many-lived Kamaraj from Madras succeeded in being re-elected. The strange anti-Gandhi alliance—the Old Congress, the Jan Sangh, the business-oriented Swatantra Party and the Socialist Samyutka Party—lay in ruins before her. And under "the Lady's" leadership, India was politically united as it had never been since her father's time. She now headed, in truth, a totally new Congress Party.

Out of 521 seats in the Lok Sabha, she was assured of at least 350 New Congress votes and was no longer dependent on the Communists or anybody else. The CPI had only 23 seats, the China-leaning Marxist Communist Party, 25. The feared Jan Sangh was reduced to a mere 22 seats, the Old Congress to 16. And a regional party from Tamil Nadu (Madras), the Dravida Munnetra Kazhagam (DMK), polled enough votes to win 23 seats. As for the Swatantra Party, with its thumping for free enterprise and a pro-West alignment, it wound up with 8 seats and its leader, Minoo R. Masani, was defeated. The Muslim League had only 4, the Samyutka Socialist Party, 3.

Outside her modest cottage in New Delhi, into which she had moved when she became a Cabinet member under Shastri, the victorious Prime Minister said, "I'm not at all surprised." But everyone else was. One prescient Indian commented: "Indira not only vanquished her enemies. She vanquished her friends." At the peak of her power, she now had all the authority she needed to put through her program for India. The people were with her.[25]

An Interview with Mrs. Gandhi

My wife and I talked with Prime Minister Gandhi at a far less auspicious time in her career, when everything seemed to be about to go against her. It was late on a hot midsummer's afternoon in 1970 when we were shown into her private office at Parliament House by her private secretary, K. Natwar Singh, a small, youthful, American-

[25] Reading the Indian papers on this election is highly recommended. Also worth the trouble are special articles in the *Far Eastern Economic Review*, March 20, 1971, pp. 5–7; *The Economist*, March 20, 1971, p. 19; *Time*, March 22, 1971, pp. 22–23; and *The New York Times*, March 11–12, 1971, p. 1.

educated diplomat. It had been six years since I had last seen her, but she hadn't changed very much. She seemed tired after a long day of Parliamentary dueling. That was obvious enough. Her dark eyes had deep shadows under them but she wasn't as tense or as nervous as I had remembered her.

As we entered, Mrs. Gandhi welcomed us with a charming smile and asked us to sit beside her desk with Natwar Singh. Because of her appearance and her bearing, she makes an instantly favorable impression—a small, fine-looking woman with a handsome, sensitive face and dark hair streaked with white that seemed to have been freshly set (or so my wife said). She wore a white vest, an expensive-looking violet-figured sari and a necklace of small dark beads, but no other jewelry of any kind.

Almost at once, the pull of her domestic responsibilities became evident when she mildly protested the widespread misunderstanding in the United States of the relations of the government of India to the private business sector. American businessmen and, of course, Indian business people share this attitude, she observed with a touch of temper. "But," she said, "what are we to do? The private sector has let us down in some important respects and simply has not pro-duced." As examples of her concern, she mentioned the relatively poor Indian production of sugar, jute and cotton by private manu-facturers.

This grievous situation, she explained, was behind her govern-ment's policy of nationalizing banks and casting about for other ways to build up the public sector of the economy—an effort that she said was directed for the benefit of the great bulk of the people and not merely a few wealthy individuals. "The Communists," she said, naming the various kinds active in India, "are trying to do this by violent means such as the land-grab movement."

With a practical eye on the tenderness of American sentiment on the general subject of Communism, she contended that she was being forced to increase the scope of the public sector in order to circum-vent the Communists. It was her position that she could not govern for very long without invoking new and drastic measures to benefit the masses of her people.

When I asked her what she thought the United States could do to improve relations over the next five to ten years, she reminded me gently that India was a poor country and needed aid for development on somewhat different terms than the United States had been accustomed to offer. Now, she said, the terms were such that India always found herself caught up in a payments problem so that fresh aid often went merely to repay old debts.

She didn't specify the nature of further aid from the United States, nor did she do more than suggest that it could be negotiated either bilaterally or through a consortium. What she seemed to be saying, in a polite way, was that too many conditions were attached to American aid for India.

It was obvious that trade in terms of dollars also bothered her. For while India could sell comparatively little to the United States, she pointed out that India was able to trade in rupees with both the Soviet Union and the countries of Eastern Europe; moreover, African and other developing lands were also willing to accept rupees. She did not refer to the already large American holding of rupees and I did not bring it up, either. But we both agreed that it would be difficult for India to compete on any basis with the Japanese as rivals in any of the developing countries.

I asked her about the widespread belief in the United States and elsewhere in the West that India was too closely allied with the Soviet Union. She replied calmly, as she always has, that the Indian-Soviet relationship was grossly exaggerated. However, she argued that India had to consider both her history and her geography in her relations with the Soviet Union. "In trade as in weapons," she said, "India pays for what she gets and I see nothing wrong with that." She repeated her usual disclaimer of anti-American prejudice, referring to her government's declared policy of evenhandedness, but she didn't make much of it.

When she returned to the question of what India could expect from the United States under such circumstances, she took the position that it wasn't a question of what was given but how it was given, and the manner in which the transaction was negotiated. "India isn't interested in receiving money alone," she said.

Turning to the defense of India, I asked her whether she believed the Indian defense effort could be conducted independently of the

Soviet Union. Then as now, Indian dependence on Moscow was a sore point with the prime minister. With a touch of impatience, she replied that requirements for defense were always increasing so it was difficult to say what constituted self-sufficiency. But she left no doubt that she wanted the Americans out of Asia militarily, a policy aim she shared with the Soviets. "One military presence brings about another military presence," she said, "and this sort of thing can go on indefinitely."

Throughout our discussion, she was courteous and considerate and even gracious at times, but she continually demonstrated her mastery of the art of political journalism by shading her observations to the precise degree of meaning that she wanted to convey. Only once did she permit herself to become enthusiastic over anything, and that was when I referred to our discussion in 1964, when she was in the broadcasting and information ministry, about the future of television. Relieved of the onerous task of fending off inquiries about the extent of India's friendship for Moscow and hostility toward Washington, she dropped her mask of immobility and her dark eyes fairly danced with pleasure.

"Television is a very powerful and useful way of transmitting information on family planning, rural development and other subjects," she said. "I myself have gone into a village near Delhi and heard one of our television programs on rural development. After it was over, we had a technical expert available to answer questions and then we had a general discussion with the villagers. I thought the whole performance was effective and I intend to pursue it."

She sighed. It was evident enough that all her more serious problems were crowding in on her, from feeding her people to staving off the ever worrisome Pakistanis. "It will be a long time before we can have television on a nationwide basis," she added. "Right now, we are extending service from the New Delhi area but it will be limited to a few of the larger cities for the present." And did she believe that television could become a powerful political instrument in India, as it now is in the United States? Again she smiled and repeated, "It will take a long time."[26]

There was no nonsense about Indira Gandhi. And no wishful

[26] Our visit with Mrs. Gandhi was on August 7, 1970.

thinking, either. She was, as one of her opponents had said, the "best man in the government." If there was nothing in what she had said that could have raised hopes for an improvement in Indian-American relations, it was also true that she seemed concerned that they should not become much worse. And that was about the best that could be expected. Mrs. Gandhi, like her father, has never been an admirer of the United States and has never pretended to be anything but a critic of the American presence in Asia.

India and the United States

It is perhaps symbolic that V. K. Krishna Menon, India's angry man and the scourge of the United States at the United Nations for many years, was returned to Parliament in the 1971 elections. As the Indian defense minister accounted chiefly responsible for the failure to prepare the Indian armed forces to withstand the Chinese in the 1962 border war, he had been dropped from Nehru's Cabinet. He was, as a Cabinet colleague said at the time, "allergic to the West." His views have not changed.

If there is no one in the Indian government today who is quite as vitriolic as Krishna Menon in his prime, the Cabinet nevertheless does not lack for articulate critics of American policy. Generally, however, they do not like to express their views for publication without clearing first with the Prime Minister, for understandable reasons. One minister, however, seemed to me to sum up the actual, as opposed to the declared, Indian position toward the United States in a private conversation.

First of all, even before the signing of the India-Soviet pact, he didn't even bother to defend the stated Indian position of even-handedness toward Washington and Moscow. Instead, he readily conceded that the balance in India had shifted away from the United States because of consistent American favoritism for Pakistan, including weaponry. This seemed to him to outweigh in importance the massive American shipments of food grains to India to avert mass starvation and other past forms of American economic assistance. The reality of Soviet military aid for India and other forms of support made a much deeper impression on him.

When I asked him what he thought could be done to improve Indian-American relations, he suggested two unrealistic moves:

1. The United States should support India for a permanent seat on the United Nations Security Council.

2. The United States should help India develop a nuclear capability.

As to the former, he agreed after some discussion that India could not hope for parity with China in wielding the veto in the Security Council. The latter proposition, it seemed to me, would mean that both the United States and the Soviet Union would be helping India to become a nuclear power, which would please neither Washington nor Peking. Certainly, I argued, if India wished to go nuclear as a counterweight to China, Moscow would be delighted to help but it would be unrealistic in the extreme to expect American aid.

The blunt-spoken minister shrugged. He was well aware that India, with all its Soviet commitments, could expect little from Washington in the foreseeable future.

This posture has not made life very pleasant for a succession of recent American ambassadors to India, including Ellsworth Bunker, John Kenneth Galbraith, Chester Bowles and Kenneth B. Keating. But each in his own way tried to make a contribution, although none was able to escape criticism from the Indians. One of Morarji Desai's happiest recollections was an occasion when he told off the less than humble Galbraith, who accepted the situation with a stoic Harvard calm. The more friendly Bowles, who was fond of reproaching correspondents from the United States for being too critical of India, also had a difficult time when he and Mrs. Gandhi argued over whether India had backed the Soviet Union more often than the United States in the United Nations.

Keating, the most practical politician of the lot, with a long record in Congress as both a Representative and a Senator from New York, was in the most difficult position of all. As a former law partner of the Secretary of State, William P. Rogers, he might have expected his advice on American policy toward India in 1971 to be considered in the higher reaches of both Foggy Bottom and the White House. It wasn't. In a cable of protest to Washington that was promptly leaked to the press after the 15-day India-Pakistan war, Keating informed his superiors quite candidly that their anti-India, pro-Pakistan policy neither strengthened the American position in South Asia nor added to American credibility.[27]

There was no indication that his views led to any reconsideration of the Nixon "tilt" toward Pakistan in early 1972. Nor could he soothe the angry Indians, even though some American aid continued to dribble through the pipeline after a Washington cut-off. As for the bulk of American public opinion, aside from a thin stream of liberal protests, it didn't seem to matter what the Indians did or did not do.

If the mood of the early 1970s is any indication of the future of Indian-American relations, they will be cool for some time to come. This does not have very much to do with what the Americans have or have not done in Vietnam or what they will or will not do to improve their relations with China. It has everything to do with the great-power struggle for influence over South Asia, in which the Soviet Union, for the time being, holds the winning hand through its alliance with India, and the United States and China are left with a bleeding and truncated Pakistan.

Three Wars—No Settlement

Three times since India and Pakistan won independence from Britain in 1947, they have fought short and bitter wars without coming anywhere near a final settlement of their disputes. The Kashmir war of 1947 gave India the best part of that fabulous land, so prized by Jawaharlal Nehru. The 1965 border conflict in the western part of the subcontinent settled nothing. But in 1971, roaring into East Pakistan in overwhelming force, the Indians succeeded in tearing their old enemy apart and setting up a new nation, Bangladesh, as a kind of satellite state.

Yet, despite India's demonstrable superiority, all manner of obstacles continue to block a final settlement with Pakistan that will insure peace on the subcontinent. If anything, the problems of South

---

[27] Mrs. Gandhi is the source of the story of the argument with Bowles. She told me it was not true India supported the Soviet Union more often than the United States in the U.N. As for the Keating cable, it was leaked to *The New York Times* by Jack Anderson, syndicated columnist, and published January 8, 1972, p. 17.

Asia are even knottier than those in the Middle East, where the Arab states and Israel have refused for more than two decades to resolve the issues that separate them. In both the Middle East and South Asia, the problem of resettling refugees and caring for them is basic, but nobody is quite sure how it can be done and who will provide the funds for such an enormous humanitarian undertaking.

The first time India had to grapple with the refugee issue was in 1947–48, when a human tidal wave of 14,000,000 refugees inundated its eastern border with Pakistan. Somehow, the Indians managed to absorb that shock and survive. What relieved the pressure then, in large part, was the flight of millions of Muslims from India into East Pakistan—already an overcrowded and impoverished land.

In 1971, following Yahya Khan's attempted suppression of the Bangladesh secessionist movement, there was no relief for India when another 10,000,000 refugees, all but 2,000,000 of them Hindus, stampeded across the eastern border. India rightly appealed to the international community for help in order to absorb her new charges and care for them, but comparatively little was forthcoming and most of it came too late.

If India had had any hope of achieving self-sufficiency, the magnitude of the emergency and the resultant fighting dissipated it. For with a budgetary deficit of $290 million and costs of well-nigh $1 billion a year for refugee relief, India went deeply in the hole. The United States initially gave $70 million for Indian refugee relief, and another $35 million for East Pakistan, but the scale of international giving was much lower and less effective.

India's hope for a worldwide effort to defray the added expense on humanitarian grounds went glimmering. Due in part to a curtailment of the American aid program, India was receiving outside economic assistance at the rate of only about one per cent a year of national income in 1971, a 300 per cent reduction from the glory years under Nehru. And the crucial matter of debt repayment that so worried Indira Gandhi was running at the rate of 30 per cent of India's annual exports.[28]

That difficult economic situation was not at all changed by the great Indian victory over Pakistan in the 15-day war of 1971 and the

[28] *The Economist,* June 12, 1971, pp. 67–68.

resultant creation of Bangladesh. If anything, it was intensified. For it was up to the Indians to move 10,000,000 refugees back into Bangladesh, rebuild the ruined villages and towns and burned-out houses, re-establish transport and food supply, reconstitute a shattered agriculture and industry, and set up and support a new government. A force of 100,000 militia had to be trained to replace the Indian Army's peace-keeping units as they were withdrawn. Basic health and hospital services had to be restored, schools reopened and a civil service put together. Realistic Indians were well aware that the task would take years, if indeed it was at all possible to accomplish.

Trouble in West Bengal

The formation of Bangladesh created new uncertainties for India in chaotic West Bengal and its great port city of Calcutta. Even before the 15-day war, some 2,000,000 people were unemployed in the area and local government was near breakdown because of abysmal mass poverty and the destructive attacks of roving bands of Naxalites, or anarchists. In 1970 alone, more than 200 industries employing 25,000 persons closed in the Calcutta area. In the following year, a shaky local government took office—a six-party West Bengal coalition that included a dominant segment of Mrs. Gandhi's New Congress Party and excluded the Marxists. The trouble was initially that the group had only 140 out of 276 seats in the state's parliament, not much for Calcutta's first non-revolutionary government in four years.[29] With so weak a regime, the example of secession in the east could not help but be seized upon by extremists as a desperation solution for West Bengal, as well.

When the millions of refugees from East Pakistan fled over the border, the New Delhi government had to step in or West Bengal would have gone under then and there. Even so, Indira Gandhi's regime had all it could do to maintain minimal standards of living for the 3,000,000 people of Calcutta and the additional 10,000,000 in the surrounding region while the refugees were dispersed into camps. When the international community withheld the kind of help that was

[29] *The Economist*, April 10, 1971, pp. 20–21.

needed, India was up against the wall. As long as Yahya Khan's repression continued in East Pakistan, it was certain that more and more millions would come over the border. At first, India tried to enforce restraint on Yahya by arming the Mukti Bahini—a risky move in view of the known secessionist sentiment in West Bengal. When that course proved unavailing, open armed intervention was virtually forced on Indira Gandhi by a virulent combination of Indian hawks and a deteriorating situation in West Bengal.

Victory in the east did not end the Indian gamble. Far from it. Succeeding years will show whether Bangladesh can survive as an Indian client state, whether the new nation will act as a catalyst in separating West Bengal from India, and whether the secessionist example will spread to the unruly, Communist-controlled southern state of Kerala.

The Fate of Kashmir

The dismemberment of Pakistan has had other major consequences, notably in Kashmir.[30] Despite the protests of the new civilian-led regime in Islamabad, India now can do pretty much what it wants in the long-disputed territory. Only Chinese intervention could give Pakistan any hope whatever of recovering any part of the India-held land in which Muslims form a majority. And China has far more important problems to worry about.

The position of the Indian government is that Kashmir, except for the fragment still held by Pakistan, is an inseparable part of India. The claim is based on the adherence of the Maharajah of Kashmir to India in 1947 when a forceful Pakistani takeover was frustrated. To all demands in the United Nations for a plebiscite, the Indians have said no. And three wars in the area have made no difference in its ultimate disposition. In fact, in the 1971 action, brief as it was, the Indians managed to gain more Kashmiri territory.

The single world figure among the Kashmiri, Sheikh Mohammed Abdullah, has lost his chance for any kind of a settlement now. He has spent thirteen years in Indian prisons for his agitation in favor of Kashmir's dominant Muslims, and early in 1971 he was barred by

[30] Formally, the area comprises the provinces of Jammu and Kashmir.

the Indian government from visiting Srinagar.[31] At the time, his influence was held so lightly that the Indians didn't even bother to arrest him. The "Lion of Kashmir" had grown old—he was sixty-five at the time—and he no longer had any standing in New Delhi.

Mrdulla Sarabhai, the faithful Indian woman who has supported the Kashmiri movement for many years, saw no hope for a change in Kashmir. She doubted that India would ever permit the Sheikh to do anything of an effective nature, such as a popular front of Kashmiri parties. Just about the only way the status of Kashmir can be changed, she said, was through some sort of a confederation and common market of the nations of the subcontinent—a far-off vision.[32]

The Future for India

Through a rare and unlooked-for cooperation between the Gandhi regime and the rightist Jan Sangh, New Delhi has begun to take on the gracious air of a world capital. Wandering cows have been banished from its wide and tree-lined thoroughfares. Fine new suburbs are thrusting into the countryside. Beautiful new commercial buildings are rising in many sections, reflecting a new sense of well-being among India's upper classes. Even the crowded old city of Delhi is able to boast that its main streets are clean and passable and, with the new city, looks a lot tidier than many parts of New York City.

Compared with the horrors of Calcutta and the less publicized but equally tragic misfortunes of many people in Bombay and Kerala, New Delhi seems like a part of a different country. But Indians cannot deceive themselves. When 80 per cent of India's children suffer from malnutrition and almost half the population earns less than the equivalent of 20 cents a day, there can be very little optimism. Nor can the cheers over fallen Pakistan delude the needy into a belief that they are approaching Nirvana.

What India will have to do is to work by every conceivable means to increase agricultural production beyond the current rate and take another look at the repressive measures that have kept industrial production to a minimal increase of less than 5 per cent a year when

[31] *The New York Times*, January 10, 1971, p. 10.
[32] I last saw Miss Sarabhai on August 10, 1970, in New Delhi.

it should be at least double that total. The crackdown on tax evasions and easy-going government servants is long overdue, but these things in themselves are not going to stimulate a lagging, war-burdened economy. Nor will they bring in the flow of capital that India so urgently needs. The public sector of the economy cannot carry India forward by itself. A change in the continual government harassment of the private sector is strongly indicated, provided Indira Gandhi can discern that no "March Toward Socialism" can be successful with capital in flight and factories closed.

In India's foreign relations, the first and most urgent business is a settlement with Pakistan and a viable relationship with Bangladesh. Obviously, with the great powers exerting influence wherever they can over the subcontinent, negotiations are going to take a lot of time and an enormous amount of patience. If India remains in the Soviet orbit and Pakistan continues to depend on China, the hope for an accommodation in South Asia will be very small for as long as the two Communist giants are adversaries. The role of the United States, in such circumstances, could be crucial if Washington finds the will and the means to be more flexible.

3. DISASTER IN PAKISTAN

In the beginning, Pakistan was a beautiful theory. Some called it an abstraction. It was based on the principle of Muslim brotherhood, now a somewhat dubious premise. There was, in addition, an even more compelling reason to hope that Pakistan would survive: fear of India. This, it was reasoned, would hold together the unequal parts of a country separated by more than 1,000 miles of Indian territory.

Prime Minister Clement R. Attlee's Labor government in Britain approved the new arrangement for the subcontinent on June 3, 1947. To Mohammed Ali Jinnah and other founders of the Muslim League, it was a great victory over the Indians. No true Muslim would listen then to suggestions that Pakistan would be in trouble over differences of culture, language, regional interests and economic potential between the eastern and western halves of the country. And so with

India, Pakistan—a name founded on an acronym[33]—won independence August 15, 1947.

For twenty-four years, the Pakistanis confounded their detractors. Their economy proved to be proportionately stronger than India's. Despite population gains of almost 3 per cent a year, Pakistan's per capita income grew from $67 in 1960 to $75 in 1964 and slightly more than $100 in 1970, when the GNP stood at $18 billion and the combined population of East and West Pakistan at 130,000,000.

Politically, too, Pakistan appeared stable on the surface because of the tight military rule of successive dictatorships. I well remember sophisticated Indians, viewing the political disarray of their democracy in the 1960s, saying: "What we need is an Ayub Khan." Yet, all the time, the Bengalis of East Pakistan were seething because they had so little and the Punjabis of the west had so much.

The world may have been surprised by the suddenness with which the roof fell in on divided Pakistan. The Bengalis were not.

The Rule of the West

In the west of Pakistan lay 85 per cent of the nation's land, populated by only 46 per cent of its people. Yet, the 55,000,000 Urdu-speaking inhabitants of the western wing, mainly Punjabis, dominated the life of the country. They controlled both the central government and the army, the civil service and the professions. In their fruitful land of some 310,000 square miles, larger than California and Arizona combined, they were able to expand and modernize their agriculture almost to the point of self-sufficiency. With a developing industry, they proved strong enough to maintain a thriving trade, East Pakistan being their reluctant major customer, and they benefited from funds poured out by an international consortium of Western powers. In and outside this group, the United States contribution was more than $4 billion.

West Pakistan's prosperity did not sit well with the impoverished 75,000,000 people of East Pakistan, mainly Bengalis, who were jammed into 55,000 square miles of poor land. In an area the size of Arkansas, the Pakistan government crowded thirty-six times the

[33] It is derived from Punjab, Afghania, Kashmir, Sind, and Baluchistan. No eastern province was represented in the name.

population of that state. It galled the Bengalis, a proud and independent race with their own ancient language and literature and a great
poet, Rabindranath Tagore, to struggle along on next to nothing.
With less than half an acre each on the average for cultivation, they
had to depend on rice, tea and jute crops to sustain life. And in years
of devastating monsoons, they often saw starvation and death all
about them.

The whims of a cruel nature and the circumstances of science
contributed to widen the gap between the "haves" of the west and the
"have nots" of the east.[34] The dry culture of the western farmlands
was favorable to the growth of the "miracle" strains of Los Banos
rice and Mexican wheat, while the wet culture of the east was not. As
a result, production on the west's 15,000,000 acres of wheat land
almost doubled in five years, from 3,800,000 tons in 1965 to
7,300,000 tons in 1970. The west's rice land produced just as well,
rising from 1,400,000 tons to 2,100,000 tons in 1967–68. Had
Pakistan been able to hang together, there is no doubt that West
Pakistan would have become self-sufficient in a few years. Even under
trying circumstances, the western wing's growth rate was so large
that it was high on the list of stars in the GNP league, being seventh
behind Japan, Iran, Brazil, Mexico, Turkey and Spain.

The Bengalis in the east, far distant from the seat of power, had to
absorb blow after blow. The Indian embargo on Pakistani trade after
the 1965 war virtually wrecked the east's jute trade, the main source
of its income.[35] The principal market for Bengali jute, Calcutta,
dried up and many mills there closed. As if that weren't bad enough,
Bengali factories were cut off from Indian coal and had to buy it at
three times the Indian price from China or Poland. The Indian
market for fish, another East Pakistan export earner, also was
reduced.

But the worst misfortune of all to the suffering Bengalis in the east
was the discovery that the "miracle" rice, a dwarf strain, did not do
at all well in the traditional wet-culture lands. Successive monsoons
simply flooded out the low-standing rice fields, cutting production

[34] The report on agricultural conditions is from Richard Critchfield's paper
for the Patterson Fund, December 27, 1970.
[35] Phillips Talbot, *The New York Times*, March 28, 1971, p. 4, sec. 4.

instead of increasing it. Since farming provides the chief form of sustenance for 85 per cent of the people of East Pakistan, this was a calamity.

Despite the clamor from the eastern wing for relief and a greater share of the national income, the central government was insensitive to all pleas, resentful of all threats. Ayub Khan's "basic democracy," a program that wasn't anything remotely like its name, remained in force for slightly more than a decade from the time he took over in 1958 as head of the 250,000-man Pakistani Army, his main strength. The only serious challenge to his rule in those years came from the seventy-year-old sister of Mohammad Ali Jinnah, Miss Fatima Jinnah, who ran for president in 1965 and charged that the government had created an "atmosphere laden with fear and reeking with corruption."[36] Ayub Khan rolled up a 2–1 majority over her among the 80,000 popularly chosen electors. He also disregarded charges that he favored the 22 wealthy families in the west and paid more attention to these large landowners of West Pakistan than to the distressed millions of the eastern wing.

In 1969, Ayub Khan's luck ran out. Riots in the east coupled with violent student demonstrations in the west first forced concessions from him, then his resignation. But when he stepped out, he handed over power to his military successor, Yahya Khan, and the beleaguered Bengalis of the east realized then that the issue had been drawn.

The Rise of Sheik Mujib

The spearhead of Bengali opposition to the rule of the west was the Awami (People's) League, which was organized soon after Pakistani independence as a major political party of the eastern wing. Its leader, Sheik Mujibur Rahman—Mujib to his people—was an uncompromising foe of Ayub Khan's military dictatorship, having been jailed in 1958 and 1962. Nevertheless, in 1966, he was in the forefront of a movement for greater autonomy for East Pakistan and issued a six-point "freedom" program. What he demanded was internal self-government for the east, control over the east's foreign

---

[36] *The New York Times*, January 3, 1965, p. 1.

trade and taxation, and limitation of the west's power to defense and a part of foreign policy.

The furious Marshal Ayub had the impudent Mujib clapped into prison once again for what amounted to treason, but it only stirred the sheik's supporters to greater efforts in his behalf. Too late, the tottering dictator released Mujib only to find that the situation had gone far beyond the government's control. With the accession of Yahya Khan, Mujib and the Awami League reverted to their six-point program and settled into a campaign for the first free elections in the country's history.

Mujib was no wild-eyed, starving rebel, having come from a middle-class environment. He was born March 17, 1920, in the village of Tongipara, East Bengal, became a student activist at Islamia College in Calcutta, studied law at Dacca University and forthwith entered upon a career as a revolutionary by being imprisoned for supporting illegal strikes and demonstrations. With that kind of a background, it was natural for him to favor some form of Socialism—he called his brand democratic Socialism. In many respects, it was much the same as Indira Gandhi's, for the sheik's program included nationalization of banks, insurance companies and major industries.[37] No wonder Ayub Khan didn't like him! The old marshal's chief supporters, the "twenty-two families," were reputed to control four-fifths of the nation's banks and insurance companies and two-thirds of its industry.[38]

The Politics of Misery

There was no doubt that a confrontation was coming between Mujib, the most popular and magnetic figure in East Pakistan, and Marshal Yahya, the new dictator of the west. Everybody expected it but none could discern the tortured course it would take. For there now occurred one of those catastrophes of nature that swept away hundreds of thousands of lives and revealed to the world the misery and the terror of life in East Pakistan. There was forewarning of the devastating cyclone that struck the Ganges River Delta on November

[37] Selig Harrison of the Washington *Post*, in *Japan Times*, November 18, 1970, p. 14.
[38] *Time*, December 7, 1970, p. 27.

13, 1970, but evidently most of the 5,000,000 people in the area didn't know of it or, if they did, they paid no attention to it. Such storms had long since become a part of the hazards of living in the area. There was talk of taking precautions, but no one—least of all the central government of Pakistan—did anything about it.

This storm was the worst natural disaster in recorded history. When 120-mile-an-hour winds struck the low-lying delta land and twenty-foot waves dashed over the islands and the coastline, no living thing in their path was able to survive. Almost the entire population of a 3,000-square-mile area was wiped out, together with 90 per cent of the buildings and nearly the entire rice crop. The toll was somewhere between 300,000 and 500,000 people—the exact number will never be known—and the homeless and the destitute ran into the millions.

Yet, long after the storm had passed, the Pakistani authorities seemed to act as if the whole business was a colossal attempt by the world press to insult their country. Their callousness and insensitivity to the needs of the survivors seemed almost beyond belief. One Pakistani authority even denied the intensity of the storm, saying that "only 16,000" people had been killed and seemed annoyed over the fuss. It was almost two weeks before President Yahya Khan came to East Pakistan to make a formal visit of inspection, after which he ordered $115,000,000 appropriated for relief and gave $9,000 himself. But when India offered help, with the rest of the international community, Pakistan replied coolly: "We don't know if it will be needed."[39] In the face of such obtuseness, the bitterness of the people of East Pakistan against their government burst all bounds. Islamabad had resorted to the politics of misery once too often.

The Hollow Victory

One of the pledges that President Yahya had made upon assuming office was to hold the nation's first free, general election. He had given the nation assurance that he would fairly supervise the polling for a National Assembly, which would be given four months to produce a constitution suitable for the fifth most populous nation on earth. The only hitch in the proceedings, at the outset, was that the

[39] *Time*, December 7, 1970, p. 27.

President reserved to himself the right to approve or disapprove the constitution.

In the wake of the cyclone and the turmoil that it aroused in East Pakistan, there was concern that Yahya Khan would postpone or cancel the election, which had been set for December 7, 1970. He didn't. With the support of the two principal leaders, Sheik Mujib and his Awami League and the former foreign minister Zulfikar Ali Bhutto, head of the dominant Pakistan People's Party of West Pakistan, the President went through with the elections. They were, as he had promised, peaceful. They were also fair. And some 40,000,000 Pakistanis cast a free vote for the first time in their lives.

The result was an astounding Assembly majority for Sheik Mujib and the Awami League, with Bhutto's PPP as the runner-up. They swamped the other twenty parties in the field, including the Islamic parties that had hoped to rally religious sentiment to their cause.[40] The sheik's adherents began celebrating prematurely, not counting on the formidable Bhutto and his influence with Yahya Khan.

This was the Awami League's first mistake, for a reading of Bhutto's career would have shown that he did not easily submit to defeat. As foreign minister, he had been the author of Pakistan's pro-China, anti-American policy and frequently had linked the Soviet Union and the United States as "imperialist" powers. This had been based not so much on friendship for Peking as resentment of what he regarded as the pro-Indian "collaboration" of the United States and the Soviet Union on Kashmir, always the hottest political issue in West Pakistan. Bhutto's student days at the University of California in Berkeley had not notably imbued him with respect for the United States, its people and its foreign policies.

Like Mujib, Bhutto campaigned on a Socialist platform, something he first called "Islamic Socialism" and later "Musawat," which means roughly "Islamic justice and equality." He stood for an end to all capitalistic monopolies, for land redistribution, and for nationalization of industry. He also demanded national leadership to unify

[40] Out of the 313 Assembly seats, 162 were allotted to East Pakistan, and Awami candidates won 151; of the 138 seats allotted to West Pakistan, the PPP won 82. Of the 13 seats allotted to women, the PPP had 6, Awami 7. With its allies, Awami had a bloc of 167 of the 313 seats—an absolute majority—and held all but two seats from East Pakistan.

the country, quite the opposite of Mujib's summons for an autonomous East Pakistan.

Once the election results were in, it was obvious that everything depended on the ability of Mujib and Bhutto to reach a working agreement on procedures in the National Assembly so that a constitution could be framed. They didn't. From the outset, Bhutto demanded "equally shared" power between the two major parties, even though he could be consistently outvoted by the Awami League. The league, on the other hand, declared that it was "competent" to frame the constitution and to form a central government "with or without cooperation from any other party."[41]

Three days before the scheduled meeting of the National Assembly on March 3, 1971, Bhutto revealed his basic disagreement of policy with the Awami League, demanded postponement of the session and threatened a PPP boycott if the delegates did meet. He didn't like the prospect of being outvoted on every issue and made no secret of it in his broadcast to the nation. On March 1, with a "heavy heart," President Yahya agreed to the postponement, which, he said, had cast a "shadow of gloom" over the country.[42] Almost at once, rioting broke out in East Pakistan with a loss of more than 300 lives. Yahya proclaimed martial law; Mujib, a general strike.

On March 15, Mujib announced that he was assuming the administration of East Pakistan on the basis of his party's holding of 288 out of the 310 seats in the provincial assembly. He ordered the suspension of income tax collections as well as the remittance of taxes already collected for the central government in the west. His aim, he cried, was nothing more nor less than the "emancipation of the people of Bangladesh," the Bengal nation.

The proclamation was in vain. Yahya came to Dacca to make one more effort to reach an understanding with Mujib. But while they were negotiating, reports came to Awami League headquarters that the Pakistani Army already had intervened in Chittagong and Rangpur. Mujib accused the President of a reign of terror, whereupon the infuriated Yahya walked out. Assailing Mujib's non-

[41] *Far Eastern Economic Review*, January 9, 1971, p. 20.
[42] *The New York Times*, March 2, 1971, p. 1.

cooperation movement as an "act of treason," the President proscribed the activities of the Awami League.[43]

Civil War

After invoking strict censorship and expelling every foreign correspondent he could lay his hands on, the Pakistani Army's martial-law
administrator, Lieutenant General Tikka Khan, moved against the
rebellious Bengalis on March 25. Within two days, civil war raged in
the streets of Dacca, Chittagong and a dozen other cities, and refugees by the millions were streaming over the Indian border. "Resist
the enemy forces at any cost!" Mujib ordered his followers. But
without sufficient weapons, organization and resources, the Bengali
separatist movement had little chance of resisting 93,000 well-armed
West Pakistani troops.

Within eight months, casualties in East Pakistan ran into the
hundreds of thousands and India was caught with more than 10
million refugees for whom it could not afford to provide. Yahya
Khan appeared at that point to have reasserted his control over East
Pakistan. Mujib and other opposition leaders were in jail, facing
heavy punishment. Despite a formal proclamation of the independence of Bangladesh on April 17,[44] with Syed Nazrul Islam acting as
president in place of Mukib, the separatist cause languished.

It was at this juncture that India began training and arming the
Bengali liberation fighters, the Mukti Bahini, and sending them back
across the border to harass the West Pakistani Army. The government
in New Delhi turned its back on the precepts of Mahatma Gandhi,
who once warned: "War is wrong, an unmitigated evil. No cause,
however just, can warrant the indiscriminate slaughter that is going
on." Slaughter there was in East Pakistan; too much of it. Despite
the peace of Tashkent that ended the 1965 Indo-Pakistan war, a new
conflict now threatened to tear the subcontinent apart.

In a tanglefoot display of diplomatic ineptitude, the United States
once again was caught in the middle of an utterly untenable situation.
For despite assurances to Indian Foreign Minister Swaran Singh that

43 *Newsweek*, April 5, 1971, p. 31.
44 From the Associated Press file for April 17, 1971.

no American arms aid would be sent to Pakistan after March 25, when the fighting began, at least three shiploads of arms for West Pakistan left American ports after that date.[45] The stated American purpose was to prevent a new Indo-Pakistan war. It was never explained why the United States, as the chief dispenser of economic aid to Pakistan for 15 years, could not have used economic pressure instead of arms shipments to restrain Islamabad. In retrospect, Indira Gandhi charged that the United States could have prevented the war by obtaining the release of Mujib and obliging Islamabad to enter into realistic negotiations with Dacca. In Yahya Khan's bone-headed state of mind, it is doubtful that Washington could have exerted that kind of pressure on him. But at the very least, more of an effort might have been made.

Under the circumstances, the United States demand on India and Pakistan to cease hostilities over Bangladesh had all the appearance of a pious fraud. And Washington's relations with West Pakistan did not seem to be particularly improved at that juncture.

India Intervenes

Yahya Khan was fully aware that the Indians outmanned and outgunned his forces in East Pakistan, that they had superior air cover and tanks, and that his chances of supplying his troops were almost nil. The figures in themselves were revealing, testifying to India's absolute advantage. India could count on an army of nearly a million troops against Pakistan's 300,000, a force of 600 modern aircraft including seven squadrons of MIG 21s against 270 Pakistani aircraft, a fleet of nearly 1,500 tanks of new and mobile design against 1,000 obsolete Pakistani machines. Even at sea, India's modest fleet of twenty-eight small warships outmatched Pakistan's twelve vessels.

Within East Pakistan itself, the Indian advantage was even more startling. Against the 93,000 Pakistani regulars, there were six divisions of crack Indian troops, about 150,000 men, plus several thousand Mukti Bahini.[46] Even worse, the Pakistani soldiers had to

---

[45] *The New York Times*, July 24, 1971, p. 1.

[46] Figures from *Newsweek*, December 13, 1971, p. 40; *Time*, same date, p. 25.

operate in a hostile land among a populace whom they had outraged with their wanton policy of killing and burning. Yet, with an obtuseness that defied all understanding, Yahya Khan ordered a small Pakistani air contingent to bomb selected Indian airfields on December 3. When the Indians struck back within a few hours, following a midnight broadcast by Prime Minister Gandhi calling for a war footing, they gained mastery of the air easily.

The United States, nevertheless, continued to support the Pakistani cause. In the secret minutes of a December 3 strategy meeting in Washington, which were leaked to the press, President Nixon's enmity toward India was stressed repeatedly. Henry A. Kissinger, the President's deputy for national security affairs, said at one point: "I am getting hell every half-hour from the President that we are not being tough enough on India. . . . He wants to tilt in favor of Pakistan." And yet, Kissinger left no doubt that the United States knew it was backing another losing ally. "Everyone knows," he said, "that India ultimately will occupy East Pakistan." And he also didn't mistake India for just another Soviet satellite. Referring to Mrs. Gandhi, he observed, "The lady is cold-blooded and tough and will not turn into a Soviet satellite merely because of pique."[47]

It was all over a lot sooner than Kissinger thought it would be. While Indian forces contained the Pakistanis in Kashmir, a three-pronged Indian attack crushed all resistance in East Pakistan in 15 days. With Indian troops in Dacca, the Pakistani Army surrendered. And on December 18, after Yahya Khan agreed to a cease-fire on all fronts, he was forced out of office in favor of Zulfikar Ali Bhutto and soon was under arrest. As for Sheik Mujib, who had been condemned to death and narrowly escaped hanging, he was freed by President Bhutto on January 8, 1972, and two days later took up his post in Dacca as the first Prime Minister of the People's Republic of Bangladesh.

Thus Pakistan lost a majority of its people and the whole eastern part of its territory. The Indians counted 10,000 casualties in dead,

---

[47] From the texts of the records of three secret meetings in December, 1971, of the National Security Council's Special Action Group, as made public by Jack Anderson, syndicated columnist, and distributed by the Associated Press and United Press International.

wounded and missing, but they accomplished their objective. An independent Bangladesh, allied with India, was in being. And India, more united than at any time in its twenty-four-year history, had wiped out the stain of its 1962 border rout by the Chinese and established its dominance over the subcontinent. The Indians still were by no means a major military force, but they were much improved over 1962 and 1965.

The Consequences

The United States has a truncated East Pakistan on its hands in South Asia and a vengeful India, which has wasted no time in recognizing North Vietnam. Just about all that Washington can hope for is to try to bind West Pakistan into a closer relationship with Iran, Turkey and some of the Arab states. And yet, despite President Nixon's gestures of friendship for President Bhutto, the Pakistanis are well aware that they may in the end have to depend more on China than on the United States for survival.

True, West Pakistan has been relieved of a hopeless economic burden in losing the eastern wing. Moreover, American aid—with the exception of limited funds allocated to relieve suffering in the east—is going to be used from now on exclusively for the benefit of the west. Up to the time of the war, the United States was supplying $200 million of the $500 million annually contributed to Islamabad by a 10-nation consortium.[48] With the resumption of foreign assistance, West Pakistan should be able to make a fairly rapid recovery, for its industry and agriculture suffered scant war damage and its potential for growth is still very great.

President Bhutto is restoring national morale. He may talk about resuming ties with the east, but West Pakistan doesn't have any real hope of that. Its future is tied, therefore, to how well and how quickly it is able to adjust to the new realities of power on the subcontinent.

As for Bangladesh, everything hinges on the manner and method of its leadership. Here is a new nation of 75,000,000 people with a per capita income of only $75 a year, almost no industry, not enough rice to feed itself and not enough jute or tea production to earn its

[48] *Far Eastern Economic Review*, May 15, 1971, p. 7; *Wall Street Journal*, July 27, 1971, p. 1; *The New York Times*, December 19, 1971, p. 1, sec. 4.

way.[49] If India can get even half of the 10,000,000 refugees to go back, Bangladesh will have an additional half-billion-dollar task of feeding and housing them. It will cost $3 billion or more to get the country going again. In such an extremity, Mujib's leadership is the main hope for Bangladesh.

4. CEYLON'S BITTER TEA

The island of Ceylon, a land of tropical splendor, has been trying to turn itself into a Socialist paradise almost since it won independence in 1948. As the largest source of the world's tea, and a producer of everything from rubber to coconuts as well, its 12,500,000 inhabitants seriously expected their government to give them everything they wanted. And quickly, too.

Successive governments have tried. The people of Ceylon, as a result, have a subsidized rice ration, on which the government spent more than $60,000,000 in 1970 alone. Their public transportation costs them a third of an American cent a mile. Their health services are free. They also have free education from nursery through university. There are, in addition, numerous invisible subsidies that make Ceylon a welfare state of the type that is dreamed about in the Indian subcontinent.

Such a life style would tax the coffers of a state as prosperous and expanding as Hawaii, with its sugar and pineapple, its tourism in the grand manner, and its military income as the chief American defense center of the Pacific. But Ceylon, being four times the size of Hawaii with more than fifteen times the population, has neither the advantages nor the potential of the wealthy American island state. Nor do the people of Ceylon pay the heavy federal, state and local taxes that Hawaiians do for whatever benefits they receive.

Consequently, Ceylon is deeply in debt. An authoritative estimate

[49] East Pakistan's jute crop, the area's main resource for export, was down from 7,000,000 to 5,500,000 bales in 1970–71 and the rice crop was less than 10,000,000 tons in 1971 whereas the minimum requirement for the area was 13,000,000 tons. With a breakdown in transport, the internal distribution system late in 1971 could handle only 150,000 tons of rice imports a month whereas twice that amount was necessary to get food to all the people who needed it. The spectre of famine, therefore, was not an illusion.

in 1970 put its foreign obligations at $175,000,000, its domestic debt at $463,000,000. At the time, it was importing at the rate of $283,000,000 annually and exporting only $218,000,000, for an imbalance of $65,000,000 in trade. More than 500,000 people were unemployed, a number being university graduates. And shortly thereafter, irked because the government wasn't moving quickly enough toward "pure Socialism," thousands of ultra-leftist students and admirers of Mao and Che Guevara staged an unsuccessful revolution.

In mid-1971, therefore, Ceylon faced the most severe balance-of-payments crisis in its history, and the island's departure from the Commonwealth at the end of 1971 didn't make its situation any easier. Whereas its foreign exchange reserves amounted to $100,000,-000 in 1961, its Central Bank had practically no reserves a decade later. Its external assets were barely equal to the short-term debts owed to commercial banks abroad.[50] And upwards of $50,000,000 was needed merely to keep the government going on an emergency basis. Even the hard-won victory over the Guevarists didn't end Ceylon's crisis.

Its people had been living beyond their means for almost a generation. Now, the time of reckoning had come. The sweet and delicate flavor of Ceylon's tea had turned bitter.

The Perils of Sirimavo

Nothing like this had been anticipated by Sirimavo Bandaranaike, the handsome and quick-spoken prime minister of Ceylon, upon her return to power at the head of a three-party leftist coalition in the election of May 27, 1970. It had seemed to her, and to her entranced supporters, that all she had to do was to use her big majority to complete the socialization of Ceylon, lead the island out of the Commonwealth, and set up shop as an independent non-aligned republic. To demonstrate her independence of the West, she recognized

[50] For data on Ceylon's finances, I am indebted to a World Bank report, *Note on Recent Developments and the Exchange and Growth Outlook, 1970–71, of Ceylon*, published by the Government of Ceylon. Also, Ranjit Gunawardene, Hong Kong *Standard*, October 19, 1970, sec. 2, p. 11, and the *South China Morning Post*, November 23, 1970, sec. 2, p. 2; the *Far Eastern Economic Review*, October 10, 1970, p. 17, and May 15, 1971, p. 8.

North Vietnam, North Korea, and East Germany and encouraged better relations with China. As events were to demonstrate, she was a bit rash. She could not cut her ties to the West so easily; nor, for that matter, could she find Communist states that were willing to take over the financing of Ceylon's mounting debt.

Mrs. Bandaranaike has had to learn her politics the hard way, as her latest experience indicates. She was born April 17, 1916, into the prosperous landholding Ratwatte family, was educated at St. Bridget's Convent in Colombo (although she remains a practicing Buddhist), and married one of Ceylon's leaders, Solomon Bandaranaike, who became prime minister in 1956. When he was shot to death in her presence in 1959 by a Buddhist monk who objected to his support of Western medical practices, she replaced him in Parliament. In the national election of 1960, she led the Freedom Party to victory, allied with Communist and Trotskyite factions, and thus became the world's first woman prime minister.

Unhappily, the complex Ceylon electorate, 70 per cent Sinhalese and 22 per cent Tamil, was not impressed by the relatively relaxed manner in which she went about providing them with new benefits. And the opposition conservatives made out a good case against her for bungling state finances. In 1965, she went too far by trying to nationalize the press and was toppled from office. It was Ceylon's misfortune that the conservative regime of Prime Minister Dudley Senanayake was equally inept during the succeeding five years, resulting in Mrs. Bandaranaike's return to power.

Outwardly, it seemed like a landslide. Actually, it was not. For Mrs. Bandaranaike's Freedom Party received only 36.5 per cent of the votes cast, while the conservatives, the United National Party, took 38 per cent. What made the difference was the support of the Communists and the Trotskyites who, with the Freedom Party, took ninety seats in the lower house of Ceylon's Parliament, as against only seventeen for the conservatives. The lady, quite evidently, had learned something about politics from her first unsatisfactory experience.

The new and reconstituted leftist regime did not, as so many expected, go rushing headlong into imprudent nationalization on every front. The ultra-leftists had been campaigning for years to

406 : *New Era in the Pacific*

nationalize the great tea estates, for example. But the Trotskyite Minister of Finance, Dr. N. M. Perera, said, "We have agitated for the nationalization of the tea estates for the past forty years but today, after assuming office as minister of finance, I realize that it is not advisable to do so."[51]

For one thing, there was no money in the treasury to pay compensation. For another, the British interests that so largely controlled the tea trade were also important to the maintenance of Ceylon's rather uncertain financial equilibrium.

These are some of the considerations that Mrs. Bandaranaike has had to take into account in trying to restore a measure of stability to Ceylon during her second term in office.

"The World Must Understand"

Across the street from the Prime Minister's office, set down in the lush green surroundings of the Gordon Gardens in Colombo, is a white stone statue of Queen Victoria with scepter in hand, seated in celebration of the diamond jubilee of 1897. The Queen is not amused. And neither is her successor to the rule of Ceylon, so opposite in every way to her imperial majesty and so committed to leave the Commonwealth.[52] Sirimavo is everything that Victoria was not, but she has yet to learn to enjoy the uses of power. For her, life in Ceylon has been a continual crisis.

When my wife and I saw Mrs. Bandaranaike at the magnificent formal residence of Ceylon's prime ministers, Temple Trees in Colombo, we were impressed with her seriousness of purpose and the earnestness with which she discussed her many problems.[53] She had then been in office only a little more than two months, following her re-election. The future was far from clear and she realized it, for the previous administration had bequeathed to her a budget deficit of $120 million, pierced the borrowing ceiling of $234 million set by the International Monetary Fund, and left her with the unsavory task of

[51] Neville Maxwell in the *South China Morning Post,* October 23, 1970.

[52] The June 14, 1970, Throne Speech of Prime Minister Bandaranaike's second government, read at the opening of the seventh Ceylon Parliament, called for "a free, sovereign and independent republic."

[53] Interview at Temple Trees, August 14, 1970.

finding $22 million to meet the government's commitments for the remainder of 1970 alone.[54]

Mrs. Bandaranaike came to talk with us in a small, tastefully furnished anteroom, unaccompanied by the usual protective official or secretary. She was then fifty-four, a fine-looking woman of ample figure and above-average height with a mass of jet-black hair framing her expressive face. She had on a very pretty light-brown sari over a white vest, with a gold ring and two small gold bracelets as ornaments. If she wore make-up at all, there was so little of it that my wife, an expert in such matters, couldn't detect it.

Complicated as Ceylon's situation was, and still is, the Prime Minister advanced a comparatively simple argument as the basis for her program of remedial action. What she wanted to do, she said, was to build an independent country that would be governed in the interest of all its citizens and would be strong enough to be truly non-aligned in foreign affairs. "The world must understand," she said, "that we want to work out our own form of government in our own way without interference. It may be that we will make mistakes; very well, we will have to take the risk. But at least these mistakes will be our own and not those of some imperial power seeking domination over us."

It seemed to annoy her that she was being depicted in the United States, and elsewhere in the West, as either a Communist or a creature of the Communist groups with which she was allied. "I did not make a successful fight to return to power in order to sell out my country to the Soviet Union or anybody else," she said. "You may be sure of that. I am not a Communist and I don't intend to be a Communist. We are not about to go into the Soviet bloc here in Ceylon, but we are going to work our way toward a republic based on Socialism."

She did not minimize the seriousness of Ceylon's economic plight. Like India, she pointed out, Ceylon has descended into an untenable situation in which the cost of keeping up interest payments for past indebtedness is so heavy that it takes a sizable chunk of every new financial commitment into which the nation is able to enter. "Ceylon," she repeated several times, "is a poor country, a very poor country

[54] Throne Speech.

with many problems. Along with other developing countries, we have a right to expect that we will receive help from the industrialized countries at terms that we can meet."

We discussed the options before Ceylon, both economic and political, and found nothing very attractive in the immediate future. The Prime Minister herself was reserved on her continued relationship with the other Commonwealth countries, even though she was set on breaking the Commonwealth tie. Still, without knowing where Ceylon would have to turn next for financial resources, she obviously did not intend to alienate any powerful nation or group of nations. She didn't even spend much time inveighing against the United States over the Vietnam War, a cardinal feature in the lexicon of every non-aligned leader. Clearly enough, political rhetoric was one thing. Fiscal responsibility was quite another.

It was with relief that she finally turned from Ceylon's dismal prospects to more personal and congenial matters. Instead of weighing her words, she now spoke rapidly. Frequently, she smiled, showing her even white teeth, and made graceful gestures with one hand. She was still new enough to political life to be thrilled by her comeback to power and she made no secret of it. "Before the coming of imperial domination of so many Asian countries," she said, "many women played leading roles in many lands." And, with great animation, she told us the story of a queen of Ceylon who had offered herself as a human sacrifice to her conqueror and was thrown into the sea, only to be saved by a friendly king who married her and enabled her to liberate her people.

"Women today must be liberated so that they may be able to take their proper role in their country," she said. Much to our amusement, she seemed not to have heard of the women's liberation movement in the United States, for she enlarged on the many privileges that American women enjoyed. When we told her about our Women's Lib, she seemed somewhat amazed and abruptly changed the subject.

"Do you know," she asked, "that I am the only remaining national leader who still holds office and who has attended all three conferences of non-aligned states?"

She ticked off with a smile those once-powerful nabobs of the Third World who had fallen or died, Nkrumah, Sukarno and Sihanouk among them. "But," she said, with understandable vanity and a good deal of womanly satisfaction, "I have survived and come back to the head of my government." We toasted her good health in the grape juice with which she had provided us and left Temple Trees with a cordial farewell.

Neither the Prime Minister nor her government nor the supposedly watchful worthies of the American embassy appeared worried then that a rebellious movement among her own supporters would soon come dangerously close to overthrowing her and send her scurrying first of all to Britain and the United States for help.

Behind the Uprising

Ceylon's insurgency did not burst without warning upon a surprised and almost defenseless land. There had been abundant evidence, much of it published in the country's conformist press, to show that the 10,000 young members of the People's Liberation Front were preparing for trouble. Founded in 1964 during an otherwise pointless university strike in Colombo, the front had been planning—and arming its membership—for at least three years, and some accounts say even more. Locally, these hairy and wild-eyed youths were known as Che Guevarists after the late Cuban leader whom they idolize.

During our comparatively brief visit to Ceylon, there was a meeting of the National Security Council to hear reports on what was termed the continual surveillance of the People's Liberation Front. The service commanders and their CID people as well as the police chiefs were represented. The reason for the meeting apparently was a recent rally of the Guevarists at which pamphlets were distributed by the Peking branch of the Ceylon Communist Party arguing that a successful revolution depends on the participation of the masses and not merely the activities of a handful of guerrillas.[55]

However, despite the surveillance and the activities of both the police and the Army, very little was done to head off an uprising. While the Army was supposed to have 30,000 effectives, its actual strength was closer to about 7,000 and it was both poorly armed and ill-trained. As for the police, they were competent mainly to direct

[55] *Ceylon Daily News*, August 13, 1970, p. 1.

traffic in Colombo. Scant wonder that the Guevarists, as was later shown, expressed confidence that they could take over the government and become the masters of Ceylon in less than a month.

In the early spring of 1971, a bomb factory blew up in Colombo and killed some of the rebels. Next, the Guevarists demonstrated against the American embassy, always a favorite target, and did a certain amount of damage. By March 17, the Guevarists had spread so much terror throughout the villages that Prime Minister Bandaranaike finally had to move against them, even though they had been among her warmest supporters. She declared a state of emergency in a broadcast to the nation, warning that the guerrillas were planning an uprising and appealing for support for her government in the name of "the preservation of democracy and Socialism."

Much worse was yet to come. On April 5, the guerrillas launched their major offensive all over the island in a coordinated and well-planned campaign. They wrecked police stations, repulsed small groups of soldiers who attacked them, and seized a considerable amount of territory in central Ceylon. Almost at once, the government blamed the American Central Intelligence Agency, one of Finance Minister Perera's pet hates. But as the struggle continued, and Mrs. Bandaranaike applied for and received help from the United States and Britain, the suspicions of her government shifted to the activities of Communist countries in general and the North Koreans in particular. In the name of Kim Il Sung, the North Koreans had been trying to export pint-sized revolutions for some time and were said to have been in contact with the Guevarists almost as soon as Ceylon recognized the government at Pyongyang. In any event, it was North Korean diplomats who were expelled from Ceylon on charges of aiding and abetting the rebels, not the spectral operatives of the CIA.

In a speech thereafter, Mrs. Bandaranaike announced that because the North Koreans had refused to desist from aiding the rebels, she had obliged their ambassador to close the embassy and leave the country. And an excited official commented in Washington, "You see what happened in the showdown? After everything she has said about us, she had to come to us for help."

The United States didn't send very much—four helicopters and

8,000 pounds of spare parts as a beginning. The British sent in substantial quantities of other arms and ammunition. Somewhat later, the Soviet Union contributed six old MIG 17s and crews, the latter strictly for training purposes, for use against the rebels. India flew in five helicopters and 150 infantrymen to guard the airport and embassy while Pakistan, not to be outdone, supplied two helicopters.[56] Just about the only power of consequence that didn't seem concerned at first over the rebellion was China, but even Peking softened its position later.

Within a month, the rebel forces were on the defensive, their estimated strength reduced to a hard core of about 1,500 to 2,000, and the government felt strong enough to offer amnesty to those who were willing to abandon the struggle. It was one of the few times in recent history when American armed intervention in a foreign country did not produce a wave of international denunciation and domestic outcry. The United States response, after all, was minimal—less, on the whole, than that of the Soviet Union and Britain.

The United States and Ceylon

What is the American interest in Ceylon? Commercially, the United States lost interest during Sirimavo Bandaranaike's first government when Ceylon announced the take-over of Shell, Esso and Caltex by nationalizing petroleum imports and internal distribution of oil in 1962. Washington then suspended aid to Ceylon. In 1970, by nationalizing marine bunkering and aviation fuel, the Ceylonese oil take-over was completed.

There has been, in consequence, no appreciable American interest in trade with Ceylon. What does matter is the rising Soviet interest in Ceylon, particularly since the frustration of the revolt that almost certainly would have made Chinese influence dominant in the island. Both Soviet and Chinese *apparatchiks* were present in force in the Bandaranaike government before the uprising; since then, the pro-Chinese politicians have not been heard from to any marked extent.

Yet, in the familiar Peking manner, trade between Ceylon and China has continued to flourish. Next to Britain, China remains the

[56] Reuters dispatch in *Japan Times*, April 18, 1971, p. 12; *The New York Times* dispatches April 21, 1971, and April 28, 1971.

island republic's biggest trading partner and the Sino-Ceylon Rubber-Rice Pact is the most important single trade agreement in Colombo's portfolio. What it amounts to is that Ceylon annually barters about 40,000 tons of its sheet rubber for about 200,000 tons of Chinese rice, putting the two-way trade turnover at around $80 million. In addition, during 1971, China gave Ceylon a $25 million interest-free loan, just to make sure there were no hard feelings, a handsome addition to the $67 million Ceylon already had received in Chinese economic aid.

There are, of course, advantages for China in this relationship that Peking would be reluctant to lose to the Russians. Ceylon decided in 1971 to import more than half its textile needs from China, a matter of 50 million yards. That meant an increase in the balance of trade in China's favor, and in 1970 that amounted to $6 million from Ceylon alone.[57]

The Soviet Union's interest in Ceylon is, of course, to keep Chinese influence on the island within reasonable bounds. There have been persistent reports, only weakly denied in Ceylon, that under certain circumstances the Soviet Union would be interested in leasing the huge Trincomalee base for the use of the Red Fleet in the Indian Ocean. The Soviets already have Mauritius, which is sufficient for their current naval needs. If they should want to do more in the Indian Ocean than show the flag on occasion, Trincomalee would suit them perfectly.

The United States seems not to be particularly disturbed by the prospect, although the British are making a certain amount of to-do. The most the American government has decided to do so far in those waters is to construct a $20 million communications base on British-owned Diego Garcia Island, a part of the Chagos archipelago between Ceylon and Mauritius. This is being done under the terms of a bilateral agreement entered into with Britain in 1966, with the base scheduled for completion in 1974. Since the island is only eleven square miles in area, the most it could be used for would be a communications link between the Anglo-American fleets in the Indian Ocean and an airstrip.[58]

[57] *Far Eastern Economic Review*, June 19, 1971, pp. 43–44.
[58] Hong Kong *Standard*, December 17, 1970, p. 2, sec. 2.

On the available evidence, the interest of the great powers in the Indian Ocean for the present is a matter of low priority. That, too, is the case in United States relations with Ceylon, even though the U.S. Navy is now more welcome there than it has been in the past.

Another Dictatorship?

Time is running out for both democracy and socialization in Ceylon. More and more, the thoughts of disgruntled leaders in both major parties are turning to more drastic and authoritarian solutions. J. R. Jayewardene, the opposition leader, has said that to send more foreign aid into Ceylon is "like giving oxygen to a man who needs an operation." And Felix Dias Bandaranaike, a rightist in the ruling Freedom Party, is becoming increasingly disenchanted with the notion that visionary Socialism will pull Ceylon out of its tailspin. "You can't sacrifice a people for the sake of preserving a dogma," he said at the time of the Guevarist uprising.[59]

The immediate future, therefore, is not very inviting for Ceylon with its rising unemployment and debt and its declining prospects in agriculture, industry and foreign trade. While Mrs. Bandaranaike's government is planning on nationalizing almost everything in sight, the "Aid Ceylon" Club is unlikely to foot the bill very much longer. Not a great deal of additional money can be expected from the consortium, consisting of the United States, Britain, Canada, West Germany, France, Japan and Australia, until Ceylon puts its house in order. Scant wonder that the government is taking a new look at China and hoping for a better trade relationship.

Ceylon is a lovely island with a patient and hard-working people, better educated than their neighbors on the subcontinent, and far more favorably situated. Under proper management, it could be one of the most prosperous and satisfying lands on earth, a veritable Hawaii of the Indian Ocean. Whatever its governments have been doing since its independence, there is very little that has been right. Otherwise, Ceylon would not now be in an unholy mess, a worse fix than any that could be devised by the miserable foreign plotters whom the island's politicians blame for all their troubles. Actually, if

[59] *Far Eastern Economic Review*, March 27, 1971, pp. 75–79.

blame is to be allotted, the source is much closer to home. For the tragedy of Ceylon is the weakness of its government, not its people.

5. WHO WILL HELP SOUTH ASIA?

There is a monumental impatience with South Asia and its suffering peoples elsewhere in the world. Sometimes, it seems as if there is so much misery on the subcontinent, and so little hope of relief, that the international community insensibly averts its gaze and lets itself grow callous in the face of a towering tragedy. The United Nations, paralyzed by great-power rivalries, stood by helplessly while India was inundated by 10 million refugees from East Pakistan and its Security Council could not even pass an effective cease-fire resolution during the Indian invasion that led to the creation of Bangladesh. Nor did U Thant, in his final weeks as Secretary General before his replacement by Kurt Waldheim of Austria, find the intestinal fortitude to make even a mild protest against the killing and burning.

If the international community is so apathetic in the face of war in South Asia, its detachment becomes almost inhuman in times of peace. One foreign correspondent, with long experience in the coverage of the subcontinent in what passes for normal times, has said, "South Asia might in some weeks fall into the Indian Ocean for all the attention it gets in the United States." A former American ambassador, whose view was pretty much the same, said he felt that his reports from South Asia were largely ignored by the State Department except in times of extreme crisis.

Unjust and untrue though it may be, the countries of South Asia generally cut a hapless figure in the rest of the world. The Japanese, who are willing to trade with almost anybody, are not enthusiastic about the subcontinent and generally prefer to take their business elsewhere. The British, from long experience, despair of persuading such diverse peoples to agree even on plans that are to their mutual advantage. The Russians, India's allies, after going to a lot of trouble in helping set up the Bokharo steel mill, complained privately about the difficulties of working with the Indians. And in the United States, home of the most determined tourists on earth, few who have ever seen India or Pakistan want to return.

All the participants in international financing who meet periodically to dole out funds to India, Pakistan and Ceylon are not going to change such melancholy views, for the remedy does not consist of money alone. Nor is it likely that recourse to the Socialist mystique, in all its strange Asian guises and apparitions, will be sufficient to bring about a magical change in the human condition on the subcontinent. As for the United Nations, its humanitarian record in South Asia to date does not justify much hope for progress despite its developing new program of disaster relief.

If the subcontinent is to be rescued from poverty and pestilence and all the other ills that follow them, the first requirement is peace. Three wars in a quarter-century, and the resultant tensions, have created an appalling loss in human life and suffering. Another one could well prove catastrophic for the peoples of South Asia. Here, surely, the international community has a role to play in bringing pressure to bear on the great powers who have made South Asia a kind of cynical sideshow to their global rivalry. Whatever happens on the subcontinent is not going to be decisive for the future of the United States, the Soviet Union and China. But they can, if they are not careful, fragment the subcontinent into weak and warring states that will sink into confusion and chaos.

The great powers, therefore, bear the major responsibility for the future of South Asia. While they may not be able to dictate a final settlement between India and Pakistan, they can—if they will—create an atmosphere that is conducive to agreement. Should the basis for a durable peace be developed, then the subcontinent will have a chance to work out its own destiny. But if the struggle for peace is lost once more, then nothing on the subcontinent is likely to change in fifty years. In fact, the odds are that things will be a lot worse before they get better.

VII. The Emergence of China

1. THE DRAGON ROARS

During one of China's periodic domestic convulsions, which so fascinated and mystified the outside world for weeks at a time, an American reporter newly returned from Peking called at the Department of State for enlightenment. He was welcomed effusively as a seer from far places.

To his immense gratification, he was promptly ushered into the presence of the contemporary presiding genius of Foggy Bottom, Secretary of State William P. Rogers, whose first words were: "What in the world is going on in China?"

To which the somewhat startled correspondent replied, "Mr. Secretary, if you don't know, then we are indeed lost."

It was cold comfort to the Secretary of State, with the matchless intelligence resources of the United States at his command, to realize that the position of foreign experts inside China was no less disconcerting than his own. As any long-suffering member of the corps of correspondents in Peking could have told him, there were nights in the Chinese capital when they could hear immense cheering from

50,000 people in a nearby stadium without having the faintest notion of what was going on.

War or Peace?

This inconvenient Chinese practice of maintaining secrecy over the events affecting 800,000,000 people remains one of the central problems of dealing with whatever government is in power in Peking.

To be sure, the Chinese have excellent reasons for doing their best to keep their own counsel. In the late 1960s and early 1970s, they had to reckon with 1,000,000 Soviet troops strung out in menacing fashion along their common 4,000-mile border, with the support of the vast Soviet armory of nuclear-tipped missiles, a powerful air force and vast fleets of tanks and other mobile weapons. Under such circumstances, the long-held notion of the American right wing that China was an aggressive power bent on world conquest became increasingly difficult to justify.

Regardless of the satisfaction Peking may have felt over the American military pullout to the south in Vietnam, the overtures from Washington for improved relations and the heartening recognition of the United Nations, no Chinese could feel secure when he did not know if there would be peace or war with the Soviet Union on the morrow. Faced with such a continual threat over acrimonious border disputes, China grimly prepared its defenses.

Nor could the Chinese accept with equanimity the spectacle of a new and even more powerful Japan, which had developed into the third-greatest industrial state in the world under the protection of the American atomic umbrella. It made sense to the leaders of China to assume that Japan would not remain forever weak as a military force, bound by a self-imposed restraint to renounce war as an instrument of national policy. When Premier Chou En-lai sounded the alarm over the $16 billion Japanese military expansion program for 1972–76, it was perfectly evident that he had the heartfelt support of a people that had endured and surmounted decades of Japanese military savagery.

Despite the immediacy of the Soviet menace, therefore, Japan still remained the ancient enemy for China. As for the United States, branded during a quarter century of Chinese Communist propaganda as the center of all evil and imperialist encroachment, the new line of negotiation did not necessarily mean that Peking's ideas about the American giant had changed. True, the digging of air-raid shelters went on under all China's major cities in preparation for possible Soviet attack. But the Chinese did not seem to place any more trust in Washington. Xenophobia, an old Chinese ailment, could not easily be overcome in a world that China had never made and, in all probability, did not really understand.

The Chinese Pilgrimage

In the era since Mao Tse-tung had hoisted his five-starred red flag in Peking's Tienanmen Square on October 1, 1949, and proclaimed the establishment of the People's Republic, China had reversed its nineteenth-century history as a weak, corrupt nation, a prey to every predator of Europe and Asia. While it was slow in its economic development and far from the status of a great power, it had become one of the most important nations on earth. Neither the United States nor the Soviet Union nor Japan nor any lesser land could now ignore the dragon's roar.

It was no wonder, therefore, that in the period immediately after the end of the Great Cultural Revolution all roads in Asia led sooner or later to Peking. Month by month, the parade of foreign delegations and distinguished individuals into China grew longer. The hotel accommodations and travel routes by rail and air were taxed to the limit by the influx, unparalleled in twenty years, which was climaxed by President Nixon's visit at the end of February 1972.

Even China's traditionally bountiful hospitality was strained. The relatively small corps of talented young escort officers and translators in the Chinese foreign service found themselves in so much demand that they could get little or no rest. For the visiting foreigner, dignitary or not, was first of all a ferocious and insatiable tourist who wanted to go everywhere and see everything while going through the motions of transacting official business.

These new pilgrims to China came from everywhere. As was to be expected, many were from Communist lands under Russian influence and received the most solicitous treatment; to China, every such visitor was a challenge and an opportunity. At least one major

Chinese diplomatic triumph over the Soviet Union was celebrated in song and story—a theatrical production entitled *The Seduction of Rumania*.

There were others. Together with infiltration and subversion, the Chinese of all eras have delighted in the arts of seduction and they did not change their ways in a time of extreme danger. Even in a period of renewed tension marked by the sudden cancellation of the classic parade for National Day on October 1, 1971, the Chinese spared no effort to persuade their Communist visitors that Peking, not Moscow, was the capital of the only true and enduring Marxist-Leninist faith.

Important though the Communist tourists were to Chinese ideologues, the Chinese government paid increased attention as well to the less comfortable but better-heeled pilgrims from non-Communist and even anti-Communist countries. Here, a certain amount of judicious *pro forma* denunciation had to be mixed with the traditional hearts-and-flowers Chinese approach to the stranger within the Gate of Heavenly Peace. For above all else, Communist appearances had to be preserved by Peking regardless of the direction that was taken by a whirligig foreign policy. In consequence, varying formulae were developed in accordance with circumstances.

Thus, the visiting Japanese business people were obliged to listen to standard Chinese denunciations of their "militaristic" government before being admitted by contract to Chinese commercial transactions. The visiting Americans were told at every turn how much the Chinese loved the American people and despised their government, a line that inevitably had to be softened in the period of arrangements for President Nixon's announced visit. The worst denunciations of all, as might have been expected, were reserved for the treacherous Russians even while trade and border negotiations were going on.

All this was very Chinese. It had little to do with Maoism; certainly, it didn't grow out of the barrel of a gun. Quite simply put, the Chinese demanded to be accepted on their own terms. And out of their age-old belief in their innate superiority over foreign barbarians of whatever origin, based on some 5,000 years of recorded history, they expected that their curious conduct would not be challenged.

Whether it was or not, the post-Cultural Revolution changes in

China were profound. The flow of pilgrims to Peking encompassed all kinds of people, from West European capitalists to American Black Panthers. Foreign businessmen by the thousands descended on the Canton trade fairs. Ever larger delegations of Japanese shuttled between China's major cities and their own. Selected correspondents from the American news media, interspersed with other American citizens, began again to tour a land that some had not seen for two decades and others were visiting for the first time. Even a handful of Russian dignitaries, admitted to Peking for compelling reasons of state at a time of tension, were given selected glimpses of Chinese life here and there, but always under tight escort. By contrast, someone like Professor Robert Ruhlmann, a Chinese-speaking French Orientalist, was permitted to go on an unescorted bicycle tour of China's greatest cities.[1]

All this was quite a turnabout for China. It testified to the zealousness with which this new China was courting world opinion. The campaign that Peking had waged so vigorously to join the United Nations, once so despised by true Maoists, was not merely for the purpose of replacing Taiwan in the Security Council and wielding the veto, or even embarrassing both Washington and Moscow. It was conclusive evidence that China had decided to end its long isolation from the world.

Who Runs China?

The manner in which this decision was taken, and the measures that were adopted to repress those who opposed it, are still among the unsolved mysteries of China's internal politics. But there can be no doubt that the people in power, of whom Premier Chou En-lai was the most visible, were determined to maintain their course in their policies toward both the United Nations and the United States.

It was a 180-degree shift from the extreme isolation that was imposed on China at the height of the Cultural Revolution from 1966 to 1969, when all ambassadors save one (to Cairo) were recalled to Peking and members of the scanty press corps in Peking were terrorized and even arrested to keep them in line. To the outside world, the

[1] Prof. Ruhlmann visited China in the fall of 1970 and told me of his experiences thereafter at Shatin, Hong Kong, N.T.

changes came with agonizing slowness. One by one, some of the familiar figures in the Chinese government who had vanished during the Cultural Revolution reappeared, their hands roughened by honest toil. Coincidentally, many of the leaders of the frightful Maoist uprising dropped from sight without explanation.

The New China News Agency (NCNA) and other official Chinese sources periodically issued long lists of names of "responsible persons" who had reassumed power in the land. At the top level, these listings ran to hundreds of names, some well known, but including many whose backgrounds were not known abroad. With the rebuilding of the Chinese Communist Party, which had been wrecked down to the local and regional levels during the purge, additional thousands of names were put out for the record but relatively few of them provided a clue to the rationale behind the reorganization.

The only check the outside world was able to run on the Chinese power structure generally was the result of the publication of pictures, the identification of leaders atop the Gate of Heavenly Peace or the publication of the names of ranking chieftains on the two great holidays, May 1 and October 1. It was in this manner that the regime signaled the downfall of Lin Piao, who had been deputy party leader, defense minister and the chosen successor to Mao Tse-tung, as well as the purge of such leaders of the Cultural Revolution as Chen Po-ta and Kang Sheng and a covey of military men headed by the chief of staff of the armed forces, Huang Yung-sheng.

At the beginning of 1972, Premier Chou En-lai, at seventy-four years of age, had become No. 2 to Chairman Mao and was directing the day-to-day operations of the government. Chiang Ching, Mao's wife, was still high in the counsels of the Politburo, but different personalities were joining these top three in the exercise of power. Among them were listed Yeh Chien-ying, who at seventy-two apparently was exercising military authority; Chang Chun-chiao and Yao Wen-yuan, both Shanghai party leaders; Li Hsien-nien, Chou En-lai's chief aide and a deputy premier, and the eighty-five-year-old Tung Pi-wu, whose functions were ceremonial.[2]

The story of the change in the top group in China apparently

[2] This list was put together on the basis of numerous NCNA announcements and analysis by research organizations in Hong Kong and elsewhere.

began with the 1971 May Day proceedings when Lin Piao last was seen in company with Mao Tse-tung. Mao, as chairman of the central committee of the Chinese Communist Party, appeared atop the Gate of Heavenly Peace in Tienanmen Square accompanied by two nurses. Lin departed almost at once. Mao acknowledged the cheers of the crowd, but left soon afterward. The imperturbable Chou En-lai, as premier, took over. And it was Chou thereafter who took charge of the altogether pleasant chore of greeting and entertaining foreign diplomatic missions and other teams of notables. What was wrong with Mao? The infirmities of age, judging from official Chinese films of him that were distributed outside China.

During the ensuing months, it was tempting to theorize that Chou was the real leader of China because of his high visibility and his obvious direction of the brilliant diplomatic offensive that brought China into the United Nations. There is no doubt that this symbol of moderation in Peking was mainly responsible for sending more than sixty Chinese ambassadors back to their posts, as well as reorganizing the government. But he always told interviewers that he did his work at the direction of Chairman Mao.

Indeed, in the draft Constitution that was prepared for the National People's Congress[3] but never adopted, there was no mention of Chou and no provision for any regency if Mao and Lin were unable to act. This was the document that made Mao the reigning deity in the land—"the great leader of all the peoples of the entire state, the Head of State of our Proletarian Dictatorship State, and the Supreme Commander of the whole State-whole Army." As for Vice Chairman Lin, he was identified as the Chairman's "closest comrade-in-arms . . . his successor and the Deputy Commander of the whole State-whole Army."

What happened to upset this apparently fixed order of succession? Not many months after the text of the constitution became known toward the end of 1970, rumors circulated in Hong Kong of a falling out in the Politburo. Thereafter, when Henry Kissinger visited Peking secretly to arrange for President Nixon's visit, the rumors intensified. It was obvious that the extreme left did not want a rapprochement with the United States, or even the appearance of one.

[3] Text as released by Nationalist China on November 3, 1970.

But few would have guessed that Lin Piao would lead the opposition to Chairman Mao, and fewer still believed at first the widely circulated story that Lin had led an attempt to assassinate Mao and perished thereafter.[4] The whole business was so riddled with intrigue and false clues that it was extremely difficult to get at the truth.

What did survive the draft constitution's shattered delegation of power was the concept of "whole State-whole Army." It suggested the creation of an organizational trinity—a union of the People's Liberation Army (PLA), the government and a reconstituted Chinese Communist Party (CCP). But since the CCP organization was still in the process of reconstruction at the time the constitution was written, it followed that the PLA remained the principal source of authority in China and the guarantor of public order as well as governmental stability.

The power of the PLA was made evident by the presence of a group of 159 military officers on the Tienanmen rostrum on May Day, 1971. It was still another step in the annual increase in the military presence there, from 53 on October 1, 1969, to 129 on May 1, 1970, and 136 on October 1, 1970. The Chinese government's decision to cancel the National Day parade a year later was symptomatic of the falling out between Marshal Lin and the army high command on the one hand and the Mao-Chou group on the other. But while the army's leadership may have changed drastically, the army's responsibility did not.

The Mao-Chou group now had to devise ways of breaking the news to the country and they seized on a typical Chinese device of indirectly approaching bad news. To the denunciation of Mao's old enemy, Liu Shao-chi, the prime victim of the Cultural Revolution, official publications and broadcasts added the phrase, "Those of the same gang as Liu Shao-chi." At first, this was a code name for Chen Po-ta, once the devoted friend and confidant of Mao. Later, the phrase was extended to cover Marshal Lin and his cohorts.[5] It was in this manner that the public was prepared for the shock.

Yet, the PLA retained enough muscle in China to play a major role in both the government and the reconstituted Communist Party in

[4] Stewart Alsop in *Newsweek*, December 20, 1971, p. 104.
[5] It was used in all official publications and broadcasts for many months.

that confused and trying era. Military leaders appeared to dominate the lower and middle areas of the new Communist Party apparatus that was installed in China's 21 provinces, five autonomous regions and two municipalities—Peking and Shanghai.[6] Technically, the rebuilding process was completed shortly after the celebration on July 1, 1971, of the 50th anniversary of the founding of the CCP. Actually, however, Lin's fall shook the whole establishment.

It was in the Politburo that the decline of PLA influence first became evident. At one time, eight of the thirteen people listed under the names of Mao and Lin in this supreme authority were military people.[7] But in the latter part of 1971 and early 1972, some of the most prominent dropped from sight and the outside world had to wait to determine whether they had been purged, exiled or simply taken to cover. The outward movement of the military was less evident in the central committee of the Communist Party, of which the military had formed roughly half the representation at the height of Lin's authority.[8]

At the grass roots, however, the available evidence seemed to indicate that it was hard to cancel out the PLA's influence for two reasons: 1) The central government didn't have that much reach in Mao's declining days, and 2) There wasn't anybody else to substitute for the military, once the showdown came with the extreme left. The saving grace for China was that the PLA, under stress, proved to be no more monolithic than the state itself. The extent of factionalism and the strength of the pull away from central authority were carefully concealed, but the tendency was there.

One of the principal reasons for the military assumption of provincial authority, at the outset, was the manner in which the Communist Party was reconstituted. Regional party congresses, in the first instance, had elected the new provincial party organizations, which were known as revolutionary committees. They had been intended to replace the extreme left that in many cases had seized control of the People's Councils as the administrative organs of the various provinces. As time went on, the revolutionary committees showed every

---

6 Including Taiwan, China actually lists 22 provinces.
7 *The Economist*, October 10, 1970, p. 18.
8 *Far Eastern Economic Review*, October 3, 1970, p. 16.

sign of becoming a permanent part of the interwoven combination of PLA, government and party.[9]

Except for ever-independent Shanghai and several other places, this re-formed and re-grouped Communist Party apparatus therefore bore the military stamp. Joining the military were the old cadres which had survived the Cultural Revolution and now emerged to resume their accustomed activities. The extreme left *apparatchiks* were heavy losers in this process.

Many an embittered young activist who had taken part in the Red Guard uprising that tore China apart found himself shorn of power. In numerous instances, the extreme leftists were banished to distant farm communes. Now and then one would turn up in Hong Kong, having gotten past the border guards and made the long and danger- ous swim to freedom. When they told their stories, it was evident that the cause of the extreme left in China had suffered heavily through frustration, disillusion and defection.

Despite the continuing importance of the military in China, how- ever, it would be an error to assume that the military are able to do as they please. The fate of Lin and his associates would appear to indicate quite the contrary. And yet, it would be an equally grave mistake to discount the PLA as a major force in the government of China. This dichotomous role has developed because the PLA is no ordinary army. With its estimated strength of 2,300,000, not count- ing the militia, it is the most politicized armed force in the world. A dual command system dictates its every move, except in the most critical border regions facing the Russians, with a political com- missar at the side of every regional commander. This kind of organization is intended to act as a brake on the individual ambitions of China's stronger generals; in the Lin crisis, evidently the system worked.

The signals from Peking that all was not well came to the provinces in numerous ways. For example, once it had been established that Chen Po-ta was in disfavor, China's provincial chieftains learned from their newspapers, journals and radio that others also had fallen from power. The ideological journal *Hung Chi (Red Flag)* then made an oblique attack on Lin Piao as a "sham Marxist" and a

[9] *South China Morning Post*, November 30, 1970, p. 14.

"bourgeois schemer." Finally, a joint editorial of the *People's Daily, Hung Chi* and the *Liberation Army Daily* assailed Lin, although not directly by name, as a "chieftain of the opportunist line" and accused him of "illicit relations with foreign countries." The joint editorial concluded ominously:

"In our party's history, these bourgeois careerists, conspirators and persons having illicit relations with foreign countries, who clung to opportunist lines and engaged in conspiracies, could not but bring ruin, disgrace and destruction upon themselves in the end."[10]

Yet, the whole process remained infinitely puzzling to the outside world, for rumors were also circulating about Mao's demise as well. The seventy-eight-year-old Mao put a halt to rumors about his incapacity, for the time being, by receiving President Nixon at his home in Peking on February 21, 1972, and posing for television films that were circulated all over the world. That did not really dispel the widely held belief that the great helmsman's grip was weakening. In this extremity, it appeared that a collection of leaders, headed by Premier Chou, was conducting the central government in Peking, but Mao still had the power of the final word.

Hazards of the PLA

The PLA has played a major role in every struggle that has convulsed China since Mao's assumption of power in 1949. Chairman Mao, suffering from severe loss of support in the CCP after the failure of his "Great Leap Forward" in 1958, turned to the PLA and made Lin the Defense Minister the following year. It was Lin who politicized the military, but he did so with the encouragement of the great helmsman. By 1964, Mao was sponsoring a propaganda campaign, "Learn from the PLA." And when the Americans escalated the Vietnam War in 1965 and the military hard-liners sought to intervene, Mao and Lin joined forces to keep them in line.

Mao was now ready to move against the massive Communist Party organization which had, in a sense, rejected him. Once again, Lin and the PLA were behind the Chairman when he struck against President Liu Shao-chi and Peng Chen, the mayor of Peking. It

---

[10] Joint editorial, December 1, 1971; *Hung Chi* editorial, November 13, 1971. The Changsha, Chengtu and Nanning radios also were in the campaign.

wasn't enough, however, for Peng to be brought down. Mao wanted Liu's head as well, but here the PLA was in a curiously ambivalent position. At length, Mao turned loose the only force he could command, the tens of thousands of young student activists who formed themselves into Red Guard units and were only too anxious to do his bidding. The PLA waited on the sidelines. But Lin, still loyal to his chief, marched with him as the Cultural Revolution broke in full force.

Between June 1966 and January 1967, the Red Guards waged a hectic but largely ineffective war against regional Communist Party organizations to try to bring them over to the Maoist side. In this struggle the PLA acted sometimes as an arms supplier, sometimes as a restraining agent, on the hotheaded youthful activists. It depended on the commander, the region and the strategic situation. But at the beginning of 1967, when the Red Guards decided to seize power for themselves, they were brought into direct conflict with the PLA in many places. Despite orders to the military to support the Red Guards, many a commander either kept hands off the political mess or tried to form a coalition consisting of the young activists, the old and reliable officials and the PLA. In the resultant turmoil, the party organization became paralyzed.

The Red Guards, striking for total control, pressed their advantage. They succeeded in obtaining an order, issued April 6, 1967, that forbade the PLA to suppress any mass organization without direct authority from the central government and to "rectify mistakes" it had committed. The celebrated Wuhan incident of mid-July 1967 was the result and perhaps the turning point in the whole Red Guard offensive. For Chen Tsai-tao, commander of the Wuhan Military Region, disregarded orders from Peking to back a particular Red Guard faction there and was dismissed. To make matters worse, the excitable Chiang Ching, Mao's wife, demanded in Peking that the Red Guards "drag out the handful of power holders in the army."

That did it. The other regional commanders of the PLA let it be known that they could countenance no more Wuhans. The first sign of a change came with the purging of the Red Guard leader of Wuhan, Wang Li. Next, on September 5, 1967, Chiang Ching utterly reversed herself by condemning attacks on the PLA and urging the

Red Guards to restrain themselves. At the same time, the central leadership in Peking forbade further attacks on the PLA.

Military commanders now had an implicit directive to try to restore order, but they could not suppress the Red Guards for fear of antagonizing Mao and Lin and they were reluctant to turn on the old reliable CCP regional organizations, even if they were in complete disarray. As a result, the Red Guards burst loose for one more splurge between April and July 1968, bringing China to the verge of anarchy. It was too much. The Maoists in Peking tried to save the Red Guards by introducing "Worker-Peasant Thought Propaganda Teams" into the countryside to forestall a frontal attack by the PLA. But this time, despite a defiant Red Guard proclamation that the country was at last "all red" and presumably all Mao, the revolutionaries had come to the end of the road.

The PLA began breaking up the Red Guard organizations all over the land and dispatching many of the activists to the countryside and remote border areas to work at hard labor. With the sessions of the Ninth Party Congress in April 1969, the Cultural Revolution was liquidated. If the PLA remained the only unchallenged power in the land, this is not to say that it was able to exert its authority. Somehow, the Chinese were able to reconcile the forms of government on which Mao had insisted with the necessary role of the military in maintaining order. The effort was logical enough. For the truth is that the PLA, being so much a part of the new China, suffered from the same ideological strains and stresses as the people, the government and the new party-building apparatus.

Just what happened to the intricate and necessary relationship between the ruling trinity of Mao, Lin and Chou En-lai is still very much of a mystery. Chou has revealed that the central government's bureaucracy, over which he presides, was cut from 60,000 to only 10,000 officials as a result of the Cultural Revolution. In part, this could very well be attributed to Lin's zeal in urging the Red Guards to attack the old-line bureaucrats. Chou tried by every device to protect his people, but he couldn't save everybody. Neither, for that matter, could Lin; inside the PLA, there were sacrifices of key personnel, as well.

But in the end, when the Red Guards went too far, it is evident that

Chou's will finally prevailed and order was restored. The Premier was thus indebted as much as anybody to the PLA's ability to restore order in the land, although he argued subsequently that the PLA could not and should not dominate the government or party. "That," he said, "will never happen."[11] It should have been a warning signal to Lin Piao against pressing his advantage too far, but Lin disregarded it. The rest is history.

Thus, Mao's bizarre revolution in the end was turned against some of those who began it. On the surface, the great helmsman achieved his aim of overthrowing his "revisionist" enemies headed by the deposed chief of state, Liu Shao-chi. But in the process Mao sacrificed his chosen successor, the sixty-three-year-old Lin; his secretary and one-time favorite, Chen Po-ta; numerous military comrades from the days of the Long March, and others who had worked with him in the Politburo. Nor was Mao in the end able to create a new Maoist man any more than Stalin had been able to create a new "Soviet man." For just as Stalin's purge trials nearly destroyed his society, Mao's revolution came very close to wrecking China.[12]

The Chinese Economy

For a country as large as China, where even population estimates are open to question, the problem of developing a reliable system of economic statistics is overwhelming. This is particularly true because of the differences between China's system of rewards and incentives (no income tax, for one) and those of the industrially advanced countries, so that comparisons are bound to be misleading. Still, by any standard, China remains poor, with 80 per cent of her people living on the land and 20 per cent in the overcrowded urban areas. Bearing in mind the comparatively low standard of living maintained in China, estimates of an average wage of $20 a month for industrial workers and $10 to $15 a month for farm commune peasants seem credible. The Chinese officially claim that typical factory workers earn monthly wages respectively of $16, $19 and $23 for three separate

[11] Edgar Snow in the magazine *Epoca*, Milan, Italy, February 28, 1971.

[12] I have put together this all-too-brief summation of the role of the PLA from consultations with Hong Kong scholars and research groups, talks with refugees in Hong Kong, materials from China press sources and such publications as *Current Scene*, May 7, 1971.

pay grades for a forty-eight-hour week, that farm commune people earn less and that managerial staff are paid more. Some figures for supervisory help go up to $200 a month, but these rates are very high for China.

In any event, Chinese wages should be considered within the context of China's economy. In typical cases, rents today for a one- or two-room apartment run $1 to $3 a month; rice is 7 cents a pound; eggs, 30 cents a dozen; milk, 10 cents a quart; vegetables in season, 1 or 2 cents a pound; and fruits about the same. A pack of Chinese cigarettes costs only a few cents, and cereals, cooking oils and cotton cloth are rationed.[13] Even if the average annual income in China does not exceed $100 to $125 a year, people live better than they did before the Mao era and nobody starves.

One of the keys to China's economic progress is the regime's target of 880 pounds of grain per person per year, or about 300,000,000 tons a year. The base of most estimates of Chinese grain production is the 1957 figure of 185,000,000 tons. Premier Chou En-lai's estimate of 240,000,000 tons, given to Edgar Snow in 1971 as the production figure for 1970, was boosted to 246,000,000 tons for the following year in an authoritative announcement by Hsin Hua. The chances are that both figures may be inflated by about 10 per cent, foreign observers believe. In any event, despite propaganda claims of self-sufficiency in grain, China's goal of 300,000,000 tons remains distant.

There are, however, reasons other than shortfalls in domestic production for the continued Chinese imports of wheat. For one thing, millions of tons of grain have been given to North Vietnam and a few other nations. For another, China sells rice abroad (in Hong Kong, Ceylon and Southeast Asia) at a higher price than it is paying for its imported wheat and has quite a strong foreign aid program going. As a result, it may be 1976 before China approaches self-sufficiency in grain production, always assuming satisfactory progress is made in keeping the population growth rate down. For

13 Hong Kong's *Ta Kung Pao*, September 23, 1971, is the source of Chinese propaganda claims in wages. More realistic estimates were in the Hong Kong *Standard*, October 31, 1970, p. 1; *Time*, May 3, 1971, p. 27. A 1971 U.S. State Department study placed China's foreign aid spending at $709 million for 1970, exceeding the $204 million estimated for the Soviet Union.

China is estimated to require 30,000,000 to 35,000,000 tons of fertilizer a year and won't approach that figure until the end of the 1971–76 five-year plan. The 1971 figure for chemical fertilizer production was given by Hsin Hua as a 28 per cent increase over 1970; even so, taking Premier Chou's estimate of 14 million tons for 1970 as accurate, that would still make fewer than 18 million tons—far off target.

Industrially, Chinese progress has not been impressive even by Chou's optimistic estimates and the cheerful 1971 announcements. The ever-critical steel industry, for example, produced 10,000,000 to 18,000,000 tons annually for 1966–70 by Chou's estimates and 21,000,000 tons for 1971 by Hsin Hua's announcement. That is still far behind that of the United States or Japan or even Britain's modest 28 million tons for 1970. Oil production was better, rising from 10,000,000 to 20,000,000 tons in the five years ending in 1970, and showing a further 10 per cent increase for 1971, an estimate in which foreign and Chinese sources nearly concur. The one big claim that Chou makes for China is that the nation in the early 1970s had become the world's top producer of manufactured cotton cloth. If that is anywhere near true, it spells more bad news for the American textile industry, already hard pressed by competition from Japan, Taiwan, Hong Kong and South Korea.

There is, of course, no way of assessing Chou's contention that China in 1970 had a gross agricultural and industrial production of $120 billion, $30 billion in agriculture and $90 billion in industry. That would be a huge increase over the generous foreign estimates of $80 billion as China's GNP for 1970 and almost $90 billion for 1971. In view of the known difficulties of Chinese industry and agriculture in recovering from the blows of the Cultural Revolution and its 1971 aftermath, Chou's estimates would appear to be excessively optimistic. But one thing is certain: China is not to be ignored from now on in its campaign to become something more than a mere hand-to-mouth state, even though its results are not in a class with Japan's stellar economic performance, and it has not even maintained the pace of South Korea, Taiwan or Hong Kong.[14]

[14] I gratefully acknowledge the help I received in Hong Kong from American, British and other foreign sources in the analysis of the Chinese economy. The

The question is not whether China can continue to develop. That has been answered by the ability of the nation to pick itself up after the shattering experiences of 1966–71. As one American economist put the case: "There is no clear upper limit to how fast China could grow if a new leadership wanted to pay the price. Economic bottlenecks and military needs would probably keep the pace below that of Japan, but how far below is anybody's guess. The question is whether China's leaders still want to pay the political and social price for rapid growth."[15]

The New China Trade

During the slack business season of 1970 in Hong Kong, the great Chinese trade emporium in the Star House—biggest of the Communist government's Arts and Crafts stores—put out banners announcing a blanket 10 per cent reduction on all articles. Intrigued by the prospect of a Christmas sale under such auspices, my wife and I looked over the merchandise and were attracted by a beautiful figurine of serpentine stone in the store window, priced at HK $500, or about US $80 at the 1970 exchange rate. But when I asked for the 10 per cent reduction, as advertised, the salesman demurred, arguing that the price already had been cut. Pointing to the banner in the window that promised 10 per cent off on all articles, I suggested that perhaps there had been a mistake. The salesman conferred with his section chief and came back, beaming. I received the 10 per cent reduction and carried off my treasure for HK $450.

It was one of the few times, to my knowledge, that the Chinese have ever backed down on any matter of trade, large or small. Generally, they don't like to set bargain rates or give even mild discounts. Nor do they care to pay premiums for trade advantages. The Japanese, whose dealings with the Chinese are more extensive

---

latest figures at the time were from Premier Chou En-lai in the Snow interview in the magazine *Epoca* of February 28, 1971. Others have been issued since from time to time, the latest being in the Hsin Hua year-end file of 1971, quoted in *The New York Times*, January 2, 1972, p. 9. Other comparative figures are from the *Economist*, March 13, 1971, pp. 38–41.

[15] Professor Dwight H. Perkins of Harvard, *Current Scene*, January 8, 1971, p. 13.

than any others, say that all contracts are scrupulously kept and there has been no known default of contractual payments.

Unlike the difficult matter of estimating the progress of the Chinese economy, there is more certainty about the statistics of the new China trade, since they come basically from Peking's foreign trading partners. Despite all ideological concerns, non-Communist lands currently account for 80 per cent of China's import and export business. Had it not been for revolutionary disorder, there is little doubt that Chinese foreign trade by now would be well beyond the $5 billion mark. As it is, the record year of 1966, when exports and imports totaled $4.2 billion, was equaled only in 1970 and was going at a slightly better rate in 1971.

Taking 1970 as a typical year during this period, statistics based on foreign trade reports showed that mainland China exported $2.060 billion and imported $2.165 billion worth of products, for an adverse trade balance of $100 million. Of the total two-way trade, $3.385 billion was with non-Communist partners and only $840 million was with Communist countries. Sino-Soviet trade, which had exceeded $2 billion in 1959, dwindled to only $45 million in 1970 despite the signing of a new trade agreement between the Communist giants.

Trade with Japan and Hong Kong dominated all others in China, as had been the case for some time, but West Germany did a $250 million import-export business with China and became a major trading partner, as well. The United Kingdom, Australia, Canada, France and Singapore each did more than a $150 million business with China, but the United States total sagged to a mere $3.5 million.

China's largest import items were $360 million worth of machinery and equipment and 2,000,000 metric tons of steel worth $315 million, all from Japan. Another major import was 4,900,000 metric tons of wheat, 2,200,000 tons each from Australia and Canada, at a total cost of $290 million. Chemical fertilizers from Japan, rubber from Singapore, Malaysia and Ceylon and non-ferrous metals from various sources also were high on the Chinese list of imports.

The largest Chinese export, as always, was foodstuffs, totaling $645 million, most of it for Hong Kong. But China also did well in exporting $300 million worth of textiles and $200 million worth of clothing, mainly to Hong Kong and Japan. Other export products included textile fibers, soybeans, oil seeds and animal by-products ranging in importance from hog bristles to human hair for the wig industry.[16]

Regardless of China's very real fear of a reviving military spirit in Japan, that did not stand in the way of a thumping trade between the two nations. Japan's devotion to the mainland Chinese trade may be gauged by the expansion of two-way business between them from $23 million in 1960 to $625 million in 1969, $825 million in 1970, and a rate that was around $1 billion for 1971.[17] It is no surprise that the balance of trade turned out to be $300 million in Japan's favor, which probably accounts for the enthusiasm over China in Tokyo's business circles. There are Japanese who believe the trade with China may increase sevenfold before the 1970s end. In any case, Japan means to remain the leader in the China trade and there is very little prospect that any other nation will be able to come even close as long as the Chinese are willing to follow Japan's various initiatives.

What China is aiming at is a growth rate of somewhere between 8 and 10 per cent a year. With a lot of luck and a lot of help from non-Communist countries, primarily Japan, the Chinese just might make it in the foreseeable future.

The Endless Struggle

One of the most essential ingredients in Chinese progress is the adoption of family planning as an article of faith for the Chinese people. There is abundant evidence that the Chinese leadership is making quiet progress toward this goal, but the movement is being conducted without the blare of propaganda so characteristic of Peking's efforts at persuasion in other areas. The government is aiming first of all at making late marriages popular—twenty-five years of age for women, thirty for men—and calling for small families because of lack of housing. Then, too, teams of "barefoot doctors," as Chinese medical assistants are called, spread knowledge of birth control methods by house-to-house calls, public lectures and even public demonstrations. Finally, free birth control pills are

[16] Figures from *Current Scene*, August 7, 1971, and foreign sources in Hong Kong.

[17] *The New York Times*, April 26, 1971, p. 88, and July 21, 1971, p. 45.

passed out, condoms and other contraceptives are sold for minimal prices, abortions are easily available and sterility operations are slowly rising.

While most foreign authorities are inclined to agree that China's family planning campaign has achieved a substantial reduction in the birth rate in urban areas,[18] there is little available information on results in the agricultural communes as a whole. A visitor to one such place, the Machiao commune, eighteen miles west of Shanghai, in 1971, was told that twenty of eighty married women had had sterility operations, men were submitting to vasectomies at the rate of three a week, and both birth control pills and other contraceptive devices were in general use. For the entire area of 196 collective farms and 35,000 people, the birth rate was given as 15 to 17 per thousand but there were no figures on the death rate, which is also declining in China.[19] While there is no way of verifying scare stories of more strenuous methods of persuasion, tales have circulated in Hong Kong for some time that women who already have two children are obliged in some rural areas to undergo abortions if they become pregnant a third time.

The growth rate of China's population has been estimated by most knowledgeable foreign sources to be around 2 per cent or slightly less during the past few years. And while the Chinese government has generally used the figure of 750,000,000 for its total population, it was closer to 800,000,000 in 1971. The 800,000,000 figure was used in Premier Chou En-lai's presence by Prince Norodom Sihanouk, the deposed Cambodian chief of state, during a Peking mass rally on October 9, 1970.

Official statistics on the growth rate have been rare in China. During the "hundred flowers" period of 1957, it was given as 2.2 per cent. Peking's *China Youth Journal* of August 7, 1962, estimated it had fallen to 2 per cent. And on December 20, 1963, Premier Chou in Cairo told a Middle East News Agency correspondent that the Chinese population "increases at an average annual rate of about two

[18] Dr. Irene Taeuber, Princeton University demographer, made such a statement to a Tokyo conference October 13, 1970, as reported by Reuters.

[19] Tillman Durdin, *The New York Times*, April 21, 1971, p. 1. It is also reported in Hong Kong that the Chinese are experimenting with an anti-pregnancy pill, effective for one month.

per cent, that is, more than ten million." Two years later, on October 2, 1965, the since liquidated Yung Lung-kai, an economic expert, put the increase at 1.8 to 2 per cent annually when he spoke with foreign correspondents in Peking. It has been the last such public estimate for some time.

One of the latest foreign estimates is from John Z. Bowers, M.D., president of the Josiah Macy Jr. Foundation of New York, who uses statistics to show that the birth rate in China has fallen from 38 per thousand in 1960 to 32 in 1970, while the death rate during the same period dropped from 25 to 17, giving a natural increase in population growth from 13 to 15 per thousand.[20] A more alarming estimate is given by Carl Frisen of the United Nations Economic Commission for Asia and the Far East, who puts China's population for 1970 at 759,000,000 and believes it will be 893,000,000 by 1980.[21] The assumption he makes is that China can show no appreciable progress in the decade.

The pressures in China, however, are all toward lowering the growth rate by every means of popular persuasion. In the ancient Chinese tradition, children were a necessity for the support of parents as they grew old. But in China today, the older people are the responsibility of the group or commune with which they live and children become independent in their teens. Moreover, the Chinese Marriage Law of 1950 has had an enormous impact on the outward forms of Chinese society, with some 55,000,000 ex-housewives working in factories and farms and making up in all from 30 to 40 per cent of the Chinese work force.[22]

This scarcely means that women are "liberated" in China. Premier Chou himself has conceded: "Men and women should be equal, but there are still old habits that hinder complete equality. We must carry on the struggle. It may take ten or twenty years."[23] In that period, certainly, tens of millions of women are going to get the message favoring late marriage and small families, if they haven't already discovered the advantages for themselves.

[20] UPI report from Tokyo, October 13, 1970.
[21] *Current Scene*, January 7, 1971, pp. 18–19.
[22] *The New York Times*, June 23, 1971, p. 2, during interview with American correspondents.
[23] *Ibid.*

The Reforming of Education

For the young people, too, there is a different China. The educational system is rapidly banishing the demon of illiteracy. The new generation—and a majority of Chinese are believed to be under thirty today—has a relatively high literacy rating; even including the less literate older people, Japanese estimates rate China as about 60 per cent literate.

Under the spur of reforms instituted since the Cultural Revolution, the whole system of higher education has also been changed. With as many as 10,000,000 secondary and college students "sent down" to the land and new applicants chosen without the usual examinations, a new generation of students is in the colleges and universities that were closed for four years.

Like everything else in China today, the impetus for change came from Mao Tse-tung. In July 1969, he issued a directive calling for shorter periods of schooling, a combination of physical labor and classroom study, and a student body chosen from, and even elected by, peasants on the farms, the working class in the cities and the Army. Like his "May 7 Schools," named for a directive of May 7, 1966, setting up classes for revolutionary indoctrination, the selection of students for higher education now is based on political reliability rather than academic achievement, lower-class origin instead of intellectual elitism. Communal mass meetings have chosen students who sometimes have little or no background of past study, but it doesn't seem to matter. Zeal for the revolution and working experience are deemed to be more important than book learning alone.

This, too, grows out of Mao's thinking. In drawing up the new educational order, he was all for limiting higher education to technology, engineering and physics interspersed with physical labor. As he told his son Mao An-ying, later killed in the Korean War, upon the boy's return from Moscow University in 1946: "You have only acquired book learning. Now you must go to classes at the university of labor." And that is the way things are done in China today.

The theory, not unknown in the West, is that there are no bad students, only students of different cultural backgrounds. To do away with the ivory-tower atmosphere, most children have five years of primary school, four years of secondary school and at sixteen go to work for two years. If they want to enter a university thereafter, they must apply, obtain the approval of their factory or commune, and also the assent of the university itself. Of the older workers, some are selected without much primary or secondary education.

University instruction lasts only two or three years in China today, and is severely restricted. Chungshan University in Canton has fewer than 600 students, instead of the 5,000 before the Cultural Revolution. Tsinghua University in Peking, China's greatest technical school, has been reduced from 12,000 students in 1966 to only 2,800 in 1971, but 700 teachers remain. Peking (Peita) University also has been cut from more than 10,000 to 2,500; while the emphasis here is also on technology, there are some liberal arts studies. But in the new universities, liberal arts do not have much prestige.

Inevitably, there are difficulties. At the Workers University in Shanghai, where students average twenty-nine years of age, a cultural gap[24] developed, with those of high cultural level complaining the work was too easy and those of lower cultural level saying it was too hard. At a Kwangtung middle school, teachers were criticized for working more with good students and neglecting the poor ones. If there are examinations, they are taken with open books and student discussion in a number of schools. It is, in every respect, a revolution in higher education and one that is being closely watched by the outside world as well as inside China itself. For, quite evidently, academic honors and the once-hallowed Ph.D., with their Chinese equivalents, now count for relatively little. The relevance of both instruction and training to the life of the country counts for much more. Just to make certain that faculties realize the enormity of the change, a three-way rotation has been instituted under which the faculty at Peking University, for example, goes from teaching to farm commune to factory work and back to teaching again. It isn't much like the usual American trinity of teaching, foundation work and government service.

This does not mean, of course, that students have settled down to a

[24] The cultural gap was discussed in the *People's Daily*, June 12, 1971, and on a Canton radio broadcast June 13, 1971. Ilse Sharp discussed Chungshan University in the *Far Eastern Economic Review*, June 5, 1971, pp. 64–66.

peaceful life in which their every move is foreordained or that faculties have given up their age-old bickering over the control of education. For the present, these ancient struggles go on to a large extent beneath the surface. But so authoritative a publication as *Hung Chi* concedes that a "fierce struggle" continues between the "old teachers" and the "new line." It stands to reason that for as long as Mao's influence lasts in China, which will be quite a time, the "new line" will remain.[25]

The Pride of the Cities

There are major changes, too, in China's great cities—the mirrors that reflect China's progress and achievements to the world at large. No visitor of recent times comes away from his carefully supervised urban tour without being impressed by the swarming movement of the blue-clad populace on foot or bicycle, the cleanness of the streets, the initial signs of expansion and rebuilding, the end of the old ghetto life of shame and infinite misery for tens of millions of Chinese who were condemned to the equivalent of industrial slavery. Gone are the beggars, the maimed and the diseased who ceaselessly cried out for alms. And gone, too, is the fabulous night life that made Shanghai so notorious among the great cities of the world. If life is duller, it is also much safer. If there is comparatively little on which a foreigner can spend his money, he also has considerably more assurance today that he won't be cheated or robbed—although the risk of being caught in an angry demonstration for some real or fancied slight still exists.

Over and over again during the quarter century of Communist rule, these simple discoveries have been trumpeted to the world by each visitor—old China hand or wide-eyed newcomer—as if they were ancient verities that were being perceived once again by an all-knowing intelligence. To the Communist partisans who came from abroad, this new life-style was acclaimed as evidence of the superior-

[25] I am indebted for much of this material to my colleagues at the Chinese University of Hong Kong and their associates from the mainland who often discussed this fascinating subject with me. Among many reports I was impressed particularly with John Gittings' for the London *Observer* in the *South China Morning Post*, December 17, 1970, and another by Hsieh Tao-chih in the Hong Kong *Standard*, November 8, 1970.

ity of their system over the despised precepts of a dying capitalism. But to the British and the French, the Canadians and Indians and so many others from non-Communist lands, it was usually looked upon as a creditable beginning for so large and disorganized a country, but only a beginning. To so realistic a Frenchman as Robert Guillain of *Le Monde*, it was the triumph of a nation of "blue ants." To a British correspondent in Peking, it was a two-year sentence of utter boredom. But to most of the onrushing Americans who came in clusters to China in 1971 and 1972, a majority of them new hands, nearly everything that had been described so often before their advent had to be marveled over anew.

The show places were Peking, with its 7,000,000; Canton, with its 3,000,000; and Shanghai, the greatest of all, with 10,000,000 people spilling over from the main city into the far-spreading suburbs. In addition, the visitor was given supervised glimpses of other places and selected communes in the countryside, all of them calculated to give a good impression. It would have been strange, given the authoritarian outlook of the regime, if anything else had been allowed to happen, if the stranger had not been given the impression of millions of people endlessly working, endlessly moving at their tasks, massing in enthusiastic proletarian array in response to the demands of their propaganda, chanting slogans and brandishing Mao Tsetung's little red book.

"You are taken in hand, shepherded around, shown sights and politely ushered out—with an impression of a country that doesn't exist," wrote Jacques Marcuse of Agence France-Presse after a two-and-a-half-year tour of duty. And Mark Gayn of the Toronto *Star*, who had been in and out of China several times, commented: "Mainland China is seemingly involved in a perpetual demonstration. It is a rare day that people aren't called out to march in protest against something or other, to shout defiance, to listen to words of hate and anger." To John Roderick of the Associated Press, returning after an absence of twenty-five years, China had made progress but remained a "have-not" nation: "The filth has been replaced by a clean but shabby gentility. The rich and the very poor are no more. Instead, there is a uniformity that never existed before . . . Hovering above everything is the conviction that their [the Chinese] way is the only way." And Theodore H. White, another old China hand who made the trip with eighty-six other correspondents to cover President Nixon's negotiations in Peking in 1972, found everything had changed. "Changed, completely," he said.[26]

Where are the political prisoners, the ordinary criminals, the narcotics addicts and the other rejects of this remarkably regimented society? No one knows. If it were not for the tales that come from those who escape to Hong Kong, there would be no evidence that such anti-social elements exist under the smothering blanket of a far-reaching, all-embracing conformity. There are pockets of newly arrived refugees in Hong Kong where the eager searcher-after-truth can be—and frequently is—told almost anything he wants to hear but this is no guarantee of accuracy, either. Usually, it is quite the opposite. The China traveler, particularly those who venture upon this broad and mysterious land for the first time, can only judge from appearances and at the same time continually question his own judgment.

For a sympathetic writer such as Han Suyin, making her sixteenth visit to China, it is a land of continual wonderment: "There is an effervescence about Peking which is very stimulating; the Cultural Revolution has been a success; but what to someone like me is most striking is the new sense of freedom, a real grass roots democratic spirit, which is evident everywhere."[27] Few others have made such a novel discovery. More often, the visitors' reactions are akin to that of the Indian scholar Dr. Sripati Chandrasekhar, who found China's regimented life intolerable and wrote: "The citizen does not have a minute of silence in which to rest his mind or reflect on his new life."[28] And despite all the praise for the pervasive effort to keep China clean, there are also observations of failure, such as a report of

---

[26] Marcuse in *Editor & Publisher*, December 26, 1964, p. 40; Gayn in *The New York Times*, June 7, 1965, p. 3; Roderick in the AP file from Canton, April 18, 1971. I have gone over many accounts of visitors to China in the past two decades as well as the more recent material from American correspondents briefly admitted to China from the AP, *Time*, *Newsweek*, *The New York Times*, *Newsday*, *The Wall Street Journal* and other publications.

[27] Han Suyin in *The New York Times*, September 21, 1970, p. 43.

[28] Dr. Chandrasekhar in "Red China Today," written for the AP and published in the Boston *Globe*, February 16, 1959.

pollution in Shanghai by Norman Webster of the Toronto *Globe &
Mail:* "Soochow Creek is filthy where it empties into the Whangpoo
River at one end of the famous Bund in Shanghai's center . . .
Smoke from factories sometimes makes the air hazy and a ride past a
row of them can be an experience in new and unpleasant smells."[29]
It is fresh evidence, if evidence were needed, of the validity of the old
journalistic rule to beware of generalities in observing a newer and
better China.

The most reliable observations, as might be expected, have come
from the older China hands with a continuity of experience in their
Chinese travels, such as Professor Robert Ruhlmann, of L'Ecole
Nationale des Langues Orientales, Paris. After six weeks in China,
his first visit in sixteen years, he remarked that the changes in the
land were enormous and all for the better. The people, in his view,
were better clothed and fed, the cities cleaner and busier. In Peking,
he noted how nearly all the old city walls had been pulled down and
how rapidly the population was spreading out into the suburbs. He
also liked the widespread planting of trees in Peking, minimizing the
dust and creating an image of coolness and graciousness. To his
thrifty French soul, it was also worth recording that travel in China
was cheap—no more than $40 a month if you were careful.[30]

To China-born Peter Stursberg, a Canadian journalist, the great
showpiece in Peking is the new subway, of which a fifteen-mile
section has been completed and is under operation by the People's
Liberation Army. Begun in 1965, the system's test runs began in
1969 but it still was not open to the public two years later. All the
stations are decorated like museums in the manner of the Moscow
subway and the shiny six-car demonstration trains are continually
scrubbed, as are the platforms. To the PLA, the system is a fine
underground shelter in the event of war; to the Red Guards, it was a
waste of money.[31]

Like Peking, Canton arouses many varied reactions but few are
particularly favorable. For Canton is a gray city, China's principal
market center, with its semiannual trade fairs, and it has few other

[29] Norman Webster in the Washington *Post*, April 16, 1971, p. A–22.
[30] Interview with me November 7, 1970, in Shatin, N.T.
[31] *Newsweek*, May 17, 1971, pp. 48–49.

attractions. To Ilse Sharp, a British journalist, life for the foreign businessman in Canton is unbearably dull. He sits in his hotel room, waiting for word from the Chinese that their deal has been consummated, and seldom dares venture out except to cable his home office. Sometimes, the Chinese may throw a party but it in no sense resembles the freewheeling affairs of New York's garment trade. It may be a visit to a Chinese opera, a tour of a Chinese factory, a propaganda film, a dinner of cold cuts, or a concert or ballet. But to business people who don't understand Chinese, and are interested only in trade, such things have little meaning.[32] Shanghai, by all accounts, is much livelier, although it is far from the glamorous and wicked metropolis of yore. Like Canton and Peking, Shanghai has little automobile traffic to date; if there were any of consequence, it would be hopelessly snarled because people walk everywhere in enormous numbers—on streets and sidewalks. It is all that electric and motor buses can do to get through their appointed routes slowly, for between the people on foot and the people on bicycles, transportation represents a continual hazard.

As China's major industrial center, with a work force of 1,200,000, Shanghai is far more provincial than cosmopolitan. Today, there is more smoke than garish nighttime illumination. The buildings along the Whangpoo River waterfront are still standing, but they have changed character to conform to the Maoist age. The Chinese equivalent of City Hall is a former bank, the old Cathay Hotel is now the Peace Hotel, and so on. As for the shops, once a testimonial to the elevated tastes of Shanghai's international society, they are now mainly utilitarian and full of cheap and necessary goods for a mass public subsisting on a low standard of living.

Iron and steel factories, shipbuilding, chemicals and textile plants give Shanghai its character today, not the sordid night spots of yore. And more visible than anything else is the activity of the port area, the key to so much of China's foreign trade. By contrast, the fine international airports at Shanghai, Canton and Peking are little used because world air traffic still has not come to China. The Chinese railways, with their big blue-and-white German-made cars, are in much greater demand than the propjets used on the domestic Chinese

---

[32] Ilse Sharp in the *Far Eastern Economic Review*, May 29, 1971, pp. 6–8.

flights, particularly the trains on the well-run Canton-Hong Kong line. Many a foreign air line, however, would be willing to gamble on a big future rise in Chinese air travel if the Chinese government would accept new routes and extend old ones. But the Chinese remain cautious in the extreme. The old isolationist mentality cannot be easily overcome.[33]

The Defense of China

At the root of every major policy of the Chinese government, whether it is purely domestic or in the foreign field, is a very conscious and understandable concern for national security and the preservation of the state. That is what makes China's posture largely defensive. And it is likely to remain so for years to come. The heavy losses in the Korean War, an estimated 900,000 casualties in dead, wounded and missing, were a salutary lesson to Peking on the cost of a conflict with a major world power. Scant wonder that both Mao Tsetung and his deputy, Lin Piao, are reported to have opposed so fiercely the effort of the "hawks" in the PLA to intervene with military force on the side of the North Vietnamese in 1965 when the United States escalated that war. As events have shown, the Chinese decision to give all support to Hanoi short of outright military intervention was eminently correct, particularly after the Soviet Union decided to continue as the main supplier of North Vietnam's military machine. Despite all the differences between Peking and Moscow, they found common ground in resisting the United States armed forces on the Asian mainland.

But with the coming of border conflicts involving Chinese and Soviet troops, the concentration of vast Soviet forces along the Chinese border and the winding down of the Vietnam War, China has begun a cautious policy of seeking new approaches to the United States. This does not mean that the Chinese have altogether aban-

[33] In so brief a space, I cannot do more than suggest the broad outlines of the grand reportage, and some of the not so grand, that has emanated from China recently. A close study is recommended of such 1971–72 materials as the work of John Roderick, AP; Robert Keatley, *The Wall Street Journal;* William Attwood, *Newsday;* Tillman Durdin, James Reston and Seymour and Audrey Topping, *The New York Times;* John Saar, *Life* magazine; and Norman Webster, Toronto *Globe & Mail.*

doned their old propaganda line of opposing both Soviet and American power at all costs. The line invariably appears whenever the Chinese, for one reason or another, rally their people for defense against possible nuclear attack.

Despite continued atomic testing, however, China still does not have a credible nuclear deterrent and knows it. That is the main reason for Peking's refusal to sign the limited atomic test ban treaty. As Premier Chou put it in defending Chinese policy: "We do it precisely for the purpose of breaking down the nuclear monopoly and blackmail and to bring about a complete solution of this problem." But he has no illusions of the extent of China's still rather primitive nuclear effort. "We are not a big power although the extent of our territory is vast and we have a vast population," he said recently. "From the point of view of power, we are rather weak and backward . . . We are in an experimental stage of our testing of nuclear weapons. We cannot call ourselves a big nuclear power."[34]

If it is true that China at best can accumulate no more than 15 to 40 operational intercontinental ballistic missiles plus 100 to 200 medium-range ballistic missiles by the latter 1970s,[35] it then becomes difficult for any realistic foreign observer to understand how China expects to reach parity in atomic arms with the United States and the Soviet Union. Each of the "Big Two" possesses more than 1,000 ICBMs plus many thousands of additional nuclear weapons deliverable by missile, aircraft or submarine. A Chinese atomic attack on either of the two great powers, under such circumstances, would be suicidal for Peking since retaliatory strikes would be swift and frightful in result. Nothing has been heard in recent years of Mao's reported boast to Tito that China could absorb hundreds of millions of casualties in an atomic war and still survive. The fact is that it couldn't, and the Chinese leadership has come to realize it.

This explains the broad Chinese program of air-raid shelter construction, ranging in importance from the vast tunnels of the new Peking subway to the primitive caves of the rural communes. Premier Chou En-lai, on almost every important occasion, refers to such

[34] *The New York Times*, June 23, 1971, p. 2.
[35] Estimate by Doak Barnett in *Foreign Affairs*, April, 1970, p. 428.

preparations in the event of Soviet atomic attack and his countrymen take him with the utmost seriousness. What the Chinese are doing, on a limited scale, is to work on the familiar atomic equation for survival—the development of large-scale nuclear weapons plus delivery systems together with increased protection for the home front in the form of air-raid shelters.

Having touched off almost a dozen nuclear tests up to the end of 1971 and orbited a space satellite, China has demonstrated a capability for every aspect of nuclear war except the creation of an anti-ballistic missile system. That will require even more time and money, which China can ill afford to take away from national economic development.

The Chinese refusal to enter into any kind of atomic accord with the United States and the Soviet Union, in consequence, can scarcely be based on any hope of attaining parity. Rather, like France, China remains outside the scope of negotiations to try to maintain a bargaining position on a global level, however meager. The real basis for Chinese defense remains what it always has been—the threat of unlimited manpower operating in a vast territory as a guerrilla force with massive popular support. As the Vietnam War has shown, such a conflict can render a great power impotent to impose its will on a fourth-class military force except at an unacceptable cost.

As a result of China's intense preoccupation with defense in the era since the Cultural Revolution, most China specialists are pretty well agreed that the prospect of a Chinese offensive strike in Asia is unlikely very soon. China is believed to have attained its territorial goals on the Indian border, and it made no military gesture to help Pakistan in 1971. Having absorbed Tibet by military force and neutralized Nepal and Sikkim, the Chinese have nothing to fear in that area. In Southeast Asia, China can do very well by encouraging indigenous Communists to fight for a pro-Peking government in their respective countries without risking Chinese troops. Infiltration and subversion are better bets, although in such places as Thailand, Burma and Malaysia even these techniques seem to have a fairly low priority.

China can afford few risks. It is not likely, if the Peking government intends to push for development at home, that its leaders can plan for costly military adventures abroad. The game is too dangerous over the long haul.

2. THE BAMBOO CURTAIN PARTS

The decision of the United States and China to seek a new alignment by abandoning impractical and outworn policies is one of the historic turning points in the declining years of the twentieth century. Like the break between the Soviet Union and China that preceded it by seven years, the Sino-American decision indicates a shift of global forces is under way that will have profound consequences, particularly for the Indo-Pacific area.

It has assured, as a first step, China's entry into the United Nations. Diplomatic recognition between Washington and Peking may be farther down the road because it depends on an accommodation on the issue of Taiwan. And in the distance, if all goes well, lie possibilities for mutual benefit through exchanges in every field, from science and education to trade and development, that would do much to restore old and valued ties. The initial enthusiasm of the American public for President Nixon's trip to Peking showed how well this new policy move was understood in the United States. And Premier Chou En-lai's triumphant return to Peking, after capping President Nixon's week-long visit to China with the Shanghai communiqué of February 28, 1972, underlined the Chinese leadership's satisfaction with the new policy. The agreement of the Americans to consider Taiwan as China's territory and begin removing American troops there was an augury of broader moves yet to come.

The Soviet Union, of course, did not neglect precautions as its two principal opponents began to feel their way toward improved relationships. While *Pravda* said that the Soviet also sought better ties with the United States and China, it warned against any attempt between Peking and Washington to collaborate against Moscow. In less formal ways, as well, the Russians showed both their suspicion and their displeasure. The prolonged border negotiations with the Chinese and the strategic arms limitation talks (SALT) with the United States gave Moscow considerable leverage for whatever it chose to do. Nor were the Japanese likely to limit themselves to a fit of the sulks over not being consulted in advance about the dramatic American change in policy toward China. As long as Japan remained China's major trading partner and the keystone in the arch of American defenses in the Pacific, Tokyo was bound to exercise influence in both Peking and Washington.

There are, in consequence, many hurdles that will have to be taken before any Sino-American rapprochement becomes a reality instead of a mere surface accord. But if the unthinkable of the days of John Foster Dulles and Joe McCarthy comes to pass and Red China settles into an accord with the once despised "American imperialists and their running dogs," a new era will come to the Pacific beyond anything heretofore contemplated.

This is not to say that China will give up its doctrine of perpetual revolution at home and abroad or that Washington will yield in its distaste for Communism, Mao's or any other brand. But both appear to have decided, at about the same time, that it is foolish and unprofitable in the extreme to pretend that the other either doesn't exist or doesn't count in the scale of world relationships.

A time of transition is therefore at hand. The uncertain trumpets in Washington and the ideological brass band in Peking are not likely to burst into harmony soon. Nor should new visits to Peking or Washington be regarded as harbingers of instant peace and good will. Both Mao Tse-tung and Chou En-lai wanted to come to the White House in 1945 and were turned down, with deplorable results; but even if they had been received at the time, the chances are that history would not have been changed to any degree. The times were not propitious.

What may now be possible, and even probable, is a lessening of tensions between China and the United States that may eventually contribute to a long-deferred Pacific settlement. If it comes at all, it is going to be one step at a time. And the steps initially may be quite small.

Ping Pong and Noodles

The truly surprising part of the new turn in Sino-American relations is that it was so long deferred. Even the break in Soviet-American ties, from the overthrow of the Czar in 1917 until the Roosevelt

Administration's recognition of the Soviet government in 1933, took less time—a matter of sixteen years.

The difference is that American intervention in Soviet affairs at the outset was minimal, being restricted to American forces in Siberia, which were withdrawn shortly after World War I. But in China, American intervention was on such a massive scale in favor of Chiang Kai-shek that Peking bristled, especially after the Seventh Fleet took up the defense of Taiwan. For more than a decade after Mao's takeover in 1949, the improper question "Why did we lose China?" dominated American politics. There were many answers, the most truthful being Dean Acheson's: "China was never ours to lose."

Despite that, the State Department's China service was wrecked. Some of the most brilliant and perceptive diplomatic careerists were purged from government service because they had dared to predict a Maoist victory and to urge Washington to come to terms with the new rulers of China. Even twenty years after the event, Barbara W. Tuchman's history of American misadventures in China was a best-seller among the American reading public.[36] And it was curious, too, that Chiang Kai-shek, in his eighties, still had enough political clout among American conservatives to attract defenders in the U.S. Senate.

All this was due in part to a kind of mystique in the American perception of China. From the time of the departure of the 360-ton *Empress of China* on the first American trading voyage to Cathay in 1784, there has always been a romantic glow about the China trade that shed its dubious luster on other aspects of Sino-American relations. Congregations of the pious could take up collections for missionaries to save the souls of the "heathen Chinee" in rural America. But at the same time, the first American commissioner, Caleb Cushing, could unblushingly force Chinese adherence to the trading pact of Wanghia in 1844, backed by the persuasive force of four American warships.

Nevertheless, through the churches, the schools and the press, from the latter part of the nineteenth century onward, Americans were told that they had a special responsibility for China. This was, no

[36] Barbara W. Tuchman, *Stilwell and the American Experience in China, 1911–45* (New York: Macmillan, 1971).

doubt, compounded of a mixture of high-flown American morality, Christian charity and the old-fashioned Yankee trader instinct for buttering up a good customer. It led to such contradictory policies as the Chinese Exclusion Act of 1882 and the Open Door policy, which was pointed to as an example of American selflessness and virtue in Asian affairs.

In any event, from the time of the Japanese attack on China in 1931, American sympathies were with the Chinese. And throughout World War II, Chiang Kai-shek was a hero to the American press. Aided by the well-heeled China lobby and the political terror spread by Senator Joe McCarthy, Nationalist China continued to maintain its hold on the American government long after its defeat by the Communist armies. And Mao Tse-tung remained a bogeyman. When Lyndon Johnson at last sought a way out of the Vietnam War, he became the first president in a generation to call for a "reconciliation" between China and the United States. And when Richard Nixon put out his first feelers to Peking, he was the first American President in history to utter those fateful words, "The People's Republic of China."

There was, however, no notion among the public at large that a break in the long diplomatic deep freeze was imminent. On December 10, 1970, President Nixon called for "communication" with China but few took him seriously. In a foreign policy message to Congress on February 25, 1971, the President added, "We are prepared to establish a dialogue with Peking." Once again, it was regarded as just another ploy by an anti-Communist President who was in deep trouble with the American public.

Nothing appeared to be happening. Inside and outside Washington, the Nixon initiative was regarded as the usual high-flown American rhetoric, full of sound and sometimes fury but essentially signifying nothing. The President, some of the cynics said, was just trying to con the public into believing that he really wanted Chinese help to end the Vietnam War. His critics also pointed to the Warsaw talks between the United States and China, stalled at the time, as an opportunity that had been callously overlooked by an administration that said one thing but often did another.

As hindsight has since demonstrated, the Warsaw talks actually weren't so important at that stage in the slowly evolving diplomatic scenario. What did impress Peking was the crumbling American opposition to Chinese membership in the U.N.—the 51–49 vote with 25 abstentions in the 1970 General Assembly[37] and the wholesale switching of positions in China's favor thereafter.

To people as subtle as the Chinese, the time seemed exactly right to apply pressure where the American government was most vulnerable—the wide-open arena of American public opinion. After all, the rulers in Peking had good cause to remember how Chiang Kai-shek had used the big parade of distinguished American politicians and journalists to Taipei to generate greater American support for his failing cause. But now, times had changed. Chiang was faltering and on the verge of retirement. The North Vietnamese had demonstrated how successfully a small enemy nation could appeal to the American people over the head of the American government.

It is uncertain at exactly what time China decided to stage its own campaign for American public support for Chinese sovereignty over Taiwan and admission to the U.N. But evidently, it was not too long after the liquidation of the Cultural Revolution. Chou En-lai has said that the decision to open the door to the Americans was made by Mao Tse-tung himself at a time when both the Chinese Foreign Ministry and the American State Department were cool to the idea.[38]

The opportunity for the break came in Tokyo, at the international ping-pong tournament that brought Chinese and American players together in the spring of 1971. Chou cordially invited the American table-tennis team to China for a week and also raised the bars for three American correspondents. When the eighteen people crossed the Chinese border from Hong Kong on April 10, it was a world-wide sensation.

Four days later, when Premier Chou En-lai received the Americans in the Great Hall of the People in Peking, he underlined the importance of the event by telling them that they had "opened a new page in the relations of the Chinese and American people." Just to make certain that the fraternity of foreign correspondents also got the message, he turned to the veteran China specialist of the Associated

[37] The two-thirds vote still applied to the issue in 1970.
[38] Julian Schuman in UPI file from Peking, October 6, 1971.

Press, John Roderick, making his first visit to the mainland in twenty-three years, and remarked that more American correspondents soon would be admitted. "Mr. Roderick," the Premier said, "you have opened the door."

President Nixon needed none of the eager young China specialists in the State Department to interpret these signals from Peking. That same day, he announced a relaxation of the twenty-one-year-old trade embargo against China, principally on non-strategic items. He also ordered visas expedited for Americans visiting China, permitted the Chinese to use dollars to pay for imports, let American oil companies supply fuel for China ship and air travel, and permitted American ships and aircraft to carry Chinese cargoes between non-Chinese ports. Added to the removal of restrictions on American purchases of Chinese goods, a step previously taken, the Nixon program marked a considerable change in the old stand-pat Washington attitude. The President's press secretary, quickly claiming credit for his boss, announced that "the initiatives of President Nixon have turned a new page in our relations with China."

All this added up to a lot of publicity, but few practical consequences at first. It was amusing, after so long an estrangement between China and the United States, that the first renewed contact led to a friendly confrontation between Premier Chou and a youthful California hippie, with shoulder-length hair and purple bell-bottomed pants, who breathlessly asked Chou what he thought of the hippie movement in the United States. The reply was typically Chinese: "We agree that young people should try different things but we should try to find something in common with the great majority." While it was not a deathless exchange in the annals of diplomacy, it had the merit of demonstrating Chinese good will under somewhat strained circumstances.

A few more American correspondents were admitted to China for a limited time with the departure of the table-tennis team, but the phrase "Ping-Pong Diplomacy" had become imbedded in the English language by the time the incident was over. Referring to the lavish spread of Chinese hospitality for the visiting Americans, Foreign Minister Adam Malik of Indonesia somewhat caustically added that the Chinese had also instituted "Noodle Diplomacy." And the Japanese, in a restrained manner, commented on China's new diplomacy of smiles while Taipei darkly regarded the whole business as a political plot. The most nervous of all, for understandable reasons, was the Soviet Union, with Moscow showing annoyance and even anger over the proceedings.

The American Secretary of State, William P. Rogers, tried to soothe the Russians by saying the American initiatives toward China had not been undertaken "with the idea of irritating the Soviet Union in any way." But the dour old Washington lawyer fairly beamed when he reflected on the changed atmosphere between the United States and China. Nor did Chou, at a party for the deposed Prince Norodom Sihanouk of Cambodia, do more than repeat the stock accusations against the United States in Indochina, dropping the usual invective and softening the Chinese line accordingly.

If he hoped for an immediate American signal on the Taiwan issue, however, he must have been disappointed. For when a special Presidential commission made its report on April 26, 1971, its conclusions in effect were that Peking's entry into the United Nations must not be accomplished at the cost of excluding Taiwan. It was not a line that proved to be very popular in the United Nations. Evidently, it didn't particularly disturb Peking, especially when the United States ended the long China trade embargo on June 10 and lifted all controls on imports from China. It wasn't likely, however, that the $200 million annual trade between the United States and China in 1950 would come back very quickly.

The signals by this time were being exchanged at a furious rate between Washington and Peking. The result was the secret trip of the Presidential adviser Henry A. Kissinger to confer with Premier Chou in Peking from July 9 to 11. Four days thereafter, Washington and Peking simultaneously announced President Nixon would visit China to "seek normalization of relations between the two countries." The President's 90-second statement on nation-wide television on the night of July 15 set off weeks of speculation in world capitals and created a kind of euphoria in Washington.

But in the midst of the dickering over arrangements, another political crisis blew up in China. Following the mysterious crash of a

Chinese air force plane on September 12 in the Mongolian Republic, with nine dead, all Chinese aircraft were grounded for three days without immediate explanation. Thereafter, the Chinese canceled their traditional reception on the eve of their National Day celebration and the usual big parade the next day. Aside from a former army marshal, Yeh Chien-ying, all top military leaders vanished; except for Premier Chou, only the Deputy Premiers Tung Pi-wu and Li Hsien-nien were in evidence. Soon afterward, reports of Lin Piao's fall began circulating.

The United States became so concerned that Secretary of State Rogers publicly questioned whether the President would be able to go through with his announced plans. It must have created consternation within the Chinese government, for within three days Washington and Peking again were able to make a simultaneous announcement, this time of Kissinger's return visit to Peking to make "concrete arrangements" for the President's 1972 trip. The energetic Kissinger took off promptly enough in a United States Air Force plane, with numerous Presidential assistants, for a pleasant sojourn with his host, Premier Chou, toward the end of October.

It was at precisely this time that the United States was trying once again, with disheartening results, to pump up its "two Chinas" policy in the United Nations to save Taiwan from expulsion. Just how President Nixon hoped to accomplish anything of substance by maintaining his friendly overtures to Peking on the one hand, and trying to save Taiwan from disgrace on the other, defied all rational understanding. The seating of Peking had, for all practical purposes, become a foregone conclusion. Consequently, the Chinese didn't let themselves be disturbed by the twisting and turning in Washington as the Americans slowly divested themselves of an outworn policy.

Despite all the Nixon Administration's efforts to soften the blow, the final United Nations action in the China case came as something of a shock. Late on the night of October 25, the adherents of Peking forced the issue because they feared the American program of persuasion might yet save Taiwan temporarily if given enough time. The United States, in a last-ditch effort, called upon the General Assembly to declare the motion for the expulsion of Taiwan to be an "important question" within the meaning of the Charter, which would require a two-thirds vote. It was this device that had been successfully used for a decade to keep Peking out of the United Nations. The Americans failed by four votes, 59–55 against the two-thirds rule, with 15 abstentions. What really hurt was that every NATO ally, with the exception of Greece, Luxembourg and Portugal, deserted the United States on this question by either voting no or abstaining.

A joyous victory demonstration, with anti-American delegates hugging each other and dancing, preceded the climactic vote ninety minutes later when China at last was voted into the United Nations by 76–35, with 17 abstentions. The delegation from Taiwan marched out of the excited General Assembly hall just before the decision to expel them. Their "last hurrah" was delivered with a flourish next day from Taipei by Chiang Kai-shek.

The practical-minded Chou En-lai didn't let China's long-deferred victory change the direction of his foreign policy. Even as a new Chinese delegation took over in the United Nations, and Washington's overtures persisted, the Premier insisted on the reunion of Taiwan with China. Only then, he said, would it be possible for China to establish diplomatic relations with the United States. He did not accept, any more than Chiang Kai-shek did, that it would be possible to have more than one China in the world. It was foreordained, in consequence, that the eventual settlement of the Taiwan matter would not be within the United Nations; instead, it became, by common consent, an internal Chinese affair.

This was the chief outward result of the Nixon-Chou meetings on February 21–28, 1972, which received the blessings of Mao Tse-tung, and it did much to smooth the path of both nations toward an eventual accommodation of sorts and mutual diplomatic recognition. The conversations between the American President and the Chinese Premier, however, ranged far beyond Taiwan. If the week did not exactly change the world, as the enthusiastic Nixon contended, it did usher in a period of negotiations among the great powers that took little account of past differences.[39]

---

[39] For an understanding of the changed positions of China and the U.S., a detailed study of the American press and official Chinese statements is recommended from April 10, 1971, onward.

The Sino-American Options

All manner of options, therefore, lie ahead for the United States and China, as well as for the Soviet Union, Japan and the European Economic Community. As the least developed of all the relationships between the great powers, the future course of the United States and China offers the most room for maneuver.

By trading with American subsidiaries through third parties even before the lifting of the trade embargo, the Chinese have shown themselves to be flexible. Such firms as General Motors, Hercules, American Optical and Monsanto have been among the first to take the lure of fresh business. There is little doubt that others among the principal American global concerns will be working out arrangements with the Chinese. But it is also true that cheap mass-produced Chinese consumer goods, notably textiles, will present problems of sorts for the American economy. And in any two-way exchange, China is not going to be left far behind.

Similarly, the limited advances China has been able to make in science and technology do not necessarily circumscribe cooperation in such fields. The simplest suggestions for regulating urban traffic, offered by an American scientist, Professor Arthur W. Galston of Yale, were gratefully noted by Chinese interviewers during his brief visit to Peking. How much technical assistance from the United States can be offered and used by China is something that defies quick analysis and decision. Expert counseling on how to increase agricultural yields alone would be an attractive proposition to the Chinese. Just as important to them are methods of improving factory operations, hospitals and public health, family planning, the mass construction of homes, road building, the creation of a national electric power grid and the avoidance of the spreading pollution that comes with industralization.

Why should the United States offer such aid after fighting China in one war in Asia and struggling against Peking-supported North Vietnam in another? And above all, why should China accept if it continues to be Peking's policy to try by every means to curb the power of both the United States and the Soviet Union? The question might as well be phrased: Why not? Through wise and generous policies, the United States stimulated and helped restore both West German and Japanese economies after destroying them as enemy nations in World War II. Thus, former enemies became allies, lucrative trading partners and strong points in the American defense system. Granted that such a quick turnabout in Sino-American relations is scarcely possible under present conditions, must there be another war with China before the United States can decently consider offering minimal help to Peking in the name of the Chinese people? The premise is unthinkable.

The Chinese have shown that they do not consider differing principles of government and clashing ideologies to be a valid reason for limiting their approach to other nations. Despite China's own needs at home, Chinese foreign aid in 1971 alone probably amounted to more than $1 billion to developing countries elsewhere in the world with whom Peking sought to build a united front. China's interest in the United Nations has increased despite a 1951 Security Council resolution, still on the books, condemning the Communist side for aggression in the Korean War. China has applauded the European Common Market's invitation to Britain to join its ranks, supposedly because it limits Europe's dependence on the United States, but has also encouraged the independence of Yugoslavia and Rumania of Soviet foreign policy. Even so, the Chinese have entered cautiously into the expansion of their trade with the Soviet Union, very possibly as a counterweight to China's present heavy dependence on trade with Japan.

All this demonstrates a growth of Chinese sophistication and pragmatism in world affairs that the United States can scarcely ignore. In fact, the United States would do well to take advantage of the opportunity that such a policy offers. For one thing, with the removal of the American military presence on China's borders, the United States offers China a practical alternative in such fields as diplomacy, trade and aid to both Soviet militarism and Japanese economic expansion in Asia. Moreover, a strengthening of the slender Chinese ties with the United States would tend to pull Peking back into the mainstream of world affairs and away from its policy of tampering with its neighbors to the south, now in declining favor.

With the winding down of the Vietnam War, in summation, there are many more reasons for a drawing together of the United States and China than for a renewed separation. Both have suffered grievous political setbacks in their foreign adventures in the 1960s, China in the Third World and the United States in Indochina, and could use a period of peace and consolidation of interests. Both are troubled by economic problems of widely varying degree that could be reduced by the adoption of mutually helpful policies. Both are quite willing, up to a point, to work through international organizations to advance their mutual interests. And the American withdrawal from the Asian mainland, undoubtedly eases Peking's fear of an aggressive and vengeful America.

Given increased good will and an end to the long period of recrimination and hostility between China and the United States, there is no doubt that even the knotty problem of Taiwan can be resolved in time. Peking already has shown that it is willing to accept such halfway measures as Canadian and Italian willingness to "take note" of its claim to Taiwan. Nor is there any reason now to fear that China, even with the removal of the Seventh Fleet, will launch a military move to recover Taiwan. It won't be necessary.

Premier Chou has done much to allay the fears of the people of Taiwan by pledging that no harm will come to the 12,000,000 Taiwanese and offering the 2,000,000 Chinese a chance to return to their native provinces. In addition, it is hardly likely, in view of the practical manner in which Peking has handled its relations with Hong Kong, that the People's Republic would want to do anything that would interfere with the prosperity of Taiwan. It follows that a general recognition of Taiwan as an autonomous province of China could conceivably be a first step toward an eventual solution of the problem. Regardless of United Nations action, China and Taiwan could continue their separate existence for years to come while being joined in principle. In a more benign political atmosphere, they could be reunited.

3. CHINA AND THE SOVIET UNION

There is no hopeful augury for a quick solution of China's problems with the Soviet Union. For what China wants is nothing more nor less than admission from Moscow that the Czarist seizure of vast Chinese borderlands in the nineteenth century and their incorporation into Russia resulted from unequal treaties that were in effect imposed upon Peking. In return for such a signed concession at the Chinese-Soviet border talks, which began in 1969, the Chinese are willing for the present to accept present boundaries with minor rectifications. Premier Chou En-lai, for example, objects to the Russian tendency to let some boundaries run along the middle of border rivers and others on the Chinese side of such rivers.

The Soviet Union, naturally, fears that the consequences of a concession of wrongdoing by the Czars would result in the gravest consequences for the Communist successor government. For while China might not now press its claims for the return of its land, so urgently needed to support its growing population, the chances are that such demands would be made at some future time. As a result, having admitted to the possession of stolen territories, the Soviet Union would be placed in a difficult position before world opinion if it did not make some kind of restitution. The continued presence of impressive Soviet armed forces on the Chinese border is Moscow's answer to China's demand and China's nation-wide construction of air-raid shelters is one form of Peking's response. Without doubt, there will be others.

The Great Schism

This was not what the world expected during the eight years of the uncertain honeymoon of the Red giants between 1949 and 1957. True, the Soviet Union had never been enthusiastic about Mao before his accession to power and Mao, almost from the time of the founding of the Chinese Communist Party in 1921, had had more cause for suspicion and complaint in his relations with the Soviet Union than for unbounded satisfaction. But in the period when Mao was consolidating his victory, Peking and Moscow seemed to have entered into an unbreakable alliance.

The first cracks in what seemed to be a monolithic power structure appeared in 1957. Premier Chou En-lai since has blamed the Russian policy line adopted by Nikita S. Khrushchev when he blasted open the "de-Stalinization" era in 1956 at the 20th Congress of the Communist Party of the Soviet Union. At a Moscow conference in the following year, Chou revealed, the Chinese protested in vain against the voluble Khrushchev's policy of coexistence with capitalism and what they believed to be his attempt to restore some of the principles of capitalism in his own country. This they called "revisionism."

But Khrushchev wouldn't listen, much to the annoyance and even the uneasiness of the Chinese. They saw that they had contracted for a rather peculiar ally. When Khrushchev canceled the Soviet-Chinese agreements for atomic cooperation in 1959 and withdrew all Soviet experts and technicians the following year in violation of industrial and construction agreements, Peking became downright angry. With the expulsion of China-allied Albania from the 22nd Congress of the Communist Party of the Soviet Union, Premier Chou responded with bitter scorn: "We hold that if a dispute or difference unfortunately arises between fraternal countries, it should be resolved patiently in the spirit of proletarian internationalism and on the principles of equality and unanimity through consultations. Any public, one-sided censure of any fraternal party does not help unity and is not helpful in resolving problems. To lay bare a dispute between fraternal parties or fraternal countries openly in the face of the enemy cannot be regarded as a serious Marxist-Leninist attitude."

The Soviet Union struck back. In the Chinese-Indian border war of 1962, Moscow was said by Premier Chou to have sided with India and condemned China. No wonder, therefore, that the Chinese took a savage delight in Khrushchev's failure in the missile crisis over Cuba with the United States that fall. Despite continued skepticism in the American press over the mounting differences between Moscow and Peking, there was little doubt among informed Europeans that the once-solid Communist world was coming apart.

The break came on June 14, 1963, when the central committee of the Chinese Communist Party assailed Khrushchev as a "coward" for withdrawing Soviet missiles from Cuba. In a letter to Moscow, the Chinese argued it was an illusion for Khrushchev to hope for peace while "the system of imperialism and the exploitation of man by man still exists."

One month later, on July 14, 1963, the central committee of the Communist Party of the Soviet Union accused the Chinese of wrecking Communist unity, saying, "This is no longer a class approach in the struggle for the abolition of capitalism but for some entirely different aims." Then the Russians demanded, "If both the exploiters and the exploited are buried under the ruins of the old world, who will build the 'bright future'?"

The fall of Khrushchev on October 16, 1964, which nearly coincided with China's first atomic test, gave the Chinese hope that it might be possible to piece together the old alliance. But when they went to Moscow for the anniversary of the Soviet revolution that year, they learned that the policies of the new Soviet party leader, Leonid I. Brezhnev, and the new Soviet Premier, Aleksei N. Kosygin, were just as objectionable as Khrushchev's had been. Premier Chou tells the story that Mao, in a meeting with Kosygin in February 1965, warned the Soviet leader that Chinese-Soviet differences in principle would result in polemics for 10,000 years. And when Kosygin objected that that was too long, Chou related, Mao deducted 1,000 years, still leaving 9,000 years for the continuation of the dispute.

As the conflict widened, China rejected a Soviet invitation to attend its 23rd CPSU Congress in Moscow and charged that the Soviet Union was working "hand in glove with the United States in a whole series of dirty deals inside and outside the United Nations." This, the Chinese concluded, meant the Russians were trying to create a "Holy Alliance" against China and "sell out the struggle of the Vietnamese people against United States aggression."

By 1969, Premier Chou relates, tensions had become so great that the Soviet Union's troops on the Chinese border were more than 1,000,000 strong and some had gone into the Mongolian People's Republic. From the Soviet side, it has since been established that the Russian forces consisted of twenty-five divisions of 20,000 troops each, with another twenty divisions in reserve, the whole being backed by enormous air power and a sophisticated system of air defense. Nor did the Russians bother to conceal their preparations. They wanted the Chinese to know what kind of strength was being mobilized against them.

The Threat of War

The border conflict of 1969, in which Chinese and Russian troops fought over an island in the Ussuri River, emphasized how much relations between Peking and Moscow had deteriorated. In Peking, that was the year of greatest danger. The Chinese seriously believed that the Russians might launch a pre-emptive strike against them in overwhelming force. The best units of the PLA were positioned in Mongolia and along the approaches to Peking, as well as at the heart of the atomic arsenal in Sinkiang. But elsewhere, militia and local forces had to face the Russians with minimal equipment along thousands of miles of the Chinese-Soviet border.

When Premier Kosygin attended the funeral of President Ho Chi Minh of North Vietnam later in 1969, he went home by way of Peking and talked with Premier Chou on September 11 for three hours at the airport there. The upshot was an agreement to begin border negotiations and try to normalize relations through an exchange of ambassadors and other measures. But the slow pace of the border talks and the brief reopening of American-Chinese meetings in Warsaw on January 20, 1970, caused *Izvestia*, the organ of the Soviet government, to resume its attacks on Peking. And on May 18, 1970, *Pravda* followed up with a twenty-four-column blockbuster that compared Mao with Hitler and Chiang Kai-shek.

The propaganda war spread with such fury that it dominated the arrangements for the 24th Congress of the CPSU in Moscow on March 30, 1971. A little less than three weeks beforehand, on March 10, the Soviet-controlled "Radio Peace and Progress" accused the Chinese leadership of making China militarily impotent and helping the United States to "neutralize China as a revolutionary factor in Asia." Commemorating the centenary of the Paris Commune on March 18, China responded with a triple-header attack on the Russians in an editorial printed in the *People's Daily*, *Red Flag* and the *Liberation Army Daily*. Here, the Soviet chieftains were accused of having "usurped the leadership of the Soviet Party and State" and of having turned "the dictatorship of the proletariat into the dictatorship of the bourgeoisie and put social-imperialism and social-fascism into force." In a direct attack on Brezhnev by name, the Chinese editorial called his pretensions to "Soviet democracy" nothing but "humbug." Tass, four days later, came back with a rebuke to the Chinese for "a rude attack and slander" against the Soviet leadership.

To no one's surprise, the Chinese refused to attend the unremarkable 24th CPSU Congress. But the Soviet Union's criticism of a coming Chinese rapprochement with the United States must have hit home, for on May Day, 1971, in the midst of the Chinese campaign of smiles toward visiting Americans, another triple-header editorial attack in Peking was aimed at "U.S. imperialism and its running dogs," the same old line. These Chinese were ever adept at denying the obvious.

By that time, the new Soviet ambassador, Vasily Tostikov, was in place in Peking and China had rehabilitated Lin Hsin-chuan, a victim of the Cultural Revolution, to be the first Chinese ambassador to Moscow since 1966. In addition, a new trade agreement between China and the Soviet Union was in effect and the cooperation of the Communist giants apparently continued in support of North Vietnam. There was, however, a slight difference in meaning that did not escape Hanoi's attention. For when Premier Chou visited the North Vietnamese capital on March 5–8, 1971, his language and his tone were considerably more moderate than that of the Soviet Union, although he gave assurance that China's support was as strong as ever. And Mao Tse-tung went out of his way thereafter to emphasize that any who disapproved of Chinese backing for Hanoi were committing an act of "betrayal," a theme he repeated on May 1.[40] The identities of the supposed opponents of continued Chinese aid were not revealed, but it was clear enough that Peking was less enthusiastic about continuing the war than Moscow. Subsequently, during a Peking visit by Gough Whitlam, leader of Australia's opposition Labor Party, he quoted Premier Chou as having been willing to commit China to participate in a new Geneva conference. Moscow was deeply annoyed and sent a high-level mission to Hanoi, pledging full support to the bitter end. The Chinese couldn't do much less,

[40] *The New York Times*, May 21, 1971, p. 10, quoted Chou's account of the great schism.

pending some more practical arrangement with the United States.

The curious Chinese line thus continued to zig and zag, first aimed at arousing fear in Moscow of a détente with the United States, then striking a glancing blow at Washington just to remind the hopeful Americans that China could never be taken for granted. It was hardly likely, however, that the Chinese could come to any understanding with the Brezhnev regime without major concessions that Moscow was in no mood to offer. The invasion of Czechoslovakia in 1968 had been sufficient evidence for Peking that Brezhnev meant what he said when he warned that the Soviet Union would intervene militarily in any state where it believed Moscow's principles of Socialism were being undermined and in danger of being overthrown. The subsequent softening of this doctrine to accommodate Tito didn't make it any easier for Peking to accept. But after Mao's passing, no one could foretell what would happen in the rivalry between the Red giants.

4. A CRISIS OF LEADERSHIP

In the rebuilding of the Chinese government following the end of the Cultural Revolution, the "responsible persons" in charge of key departments turned out for the most part to be the experienced elderly functionaries who had come to power with Mao Tse-tung in 1949. Of the 170 full members of the reconstituted central committee of the Chinese Communist Party named after the Ninth Party Congress, moreover, data available on 118 of these functionaries showed their average age to be sixty-one.

There was no doubt that China's government was in the hands of old men, from the septuagenarian Mao and Chou to the tough top military leaders who were in their mid-sixties. Aside from the ideological wars that appeared to be endemic to China, the major problem of China's leadership was to introduce younger men into the line of succession. It had been all very well to glorify Lin Piao as the personal choice of Mao to carry on, but it had never been very practical because of his constant battle against tuberculosis. At most, Lin could have been expected to stay in power only a few years, had he not fallen out of favor.

If there were promising younger men among the recruits to the ranks of party or government, many must have been trapped in the fierce internal wars of the Cultural Revolution. No one can say how many were sent down to farm communes among the dispossessed Red Guards. Nor can there be any calculation on how many will be able to return to power in the foreseeable future. But the chances are that few will make it while the generation of the "Long March" wields authority. The Chinese old guard, too, dies but never surrenders.

Again taking the central committee of the CCP as a standard, the proportion of members more than seventy years of age dropped from 34 per cent to 17 per cent between 1956 and 1969, while members aged fifty to fifty-nine rose from 10 per cent to 37 per cent. Even among the Communist mandarins whom Mao brought to power, it takes a long time to break through China's age-encrusted ruling system.[41] All the tremendous changes that have occurred in an era that witnessed the fall of a corrupt and venal government in China have not overcome the inherent Chinese mistrust of youthful and inexperienced people. It is not likely that youth will be served through the consolidation of the central government's ninety departments into twenty-eight and the reduction of central government administration personnel to 10,000, only 16 per cent of the total before the Cultural Revolution.[42] In the provinces, factories and communes, administrative structures also have been simplified and reduced by 50 per cent or more, making it even more difficult for a younger leadership to gain essential training.

By 1980 to 1985, the elementary facts of human existence will oblige the Chinese to turn for leadership to an entirely different generation. By that time, the old soldiers of the "Long March" will be fading away and the generation born during that historic movement will be in its forties. To the younger people, the agonies of World War II will be, for the most part, dimly remembered scenes from their childhood and Mao and his works will be dry subjects to be

[41] *Far Eastern Economic Review*, October 3, 1970, p. 16.

[42] Premier Chou En-lai is reported to have made this statement to a visiting Canadian delegation. It was published in the *South China Morning Post*, July 5, 1971.

discussed in the classroom. In the development of China, the insistence on perpetual revolution will have about as much chance of survival as the beliefs of Leon Trotsky in the Soviet Union. For sooner rather than later, the essential conservativeness of Chinese society is bound to reassert itself.

This assumption could, of course, be upset by the possibility of war between China and the Soviet Union, which cannot entirely be dismissed. It could be triggered by an accident or a maniac militarist who seized power in either country. But the ultimate result to both, as all but maniacs and idiots have come to realize, would be a disaster of such colossal magnitude that any reasonable government would shrink from contemplating it. Perhaps there was a time when it might have been possible. It was during the era of the Red Guard uprising, when China lay well-nigh helpless before hordes of rampaging and ferocious young people. It is less likely that even a superconfident Soviet militarist, rattling his missiles and boasting of his atomic arsenal, would want to take on China today.

If there is a possibility that China's return to a more stable government may be blocked in the next decade or two, it will stem as always from internal weakness rather than external causes. For despite Mao's success as an authoritarian administrator, it remains to be seen whether so huge and populous a country will continue to permit itself to be organized along central lines of power after his death. If the pull of regionalism can be resisted by Mao's successors, then there seems to be a good chance that China can continue with its development into a power of the first rank and a major force in the Pacific.

The rulers of this future China are now in the lower ranks of the administrative structure, the Army, or perhaps still in school. What their view is of the world at large and their country's place in it may be very greatly influenced in the next decade by the manner in which the other great powers of the Pacific—the United States, the Soviet Union and Japan—treat the interests of China. Thus, it is no longer as important as it once was for Americans to worry over the differences between Mao Tse-tung and Chiang Kai-shek. Very soon, that will be ancient history, if it isn't already. Nor are the ideological differences between the United States and China so monumental that they should be permitted to block the rational development of mutual interests. It is to the China of the next generation, rather than the fading one of the present, that a realistic American policy must address itself in the years immediately to come.

VIII. New Era in the Pacific

1. A FRESH START FOR AMERICA

After fighting three Asian wars in thirty years at a cost that finally became insupportable, the United States needs a new set of policies for the Pacific. The old strategy, with its dependence on direct military intervention, shaky Asian allies and unpopular foreign bases, is bankrupt. It can no longer be sustained.

The withdrawal from Vietnam, accompanied by a changed American posture toward China and Japan, marks the beginning of a new course for the United States. It cannot be the end. For the tactics of temporary accommodation, as exemplified by the Guam Doctrine, can fulfill only a temporary need. That course can scarcely serve as the sole strategic guideline of the United States in the Indo-Pacific area.

The world that is heading toward the twenty-first century no longer is dominated by two superpowers, as it was for two decades after 1945, for new power centers are growing in Western Europe, to which Britain has now committed itself; in a resurgent Japan, and in a developing China that has assumed great authority in the United Nations. Both the United States and the Soviet Union must reckon with these new giants in the foreseeable future, particularly in formulating policies in the Pacific.

Essentials of a Policy

There is a limited amount of time at the disposal of the United States to develop new policies that are realistic, workable and worthy of basic public support. For peace in the Indo-Pacific is very fragile today; neither the United Nations nor any international conference can guarantee how long it will last.

Any new American posture, therefore, must be aimed realistically at preserving peace, primarily through collective action and not merely through American armed might. This time, there must be a clearer public understanding of what the United States can and cannot do in the massive Indo-Pacific crescent that encompasses one-third of mankind in its sweep from Japan through Southeast Asia and on to the Indian subcontinent.

Such policies must also take into account the hard facts of geography—that the Pacific is as important to American security in the largest sense as the Atlantic, and that the states of Hawaii and Alaska, the island territory of Guam and the Trust Territory are outposts as vital to the United States as the Mediterranean and the Rhine.

Such policies cannot ignore the lessons of history and fall into the neo-isolationist gaucherie that the non-white peoples of the Pacific, with the exception of Japan, do not count for much and that the United States can turn its back on them. The terrible reality is that war came to the United States from the Pacific in 1941, 1950 and 1961.

Such policies, moreover, can scarcely nullify existing commitments. If current treaties or understandings in the Indo-Pacific are inconvenient, if they are unrealistic or outdated, there are well-defined methods of renegotiating such matters without discrediting American diplomacy and repudiating American pledges.

The slow and sometimes painful resolution of the changed relationships between the United States and Japan, the United States and China, and the United States and the Soviet Union illustrates the problems that are involved.

In short, in any unfolding American policies for the Indo-Pacific, the crucial elements to be considered are whether they will command the trust of our allies, the respect of our enemies and the support of the American public. As hindsight has long since demonstrated, it was precisely these elements that were missing in the policies that plunged the United States into the Vietnam War and created the worst civil strife in America since the draft riots of 1863.

No American government of the future can afford to risk the nation's survival again on such poorly conceived and stealthily executed plans. The days of American empire building in the Orient are over.

What the Public Can Do

The American public should not be regarded as an insuperable obstacle to the decision-making process, as some of the more eminent careerists in the State Department have sourly concluded. Such officials have, in their time, acted as if Congress existed solely for the purpose of cutting their representation allowances and reducing the staff cars at their disposal. No doubt, it is annoying to one nurtured on the theory of rule by a superior elite to find that the public doesn't believe a word of it. But then, the public has to put up with a lot of nonsense from the State Department and can't be blamed too much for refusing to be spoon-fed on even such intricate matters as foreign policy.

More often than not, the American public does react positively to leadership for causes of which it approves, whether the response is to the gaudy imperialism of the trumpeters of Manifest Destiny or the self-interest implicit in Franklin Delano Roosevelt's New Deal. It is only when the public is outraged and frustrated and determined to exercise its veto against policies of which it disapproves that it throws off all restraint and resorts to violence.

From the Boston Tea Party to the abolitionists who smuggled slaves into freedom, and from the architects of the war against Spain to the "little group of willful men" who whipped up public sentiment against Woodrow Wilson and the League of Nations, the calculations of a less than omniscient power elite in the United States have on occasion been blocked, changed or upset by public action. And that was particularly true of the Vietnam War, for an adverse public opinion virtually forced Lyndon Baines Johnson out of the White House for his share in that ineffable but avoidable tragedy.

What the Public Cannot Do

Outwardly, the American democratic ideal is based on the concept of a strong Presidency and not much attention is given to the Constitutional system of checks and balances until a crisis bursts all bounds. Thus, the Asians who depend on Presidential assurances of support suddenly find that the Senate must "advise and consent" to the exercise of treaty-making powers in foreign affairs and the House holds the purse strings. But just when foreign sophisticates triumphantly point out how hopelessly divided American society is when Congress and the President are at odds, the Supreme Court will hand down a whole series of new policy-making decisions on such matters as press freedom and school desegregation.

In the American system of separation of powers, quite clearly, there can be no hope of any major policy development of a positive nature from a protest movement. No strike, no boycott, no march or street demonstration, no appalling outburst of fighting and shooting by a public galvanized into action can possibly serve as a substitute for the flexible relationship between the three coordinate branches of the American government. A protesting group, regardless of the nobility of its leaders, cannot draft the simplest law, let alone a complicated tax structure on which American financial order rests; nor can it, in its rage and fervor and impatience to get things done, devote the necessary care to the development of weapons systems for the national defense or wise policies for the conduct of affairs of state.

It is to the orderly processes of government, in consequence, that appeals must be made for the fresh start that the United States so urgently needs in its changed relationship with the nations of the Indo-Pacific. And yet, when I made probes in Washington during 1971 for something beyond the new approach to China, the Southeast Asian withdrawal and the graceless treatment of Japan, I found no evidence of the growth of a coherent Asian policy. I learned, instead, that the ablest and most innovative minds had to concentrate on day-to-day matters. As one key official said to me, "I haven't had a chance to look beyond the first turn in the road." Nor was there evidence of coherent action between the White House and the State Department. In making his approaches to China, for example, President Nixon acted almost alone.

The Battle for Asia

There are enormous difficulties in creating an improved posture for the United States in the Pacific, let alone an entirely new one. For the division between the "have" nations of the Northern Hemisphere and the "have-nots" of the Southern Hemisphere has become as acerbic in its own way as the more familiar struggles between East and West. In addition, nearly everywhere in Asia, the United States is usually made the symbol of the "haves," who hold so much of the world's wealth in their grasp. It is neither a pleasant nor a tenable position for the United States in a part of the world where hunger is still a more pervasive issue than freedom.

It would, of course, be marvelous if the United States had the wealth, the will and the power to create unilaterally a new era of peace and plenty in the Pacific. Such an age, so eagerly sought by the developing lands of Asia, conjures up the glamorous image of contented peoples living everywhere in the grand American style with embellishments. It presumes the presence of expanding industrial economies and farm production. It implies, in so happy a time, that governments will be distinguished by their restraint, purity and wisdom and selfless leaders will be motivated only by the advancement of the public weal.

The dream is very pretty but unrealistic in the extreme. For it is beyond the power of the United States, or even a union of the great industrial nations, if such a thing were possible, to soon bring about so profound a change in the status of a substantial part of the world's population. The United States, in its libertarian zeal, has worked itself into an economic fix by trying to provide sufficient welfare money for every American to live at least at the poverty level. What would happen if this kind of scheme were tried on a world-wide scale fairly boggles the imagination.

It simply isn't possible as the world is constituted today. For there is no peace in Asia, despite the American withdrawal, and there is no truly abundant life for the Asian masses in the Western manner outside Japan. While there has been economic progress in South Korea, Thailand, Taiwan, Malaysia, Singapore and Hong Kong, it has brought political unrest in its wake. And in many a less-favored land, even a modicum of stability is a far-off vision.

On such a shifting and uncertain foundation, it would be difficult to build a new set of relationships based on the old formula of offensive-defensive alliances and balance-of-power interests. Nor are existing obligations very easily maintained by either the United States or any other industrial power. In fact, since the beginning of the American withdrawal from Vietnam, tensions actually appear to have increased elsewhere in the Indo-Pacific for a variety of reasons.

The battle for Asia is far from over, in consequence. At the height of the American pullout, there was fighting on the territories of eight of the twelve non-Communist countries from West Pakistan to South Vietnam. Both peace and plenty are therefore remote from truncated Pakistan and Ceylon, shaken by civil war; the war-ravaged Indo-china states of South Vietnam, Laos and Cambodia; and three others still troubled by border insurrections, Thailand, Malaysia and Burma. India, the victor over Pakistan, remains subject periodically to violence in West Bengal, Kerala and Kashmir, while unstable Bangladesh represents a new source of danger. In East Asia, South Korea and Taiwan are garrison states under continual threat, the Philippines is still fighting the Huk rebels, and Hong Kong can never feel truly secure.

All that the removal of the United States military presence can accomplish in such a situation, as far as Asia is concerned, is to intensify the rivalry among the remaining major Pacific powers for influence in the area. To some extent this is already happening. The Soviet Union, through a combination of military assistance, trade and economic aid, is trying to build a wall of hostility around China. In India, to date, the Soviet policy has succeeded brilliantly. The Chinese, with much less to offer, are gambling on a dual policy toward some of their non-Communist neighbors, offering trade and aid while at the same time giving comfort to indigenous rebel movements. And some Asians have begun to play off one against the other.

However, it is Japan—minus an aggressive army or fleet, minus offensive air power or atomic weapons or missiles—that is making the greatest progress in the Indo-Pacific through the sheer pressure of its economic power. True, the Japanese greatly benefited as an American supplier in the Korean and Vietnam wars. But Japan needs the United States far less today than it once did, except as a trading partner, and even that link is declining in importance. There may come a time, perhaps before the decade is out, when the United States will need Japan more than Japan will need the United States.

For the role of Japan is ever expanding in the Pacific while the United States is retreating from its once dominant part in the affairs of Asia. Its position at the pinnacle of world leadership is threatened and may already be diminished, if not completely undermined.

Why Not Isolation?

There is a widespread conviction among Asian leaders that the American withdrawal will be followed by a slide into isolation. Most of those to whom I have talked believe that the trend is irreversible. They base their analysis on the revulsion of a very large section of the American public against the wars in Indochina, the profound antimilitary feeling in the United States and the steep decline in foreign aid as a part of American policy. Some in Japan and Thailand are all for cutting loose from the United States now.

Many Asians also see the specter of a protectionist wall being erected by the United States against their products, primarily because of their experience with the 10 per cent import surcharge that was imposed and withdrawn in 1971. Many already have experienced the effect of drastic cuts in foreign aid from the United States and see no hope that it will increase soon. But most of all, they are depressed by the distressing evidence of American division and disorder at home and the feeling of leading Americans that the country must attack its internal problems instead of spreading its resources around the world. Despite the new economic program on which Americans embarked in 1971–72 and the devaluation of the dollar, few influential Asians believe that the persistent malaise of the American economy will disappear overnight.

This is all perfectly true as reportage, but it doesn't depict the situation accurately. There *is* an ugly mood in the United States today that, for want of a better term, is called neo-isolationism. But it no more resembles the old isolationism of the long armistice between the two world wars than the United States of the 1970s resembles the United States of the 1920s. The Chicago *Tribune,* that pillar of the old isolationism, is unhappy with the neo-isolationists and fights them at every turn. *The New York Times,* the old crusader for intervention in World War II and the champion of world trade, is the great organ of the peace movement, with which the neo-isolationists identify themselves.

The shifting of forces is even more marked in the political arena. Here the Democrats—the party of Wilson and Franklin Delano Roosevelt—have labored mightily to become the peace party of the 1970s and the champions of domestic progress. The Republicans— the party of Warren Gamaliel Harding and Henry Cabot Lodge, Sr.—have supported the long effort to deny victory to the Communists in Indochina by fighting an extended and increasingly perilous retreating action. Behind the party labels, moreover, there has been still further shifting of ground, with the liberals of both parties generally grouped behind the peace movement and the conservatives ranged in fundamental but declining opposition.

But let American interests be touched in Europe or the Middle East and an electric shock runs through the body politic. Overnight, there is a furious changing of sides and the nation suddenly finds the old political line-up still holds, with the Europe Firsters of the liberal Eastern establishment holding off the challenge of the Asia Firsters from the old isolationist Midwest. Nothing more strikingly illustrated the kaleidoscopic nature of foreign policy in the United States of the 1970s than the Senate's voting on two troop withdrawal amendments offered by Senator Mike Mansfield, the Montana Democrat and Senate majority leader, in 1971. The first, calling for unilateral withdrawal of American troops from Europe, was decisively beaten by a coalition between supporters of the Nixon Administration and the Eastern liberals. The second, demanding a complete pullout from

Vietnam nine months after the freeing of American prisoners of war, won easily despite Administration opposition.[1]

The available evidence would seem to indicate that, despite the obstacles created by American misadventures in Asia, there is still a strong current running in the United States toward continued commitment to Western Europe and Britain in opposition to the Soviet Union. It is clear that the tide is ebbing as far as support for Israel in the Middle East is concerned. But for the rest of Asia, Latin America and Africa, even the suggestion of American military intervention would run into headlong public opposition.

It can scarcely be argued, therefore, that the old isolationist fervor has gripped the United States once more. This is not the country that turned its back on the League of Nations and gloried in the restrictive Smoot-Hawley Tariff Act. Despite all the failures of the United Nations, it retains majority support among the American public. And despite wide disillusionment with the usefulness of all the post-World War II treaties into which the United States entered, they cannot be lightly shuffled off and discarded because the public doesn't like them. There is no thought among the great global corporations in the United States of cutting back their operations to the water's edge; nor is there any sign, for that matter, that the millions of American tourists have lost their zest for adventuring abroad.

Why not isolation? In a few words, it isn't possible in the United States of today. What has happened, in effect, is that both the American government and the American people have slowly come to the realization that the United States is badly overcommitted in the world and will have to reassess its priorities. But there is not a chance that Uncle Sam will be permitted to stick his head in the sand and pretend that the rest of the world doesn't exist. If nothing else deters him, the sure knowledge that Russian long-range missiles are constantly pointed in his direction will oblige him to maintain his strength in the international community for as long as he is able to do so.

The Asians have a point in complaining about American isolation,

---

[1] The Senate's vote on May 19, 1971, on the European pullout was 61–36 against. On June 22, the vote in favor of the Vietnam pullout was 57–42. It was later compromised in conference with the House before the bill was finally approved.

but they are confusing the issue. It is not isolation from the world that Americans so ardently desire. What they quite rightly seek is a period of disengagement from an involvement in Asian affairs that became too heavy a burden for even the United States to bear. But the era of detachment, if it can be called that, will not last forever. It may not even continue for the remainder of this decade, for it is not in the national interest of the United States to turn its back on Asia for very long. It is not a very practical posture from which to defend the Pacific, as the Japanese demonstrated at Pearl Harbor.

The New Colonialism

There is a persistent feeling among the members of the old Eastern liberal-intellectual coalition that the basis for a new American policy for Asia should be a union of interest with Western Europe and Japan. The might of this industrial combination, so the argument goes, could stand off challenges from both the Soviet Union and China in giving practical assistance to developing countries. As one American ambassador in Asia put it to me, "Why shouldn't we work with the Europeans and the Japanese for the benefit of developing countries? The Europeans know how to handle national development. With our support and Japan's, they could do a better job than any of these people who depend on Socialist slogans."

It is, at first examination, an attractive idea. The assumption is that the developing countries would be under expert tutelage if Japan and Western Europe plus Britain could be persuaded to join the United States in a kind of super Marshall Plan for the Indo-Pacific area. It would be expected, of course, that the influence of the industrial countries would be benign and that the Asians would meekly do as they were told in return for a supposed cornucopia of benefits. Naturally, there would also be a workable financial proviso under which loans from the industrial powers would be repayable in time by the grateful recipients out of the proceeds of their modernized plant and commerce. Thus, every party would benefit. There would be no losers. And Asians—two and a half billion of them—would live happily every after.

Unfortunately, the scheme won't work. In the first place, the Asians aren't likely to accept any new colonialism—paternal or not—only a generation or so after having expelled their former European masters. In the second, Japan and West Germany are doing very well individually in their programs for trade and aid and could not be expected to subordinate their interests to those of the United States in a superindustrial combine. Finally, the assumption that Europeans, the British, the Japanese or the Americans are masters at the business of national development requires quite a bit of examination. Indochina, the Indian subcontinent, China and the Philippines, among others, can scarcely be said to admire their former colonial rulers to such an extent that they would want them to return en masse. The bearers of such gifts as the industrial nations have to offer are not generally welcomed in Asia without suspicion.

There is something to the notion of a limited partnership between developing lands and industrialized countries on mutually satisfactory terms. But such an arrangement does not grow out of any grandiloquent scheme; rather, it is more in the nature of a consortium, operating under the World Bank to handle loans on a country-by-country basis. And even the modest consortium, with its limited powers, runs into trouble when the beneficiary can't keep up the payments, as has sometimes happened. Then the industrial countries either lose their money or have to settle for less than the original bargain, the beneficiary hates them for it, and there is very little to show for all the effort.

A Change of Direction

The United States has been accustomed since World War II to be regarded as the leader of every enterprise upon which it embarks with other nations. Americans have been continually reminded, at home and abroad, that they are the leaders of the free world, the mightiest and richest nation on earth, the leading industrial state and the most advanced in the development of science and technology. No wonder, therefore, that American aims in foreign policy have been stated in such all-embracing terms and that successive American governments since World War II have predicated their international strategy on a global commitment. The notion of an American century and an American guardianship over the peace of the world was accepted by many in the United States almost as a matter of course.

The success of the Marshall Plan in rebuilding Western Europe and saving it from Communism seemed to confirm the God-given sense of mission so prevalent among many Americans of the older generation.

But over a quarter century of fighting the world's battles and filling power vacuums wherever they occurred, the United States has had to pay dearly in terms of declining political and military influence abroad and disunity at home. The once-almighty dollar is almighty no longer, but a devalued and vulnerable unit of currency on a world market that prizes the West German mark, the Japanese yen and the Swiss franc. Serious challenges to American dominance in world markets are developing in both Japan and the European Common Market. The United States already has lost leadership in the race for supersonic air transport to the Soviet Union and the Japanese today have the world's largest steel company. Even the mighty American automotive industry is having its troubles with rising foreign competition. And in the United Nations, where the United States once merely had to give the signal to roll up an automatic voting majority, it is becoming increasingly difficult for an American proposal of substance to get through the General Assembly.

All these signs add up to a positive warning that the American superpower mentality had best be dropped and that the United States would do well to moderate its posture before the world. The hard truth is that there never was an American century and never will be, and that American dominance of the world existed only in the imaginations of Fourth of July orators. It is all very well to say that the United States, despite its declining influence, remains a great power and cannot very well avoid the responsibilities of leadership. But this scarcely means that the tradition of John Foster Dulles should dominate American foreign policy initiatives, as it has for too long a time. A change of direction is badly needed.

In response to such counsel, it is only to be expected that there will be yawps of protest from the thinning ranks of the old Cold War warriors who argue that it is the American destiny to oppose the spread of Communism in general and the Soviet Union and Communist China in particular. However, even the most ardent of patriots must agree that the United States can scarcely act alone in so formidable an assignment. Allies for the anti-Communist crusade are regrettably few outside Chiang Kai-shek, Nguyen Van Thieu, Balthazar J. Vorster and a handful of Latin-American dictators. And pacts like NATO, SEATO, CENTO and the rest will be as dead as the Peace of Westphalia before the coming of the twenty-first century.

This is not to say that Communist societies represent the wave of the future. For the Soviet Union, too, is having an increasing amount of trouble in maintaining even the semblance of leadership behind what once was an Iron Curtain. There are as many kinds of Communist parties and beliefs as there are nations, and almost as much ferment as there is in the Western world. In Eastern Europe, despite the menace of the Red Army, Yugoslavia already has broken away and Rumania is making a brave attempt; and while the Czechs, Hungarians, Poles and East Germans have been crushed for asserting themselves, their day will come again. As for the regimes that govern in Asia in the name of Socialism, many are trying to play Peking off against Moscow in an effort to avoid domination by either. No nation, developing or not, is comfortable in the role of a helpless satellite.

In so fluid a situation, there is no possibility for the reconstitution of an American-led grand alliance. The best effort that the United States was able to make came during the Korean War, and it worked—after a fashion—only because it was done under the auspices of the United Nations. Even so, foreign troop contributions at best were only one-sixth of the American forces and the economic funding for the effort from foreign nations was even less. The attempt to create a facade of international support for the Vietnam War was an even greater failure for American policy.

That, in consequence, is not likely to be tried again for the foreseeable future. Instead of shooting out old-fashioned lines of power to allies and client states in the Indo-Pacific from now on, the United States will have to depend more on the formulation of a consensus policy. Washington has been placed once too often in the ludicrous situation of George C. Marshall's general who went charging uphill toward the enemy crying "Forward, men!" only to find that nobody was following him. It won't do any longer. The United States will have to develop policies of mutual benefit to the nations of the Pacific, on which it can offer to stand with them in a common front, or it will forfeit what remains of its influence and leadership.

There is nothing very dramatic or appealing about such moderation, but the "giant leap forward" has not enjoyed notable success in Asia. A number of small beneficial projects often add up to improvements in the lives of more people than one massive structure. The many small dams and other installations in the Mekong River Delta eventually will become a mighty flood control and water conservation system that will bring more benefit to the people of both Vietnams, Laos, Cambodia and Thailand than all the wars in their history. The support that the United States could give to such a development, in common with other industrialized nations, would signal a welcome change in direction both for the people of Indochina and the people of the United States. If it is in the American tradition to help rebuild Western Europe regardless of whether destitute nations were allies or enemies, it is equally vital for the United States to extend such assistance to lands that its war-making powers have devastated in Asia. The pledge was implied in President Johnson's Johns Hopkins speech in the period of the escalation of the Vietnam War. It is now time to make good, but not solely as an American effort.

There are possibilities for numerous other such policies of mutual benefit in Asia, in which the United States can participate without prejudice against governments of differing or even opposing political and economic beliefs. But the motivating principle in Asian policy should be cooperation among a group of nations rather than major responsibility for any single country. Fishermen have long demonstrated that a network, however slender its binding cords, is more efficient and productive than a single strong line. It is time that statesmen learned the lesson.

2. THE LIMITS OF AMERICAN SECURITY

It is a part of the mythology of developing countries, particularly in Asia, that if the United States and other industrial powers cut military spending, the proceeds would increase the flow of foreign aid. The underprivileged American masses of the urban ghettos oppose military expenditures on the same basis, hoping to obtain more funds to relieve their own hardships. But alas for the poor of all lands, the largesse of government is distributed by political rule of thumb on the basis of national requirements rather than social justice.

It is both unnatural and cruel, therefore, to foster the delusion that the end of the Vietnam War means an appreciable cut in the American defense budget that can then be put to more humanitarian uses at home and abroad. Nothing short of an American demobilization on the post-World War II scale, with the mothballing of a substantial part of the Navy and dismantling of the aerospace program, would make possible a major reduction in the American defense budget during an inflationary period. With the reduction of American troops in Vietnam past the halfway mark, the defense budget for fiscal year 1972 was still more than $71 billion, with little hope of sizable cuts in years to come. This was the cost of maintaining armed forces of nearly 3,500,000 personnel on active duty, a fleet of almost 900 warships and some 35,000 aircraft in all branches of the service plus a mammoth aerospace program. Moreover, with the nation moving toward the end of conscription and an all-volunteer Army, a pay increase of $1.8 billion was approved that assured a raw recruit of nearly $5,000 a year plus other benefits.

A despairing liberal, Senator Walter F. Mondale of Minnesota, complained against the allotment of $13 billion to develop a reusable launching device to shuttle payloads into space to sustain American astronauts. "For that," he said, "we could quadruple the federal government's combined annual outlays to fight crime, pollution and cancer. Is a space shuttle four times more important than safe streets, clean air and water and freedom from deadly diseases?"

As far as the executive and legislative branches of the American government were concerned, the answer was yes. With unemployment somewhere between 5 and 6 per cent and the economy in a sluggish state, it was not a time when anybody wanted to vote down appropriations that would put still more factories out of business. Returning Vietnam War veterans, mustered out of service, were having such difficulty finding employment that special Presidential appeals were being made in their behalf.

From the Communist camp came charges that the United States

could not be prosperous without a war. It wasn't necessarily so. The troubles of the world's first trillion-dollar economy weren't due primarily to deep cuts in defense spending but to the inexorable self-generating pressures of inflation, tolerated for too long by a timorous government that finally clamped on partial controls late in 1971 at the eleventh hour. In a world with 23,000,000 men under arms, more than half of them in developing areas, and with the world's military spending exceeding $200 billion a year, the United States remained most reluctant to cut its military strength.[2] Thus, the Defense Department—despite the strain on the economy—still planned to run military bases all over the world and proposed to maintain air bases and naval forces in the Southeast Asia area beyond the end of the Vietnam troop withdrawals.[3]

Are Foreign Bases Necessary?

The period is fast approaching, nevertheless, when the United States will have to bring home its troops and close down the bases it has maintained since World War II, either as a whole or in large part. Even if humanitarian considerations are ignored, the dictates of an uncertain economy cannot be swept aside. In addition, the continued American occupancy of foreign bases is such a sore point with most foreign governments that they become a distinct American handicap. Foreign Minister Carlos P. Romulo of the Philippines, for example, regards Clark Air Base as the single most divisive factor in American-Filipino relations. Other statesmen elsewhere have similar, but more discreetly phrased, complaints.

After the armistice of Panmunjom, it is true that there was good cause to keep American troops in South Korea. The same rationale had dictated the United States military deployments in shattered Japan and West Germany immediately after World War II. Probably, there remains good reason to maintain an American military presence today in such major trouble spots as Berlin, but such points of international tension are very few and could as well be serviced by a symbolic international force. Outside such centers, near the end of the

[2] U.S. Arms Control & Disarmament Agency survey quoted in *The New York Times*, May 6, 1971, p. 7.

[3] Washington *Post*, April 14, 1971, p. 1.

third decade after World War II and the second since the Korean War, it becomes difficult to defend the presence of American occupation forces in either Europe or Asia and without any justification elsewhere. We have here no Tenth Legion of Rome, destined to be stationed in the Middle East for 400 years, nor Spanish conquistadores, who occupied the Philippines for almost as long. The dictates of both politics and prudence should be sufficient ground for the conclusion that any prolonged American occupation of foreign territory is self-defeating.

One of the reasons for the maintenance of foreign bases by the United States is that American military leadership has stubbornly insisted that they are necessary, although a few have been given up here and there voluntarily. It was at Japanese insistence, finally, that a proper program of reversion of bases to Japanese control was instituted. And in France, the only thing Charles de Gaulle could think of to get the American military off French soil was to dispatch them and NATO, as well, out of the country. Not many other countries have had either the desire or the will to dispense with their American military guests in such summary fashion, some because they liked the extra income and others because they wanted leverage to pry more aid out of Washington. But nobody did it for love of the American GI, who can be a mighty troublesome visitor when he is bored and has nothing to occupy him.

Until the disastrous division over the Vietnam War, not many American public men would take the risk of challenging the military's need for foreign bases. For the response was an accusing reminder that any question about foreign bases played into the hands of the Soviet Union, which for a quarter century annually raised the issue in the United Nations by demanding an end to all such occupation forces. To be called a Communist in those days was the equivalent of being convicted of espionage or worse.

Yet, no less an authority than John Foster Dulles warned that it was "dangerous to let military factors determine foreign policy." He conceded that it was always tempting to accede to military requests because they were so tangible, whereas the disadvantages to military proposals were frequently intangible. "To get an air base at the price of good will," he wrote, "may be a very bad bargain." He agreed, too, that the military emphasis in American foreign policy "has greatly helped Soviet Communism to win victories and has helped Communists in other lands to exert more influence and increase their following."

This was his conclusion: "It is, I think, a fair question to ask: Who has been helped most by seeming to give our foreign policy a militaristic pattern, the United States or the Soviet Union? We have, perhaps, gained some military advantage. But we have paid a high price in moral and psychological disadvantages. Just how high that price is, we can only guess, for only a small part of the cost has been revealed."[4]

In Vietnam, the cost was very great—about 50,000 American combat deaths and several times that many wounded and missing, an expenditure of $150 billion and a deep and enervating division among the American people.

Whatever foreign bases may be worth, they aren't worth that much to the United States. With a few prime exceptions such as Berlin, Panama and the like, where the American national interest is intensely committed, they should be closed down as quickly and expeditiously as possible. The bases have long since reached the point of diminishing returns. Most of them have been retained for years at an insupportable cost to American global relationships as well as to the American economy.

There has been, as well, a decided change in many of the assumptions behind the American defense posture, which gave rise to the base system. The issue of ideology no longer is as important as it once was and rivalry in the Indo-Pacific may assume many different forms. Nor can the area be neatly divided into power blocs or spheres of influence in an era when an intercontinental missile with multiple atomic warheads can cross the vast Pacific in thirty minutes. Merely to mention the notion of containment today arouses derision; it never was very practical to think of walling off the 250,000,000 people of the Soviet Union or the 800,000,000 people of China. Even the traditional functions of the nation-state itself are weakening in a time of developing commitment to an international community.

[4] John Foster Dulles, *War or Peace* (New York: Macmillan, 1950), p. 239.

The time has not come for world government; in the Utopian sense, it is an impractical ideal. But no nation can exist any longer in the modern world as a law unto itself, brushing aside all considerations except the will of its rulers. The uses of power are limited. And while the meek have not exactly inherited the earth, small nations are not always overawed by the big ones. The Soviet Union has had its problems in Albania and Yugoslavia. The United States has failed in Cuba and in Vietnam. And in many an international crisis, from Czechoslovakia to the Dominican Republic, the use of force has proved to be counterproductive.

It would be foolish to assume that war will soon be abandoned by the nations of the world as an instrument of policy. But it would be downright insane to conclude that the United States must continue to risk involvement of its armed forces in so many distant conflicts where its enemies appear to have a fair prospect of winning some temporary advantage. There are too many centers of power in the Indo-Pacific area now to fear that any one will be able to dominate all others and arise as a menace to the security of the United States. The old power-bloc game isn't what it used to be. There are too many players and they can—and will continue to—change sides with dizzying frequency. And some will pursue a double or even a triple course if it seems to be to their advantage to do so.

In such a revolutionary situation, the only posture the United States can reasonably consider is one of caution, restraint and great flexibility in the Indo-Pacific.

Is There an American Defense Line?

The "big island" chain of American defenses in the Pacific, studded with bases and reinforced by roving naval and air units, has been an article of faith with the American military for a quarter century. On paper, it made a very neat pattern from Japan and South Korea on the north through Taiwan and the Philippines with a mainland anchor in Vietnam and Thailand, after which the line ran off across Indonesia to Australia and New Zealand, the southern outposts. To keep China on notice that American power was in the area, there were atomic bases on Okinawa and the Seventh Fleet patrolled the Taiwan Strait. To restrain the Soviet Union, there were Polaris submarines and thousands of intermediate and intercontinental missiles suitably positioned for attack or counterattack.

As a military theory, all this was beautiful. It was in accord with textbook strategy and might very well have discouraged a Japanese attack on Pearl Harbor in the pre-atomic era before World War II, even with less armament and more distant bases. But in today's changing world, the system simply did not work. A far-off defense line based on the principle of atomic deterrence had no effect at all on tens of thousands of determined little Asian guerrillas in black pajamas. Nor did day-and-night bombing from the air disrupt primitive routes of transport and supply for very long or interfere with the rudimentary economy of North Vietnam. The jungles, mountains and vast river systems of Southeast Asia proved to be a better defense than all the artificially constructed lines and strong points put together by the United States over so many years and at such enormous cost. Like the Maginot Line of France during World War II, the American "island chain" of defense was rendered useless without ever being directly attacked.

With the reversion of Okinawa to Japan, and the liquidation of bases in the home islands on an orderly time schedule, the Japanese are taking charge of their own defense. Just how much the United States will be able to count on Japanese military cooperation in the next decade or two remains an open question. Similarly, the American military withdrawal from South Korea has the effect of forcing the Koreans into greater dependence on the Japanese. The Filipinos, characteristically, never know quite what to do and talk a great deal about cutting their ties with the United States but can't quite bring themselves to do it. And Taiwan, in the foreseeable future, will be of dubious reliance. As for bases on the mainland of Southeast Asia, the chances are that they won't be available for too much longer, and Indonesia isn't likely to settle easily into a solely American defense pattern. Thus, Australia and New Zealand remain the only reliable allies for the United States in the Pacific during the next generation or so.

It isn't a pleasant picture, but it is reasonably accurate. And while it does not accord with sonorously optimistic military pronouncements from the Pentagon, it takes into account the considerable reaction against the United States in the Indo-Pacific area. None of the defense treaties into which the United States has entered with the nations of the region have very much meaning any more, and that goes for the mutual defense pact with Japan as well as others. Realistically, therefore, the "big island" chain of American defenses in the Western Pacific continues to exist only on military maps with menacing red areas for the Communist side and more patriotic coloration for the United States, its allies and clients.

There is actually no single, practical line of defense for the United States in the Pacific any longer. It is doubtful, in fact, that any realistic defense perimeter of American interests could be drawn, as Dean Acheson did on the eve of the Korean War. This is not so much because the military can find no place for the United States to take a stand. Rather, there is utter uncertainty in the highest military echelons that Congress and public opinion would support any recommendation by the Pentagon that might entrap American forces in another unwanted Asian conflict. Even if such support were possible, in the poisonous atmosphere that pervades American public life, no sensible occupant of the White House would readily consider initiating military action in Asia for some years.

In a very real sense, because of the limiting processes of an open society at war with itself, the Pentagon is entering a period when it may not be able to do much more than offer a response to foreign military initiatives that directly clash with American vital interests. It is a dangerous time and its span is very likely to be prolonged. For the global grasp of the United States, militarily, is simply not up to its reach. The high point in American military history may well have been that heroic September day in Tokyo Bay in 1945 when General Douglas MacArthur accepted Japan's surrender aboard the U.S.S. *Missouri*.

Despite the mighty American arsenal of nuclear weapons and missiles, therefore, it is entirely possible that the United States will have to fall back eventually to Guam and the Trust Territory in the central Pacific, with Alaska and the Aleutians as a northern front and

Australia as a southern front (if the Australians still agree) and Hawaii as a rear support base. But that would by no means be a forward defense line, in the World War II sense in which so much military thinking is still conducted. Nor would it be as calamitous as the military will make it sound.

American naval and air forces still retain an admirable capability for patrolling the Western Pacific, and the Indian Ocean as well, if need be. The strategy of a blue water and air defense is not to be despised; its very mobility gives it a great advantage over land-based units on either the Asian islands or the mainland. It has the added attraction, moreover, of far greater security than forces that are tied to a finite point of land. And it would be difficult, to say the least, for any publicity-minded activist to organize a picketing or stone-throwing demonstration against American units far distant from his land. Merely to stone American embassies or burn American books under such circumstances would not have much effect even among Asians.

It is also worth noting that the technology of warfare is not frozen by any means. To Americans brought up on the theory that a strong offense is the best defense, there is something heretical about maintaining a defensive strategy in a world where the hydrogen bomb is the ultimate offensive weapon and the missile is regarded as unstoppable. For whatever it may be worth to bolster the argument for a defense-oriented strategy, it should be pointed out that the chief result of the development of nuclear arms since World War II has been the "balance of terror" that has staved off a nuclear war to date. If the world is lucky enough to contain the spread of nuclear arms and bring about a reduction in the arsenals that now exist, there will be more time for the development of a stronger defense technology.

The great uncertainty, of course, is whether a truly effective anti-ballistic missile system can be perfected and matched against incoming missiles. It does not exist as yet but the Japanese, for one, believe it to be worth further examination and work. This is one area of major military technological development to which the United States should be giving far more attention than it does. All nuclear powers are well aware that the United States possesses a highly credible second-strike capability. But if a better defensive posture is to be adopted, potential American losses through an enemy first strike will have to be minimized.

There is no implication here that a "Fortress America" will have to be created to protect the United States of the next generation. It would be absurd to postulate that this would be the result of the retreat from long-occupied American bases on the Asian mainland or islands, or even the withdrawal of all American forces in Europe. The United States managed quite well before Commodore Dewey won the battle of Manila Bay and created a ready-made Pacific empire. Nor did Wilson's great crusade to make the world safe for democracy lay down a precedent for the presence of American troops in a warring Europe, although the belief is now enshrined in Foggy Bottom.

It is the better part of wisdom in a highly volatile period in Asian history not to have the Marines land at every outraged cry for help and try to take the situation in hand. If there are many more such unwise involvements in Asia or anywhere else, the backlash of an aroused American public opinion would do more to stimulate the rise of a "Fortress America" psychology than any prudent and necessary withdrawal of American armed forces.

In casting about for a substitute for American intervention to maintain order here or there, more than one American policy-making official has observed that a breakdown of the orderly processes of government in an Asian land really benefits nobody and it is as much in the Communist as in the American interest to see that anarchy is contained. The response to the rebellion of the Guevara groups in Ceylon is a case in point, for, within a short time after the government appealed for help, there was tangible assistance from the United States, Britain, the Soviet Union, China and almost a dozen other countries of all shades of political opinion.

It is tempting to conclude, in consequence, that a world force to suppress anarchy could be created in the interest of all nations directly concerned whenever the need arises. But there aren't many lands quite as helpless as Ceylon and there is no guarantee that the rival nations will respond with equal facility and effectiveness. There is more than a suspicion that this was the case in Ceylon. But even if there were to be a movement to suppress anarchy, in the Ceylon manner, it probably wouldn't last very long. Metternich, that great defender of the status quo, would revolve in his grave like a pinwheel at the notion that the United States, Britain, Russia and China could be joined together in a new "Holy Alliance."

One possibility for intervention in legitimate and necessary ways of meeting emergencies is either to expand the current United Nations peace-keeping forces or provide for their regional equivalents under international control. The record of the United Nations in Palestine, the Congo, Kashmir, Indonesia and a number of other trouble spots is a mixture of success and failure, it is true. But on balance, it is better than anyone had a right to expect from so weak and divided a world organization. The fuss over Article 19, during which France and the Soviet Union were threatened with loss of their vote for failing to pay their share of U.N. peace-keeping costs in the Congo, may very well be repeated in other crises yet to come. But it is a risk well worth taking under prevailing circumstances.

When the international atmosphere is more propitious, it would be worth the effort to review the conditions under which a United Nations armed force (not on the Korea model) could be created and the outer limits of the contributions that could be made to such an organization. In any event, whether United Nations peace keeping can be enlarged or not, it is very much worth retaining. The blue-and-white banner of the world organization is still welcome in many places where the Stars and Stripes and the Hammer and Sickle are not. It is one viable alternative to the nightmare of American intervention in Asia. There are others of a regional nature that can be developed, such as the Indonesian initiative that drew together many nations of Southeast Asia to try to mediate the war in Cambodia.

These are among the elements of a less aggressive American military posture that would be more welcome both in Asia and at home. It would, if adopted, help dispel the objectionable image of an angry and bristling Uncle Sam, rattling his missiles and glowering at an Asian world of brown and yellow men from bases on their own territory. Instead of breaching a mythical American defense line, it would tend to restore a measure of assurance that American military strength in the future would be more wisely and less frequently exerted in Asia.

3. THE CRISIS OF THE ECONOMY

Unlike the American military's relatively limited area of current effectiveness, the American economy remains truly global in scope and subject to global ailments. The very rumor of a trade war between Japan and the United States, or between the United States and the European Common Market, is enough to set off jitters on the world's stock exchanges. It is not fear of American trade competition or even temporary trade barriers that is now so deeply felt abroad, for the United States has been at a distinct disadvantage as a competitor of Japan and West Germany for some years. What is of deeper concern is the rise of a vengeful protectionist spirit among broad elements of the American public, especially labor. This poses the most serious threat to the principle of American free trade in forty years. The juggling of the value of the dollar is a symptom of the malaise, not the cause of it.

The American Hard Line

There are a variety of reasons for the spread of this massive protectionist spirit in the United States. The inability of successive American administrations to halt inflation plus the rise in unemployment in the early 1970s are perhaps the most important. A loss in labor's productivity in key industries also did some damage, as did excessive competition among too many American industrial units. The inevitable result was to undercut American leadership in world markets and weaken faith in the ability of the United States to keep pace with its competitors. It was said, and widely believed, that Japan would surpass the United States within a few years as the world leader in steel production. The Soviet Union already has done so.

For a long time, the United States failed to put together any kind of a policy to meet this slowly intensifying crisis. Although sensible economists warned continually that a stern policy on incomes was needed to check inflation, the drift in the Johnson Administration was all toward voluntary effort and the succeeding Nixon Administration did little more for the better part of three years. At home, there were increasingly frantic appeals to hold the price and wage line—pleas that were invariably disregarded by tough industrialists and labor leaders. Abroad, particularly in Asia, the United States instituted a series of voluntary agreements, which really weren't voluntary at all, that obliged foreign manufacturers of products sensitive to the United States economy to limit their American sales.

The whole rickety economic structure was so palpably weak and impractical that the effect on the American dollar was depressing. As one monetary crisis after another built up, American travelers abroad found they were unable to exchange their dollars for once-despised foreign currencies—marks, francs, yen and even lesser units that had once been known in lordly American terminology as "funny money."

As time went on without even the semblance of a move by the American government, the dollar itself sank into the "funny money" stage. News reports dwelt on the panicky flights from the dollar into more solid currencies in every financial center from Zurich to Hong Kong. If the average American at home did not feel the immediate effect, his government did. It put pressure on its trading allies to value their currencies upward, instead of cutting the dollar's value, thus hoping to maintain an artificial standard. It didn't work, even though West Germany was most obliging and other Western trading partners of the United States took to floating their currencies. Japan held out, and the Japanese trade balance was climbing to unexampled heights.

Despite all the behind-the-scenes maneuvering, considerable American goods were priced out of the competitive market and numerous mills and factories had to close. The call for protectionism became a roar. A powerful Congressional group favored better tax breaks for industry and big government loans to distressed firms on the Lockheed aircraft pattern. Others wanted antitrust laws relaxed to permit still more monopolistic growth. There was a lot of griping in big industry about the consumers' unwillingness to buy at high prices and labor's unreasonableness in seeking ever higher wages. But the industrialists didn't show moderation, either. They kept jacking up prices for as much as the traffic would bear.

The cost-of-living index continued to rise so that the rate of inflation for 1970 was 5.3 per cent as against 4.7 per cent in 1969, and 1971 promised to be just as bad. In a preliminary estimate, the nation's gross national product dropped by five-tenths of 1 per cent in 1970 at a time when the government was hailing the advent of the world's first trillion-dollar economy. It wasn't much of a triumph, for at the end of the fiscal year, June 30, 1971, the United States Treasury was obliged to report a near-record deficit of $23.2 billion. Worse still, the estimates for the succeeding fiscal year ran to a deficit as high as $25 billion.

It was no good. Jawboning, the homely American term that denotes attempted persuasion without power, had failed completely. Nor did the Nixon Administration's attempt to support a system of voluntary cuts in imports from abroad make it any easier for American industry to compete with foreign traders. Repeated efforts failed to convince manufacturers in Japan, South Korea, Hong Kong and Taiwan that it was in their best interests to withhold some of their cheap textiles from the American market.

In what amounted to an emergency, President Nixon acted suddenly and with drastic effect on August 15, 1971, by cutting the dollar from its gold base and thereby wrecked the world currency exchange system that had been fashioned at Bretton Woods in 1944. It was a move that aroused more foreboding abroad than any economic decision by any American President since 1933, when Franklin Delano Roosevelt torpedoed the London economic conference with appalling results. The United States further increased the tension with its temporary 10 per cent import surcharge, a blackjack used against friendly governments to force them to revalue their currencies against the dollar or let them float to reach their own level. In the bitter jest of the day in Washington: "We are building bridges to our enemies and burning them to our friends."

It soon became apparent that the dollar would have to be devalued and that the world currency system would have to be rebuilt if the threat of a new American protectionism was to be allayed. But the rejoicing was brief and the cheers from Britain, Western Europe and Japan were mainly synthetic when, on December 18, 1971, the United States consented to an effective 12 per cent devaluation of the dollar as a part of the rematching of world currencies and lifted the surcharge. The knowledgeable public did not have to be told by economists that it would take a long time to reconstruct the shattered system and that the United States was far from economic rectitude. Despite the good cheer of press agentry that emanated from Washington, the mood of the nation remained somber. Like Herbert Hoover's celebrated pledge that "prosperity is just around the corner" in 1929, the United States still had to turn the corner in 1972 and thereafter.

The end of the surcharge did not by any means dispose of the determined drive of the protectionists, however. That part of the emergency program to bolster the economy had been much more popular than the wage-price freeze and the ponderous machinery that was created to implement it. A large section of the American public was deeply troubled by the presence of so many foreign automobiles on the nation's highways and so much foreign goods on the shelves of stores at a time of high unemployment. The danger remained, long after the adoption of new currency rates, that the United States for the long term might yield to the domestic fervor for greater protectionism.

The Textile Battle

The struggle over textile imports from Japan was the key engagement in this opening test of strength between American free traders and protectionists. It towered in importance over much more significant issues even though only about 6 per cent of American consumption of textiles in terms of value was attributable to imports and Japan's textiles constituted only a quarter of these imports.

The reason for American persistence in hammering at the Japanese textile industry with everything from import surcharges to ultimatums was an injudicious pledge that had been made by Richard Nixon during his 1968 Presidential campaign. Since he deemed the American South to be important to his candidacy and since the textile industry was largely based in that region, he agreed to help American textile manufacturers by curbing Japanese imports. It was obvious enough that the issue was political and not economic, and so it has remained.

After prolonged negotiations during which the White House turned down every effort by the Japanese government to seek a compromise, the Japanese textile industry unilaterally instituted its own program of voluntary quotas on July 1, 1971. Approaching a campaign for reelection, President Nixon once again refused to accept the Japanese move, but they went ahead with it anyway. What the United States then did was to send high-level negotiators from Seoul to Taipei and Hong Kong, and back to Tokyo, hoping to win some kind of agreement from all these textile producers to hold back on their exports to the American market. The notion was that the smaller producers would cave in, thus bringing pressure to bear on the Japanese. It didn't work. Next, the Americans tried political blackmail, intimating that the Senate might hold up ratification of the agreement for the reversion of Okinawa to Japan. It was only the imposition of the import surcharge, which preceded the devaluation of the dollar and revaluation of the yen, that finally produced the kind of textile agreement the White House could accept. How long that would last was problematical.

Throughout the struggle there was doubt that the American textile industry's plight was as serious as it was represented to be. The industry's critics argued that it was in the doldrums, not because of Japanese competition, but because of its own inability to stimulate domestic consumption. Its sales had not improved. They were running at the rate of $21.5 billion in 1971, about the same as 1968, with higher prices and volume up 3 to 5 per cent. As a result, net earnings were down in 1971, less than the $413 million of 1970,[5] and all the hoopla in Washington did little to reverse the trend.

The whole business would have been ridiculous if the new American protectionists had not made textiles the No. 1 issue. It cheapened the government of the United States to be using all its prestige and power for the benefit of a single politically motivated industry and it demeaned the presidency as well. Not that the Japanese were without blame in permitting the issue to take on such grave implications. Had they moved earlier for a workable compromise, their end position might have been better. But despite a government reshuffle that eliminated some anti-American cabinet ministers, Tokyo remained unwilling to lower its own protectionist stance and thereby invited American retaliation. The end result left both sides dissatisfied.

[5] *The New York Times,* July 4, 1971, p. 9, sec. 3.

The Development of Asia

The struggle over textiles is only a foretaste of what the United States faces in Asia. Before the coming of the twenty-first century, there is little doubt that many of the processes of modern technology will be mastered by Asians outside Japan and the few other smaller centers that now figure in world trade. While it would be impossible to calculate growth accurately for so large and diverse an area as the Indo-Pacific, an annual growth rate of 6 to 7 per cent by 1980 for most of the developing countries there is not unreasonable. That should be more than enough to sustain a projected population for the area of 3,000,000,000 people by 2000 A.D. and perhaps allow a modest gain in per capita income, perhaps on the order of $250 to $300 a year, with more in some places. By American or even Japanese standards, that isn't much; but to Indians or Pakistanis who have been living at the hunger level or worse, it will seem like a better world.

Less than one-third of American trading abroad, both imports and exports, is concentrated in Asia and Oceania and much of that goes to Japan, Australia, South Korea, Hong Kong, Taiwan and Singapore. China, India, Pakistan, Indonesia and Southeast Asia (except for military goods) account for comparatively little even though together they represent the bulk of Asia's population. Necessarily, in the declining years of the twentieth century, these are the countries that will be turning increasingly to the industrialized lands in matters of trade and development.

Judged by its performance in Asia during the early 1970s, the United States may not play as great a role in this process as it should. The Japanese have shown rather conclusively so far that almost anything the United States can do in Asia, they can do as well or better. (This, of course, does not include war making on the Asian mainland, at which both have failed.) Other Asian lands have no particular affection for either of the two Pacific trading giants; very possibly, especially in countries that were occupied by the Japanese during World War II, sentiment would tend to favor the United States as the lesser of the two evils.

But in pricing, efficiency, availability of materials, prompt delivery and the ability to deal with other Asian governments, the Japanese have the advantage over the United States in numerous fields. Even some of the Europeans, notably West Germany, are improving their position in the Asian trade at the expense of the United States. Despite the bludgeon of protectionism and the juggling of the dollar, the American economic prospect in Asia, therefore, is not encouraging. Whatever advantage the United States has gained from its new economic policy is likely to be temporary in the Far East.

There are some who say, quite recklessly, that the United States doesn't really need the Asian trade, except for Japan, and even dealings with the Japanese could be reduced. They echo the familiar argument that Asians need the United States and most nations are dependent on the American market. It is a dubious premise, in view of Japanese progress, and is likely to grow increasingly less tenable. To a nation like the United States with global interests, it would be a grave error to hold the Asian trade cheaply merely because it is so difficult to make practical arrangements with Indo-Pacific nations.

This lofty attitude leads first of all to a natural resentment against American products. It also causes many prominent Asians, always so sensitive on the issue, to suspect a basic American discrimination against them because of differences of color and race. Where they normally would tend to be critical of the Japanese, they seem to take comfort in the staggering Japanese-American trade imbalance, which was still running very heavily in Japan's favor in the early 1970s. Clearly, the American economic posture in Asia calls for a lot of reassessment.

What the United States Can Do

It must be emphasized that the revival of protectionism, plus the juggling of currencies and interest rates, can scarcely be a solution to American economic problems in the Indo-Pacific. What the United States has to offer is considerably more—an advanced and highly sophisticated technology, the ability to organize and participate in funding for development, an unsurpassed expertise in communications and the drive and imagination to create a skilled work force capable of operating everything from steel mills to computers. In the long view, American services are going to be more important than

American goods in restoring the United States to a stronger economic position in Asia.

One of the abysmal features of the American economic recession and slow recovery has been the tendency of both the American government and private industry to cut back on research and development, which have been so largely responsible for American leadership in the past. It is a stunning reversal for a power that considers itself the leader in stimulating a global technology. Private industry devotes only about $10 billion annually to research and development today, a fraction of its capital expenditures. As for government, it has closed out its research arrangements with many leading universities and heavily cut back on its own programs in a mistaken effort to reduce budgetary deficits. Research and development should be the last place for such reductions, constituting as they do the main resource for continued American technological development.

It is of course true that much of the government's cutback on university research was forced by student revulsion against the American role in the Vietnam War. In addition, leading scientists in the universities were so dedicated to the peace movement that they would no longer work on projects that might have, in some indirect way, had a bearing on continued American participation in the conflict. But with the American withdrawal from Indochina, it becomes imperative to enlist the best in American science and technology for the long and difficult process of rebuilding devastated areas and reconstituting governmental and other disrupted services.

This could well serve as a starting point for new joint ventures in science and technology between Asians and Americans, either under joint governmental arrangements or international auspices. It is a far-reaching project in which American universities, the powerhouses of research, could join with enthusiasm. Properly organized and reasonably financed, such a move might be taken as a useful approach to a revival of American interest in research and development at all levels, both public and private. Certainly, this is an area in which Asians have an overwhelming interest; it is also one in which the Japanese, despite their brilliance, are often at a disadvantage when working with other Asians because of the forbidding nature of the Japanese language.

Second only in importance to a fresh stimulus for technological development in Asia is the prime need for working capital for development. Foreign aid, as such, is unpopular in all industrial countries—the Soviet Union no less than the United States and Japan—because there is seldom any way of showing the home front any tangible return for the funds that are given, invested or loaned. Moreover, the recipients are not often prone to display a proper amount of gratitude to their foreign benefactors but keep complaining that what they get isn't enough, or the terms are too stiff, or the strings attached to the money are too obvious. For all these and other reasons, it is becoming more and more difficult to obtain sufficient foreign economic assistance through the democratic processes of open societies; as for the closed ones, they are even less philanthropic about such ventures, and with good reason.

In the United States, the trend toward lower foreign aid appropriations has been particularly marked. The government couldn't even get the Senate in 1970 to approve such financially sound measures as a commitment of $100 million for the Asian Development Bank and, closer to home, $900 million for the Inter-American Development Bank. Seeing disaster ahead, the Nixon Administration proposed a full-scale reform of the American foreign aid program[6] but an angry Senate on October 29, 1971, killed a pending $3.2 billion foreign aid authorization bill, 41–27. All the patching that followed couldn't really put the Humpty Dumpty concept of foreign aid together again.

However foreign aid may eventually be restructured, it must be taken for granted that the United States no longer can be counted on to pour out money lavishly to developing lands. The incentive for giving in Asia, in particular, is terribly low; the availability of working capital for loans, still less. Despite the need, the American electorate is bound to consider it a dubious proposition to invest a lot of money in Asian development when such funds are more urgently required at home.

What will have to be done, therefore, is to explore new directions for foreign aid, primarily through the mobilization of international resources. The World Bank, the regional development banks, the

[6] Message to Congress, April 21, 1971.

spread of the consortium for assisting developing nations and the use of United Nations specialized agencies all will have to be tried to a greater degree than in the past. The United States simply is not going to foot gigantic foreign aid bills by itself from now on.

The time has passed when a native leader could jump on a café table, scream that his nation was about to be taken over by Communists, and then hope for a fat grant of American aid. It did happen in several places, unfortunately, but the United States was neither as gullible nor as prone to be stampeded as the caricature suggests. Today, anti-Communism is not a sufficient reason for propping up weak, corrupt governments. Nor are deceptive claims in favor of such governments likely to be accepted at face value any longer.

The course open to the United States for the enlargement of foreign aid available to Asian countries is to stimulate greater participation in the effort on an international scale. No government yet accepts the principle of international taxation or assessment without some knowledge in advance of the specific uses that are to be made of the funds; and yet, this seems to be the only viable and universal system through which development money could be raised on an equitable basis.

If no strings are to be attached to such assistance, as all givers so volubly insist (without supporting evidence), then why should American dollars be any different than Soviet rubles in an international aid fund? And why should givers be limited to industrially advanced countries with surplus funds at their disposal? China is one example of a poor developing country that still manages to spread its foreign aid around where it will do Peking the most good. Israel, one of the smallest of industrial nations with a war-burdened economy, also seems able to give assistance to its friends among developing lands.

It has been familiar world procedure for more than a hundred years to pool funds for international aid or rescue efforts whenever there is a catastrophe, natural or man-made. Rich and poor nations alike, political opponents and economic rivals, and even foemen who are at war will endeavor within their means to make a contribution for the relief of suffering humanity. It passes all understanding why the same principle cannot be invoked without delay and special pleading when people by the hundreds of thousands live and die on the streets of Calcutta or starve in Bangladesh. The United Nations has belatedly recognized the principle but has yet to put it to effective use.

Perhaps it is unrealistic to expect that international taxation will be acceptable in an era when nations still persist in using foreign aid for political and other purposes. But eventually, unless stability can be established in Asia by other means, the issue will become so overwhelmingly important to the maintenance of international peace and security that the world community will have to act in self-interest. It is beyond the means of one nation, however great and powerful, to take on sole responsibility for such a cause in Asia.

What the United States can do, and do with consummate skill, is to spread modern communications methods in Asia's developing lands. The principle of using orbiting satellites for a nation-wide education program by television scarcely need be limited to India alone. Under appropriate circumstances and with funding from diversified sources, not necessarily governmental, a great deal can be done to lift the educational level of Asian masses through advanced communications techniques. If the science of optical transmission by laser beam along glass-thread channels is sufficiently advanced in the next decade, it could be possible for millions of people to leapfrog over the era of the telegraph, telephone circuit and radio into a time of cheap and almost limitless communication by light beam.[7]

The advantages of a system of Asia-wide communications would be manifold. From instruction in family planning to the propagation of new techniques in agriculture, it would serve a continuous educational purpose. In the transmission of news and opinion, it would make Asians more aware of their common interests on numerous levels. And while without doubt the system would intensify the preoccupation of people with their own national or regional language, it also would solidify English as the principal international language—the lingua franca—of Asian lands. In his way, over a period of time, perhaps a start could be made on breaking down the language barrier that so often serves to separate Asians from the West.

[7] "Light, the Long Distance Answer," *New Scientist,* July 16, 1970, pp. 14–19.

There is, finally, a moral obligation confronting the United States as it contemplates the extent of its economic commitments in Asia. As the consumer of 40 per cent of the natural resources produced on earth for the benefit of only 6 per cent of the world's population, the United States must ask itself how wisely such precious materials are being used. The answer is bound to be disturbing to Americans as well as Asians. Every year, in maintaining the most luxurious standard of living the world has ever known, Americans junk 7,000,000 automobiles and trucks, 20,000,000 tons of paper, 48,000,000,000 beer, soft-drink and food cans, and a mountain range of other waste that costs them $3 billion annually merely for disposal.[8] It is a way of life described by the scientist René Dubos as "the whirling dervish doctrine which teaches: produce more so that you can consume more so that you can produce still more."

The callous spectacle of promiscuous overconsumption and waste in the United States is not calculated to improve the American prospect in Asia. Nor will it be very easy over a period of years to persuade both American industry and the American consumer that reckless buying and spending on goods and services without some rational social purpose behind it all will be self-defeating over the long haul. Consumption for social uses is something that wise men frequently talk about without having the faintest idea how to bring it about in a country like the United States.

Like almost everything else in a nation with such a gigantic economy, change is likely to come with infuriating slowness except in periods of great emergencies. Here and there, perhaps, in an industry or a company with some slight degree of social consciousness, it may be possible to work out a more equitable sharing of materials between "haves" and "have-nots." In the paper industry, for example, where a single great American newspaper uses more newsprint annually than the entire Indian press, a better distribution arrangement should be possible without resort to an unacceptable quota system. Many such situations exist, notably in the fields of medicine and public health, food processing and public transportation. But mere moral persuasion will not be enough to get the process of readjustment under way in any meaningful degree.

[8] Figures from *The New York Times*, December 17, 1970, p. 46.

What the Japanese did to solve this dilemma, starting with a ruined industry and a devastated land in 1945, was to develop new industries and revive old ones, some with American and other foreign help, and others through their own resources. From optical goods to chemicals, and from automobiles and electronics to watches and wigs, the Japanese output was of such quality and moderate price as to be able to compete with the best on world markets. That solved their raw materials problem, for the world's producers were eager to do business with Japan. But the great miracle would not have been possible without the prior existence of a well-trained and thoroughly disciplined work force. It was, and is, Japan's greatest industrial asset.

No other country in Asia is as fortunate as Japan in this respect. The hot competition between smaller industrialized lands for skilled labor, with all kinds of inducements being offered to fill gaps in the industrial work force, indicates the extent of the problem. Nor can it be said that any immediate solution is possible. The hard business of creating a readily available pool of skilled labor in Asia is a long-term proposition, as the developing countries already have discovered for themselves. To those who so quickly point to the large numbers of Asians studying in American and other foreign universities today, it should be made clear that many of these are intellectuals who have an acute distaste for working with their hands. More likely than not, most industrial recruiting, from West Pakistan to Indonesia, will have to be done at home at the secondary school level.

There is no ready recipe for American participation in such a broad effort. As experience with the Peace Corps volunteers has shown, the reaction to American tutelage—even on so simple a level as the development of a cottage industry program—varies widely and the instruction is not always acceptable. It is not that Americans lack good will or instructional skill or the willingness to work long hours at unrewarding tasks. But not all of them can adjust easily to wide variations in language, custom and work habits in Asia. Some of them, in addition, appear to have a genius for creating misunderstandings where none previously existed.

There are, as well, many things about management operations and labor organizations that cannot be taught, but must be learned through often torturous experience. In consequence, American assistance in the necessarily extensive process of technical training is likely to be most acceptable to Asians in a binational or even a multinational arrangement. Demonstration teams, motion pictures and a variety of other training devices have been used in the past and are likely to continue to be effective. Once television is available, it could become the most valuable of all instructional tools.

The touring expert and the learned lecturer, the visiting captain of industry and the experienced labor organizer, all have much to offer in theory, but in practice few have proved to be very effective among audiences of Asian workers and managers. For better or worse, there seems to be no substitute for a long-term commitment to on-the-job training, as Americans in Asia have discovered for themselves. There is no doubt, if past and present training commitments can be suitably expanded, that this will be as important as anything else the United States can do in the development of the Indo-Pacific area. No new industrial state can arise without the creation of a skilled work force with a reasonable degree of stability. It is the basic requirement that makes all others possible.

4 . A COMMUNITY OF INTEREST

The United States has learned to its cost that there is a limit to the effectiveness of any purely political, economic or military approach to the problems of Asian lands. Collective security, as it was defined in the middle of the twentieth century, is not enough. The notion of a grand alliance against Asian Communism, which so bedazzled John Foster Dulles and left such wreckage in its wake, is neither practical nor even possible at this juncture. What the United States will be obliged to do, instead, is to consider a more modest and potentially a more effective posture in its dealings with the nations of the Indo-Pacific in all their diversity.

The basis for such a new approach is the establishment of a community of interest among Americans and Asians in the Indo-Pacific beyond the relatively small and ineffective steps that already have been taken. It would be an effort to seek a different form of collective security, an attempt at a union of mind and heart rather than a call to arms, an appeal to self-interest rather than the construction of the universal bomb shelter. The enemy would not be one nation or another, or a group of nations, but all the ills that beset humankind from the prospect of an overcrowded and dying earth to the poisoning of the environment, from hunger and lack of shelter to pestilence and ignorance.

This could not, by its very nature, be a venture intended exclusively for free peoples or those who are willing to try to make themselves over in the American image. Unfortunately, the not-so-free are in the majority by far in Asia and very few have the slightest comprehension of what the American form of government is all about. What is more to the point, not many care; the struggle for life itself is of the first importance to them.

A policy based on a community of interest does not imply that a hopelessly impractical series of benefactions is to be attempted in Asia in return for a mild possibility of a revival of good will for the United States. Such a program, properly worked out, is as practical and necessary as domestic urban renewal or the conservation of natural resources. Instead of being applied to one nation only, it encompasses the world and invites the cooperation of all nations on a mutually agreeable basis. Conceptually, it is no more visionary than the Marshall Plan, to which Czechoslovakia would have immediately adhered had it not been for the violent objections of the Soviet Union.

The probability that the Soviet Union, China and their respective allies and client states might not at first participate in a venture to improve the entire Pacific community does not present insuperable difficulties. If an American-sponsored policy proves to be successful in Asia or anywhere else, it will be imitated quickly enough by Moscow and Peking, each by its own lights. And who is to say that differing ideologies will hamper man's effort to improve the condition of life on earth until the end of time? It isn't even thinkable. The attempt to marshal a union of forces in a common cause is bound to be made sooner or later. And if the United States does not do it, then some other nation or group of nations will.

To conservatives, of course, the effort will seem like just another summons to a cause led by woolly-headed liberals and "bleeding hearts," a program that will funnel more money down a whole series of "Asian ratholes" to the further disadvantage of the American taxpayer, and weaken the security of the United States. These weary and threadbare arguments have been advanced from the same sources against nearly every progressive step that has been taken by the United States, from the outlawing of child labor to social security and from the rise of antitrust legislation to the Wage-Hour Act. In reality, these are the programs that strengthened the internal security of the United States and made possible the growth of an industrialized economy without parallel in the world's history.

What is suggested here is an extension of the principle of a community of interest among peoples to the global level, certainly not a world-shaking notion. The innovative idea is that the United States should make a serious attempt to develop a pattern of new and practical working arrangements on some of the more urgent global necessities of our time. Some of these activities could be carried out under international control, others through regional arrangements, still others by groups of nations in twos or threes. And out of the whole, a network of interest would be woven that could bring the Indo-Pacific peoples closer together and eventually break down some of the animosity and suspicion that separate the component nations.

There is no implication in such an effort that American military strength would be weakened or national security breached. So far as the effectiveness of a policy of mutual national benefits is concerned, the United States could very well remain armed to the teeth if it chose to do so. The world is perfectly aware that American missiles and warheads have a global field of fire and that American divisions can be ferried by air to any spot in the world within a few hours. But such forces today are not going to advance the American interest in the Pacific if they are aggressively used; as the basis of American defense, they are bound to compel respect.

On every score, therefore, an advance toward a community of interest in the Pacific is overdue. There will naturally be an argument over where and how to begin, and to what degree the United States should commit itself to new and even experimental ventures in the field of global social action. That is not of prime importance at this stage. The important thing to do is to begin.

A Union Against Pollution

It is perfectly apparent that some of the areas in which the peoples of the Indo-Pacific have a community of interest are covered by existing world or regional organizations. But in practice, very little has been done about most such matters except to hold learned discussions far above the level of comprehension for a mass public. The files of the world press are overloaded with records of conventions, assemblies, convocations and the like that have talked at length about vital issues, made a long list of recommendations and then adjourned sine die. Years have gone by before the first halting steps could be taken toward a global era of good feelings—the Antarctica Treaty, the limited atomic test ban treaty, and agreements against the use of atomic weapons in outer space and on the seabed. The only quick agreement since World War II was one that was so obviously in the interest of both the United States and the Soviet Union that they leaped at the idea and quickly implemented it—the vital and ever-useful "hot line" between Moscow and Washington.

If one issue is to be selected from among all those that so deeply concern the Indo-Pacific area and used as an illustration of what is intended, let it be pollution. For the monumental rise in the pollution of the environment presents the gravest problems for Japan and the United States, very difficult ones for Hong Kong and Singapore, and situations of developing intensity that could be overwhelming in years to come for China and India, Pakistan and Indonesia. It is evident beyond all doubt that every nation and every popular interest in the Indo-Pacific will be affected.

The point is beyond debate. The pollution of the Pacific and Indian oceans and the rivers that empty into them presents a challenge that transcends the consideration of nation-states alone. It knows no borders. It has no limits. If the United States and Japan choose to poison themselves with automobile fumes or incredible waste in their waters, they also endanger their neighbors at the same time. Patriotic orators may thunder that what their nations do within their own borders concerns no one else. But if pollution is an internal matter, so was the Black Plague. Potentially, it is even more lethal and it affects hundreds of millions more people than those of medieval Europe. The Stockholm conference represents a start, but only a start, toward a global attack on the problem.

Pollution is the type of issue on which neither national nor ideological considerations should prevent action. The pollution caused by a Communist factory is no more desirable than the evil waste that flows from a mill operated by a capitalist entrepreneur. The destruction of marine life in Lake Baikal is no more acceptable than the poisoning of Lake Michigan or the South China Sea.

True, so difficult and troublesome an issue could be left to the United Nations and its affiliated specialized agencies, notably the World Health Organization. It is, after all, a familiar and disheartening international procedure to dump seemingly insoluble problems on the United Nations without providing either the funds, the trained manpower or even the basic moral support to attack them realistically. To work for an improvement in the environment of the Indo-Pacific area, the nations directly concerned are likely to find that, if they mean business, they will have to yield a portion of their sovereignty to an international agency, probably a new one. It should have the character of the Universal Postal Union and the technical competence of the International Telecommunication Union or the World Meteorological Organization.

A Pacific Organization for the Environment, well manned and funded, would represent the will of the nations and territories of the Indo-Pacific and Oceania. It would be a vital demonstration of the usefulness and the practical nature of applying the test of a community of interest to new American ventures in the area. The nagging question of whether the Communist nations will come in is likely to provide its own answer. In the Mekong River Valley, it is a dead certainty that North Vietnam is not going to be left out of whatever arrangements are made by Thailand, Laos, Cambodia and South Vietnam. Its interest in controlling the Mekong is not going to be invalidated either by its ideology or its role in the Vietnam War. The same thing would be true of North Korea for the Yalu and the Han rivers, and China for the Amur, Ussuri and Salween among others. The notion that air space or the sea can be neatly sectioned off to conform with national boundaries is a part of the ancient lore of international law, which hasn't yet caught up with the modern world and probably will take most of the next century to do so.

The Range of Interest

Just as pollution calls for concerted international action by concerned nations, so does many another issue of vital import to the future of mankind. The range of interest in the Pacific is so broad and the need so great that it is, without doubt, the principal part of the earth that requires community decision and response.

The advantages of an integrated movement for population control among the nations of the Indo-Pacific are so obvious that neither argument nor discussion is necessary. The mere participation of China in periodic conferences on family planning, for example, would be both a stimulant and an incentive toward more effective performance on the part of neighboring nations. That such action eventually will be taken by Peking cannot be doubted in view of China's United Nations membership. If China can be persuaded to join with India, Indonesia and Japan to try to establish some degree of international responsibility for population growth, the rest of the world in general and the United States in particular had better be ready to help. The opportunity, if it develops, will not soon come again should it be brushed aside by international indifference. Massive overpopulation in one country is a menace to all countries. And in years to come, it is likely that the decision of any nation to resort to unrestricted population growth will be viewed as a crime against humanity. This may not be a popular doctrine in large segments of the Christian and Muslim worlds, but it is nevertheless based on truth.

While the American share in improving the environment and limiting the population of the Indo-Pacific must of necessity be moderate, the United States can and should take the lead in clearing the way for the opening of greater resources of power for the developing lands of the area. One of the greatest and most urgent needs in such areas is a safe, dependable and inexpensive source of atomic power for the years to come. As the United States already has discovered, neither oil nor gas nor water power can generate sufficient energy for the unfolding requirements of the modern industrial state. And just as the United States today is experimenting with enlarging the sources of atomic power and reducing the cost, so are other nations with the capability for making nuclear progress.

Yet, for rather dubious reasons of state security, much of what is going on is compartmentalized and kept secret within each nation. It is, however, a reasonably safe bet that anything American scientists can do in the nuclear field can also be accomplished by the scientists of the Soviet Union, China, Japan, India and even tiny Israel among others, given the proper support. The time has long since passed when nuclear secrets are the property of any one nation or group of nations. And the world's need for atomic power is so great that it would seem to be to the advantage of all concerned to pool their greatest talent and their experimental resources to work at the problem on an international level. What is being done by the current international agency is far too limited in scope.

The United States has not been afraid to innovate in the experimental atomic field. The American program for encouraging small-scale experiments in the peaceful uses of atomic energy, notably in the fields of science and health, has been going for more than two decades without breaching American security. Surely, with all the interchanges that now take place between the world's scientists, ways can be found for joint ventures in the development of safe and inexpensive nuclear power resources. The Indo-Pacific offers a very wide and useful field for experimentation, for it is here that the need is demonstrably the greatest.

There are numerous other areas for global action that will be of particular benefit to the Indo-Pacific.

The age of supersonic air transportation is upon us, even though the United States has refused temporarily to recognize it, and a vast supporting infrastructure will have to be created for international use, both passengers and freight. One immediate result will be to shrink the largest of continents—the area, in Ernie Pyle's phrase, of magnificent distances. Another will be to intensify the desire for high-speed rail lines, more highways and faster travel by water in industrialized lands and their neighbors. Just as the Soviet Union has surpassed the United States in high-speed air transport, the Japanese have shown the way in building much faster railways. It could be, in such fields, that the United States will find itself a rather backward participant rather than a leader in a few years. International action, in fact, could well be required to shake Americans out of their lethargy.

But in the advancement of global communications and education, science and health, urban renewal, agricultural advancement, housing, marketing methodology and international law enforcement, the United States has much to offer to its neighbors in the Pacific. And they, in turn, can contribute measurably to the ultimate benefit of the United States and the other nations of the eastern Pacific. This is very far from a one-way relationship, as so many Americans appear to believe. For while it is true that the United States is in a position to make a maximum contribution to international peace and security through its talks with the Soviet Union and other nuclear powers on strategic arms limitations, American power is relatively helpless before the narcotics smuggler and the airplane hijacker among other international outlaws. Here, as in other matters of global importance, the cooperation of the lands of the Indo-Pacific is mandatory if any kind of concerted action is to succeed.

The Pacific Community

The Japanese, among others, have tried to popularize the notion of a Pacific Community in the years since World War II and the phrase has, as a result, gained public currency. Yet, in the sense of a group of nations bound together by common ties of history, language, laws, customs and belief, the basis for such a community does not now exist in the Pacific. Nor are the chances very good that it will ultimately arise in some grandiloquent form. Among the nations of Western Europe and North America, where there is a much greater common heritage, men of good will have tried for years to create an Atlantic Community without perceptible success. The oceans, like natural and man-made boundaries on land, no longer serve to partition off the forces that affect humankind.

What is useful and desirable about the concept of a Pacific Community is the recognition it implies of the potential power of regionalism over nationalism as a political entity. For regionalism, as it is slowly evolving in Europe, is a halfway house between the declining authority and influence of the nation-state and the relatively weak global organizations that are now in existence.

The Asians may not be ready yet for a coal and steel community or an atomic energy community, let alone a common market, but they are well aware of the advantages of such cooperative action. They will not be forever divided among themselves, any more than will Americans. Nor is it foreordained that they are to be poor and relatively weak with the exception of a giant Japan. Through such consultative organizations as the Asian and Pacific Council and others, the Asians today are testing various regional approaches to their problems with a modest degree of success. Tomorrow, they may well be ready for something better—and it is unlikely that whatever emerges from their consultations will be based on the old Cold War line-up. In revolutionary Asia, there will be many surprises and not all of them will flow from the rising sun of Japan or Chinese Ping-Pong balls.

In this extremity, it will not do for the United States to mourn its past errors in Asia or to wear sackcloth and ashes before the world indefinitely. The time for dissent and division has passed. The time for reassessment is at hand. And in any recasting of national priorities, it would be well for the United States to think first of Asia. Certainly, new American policies based on a community of interest with the peoples of the Indo-Pacific can do much to retrieve declining American influence in Asia. By contrast, there is no advantage in a maximum disengagement. And as for isolation, it could bring only dissolution and death.

In the new era that is advancing across the broad Pacific, the most practical recourse for the United States is to increase American ties with Asian lands instead of lessening them, to offer help to disadvantaged countries in a reasonable measure instead of snatching it away, to conduct a program of mutual trade on the basis of fair dealing and equitable currency exchange instead of political and economic aggrandizement, and to abjure the use of aggressive force to advance the American cause in the Indo-Pacific.

In opposition to so moderate a position, it may be argued that the Soviet Union is now advancing in Asia as the United States retreats, that Russian power is expanding east of Suez and that the Red Fleet in the Indian Ocean represents a threat for the future. This may be so, but it would make no sense at all at this juncture in history for the United States to seek a confrontation with the Soviet Union in the Far East. Nor would it advance American interests to be rashly drawn into the Soviet-Chinese quarrel.

A wiser American course would be to develop a more effective approach to the long effort to achieve progress toward arms reduction, arms control and the moderation of a quarter century of great-power rivalry in the post-World War II period. This does not by any means commit the United States to an unrealistic disarmament, in whole or in part. Nor does it in any respect undermine either American armed strength or American defenses, which must keep up with the times. What this posture could do, with the liquidation of the Vietnam War, would be to place the United States in a less belligerent and more reasonable attitude before the world. It would be one American program that Asian lands, in common with developing countries everywhere, could support.

The measures that have been suggested here form a part of the answer to the question, "What is the national interest?" They cannot make up a final pattern in themselves. For there is no single path to peace. And no power, acting unilaterally, can lead the world away from the ultimate disaster of atomic war. If there is no hope in the old balance-of-power game, it is equally true that no ready-made device of statecraft is available as a replacement for either this or other outworn tenets of international existence. New policies do not spring into being in a flash of divine revelation; nor can one international conference settle all the world's tangled affairs. Often, years may elapse before something of substance develops from the vagrant processes of world diplomacy.

This much is certain, however: No power is going to be able to maintain a drive toward global superiority from now on. And even the best-made arrangements for maintaining a regional sphere of influence are likely to be upset, particularly in Asia. The relaxation of tension, therefore, will require something more than a settlement in Vietnam or even an agreement, however much it may be desired, between the forces of NATO and the Warsaw Pact countries. For Japan, China and India, in common with the rest of Asia, are not likely to permit Washington or Moscow to exert a major influence over the terms of their existence and development for the indefinite future.

A new era is indeed dawning for the Pacific, but it is not an age that will be cast either in the American or Soviet image. This era belongs to the Asians themselves in all their diversity and manifold aspirations. They will make of it what they wish, for they must eventually become the masters of their own continent. What the United States can do, and in all good conscience and enlightened self-interest should do, is to join with other leading nations of the Western world in creating a sense of common cause with the nations of the Indo-Pacific. That slender but indispensable link, once it is forged, could mark the beginning of a better and more enduring global relationship. It remains the basis of whatever hope there may be for the future.

Index

ABOUT THE AUTHOR

John Hohenberg spent twenty-five years as a working newspaperman in New York City, Washington, at the United Nations and abroad and is the author of eight books, two of which won distinguished service awards from the journalistic society, Sigma Delta Chi. He is a professor of journalism at the Columbia University Graduate School of Journalism and has had a special interest in Asian affairs since 1946. He served in Asia in 1963–64 under the American Specalist program of the Department of State and was a research fellow in Asian affairs for the Council on Foreign Relations in 1964–65, a senior specialist in Asian affairs at the East-West Center in Honolulu in 1967 and a visiting professor at the Chinese University of Hong Kong in 1970–71.

John Hohenberg, a seasoned Asia expert, sets out the facts of the past and the issues of the future, demonstrating how we can rebuild our shattered relationships with half the human race. Where others offer only sound and fury, he offers sound common sense. Is anyone listening?

—JOHN BARKHAM,
Saturday Review Syndicate

New Era in the Pacific points out that the old American strategy, with its dependence on direct military intervention, shaky Asian allies, and unpopular foreign bases, is bankrupt: we can afford no more Vietnams. This important book provides the basis for a *new* American policy of peace and cooperation in the Pacific. It poses a challenge to the concerned citizen to take a more active role in shaping such a posture.

John Hohenberg, Asian specialist and Professor of Journalism at Columbia University, undertook a three-year adventure in public diplomacy; it was a mission that culminated in an eight-month, 40,000-mile journey throughout Asia, supported in large part by the Ford Foundation. Mr. Hohenberg probes for the shape of things to come